D1565909

SEEING REDS

FEDERAL SURVEILLANCE OF RADICALS IN
THE PITTSBURGH MILL DISTRICT, 1917–1921

A John D. S. and Aida C. Truxall Book

SEEING REDS

FEDERAL SURVEILLANCE OF RADICALS IN
THE PITTSBURGH MILL DISTRICT, 1917–1921

CHARLES H. McCORMICK

UNIVERSITY OF PITTSBURGH PRESS

Published by the University of Pittsburgh Press, Pittsburgh, Pa. 15261

Copyright © 1997, University of Pittsburgh Press

Manufactured in the United States of America

Printed on acid-free paper

10   9   8   7   6   5   4   3   2   1

LIBRARY OF CONGRESS CATALOGING-IN-PUBLICATION DATA

McCormick, Charles H. (Charles Howard), 1932–

    Seeing reds : federal surveillance of radicals in the Pittsburgh mill district, 1917–1921 /

    Charles H. McCormick.

      p.   cm.

    Includes bibliographical references and index.

    ISBN 0-8229-3998-3 (alk. paper)

    1. Anti-communist movements—Pennsylvania—Pittsburgh—History—20th

century.   2. Communism—Pennsylvania—Pittsburgh—History—20th century.

3. United States—Politics and government—1913–1921.   4. Pittsburgh (Pa.)—Politics

and government.   5. Internal security—Pennsylvania—Pittsburgh—History—20th

century.   I. Title

F159.P657M38   1997

974.8'86—dc21   97–21173

A CIP catalog record for this book is available from the British Library.

For my history teachers of long ago,
especially Robert Foote Harris, Lawrence S. Kaplan,
and Roland H. Bainton

CONTENTS

PREFACE

THIS BOOK GREW out of my long fascination with failed rebellions in American history, with the government's frequent resort to undemocratic means to defend democracy, and curiosity aroused during my twenty-five-year residence in the Pittsburgh mill district. It is also an effort to address unanswered questions left by my earlier work on the effects of the post–World War II Red Scare on a small college town in the coal fields of northern West Virginia. In researching that study I was struck both by the fear of change that animated conservative elements of town and gown and by their casual (and typical, for the time) invocation of the epithet *communist* to describe ideas and individuals with which they disagreed. I could find no evidence that their so-called communists had anything to do with or were in sympathy with the party or the USSR or its cold war apparatus in the United States. Then I came across a 1952 column in a Morgantown newspaper stating that what I perceived as an overreaction stemmed from the fact that the Monongahela Valley had been in times past a "happy hunting ground" for Communists. I learned later that the writer was echoing the 1928 testimony of novelist Fanny Hurst about conditions in the bituminous coal regions before the Senate Interstate Commerce Committee. However clouded, the Morgantown columnist's reading of the past was intriguing enough to lead me back to the World War I era and to the National Archives.

The National Archives contains the principal primary sources for this study, the declassified investigative files of various federal agencies: the Military Intelligence Division (War Department-Record Group 165), the Office of Naval Intelligence (Navy Department-Record Group 38), and the Bureau of Investigation (Justice Department-Record Group 65). Particularly useful were "The Investigative Case Files of the Bureau of Investigation, 1908–1922," which are on 955 rolls of 16 mm microfilm (National Archives publication M-1085), especially the Old German Files, 1915–1920, and the Bureau Section Files, 1909–1921. Also on microfilm are useful finding aids: "Name Index to Correspondence of the Military Intelligence Division of the War Department General Staff, 1917–1941," (M-1194) and "Geographic Index to Correspondence of the Military Intelligence Division of the War Department General Staff" (M-1474). A large, but incomplete, collection of MID intelligence material has been published on microfilm as U.S. War Department, *Military Intelligence Reports: Surveillance of Radicals in the United States* (Frederick, Md.: UPA, 1984).

Although this study sheds some light on the radical Left in the Pittsburgh mill district in the early twentieth century, it is not offered as a definitive history of that phenomenon. My focus, as the title indicates, is on the federal government's efforts to define, understand, and suppress leftists in the region during the World War I era. *Seeing Reds* incorporates in greatly modified form some material from a paper I presented on Margolis and Wendell at the Duquesne Forum in October 1993 and from a short article on the Red Scare and the coal strike of 1919 in northern West Virginia in the Fairmont State College publication, *Perspectives* (spring 1991).

I am grateful for the courtesy and assistance I received from librarians and archivists at many institutions, including Carnegie Library of Pittsburgh, Pennsylvania; Cleveland Public Library, Ohio; Detroit Public Library, Michigan; Fairmont State College, West Virginia; Labadie Collection of the University of Michigan, Ann Arbor; Library of Congress (Manuscript Division, Law Library, Periodical Reading Room), Washington D.C.; National Archives I (Washington D.C.), II (College Park, Md.), and the facility at Suitland, Maryland; National Archives Mid-Atlantic Region (Philadelphia); New York University Labor Archives, New York City; Ohio University Library, Athens; Seeley Mudd Library of Princeton University, Princeton, New Jersey; Swarthmore College Peace Collection, Swarthmore, Pennsylvania; University of Pittsburgh Law School Library, Pittsburgh; University of Delaware Library, Newark; Archives of Labor and Urban Affairs, Walter P. Reuther Library, Wayne State University, Detroit; West Virginia University Library and West Virginia and Regional History Collection, Morgantown; Western Reserve Historical Society, Cleveland. Susan Rosenfeld, formerly of the FBI Research Division, provided invaluable help on the use of the Freedom of Information Act/Privacy Act. I also wish to thank two Fairmont State College librarians: Janet Salvati for her encouragement and reference assistance and Genevieve Smith for her help with my numerous, sometimes arcane, interlibrary loan requests.

I value the criticism and suggestions of the scholars who read the manuscript for the University of Pittsburgh Press and the editorial staff of the University of Pittsburgh Press for their many improvements to the manuscript and for their professionalism. Of course, I absolve them of responsibility for errors of fact or interpretation, which are my own.

In this, as in most things, without the encouragement, patience, and support of Margie K. McCormick, this work could not have been done.

SEEING REDS

FEDERAL SURVEILLANCE OF RADICALS IN
THE PITTSBURGH MILL DISTRICT, 1917–1921

.

INTRODUCTION

> First Prince, then Pauper; overwork, then underwork; high wages, no wages;
> millionaire, immigrant; militant unions, masterful employers; marvelous
> business organization, amazing social disorganization. Such are the contrasts
> of "Pittsburgh the Powerful," the "Workshop of the World."
>
> John R. Commons, "The Wage-Earners of Pittsburgh," 1914

THIS BOOK EXAMINES the origins and growth of the United States government's domestic surveillance program in what used to be commonly called the Pittsburgh mill district during the Great War and the Red Scare (1917–1921). With the Steel City at its core the district included the steel mills, coke plants, coal mines, and heavy manufactories of western Pennsylvania, northern West Virginia, and eastern Ohio. It stretched from Lake Erie in the North to the headwaters of the Monongahela and Cheat Rivers in the South, and from about Johnstown in the mountains in the East to Wheeling and Youngstown in the West.[1]

The narrative is largely drawn from the declassified files of government agents and spies for the Departments of Justice, War, and Navy. These illuminate the experience and perspectives of the government's agents and of their counterparts, the street agitators and foot soldiers of the radical Left. The scene of the action and the talk—the streets, meeting halls, recreation areas, saloons, boarding houses, and private homes—is far from the intellectual ferment of Greenwich Village and the Lyrical Left of the time. Yet it was from this gritty setting, perhaps more than the other, that government intelligence practiced "seeing Reds."

In America, along with its manifold material benefits the industrial revolution showed a side that Joseph Schumpeter characterized as creative destruction, wreaking havoc with traditional agriculture, skills, and crafts, displacing millions, and bestowing progress unevenly and unequally. Alternative ideologies found it very difficult to vie for public support in competition with corporate capitalism, which not only dominated economic relations but whose core values were embedded in the institutions of culture, information, religion, and education, the filter through which most Americans interpreted the world.

In the late nineteenth and early twentieth centuries opposition movements

1

sprang up to challenge corporate industrialism. Predominantly middle and upper class, Progressives were the most visible and influential reformers. They included Republicans and Democrats, a diverse group with so many differing agendas and disparate views on such issues as race, child labor, women's rights, labor unions, immigration, and imperialism that historians have difficulty agreeing upon a definition of Progressivism. What these reformers seem to have shared was a commitment to preserving or recasting nineteenth-century liberalism with its emphasis on individual rights, civic responsibility, and constitutional government; a statist belief that only government power could tame the trusts; and a faith in the rational efficiency of bureaucratic organization to manage or engineer mass society. While many progressives acknowledged class antagonism and sympathized with the plight of industrial workers and the poor, they recoiled from the thought of revolution and sought social justice by constitutional means.[2]

More extreme than the Progressives were the avowed revolutionaries of the Left. The least radical of them were the more evolutionary than revolutionary political Socialists who sought through various strategies of education and political organization to win majority support for public ownership of the means of production and a society based on cooperation instead of competition. The American Socialist movement blended native populism and variants of European collectivism into a serious critique of corporate industrial capitalism. The Socialist Party showed flashes of surprising strength and enjoyed its greatest success between 1900 and 1918.[3] Yet, at best, it represented an articulate minority which, although it might be able to disrupt the smooth flow of production, hardly threatened the supremacy of capitalism or the American state.

Farthest left was the anticapitalist church militant made up of "direct action" advocates that included anarchists, syndicalists, communists, and others who believed that only a workers' revolution could bring about a just society. The organization that best symbolized, although it hardly encompassed, Left extremism was the Industrial Workers of the World (IWW). It was the IWW that experienced first the repressive/protective arm of the modern surveillance state in its peculiarly American context.

In a sense, World War I was the awful flowering of industrialism. Its weapons of mass death were the fruit of invention, capitalist enterprise, and mass production. Its ethnic conflicts and workers' movements were nurtured by demographic dislocations rooted in industrialization. Competition for capitalist markets and industrial raw materials fertilized its national rivalries. The rise of the Bolsheviks in Russia who personified world revolution against capitalism was its seed. Although the United States did not suffer the carnage and destruction of Europe, the effects of its relatively brief participation in the war were profound.

The Great War came at the climax of a half-century of growing pressure upon the United States government to reshape its administrative institutions to respond to industrialization. This was necessary to cope with an increasingly complex society and to mediate struggles between capital and labor and between competing capitalist factions. To call Democratic President Woodrow Wilson (1913–1921) pro-labor would overstate the case, but his administration did sponsor reforms favorable to workers, build an alliance with conservative trade unions through American Federation of Labor (AFL) president Samuel Gompers, and appoint former coal miner William B. Wilson as the nation's first secretary of labor. In addition, he liberally staffed the government with reformers of various hues, but their efforts were often stymied by an entrenched, generally Republican bureaucracy.[4]

America's sudden and controversial entry into World War I in 1917 required organizing and mobilizing a divided people and a massive production effort. The war effort needed labor's support and Wilson appointed Gompers to the powerful War Industries Board (WIB) and set up the National War Labor Board (NWLB), which was committed to mediating labor disputes. In return for a voice in government the administration demanded that the trade unions not take advantage of the crisis to alter the status quo. But labor leaders saw a chance to increase union membership and advance their goals with the help of the state.[5] In the emergency, Wilson centralized and expanded federal power as never before, creating a wartime welfare state. Washington managed food and materiel production, conscripted an army, shaped and controlled public opinion, and limited dissent.[6] But it was not primarily the tenured bureaucrats of the merit civil service who ran wartime Washington. Instead there occurred what Stephen Skowronek calls "a massive infusion of private power into public administration" as the government had to seek academic and business leaders to manage the war. The result was an executive-professional government coalition whose role was not supervising and directing "the private sector from positions in a powerful state but mediating and coordinating the actions of a powerful private sector in a weak state."[7]

The influx of wartime managers tipped the scales of the intragovernment capital-labor struggle toward the right in the War, Navy, and Justice Departments and infused the bureaucracy with private sector concerns and techniques. To maintain production quotas and ensure loyalty and compliance with conscription laws, the consolidation and centralization that had accompanied industrial growth and now the war required the nationalization and consolidation of the surveillance apparatus. At first an illusive host of German spies and sympathizers was the target of mushrooming federal domestic surveillance. Then, given the probusiness predilections of much of the wartime bureaucracy, the focus shifted to the control and defeat of left-wing labor and political organizations. American private enterprise already had an apparatus to deal with this problem. To identify troublemakers and defeat attempts to organize the workers, it relied heavily on gathering data on suspect individuals and groups from private "secret service," paid or coerced spies. Federal intelligence had only to adapt these means to its needs, even if to do so it would violate the Bill of Rights.

"We felt that Pittsburgh bore somewhat the same relation industrially to the country at large as Washington did politically." So wrote Paul U. Kellogg, director of *The Pittsburgh Survey* in 1912.[8] Kellogg's point, couched in the cautious language of a Progressive social scientist, was that Pittsburgh was the exemplar and seat of power of industrial capitalism in the United States. The city's great wealth, power, prosperity, and culture were built on the skill and vision of entrepreneurs and innovators out of the raw materials of the earth and the heavy toil of a legion of nameless laborers. Mines and mills did not simply employ, they used up, millions of landless American farmers and migrants from Europe and Asia. In the years before World War I, the Eastern and Southern European immigrants of many nationalities who predominated in the Pittsburgh mill district resembled in some respects modern "guest workers." Neither Protestant nor middle class nor even judged to be "white" by the Anglo-conformist majority, they were despised outcasts consigned to the American industrial underclass. In his classic *The Making of the English Working Class*, E. P. Thompson describes the recognition by early nineteenth-century British governing and policing classes that the underclass subcultures upon which they depended for cheap labor and from which they expected obedience were so difficult to understand as to appear "opaque."[9] Something analogous existed in the Pittsburgh mill district in the era of the Great War.

From 1917 to 1921 the Department of Justice's Bureau of Investigation (BI) (reorganized as the FBI in 1935) and other federal agencies were called upon to clarify the opacity, to serve a panoptic function, to make the actions and intentions of foreign radical workers intelligible to the elites and thereby manageable. Such activities, controversial enough in the private sector, became all the more so when carried out in secret by the United States. Federal domestic surveillance occupies a dark and uncomfortable corner of the national psyche.[10] Deep distrust of government and distant authority goes back to the Dissenter tradition of the first

English colonies and popular hostility to federal intrusions upon privacy in the early days of the Republic, as witness the Whiskey Rebellion (1794) and the reaction to the Alien and Sedition Acts (1798). In American history the quest for order and national unity and the desire of the privileged to protect their interests have collided over and over with deeply ingrained individualism and fear of big government. Seldom did they collide with such force as from 1917–1921, and Pittsburgh saw its fair share of the action.

Part I of this book (chapters 1–4) describes the war years, 1917–1918. Chapter 1 concentrates on the establishment and Pittsburgh area activities of the BI, the Military Intelligence Division (MID) and Office of Naval Intelligence (ONI). Since little has been written about the World War I government agents, they receive considerable attention here, especially undercover man Louis M. Wendell, who infiltrated the circle of pro-IWW lawyer Jacob Margolis. Chapter 2 discusses the targets for surveillance in the Pittsburgh Left as they appeared to federal agents. Chapter 3 outlines the suppression and partial takeover by government agents of the IWW and other left-wing groups in Pittsburgh. Chapter 4 depicts an expanding government surveillance apparatus that extended from its Pittsburgh base to Erie and even to the activities of conscientious objectors at Camp Lee, Virginia.

The post-Armistice Red Scare period, 1919–1921, is the focus of part 2 (chapters 5–9). Chapters 5 and 6 examine conditions at the end of the war that returned most of the wartime government managers to civilian life and the control of the bureaucracy to government careerists, who knew that their professional survival was tied to their ability to serve congressional politicians. During the Red Scare, Congress confronted, on the one hand, a resurgent American Left that was riding high on hopes generated by the rise of Russian Bolshevism abroad and a wave of strikes at home, and, on the other, corporate interests determined to roll back labor's wartime gains and widespread popular fears that a wave of labor strikes was the prelude to revolution. Terrorist bombings in May and June 1919 provided the impetus to create the Radical Division in the Justice Department headed by young J. Edgar Hoover for the purpose of finding the bombers and undertaking mass deportations of alien radicals. These aims became joined with an assumed adversarial role toward labor unions in the great steel and coal strikes of 1919. During these strikes the Pittsburgh field office aided corporate interests by discrediting American Federation of Labor (AFL) steelworkers' strike leader William Z. Foster and, extending its jurisdiction into northern West Virginia, by associating coal strikers there with the alleged Bolshevik radicalism of the Union of Russian Workers.

These actions took place concurrently with the best-remembered part of the

Red Scare, the antiradical Palmer raids. In the Pittsburgh mill district, the raids occurred in two phases: first (chapter 7) against the Union of Russian Workers (UORW), many of whose members were deported to Soviet Russia on the U.S.S. *Buford* at the end of 1919; and second (chapter 8) against the Communist Party and the Communist Labor Party in early 1920. Mounting opposition finally halted the Justice Department's campaign against alien "Reds," but, as explained in chapter 9, not before the Pittsburgh BI orchestrated the disbarment of the radical lawyer Margolis after his value declined as an intelligence asset; and not before the public mind and the federal domestic intelligence culture were indelibly imprinted with the image of socialism as dangerously subversive, un-American, and, perhaps, unworthy of equal protection of the laws.

PART 1

WORLD WAR I SURVEILLANCE, 1917–1918

1
THE G-MEN
VIRTUE MADE VISIBLE (AND INVISIBLE)

> I have taken personal pains to inquire and satisfy myself as to the character,
> ability, and general worth of every one of the so-called under-cover agents of
> the Department of Justice . . . [and] it is a fact that we do have . . . some men of
> splendid character, of unusual intellectual attainments, and a wonderfully high
> order of physical courage, who take their lives into their hands daily in associa-
> tion with the criminal classes.
>
> Attorney General A. Mitchell Palmer, 1920

WHEN THE GREAT WAR BEGAN in August 1914, the United States government
lacked the ability to carry on large-scale internal security operations. Of the various federal agencies that had dabbled in such matters, the Treasury Department's
Secret Service was the best known. Created in the Civil War era to ferret out coun-
terfeiters, from 1914 to 1916 it conducted small-scale domestic counterintelligence,
after which it largely abandoned the field to the Justice Department. The War and
Navy Departments also conducted clandestine operations while the Post Office
Department monitored or suppressed suspect foreign and radical publications
and read the mail of alleged spies and subversives.[1]

In April 1917, when the United States entered the war, these agencies lacked the
experience, expertise, or the personnel to keep tabs on the country's vast and diverse population. There had never been a national police force, although the
Pinkerton Detective Agency sometimes acted the part on a de facto basis. In times
past federal departments had contracted detective work to Pinkerton and other
private agencies. Then in 1892 the Pinkertons' role in the Homestead Strike stirred
so much public controversy that Congress prohibited government departments
from employing private detectives. Until 1908 Justice Department policy was to
borrow Secret Service agents from Treasury when it needed investigative assistance. But then, after T-men on loan to Justice uncovered a land fraud scheme that
embarrassed prominent congressional interests, legislators prohibited the practice and banned the attorney general from collecting information for partisan po-

litical purposes. In a furious reaction to the ban, which he took as interference with the power of the executive branch, President Theodore Roosevelt ordered Attorney General Charles A. Bonaparte to staff a Bureau of Investigation (BI). In this action congressional opponents saw the beginnings of what one called a "central secret service bureau such as there is in Russia." Despite such fears, on July 26, 1908, Stanley Finch became the first bureau chief, presiding over a bureaucratic empire of twenty-three employees.[2]

In 1910, capitalizing on a "white slavery scare," Progressive social hygienists pushed through Congress the White Slave Traffic Act, or Mann Act, that gave the BI its first significant mission, the interdiction of interstate and international traffic in prostitutes. With an enhanced appropriation and a chance to prove its usefulness, the fledgling bureau waged a vigorous, high-profile battle against prostitution by applying the act to personal immorality more than commercial activity. A case in point was the arrest of black boxer Jack Johnson for crossing a state line with his white mistress. In making their cases, BI agents often relied on prostitutes, the victims of the white slave traffic, recruited as informers. A technique agents used was to file complaints against the women so as to keep them in custody until they cooperated.[3]

A premise of the Mann Act, based upon the nativist findings of the Dillingham Commission, was that both the alleged procurers and the thousands of women and girls they degraded were mostly immigrants from Southern and Eastern Europe. The act therefore permitted the deportation of unnaturalized immigrants, male or female, who frequented places where prostitutes might gather such as music halls or dance halls. As a result, by 1916, according to Immigration Commissioner Frederic C. Howe, Ellis Island had become the dumping ground for hundreds of alien women, most of whom were at worst "casual offenders who would not have been arrested under ordinary circumstances." Significantly, at this formative moment of the bureau's organizational culture just before American entry into World War I, it earned its first plaudits by addressing a "scare" and playing to an overblown and transient public fear of the new immigrants.[4]

In 1912, the Mann Act investigations contributed to A. Bruce Bielaski's promotion to BI chief when Finch temporarily took over a special BI task force to suppress the white slave traffic. During his tenure (1912–1919) Bielaski sought to professionalize the Bureau and to enlarge its role. Tall, young, athletic, and a workaholic, Bielaski was the son of a Methodist minister and the grandson of a Polish immigrant who died fighting for the Union in the Civil War.[5] He was a Washington D.C.–area native and on his mother's side could trace his roots to colonial Maryland. Like several early BI higher-ups—J. Edgar Hoover and George W. Ruch come to mind—he was a George Washington University Law School graduate. His career in law enforcement began when he was offered a job in the file room if he would play shortstop for the Justice Department baseball team. Two of his siblings also distinguished themselves as enforcers of "100 percent American-ism." Brother Frank B. (1890–1961), who styled himself a "research executive," was a detective, a World War II OSS investigator, and a key figure in the 1945 *Amerasia* case.[6] Sister Ruth Bielaski Shipley (1885–1966) headed the U.S. Passport Office from 1928 to 1955. In the cold war era she denied passports to Paul Robeson, W. E. B. DuBois, Linus Pauling, Arthur Miller, Rockwell Kent, and others on political grounds.[7]

When the war began in Europe in 1914 Bielaski had about a hundred agents to cover the entire country, many with Mann Act experience, few with spy- or radi-cal-catching experience. By 1915 BI strength had doubled but was still inadequate to serve as the eyes and ears of the nation or to foil the plans of German spies. That was brought home to Bielaski and his boss, Attorney General Thomas W. Grego-ry, when (unbeknownst to them and without Justice Department involvement) Frank Burke of the rival Treasury Department Secret Service cleverly filched the plans for a Central Powers propaganda campaign in the United States from a Ger-man diplomat in New York. By the time the United States entered the war, Bielas-ki's force had grown to four hundred agents, still far too few to watch millions of aliens and citizens who might be revolutionaries or spies.[8] Arguably, the Treasury Department, Post Office, and Bureau of Immigration were better equipped and more experienced in many aspects of such work.

However, the Justice Department required a wartime mission and the coordi-nation and control of domestic intelligence seemed to require a centralized struc-ture. Justice, with its U.S. attorneys in place in every state and many large cities, was in a good position to organize the resources of the multitude of state, local, and private police forces that constituted a national tangle of often overlapping or ill-defined jurisdictions. The role of the Bureau of Investigation in the rational hi-erarchical model of organization then in vogue was to consolidate and centralize data collection and investigation. Its agents would investigate individuals and groups from German spies to radical agitators who, in the eyes of the national elites, might weaken the war effort or subvert the nation.

Despite its woefully inadequate resources for so formidable a task, in 1917 Bielaski promoted the view that the BI was the nerve center of an omniscient se-cret service that protected Americans from the kaiser's spies and saboteurs. Its "shadows" haunted public spaces. Its "eyes and minds" worked among railway conductors, farmers, waiters, barbers, chauffeurs, chambermaids, bellboys, and underworld figures. So effective was this spy-catching apparatus it was claimed that a German spy proclaimed in chagrin, "this is worse than Russia."[9]

The army and navy would join the BI in the domestic intelligence field. Like the BI they were new to the game. The army first set up an internal security apparatus at the turn of the century during the nationalist uprising against the American occupation of the Philippines. In 1916 it had conducted limited surveillance within the United States at the Mexican border. However, it was not until May 5, 1917, shortly after American entry into the war, that Lt. Col. Ralph H. Van Deman, "the father of the army intelligence," became chief of the new Military Intelligence Division (MID) with a staff of two officers. On June 17 MID was formally assigned espionage and counterespionage responsibility, and over the eighteen months of U.S. involvement in the war it grew to 282 officers, 29 sergeants, and more than 1,000 civilian employees. In Pittsburgh the army's key spy operation was the Plant Protection Section (PPS), whose agents used the cover of fire and safety inspections to set up and oversee volunteer internal "secret service" operations in mills and plants with war contracts. In charge of the Pittsburgh office was Edward H. Flood. J. W. Payne ran PPS.[10]

Navy intelligence began in 1882 as a branch in the Office of Navigation. It was transferred to the Naval War College in 1900, where it languished until World War I brought it to life as the Office of Naval Intelligence (ONI). It then grew rapidly, until by the end of the war there were more than three hundred officers in ONI's Washington office. Its director, Captain Roger Welles, and Undersecretary of the Navy Franklin D. Roosevelt filled top ONI positions with New York socialites and old stock blue bloods, whose patriotism was freighted with the defense of class interests.[11] That description certainly fitted George E. Rowe (agent #128a), who supervised ONI's Pittsburgh branch office. He was a Delaware native who belonged to the Sons of the American Revolution and traced his roots to seventeenth-century Virginia. Before the war he had been a salesman for a Pittsburgh steel company. The other two ONI lead agents were also intimately tied to corporate and nativist ideals. Raymond E. Horn (agent #128) had been confidential secretary to Attorney General George W. Dillingham in the Taft administration and assistant director of the BI. Arthur G. Burgoyne, Jr. (agent #251) was a journalist closely connected to Republican politics and a future city editor of the *Pittsburgh Post*. Pittsburgh ONI operations centered on the Naval Plant and Contract Division, similar to MID's Plant Protection Section, but agents worked very closely with the BI and

MID and the Employers' Association of Pittsburgh. ONI's initial emphasis on plant protection soon took a back seat to plant intelligence, the gathering of information on "anti-American, pacifistic, and radical personages, organizers, agitators, and societies in or out of these plants." ONI dictated personnel policies to contractors and ordered them to "root out troublemakers, loafers, and disloyal workers who ignored the Liberty Loan or Red Cross fund drives."[12]

All of the government intelligence agencies used the American Protective League (APL), a large and controversial wartime civilian volunteer "secret service." Under the supervision of the BI, championed in the beginning by MID's Chicago director, Thomas B. Crockett, and organized and funded by business interests, the APL membership grew nationwide from its inception in the spring of 1917 to 100,000 at the end of the year and 250,000 by the Armistice. The group's ostensible function was to assist in routine investigations to free the professional agents for more pressing business and to provide auxiliaries for large tasks that required temporary manpower. APL membership conferred a pseudoauthority and encouraged a meddlesome officiousness that sometimes led to vigilantism and trampling the Bill of Rights. The role played by the APL varied by locale, and what evidence there is suggests that the Pittsburgh chapter played an active but subordinate role in government labor espionage.[13]

The wartime justification of all domestic intelligence was the legitimate need to prevent subversion of the war effort, especially in the production of goods and the enforcement of the conscription act. To accomplish this, controversial special legislation defined and enlarged the federal investigative role. The Espionage Act (June 1917), amended as the Sedition Act (May 1918), gave nearly open-ended powers to the Bureau and other federal agencies to conduct domestic spying. The law suspended First Amendment rights by imposing strict government censorship and outlawing criticism of the government or the war effort. To this was added in October 1918 the Alien Act that permitted the deportation of unnaturalized members of anarchist groups.[14]

In the wartime atmosphere of intolerant "100 percent Americanism" these acts provided a legal excuse for the BI and other federal agencies to secretly "investigate and catalogue the political opinions, beliefs, and affiliations of the citizenry [and aliens]."[15] It was left to the government to police itself against Bill of Rights abuses in the name of national security. The officials with the primary responsibility, Attorney General Gregory and Secretary of War Newton D. Baker, were essentially moderate men who wished to preserve basic liberties. Although they did not wish to take sides in disputes between labor and management, political realities and the demands of an all-out war effort blinded them to abuses and made them powerful allies of industrial management.

In the case of Pittsburgh, to keep out the unions, the steel industry led by U.S. Steel, which dominated the Pittsburgh industrial economy, promoted the open shop, expanded profit-sharing and welfare programs, sponsored Americanization classes, and, between 1916 and 1918, gave frequent wage increases.[16] If these benign incentives should fail, big steel maintained an arsenal of powerful disincentives. State government in Pennsylvania, with its iron and coal police ("Black Cossacks," union men called them), was steel's ally. Local government, especially in company towns, was its tool. In Pittsburgh and surrounding steel and coal towns, big steel controlled the police and politicians, who were capital's first line of defense against workers' organizations. The corporations also could count on the popular press and the mainline churches to hew to the management line.

The steel trust and other heavy industries also carried on a secret war with an army of informants and detectives on call to monitor the workplace. The largest companies maintained their own in-house "secret service." Others pooled their resources to make Pittsburgh an "open labor market" mainly through industrial espionage cooperatives. For example, Mesta Machine, Westinghouse Air Brake, Union Switch and Signal, and a dozen other firms did so under the aegis of the Employers' Association of Pittsburgh.[17] For employers whose need was only occasional, private firms stood ready to provide espionage agents or strike-breakers as required.

A practical question in the spring of 1917 was where the BI and other domestic surveillance agencies would find qualified investigators to fill their swelling ranks. Government officials could tap two large pools of outside expertise: police and private detective agencies. Police forces in company towns of the Pittsburgh mill district were accustomed to defending property interests and the established political order from the challenges of labor organizations and economic and political radicals, not from German spies. They were typically extensions of the power of local plant or mine executives, but experience showed that, even when augmented in emergencies by posses of armed citizens, small-town police and county sheriff departments could not deal with masses of striking workers.[18] Those required state militias or federal troops to be summoned. In wartime, military personnel were needed elsewhere.

In large urban centers such as Pittsburgh, business-police-labor relationships were more intricate, but here, too, police power was wielded more often than not against labor organizers and socialists. Also, police relied largely on brute force control, suppressing dissent with tactics ranging from intimidating surveillance to denial of meeting permits to harassment to serious head-knocking. Faced with more sophisticated and better organized adversaries, some large city forces developed "bomb squads" or "red squads." These specialized units often employed professional detectives who assumed false identities to infiltrate targeted groups. In 1914, for example, Inspector Thomas J. Tunney's New York Bomb Squad put a man inside the Industrial Workers of the World (IWW) in New York and northern New Jersey. In 1917 members of Tunney's squad working out of a safe house in the nation's capital became the nucleus of the army's counterintelligence corps.[19] Still, the numbers of such specialized police were too few to meet federal needs.

Although the Immigration Bureau, Internal Revenue, and the Secret Service provided some recruits, when the federal investigative agencies expanded during the Great War, it was mainly to the private detective industry that they turned for field personnel. By enlarging upon the myths that labor organizations were inherently violent and that immigrant workers were untrustworthy and susceptible to revolutionary appeals, private detective agencies had pioneered and prospered in the field of industrial espionage. The public disgrace that ensued from its strike-breaking role in the Homestead Strike of 1892 caused the giant Pinkerton Agency, its principal rival the William Burns Agency, and a host of smaller PI operations to adopt more sophisticated and covert methods of "harmonizing" labor-management relations. The use of these new methods and the rapid growth of the detective agencies after 1900 were directly linked to industrial management's growing fear and distrust of its workers. Industrial espionage was a highly competitive business that depended upon the detectives' ability to nurture that fear and distrust. Proof that they succeeded is the fact that by 1917 they outnumbered soldiers in the peacetime U.S. Army.[20] It was, according to historian Frank Morn, a "golden age of private detective work." "Mushroom agencies" proliferated in industrial cities, many to specialize in strike breaking, labor spying, and anti-union propaganda.[21]

In Pittsburgh more than twenty agencies advertised in the city directories between 1915 and 1919. Led by the giants, Pinkerton and Burns, their offices were clustered downtown near Pittsburgh's "Wall Street" along Fourth Avenue and in the nearby Bakewell and Berger buildings on Grant Street. There were also other detectives who advertised in the guise of "audit" or "public relations" services. Whatever they were called, most stood ready to send men into plants and mines throughout the tristate region.

Despite the popularity of detective fiction, which since the late nineteenth century had polished their image, the respectability of World War I–era private detectives was in dispute. For many, *detective* still connoted a marginal man—a shady, often boozy, sleazy liar or a publicity-seeking incompetent. The real Pinkertons, after all, were the cultural descendants of eighteenth-century British "thief takers" who served laws that protected the interests of the few and who were hated by working folk who held up "social bandits" as true heroes. By the end of the nineteenth century the values shift that accompanied industrialization and a burgeoning middle class that identified with the established business order had altered the fictional image of the detective. Readers now were asked to admire kid-gloved Nick Carter and, above all others, the elegantly eccentric and individualist genius Sherlock Holmes. Both characters celebrated the protection against the forces of evil afforded to society by solitary enlightened amateur sleuths.

In the early twentieth century American private detectives bore little resemblance to the cerebral, upper-class amateurs of fiction. Neither, except perhaps in their marginalized urban lifestyle and ambiguous ethical position, did they resemble the hard-boiled private eye character that appeared about the time of World War I in the works of Raymond Chandler and ex-Pinkerton Dashiell Hammett. Some students of the genre see the Confidential Op, Philip Marlowe, and their ilk as latter-day romantic action heroes; modern urban versions of nineteenth-century white male frontier heroes who acted out the myth of the hunter battling the savage "other" to protect civilization, relying, of course, on the quintessential American weapon, the gun. For the lone frontiersmen, metaphorically, the "other" had been untamed nature in the form of wild beast or hostile Indian. For the lonely private eye it was the beasts that stalked the brutal city: venal politicians, organized criminals, petty hoodlums, and immoral rich men.[22]

From the more recondite perspective of postmodern philosopher-historian Michel Foucault, detective literature is part of the discourse on law in the "disciplinary state." It is a branch of the ideological apparatus called culture that celebrates the repressive state apparatus called the police. For the modern, enlightened industrial state seeks to impose order, as it must, not crudely by coercion, but elegantly by means of scientific knowledge of human behavior. The ideal World War I–era private detective was a functionary of the rational regime of surveillance and businesslike reporting. Utilizing the informer and the index file, according to Dennis Porter, the detective was supposed to open society to "visual inspection down to its darkest recesses, so that dissent might be stifled, crime depoliticized, and the criminal underworld organized as a relatively harmless enclave within the established order."[23]

One doubts that many working detectives understood their calling that way.

They came largely from the status and identity-seeking native lower middle class and brought to the job the prevailing cultural assumptions of that class. They identified with the economic status quo and with corporate power. They took the enemies of big business to be the enemies of the United States. They embraced nativism. What little they knew about recent immigrants inclined them to be condescending, hostile, and suspicious and to react to aliens as threats to their own security, culture, and advancement.

Necessarily they were also greater or lesser entrepreneurs whose business was to profit from labor-management conflict. Real day-to-day detective work was often tawdry and deceitful, so astute leaders in the business rationalized and romanticized it. As he so often did, detective dynasty founder Allan Pinkerton led the way by publishing several ghostwritten detective novels glamorizing himself or dramatizing the careers of successful operatives, such as undercover informer James McPharlan, whose testimony had brought down the Molly Maguires in 1876 and who, as head of Pinkerton's Denver office, took on western miners at Coeur d'Alene in 1914.[24]

In early twentieth-century novels published in their name, two famous detectives and future BI directors, William J. Flynn (1919–1921) and William J. Burns (1921–1924), presented detective work as modern and scientific. Their message was that cutting-edge technologies of their time, including fingerprint identification and listening devices such as the detectaphone, complemented the sleuth's deductive process, making crime-solving surer and more accurate and the detective more benevolent and fair-minded.[25] The famous detective in Flynn's *The Argyle Case* rescued a damsel in distress and "quickly convinced of her innocence, . . . [took] prompt and effective steps to silence once and for all the cruel baseless rumors that had circulated about her" and for good measure threatened to sue any newspaper "which printed anything further reflecting on her character."[26]

Despite such propaganda, the public remained skeptical. Various jurisdictions enacted anti-Pinkerton laws forbidding governments from employing private detectives. In 1911 the radical Randolph Bourne characterized the work of the future BI director Burns as "a system of organized espionage, organized temptation, organized bribery, and organized betrayal. . . . The practitioner of this profession should be nameless, like the public executioner."[27] Burns himself said detectives as a class "are the biggest lot of blackmailing thieves that ever went unwhipped by justice." Federal judge George W. Anderson added that they "are necessarily drawn from the unwholesome and untrustworthy classes. A right-minded man refuses such a job."[28]

Such denunciations did not deter more than one hundred thousand Americans from working as private investigators in the early twentieth century. The appeal of the job evidently lay not only in its financial rewards, but also in the pathway it offered to voyeuristic urban adventure and identification with power and authority. Depersonalized, justified, and sanctified by licensing and behavioral standards, however loose, the detective's snooping or union-busting was made to seem almost as respectable as business leaders believed it was necessary to their control of the workplace.[29]

As Rhodri Jeffreys-Jones observes, "The industrial sleuth was out for himself. He wanted no showdown with the working class, only a permanent appearance of its immanence." Certainly undercover operatives were prone to exaggerate the militancy and radicalism of workers, inflate their own accomplishments, and neglect to separate hearsay from direct evidence. They were too much given to compiling bare lists of suspect workers. Yet, as businessmen their natural temptation to take advantage of employers' fears had to be tempered by the need for repeat business and satisfactory references. Successful detective agencies gave employers reliable, efficient, cost-effective service and provided accurate information. To ensure this, both agencies and employers evaluated reports with a practiced eye and employed cross-checks of the accuracy and performance of operatives. They set spies to spy on spies and compared information on the same assignment from several spies who did not know each other. Good operatives did not have to be unbiased, but they had to be careful observers and accurate reporters.[30]

What is known about the recruitment of BI special agents (1917–1921) is mostly anecdotal.[31] The usual account, typified by Don Whitehead's semiofficial *FBI Story,* sharply contrasts the Bureau before and after J. Edgar Hoover's ascension to the directorship in 1924. Before, goes the story, it was highly politicized and corrupt. Afterward it became a pillar of rectitude and professionalism.[32] That interpretation is accurate up to a point, especially as it applies to Harry M. Daugherty's tenure as attorney general, 1921–1924, but it slights the problems the pre-Hoover BI had to grapple with during its very rapid expansion to meet new and enlarged responsibilities in World War I. Of necessity, lacking its own training facilities or program, the BI wanted agents with legal and investigative experience who could learn on the job. So little training was provided, recalled Jacob Spolansky, who was recruited for antiradical work by Military Intelligence in Chicago in 1917 and then began his thirty-year career as a BI special agent in 1919, that his indoctrination was nothing more than a pep talk on selfless nationalism inspired by Elbert Cubberly's "A Message to Garcia."[33]

For this study the personnel files of four Pittsburgh special agents who created and maintained the "radical squad" from 1917 to 1921 provide the chief evidence of the Bureau recruitment policy. In 1915 BI chief Bielaski had found it "necessary to designate some one as Special Agent-in-Charge" (SAC) in Pittsburgh and offered the job, at six dollars a day and expenses, to Robert Simms Judge. Judge was the unmarried, twenty-six-year-old son of a Wellsburg, West Virginia, drugstore owner. After completing West Virginia University Law School in 1910, he became a law clerk in Wheeling, where in 1912 he earned a modest $1,750. His administrative experience consisted of managing his father's drugstore for a couple of years.[34]

Judge's qualifications for Pittsburgh SAC seemed as meager as his earnings from the law. True, he was physically imposing: darkly handsome, almost six feet tall, and 190 pounds. But until he finally got the job a year and a half after applying, he had only worked for the Bureau part time as the Wheeling, West Virginia, white slave officer. In that position, which netted him only $250 per year, he investigated prostitution, learned to use informers, and explored the seamier side of a tough Ohio River town. Perhaps he also gained experience with political radicals and foreign intrigue during the Mexican Revolution. In 1916 he served at the border town of El Paso with the Eighteenth Pennsylvania Infantry.[35]

In February 1915 Judge moved to Union Street on Pittsburgh's North Side and assumed his duties at the Bureau's St. Nicholas Building office at Fourth Avenue and Grant Street. That building was to be a nerve center of covert activity during the war. The Secret Service, MID, ONI, and, for a time, the APL also made their headquarters there. At the beginning of 1917 Judge's investigative force consisted only of himself and special agent John R. Dillon.[36] After the United States entered the war in April the Radical Squad came into being and grew until at its peak in early 1920 a half-dozen special agents did full-time "radical work" and managed a force of undercover informants.

The first agent to be hired specifically for radical work, in July 1917, was twenty-nine-year-old Edgar B. Speer, Judge's college classmate at West Virginia University. To become a G-man, Speer gave up a $22-a-week job as a special assignment reporter for the *Pittsburgh Sun*. He had read for the law in his native Uniontown, Pennsylvania, but he had worked on newspapers since 1911. Reporting for papers in Clarksburg, West Virginia, as well as New Castle and Beaver County, Pennsylvania, made him familiar with information sources in the coal and steel regions surrounding Pittsburgh, where Chief Bielaski expected the Pittsburgh office to do much of its work on radicals. Speer's press contacts would be useful to help the Bureau with public relations and information management.[37]

Judge justified hiring Speer despite his lack of law enforcement training by noting that he was clean-cut, well spoken, and had provided good, verifiable references. Among those references was a prominent West Virginia coal company official who was known for anti-union activity. Speer was unlikely to be drafted because he had a wife and two children, one of whom, by the way, two-year-old Edgar, Junior, would grow up to become the president of United States Steel Corporation.[38]

In January 1918 Fred M. Ames joined the radical squad. Ames was an eight-year veteran and former corporal in the Pennsylvania State Constabulary at Greensburg, Pennsylvania. He had been in plain clothes and for six months had served a sort of BI apprenticeship by feeding Judge information on labor activities. Although his education ended with grade school, which would later hamper his advancement in the Bureau, the twenty-nine-year-old Ames was by far Judge's toughest and most experienced agent. He, too, was a veteran of the Mexican border where he had served a five-year hitch (1905–1910) as a trooper in a cavalry unit.[39]

During his stint as a "Cossack," Ames earned praise from public officials and business leaders for his tenacity and courage in pursuit of suspects, particularly aliens, and for his bravery in strike situations. According to a Pennsylvania judge, Ames understood criminals so thoroughly that he "seems to be able to distinguish them from others instinctively."[40] Like Speer and Judge, he brought to the BI a strong antipathy to labor radicals and an attitude of superiority to foreigners.

For patriotic zeal neither Judge nor Ames could top Henry J. Lenon, who was hired in June 1918. A six-month assignment as BI informer, functioning as "the eyes and ears of the government at all times," as he wrote on his application, preceded his full-time employment. Before that he likely came to the attention of the BI as an undercover operative with American Audit and Inspection Company, which specialized in plant investigations in Youngstown and Pittsburgh. He had also been an American Protective League (APL) volunteer and had powerful friends among area Republican politicians. Lenon was a zealous Red hunter, a true-blue devotee of 100 percent Americanism who gave speeches before neighborhood groups, churches, Sunday schools, and the YMCA on topics patriotic, moral, and uplifting. Select titles were "Preparedness," "Thrift," "Know Thyself," "Right Living" (on the evils of venereal disease), "Walking," "Manhood," and "Christianity."[41]

Lenon, a Pittsburgh native, had lived many years in Chicago. In his youth he had been a boxer and a runner. Over the years he had built on his six years of public schooling through an ambitious, if eclectic, course of self-improvement. He had taken public speaking, general studies, and evening lecture courses. In Chicago he had taken classes at the Sheldon School of Salesmanship, the Moody Institute, and Dr. Larson's School of Swedish Movements, Scientific Massage, and Corrective Physical Culture. His job history included a number of low- to middle-level white-collar jobs, mostly clerk or salesman, and, probably undercover, blue-collar jobs at Ford Motors and several steel companies. At fifty and with grown children, Lenon was too old for the draft.[42]

In these four cases, the BI recruited men with a college degree or legal training or with police or private investigative experience. Like Chief Bielaski's brother Frank, Ames and Judge had been in the army at the Mexican border in 1916. None was likely to be drafted. Judge knew each of the new agents personally or had auditioned them as informers before bringing them on board. He picked local men who knew the labor scene, who had demonstrated allegiance to corporate interests, and who came recommended by business leaders.[43] All were of northern European stock and considered loyal to the establishment. Ames and Lenon belonged to patriotic organizations. Except for Judge, who claimed a "fair" knowledge of German, none was a student or spoke the language of the ethnic groups they were to investigate.[44]

Their work for the radical squad was different from routine BI work and required men with a taste for it. Lenon wrote that "study and research" and "locating and interviewing subjects, witnesses, and informants" took up more than half of his time.[45] Pittsburgh ONI chief Rowe described the Pittsburgh information sources as a mix of individual businessmen, workers, employee associations, trade associations, foreign societies, and detective agencies.[46] This meant that radical squad agents performed little actual legwork, relying heavily upon an array of civilian volunteers and paid undercover informants.

At the bottom of the federal undercover hierarchy was a heterogeneous lot of amateurs, a few of whom remain visible through their reports in declassified BI case and investigative files. Many were temporarily employed because their situation and willingness to spy fitted them for a particular investigation. Some volunteered; others, members of suspect organizations, were "hooked," that is, forced to inform because BI agents had something on them.

Some brought more enthusiasm than knowledge and judgment to their assignments. A bizarre example was "agent" and Harvard College student, class of 1919, and future Madison Avenue advertising executive Frederick S. Owen. In 1918, after a relative intimated to draft board members that young history instructor Samuel Eliot Morison had expressed pro-German, antidraft, and pacifist opinions, the BI asked Owen to spy on the professor. Reporting shortly afterward,

Owen characterized Morison "as a nervous, sarcastic talker . . . [who] seemed to take particular delight in criticizing most outrageously the men of . . . [the Gilded Age] and accented reading such authors as [reformer] Carl Schurz." Owen then "visited" the professor's office and made a list of incriminating "books and pamphlets of I.W.W. and pacific nature."[47] Although it took months and the intervention of Senator Henry Cabot Lodge, the BI cleared the illustrious historian and future admiral.[48] A less well-connected person might not have been so fortunate.

More useful to the BI than callow amateurs were the professional operatives who for four or five dollars a day and expenses would assume radical identities. They worked undercover as miners, mill operatives, labor union officials, or radical agitators.[49] Justice Department documents usually refer to them as "confidential informants" or "special employees." ONI called them "voluntary aides." The federal agencies, the visible government, naturally drew a veil of secrecy around information about the recruitment, numbers, pay, assignments, and demographic characteristics of their invisible support force.[50] Documents from near the end of the Red Scare report that the BI then employed between thirty-five and forty-five confidential informers at a cost of a least two hundred dollars per day.[51] It is a safe bet that during the war there were many more.

Most of these men and (a few) women must have come from the ranks of labor spies. Jeffreys-Jones argues that the market for private detectives was saturated by 1917. More and more industrial firms were operating their own "secret service" departments. Groups of companies banded together as employer associations also maintained full-time intelligence-gathering apparatus. Therefore the federal agencies did not lack for willing recruits from the PI ranks.[52]

The informants, who came mostly from private detective agencies and corporate "secret service" departments, earned their bread and butter by infiltrating the industrial workforce. MID hired hundreds, some already planted in suspect organizations, who were officially "on furlough" from Pinkerton, Burns, and other companies. For example, MID files show that in 1918 private detectives employed by the Northern Information Bureau of Minneapolis filled executive positions in the local IWW; one as the secretary of the St. Paul branch, the Tom Mooney Defense League, and the Non-Partisan League. Thiel Detective Service Company had two men who had been inside the Tulsa IWW for six years.[53]

The agencies, reasoning that informants could provide information not available to special agents on the outside, generally ignored the legal prohibitions against hiring private investigators. But relying on undercover reports to build a court case had its drawbacks, among them deciding whether or not a spy should testify and reveal his identity. In 1918 BI undercover operatives feared "being arrested in I.W.W. raids and . . . that they may be compelled to testify, thus revealing their duplicity and rendering themselves liable to personal injury."[54] Informants were even more reluctant to go to jail to maintain their cover. For example, after a Burns Agency detective "who was well up in the councils of the I.W.W." was convicted along with scores of other Wobbly leaders and spent eight months in jail in 1917 and 1918, other Burns infiltrators rebelled. They demanded "formal recognition and some credential directly from the Government which they can exhibit at the proper time if they should be arrested . . . and they also wish to have matters so arranged that they will not be called as witnesses."[55]

Despite these attitudes, the BI recruited a few clever operatives during the wartime emergency, men at the top of the special employee hierarchy, who worked themselves into midlevel leadership in radical organizations and remained there for years. They would go to jail to maintain their cover and BI field offices found them indispensable as information sources and manipulators of radicals. In 1917 the BI brought such a man to Pittsburgh. His name was Louis (Leo) M. Wendell. A collect telegram dated July 20, 1917, to special agent Judge signaled his arrival: "Pursuant to conversation with Mr. [Charles] DeWoody [Cleveland agent-in-charge] of even date regarding sending a man to Pittsburgh, will arrive . . . 9 P.M." Listing his occupation as "inspector," Wendell kept his own initials, a common practice among private undercover operatives, when he adopted the name Louis M. Walsh and moved into room number 8 of E. W. Gibson's Hotel at 512 Grant Street.[56]

Wendell's life before Pittsburgh is a blank page. A cover story planted by BI agents in Pittsburgh papers in 1918 placed him at the Mexican border in 1915 and 1916 circulating Spanish language propaganda for "I.W.W. leaders" Pancho Villa and Emiliano Zapata. Neither revolutionary fit that characterization, but the IWW was a powerful force among increasingly militant Mexican laborers, especially oil field workers at Tampico and copper miners on both sides of the U.S.-Mexican border. The border was also a focus of international intrigue. Japanese and German agents were active there at a time when the United States and Mexico seemed close to war.[57]

The story, which was probably concocted by Judge and Speer, was plausible. The Villistas had been front-page news and American Socialists and Wobblies had protested against what they characterized as American imperialism in Mexico. Even better, the area and action were sufficiently remote to make verifying it from Pittsburgh difficult. Yet if Special Employee Wendell was at the border, it was probably in connection with the U.S. Army's intelligence-gathering operation there. Or maybe he was one of the private detectives Col. Van Deman recruited from Burns and Pinkerton in the Midwest in 1916 and 1917 for undercover work.[58]

Wherever he was before Pittsburgh, at some time Wendell must have been a private detective who engaged in antilabor espionage in Cleveland and, perhaps, Detroit. It was the then Cleveland SAC, Charles DeWoody, who dispatched him to Pittsburgh. Wendell's reports show that Charles E. Ruthenberg, northeastern Ohio Socialist leader, who was later the first secretary of the Communist Party, knew him as an enemy from Cleveland. Furthermore, Wendell's arrival in Pittsburgh on July 20 coincided with the completion of the prosecution's case in the Cleveland Espionage Act trial of Ruthenberg and two others for antidraft speeches. As for his Detroit connection, genealogical data show that Wendell is a common surname in the Toledo-Detroit area and that is where he would finish his detective career in the 1930s and 1940s as a labor spy for the auto industry.[59]

Federal agencies took great care to protect their confidential sources, including purging the files to hide the identity of informants. Despite such care, in Wendell's case the investigative files still provide a relatively detailed picture of this particular anonymous spy at work. The proof may be summarized concisely. In correspondence, BI and MID officials carefully referred to Wendell only as our "special employee" or "special informant." But in case files, now declassified and in the National Archives, they retained typed summaries of his first-person reports covering almost every day from July 1917 to December 1919 along with the observations of other agents on his activities. Usually BI reports were filed on a fill-in-the-box standard form. From July to December 1917 his reports carry the name Wendell neatly typed in the upper left-hand corner of each report form in the box "Report made by." In the text of one such report Wendell notes that he has followed special agent Judge's instructions to take out Post Office Box #1381 in the name of L. M. Walsh! Early in 1918 "Wendell" was replaced by "836" and soon after he was always so identified in BI and MID reports and correspondence.[60]

But even as 836, the number of SAC Judge's post office box, one can tell that L. M. Wendell, L. M. Walsh, and 836 are the same person. Whenever 836 listed those at a radical meeting or conversation, Walsh was one of them. Once, when the BI assigned an agent to track Walsh at Erie, Pennsylvania, he proved "too clever for our man." According to the report, Walsh "jumped into a taxi and went to the NYC [New York Central] depot and boarded a train, but Agent Schlaudecker was unable to state whether he purchased a ticket for Pittsburgh, Cleveland, or Ashtabula. 836 [that is, Walsh!] informs us Walsh went to Pittsburgh." And finally there

Enlargement of newspaper photo of L. M. Walsh-Wendell-836 from *Pittsburgh Press,* June 4, 1919. (Carnegie Library of Pittsburgh)

is this in a March 1920 memo to the then head of the BI Radical Division, J. Edgar Hoover, from his special assistant George F. Ruch, not even marked confidential: "836 desires to know when you will be in New York. He is stopping at the Navarre Hotel under the name of L. M. Walsh."[61] BI agents actually allowed the publication of Wendell's photograph in the Pittsburgh papers in June 1919 after police arrested him in connection with the coordinated bombings that shook eight cities, including Pittsburgh. The *Press* published his frontal mug shot, showing a chunky man with a broad face, thick features, and light-colored eyes. According to an earlier newspaper account, also planted by the BI, he was thirty-five years old.[62]

Over the next four years, 1917–21, Wendell was to prove invaluable to BI, MID, and ONI. Even recent scholars have cited his reports in connection with matters not related directly to Pittsburgh. For example, Curt Gentry finds "836" a key figure in the BI's investigation of the early American Civil Liberties Union (ACLU). Hundreds of his reports filed from Pittsburgh pepper BI and MID records. He was one of the favored informers whose analysis influenced young J. Edgar Hoover's perception of the evolving Left. From 1918 to 1920 the Pittsburgh SAC often sent "836" reports directly to Washington. Wendell was also asked to prepare briefing documents or "books." Hoover brought him to Washington for briefings on several occasions and he was one of a number of information sources for Hoover's famous memoranda of 1919 on the Communist Party of America and the Communist Labor Party, which proclaimed the danger of international Communism and linked it to the steel and coal strikes of that year. Separate from his work with the BI, Wendell even helped Pittsburgh MID to capture draft evaders and circumscribe the activities of radical conscientious objectors at Camp Lee, Virginia.[63]

THE WORLD WAR I–ERA PITTSBURGH LEFT

> Pittsburgh has not been a particular star in the political firmament, but things
> are brewing here. Revolt, real industrial revolt, is in the air. . . . The woods are
> full of Revolutionary Socialists and Industrial Unionists and the Free Speech
> Fight is merely a skirmish in the Industrial Revolt about to follow.
>
> Jacob Margolis, "The Streets of Pittsburgh," 1912

THE PRINCIPAL TARGET of Wendell and his federal handlers in Pittsburgh from 1917 to 1921 was the Left. It was a tame Left compared to New York, Chicago, or even Cleveland; the captains of industry and authorities had seen to that. Still, if it posed a small threat of revolution, it might stir up serious labor trouble among the mostly Slavic and Italian immigrants who filled the unskilled, common labor needs of heavy industry. For, despite its power, Pittsburgh industry was vulnerable to interruptions to production by its huge, exploited, and culturally unassimilated foreign labor force. It was a force little known to management or the American workers who occupied most of the better-paid skilled positions.

There were so many centrifugal and centripetal forces at work among the foreign workers that it was not clear that the radical Left could successfully tap into what Richard Oestreicher has called a "subculture of opposition:" a workers' network of formal and informal institutions and practices based on ethnic cooperation, assistance and trust.[1] On the one hand, cultural and linguistic differences and traditional rivalries were hard to overcome. Until the outbreak of war in Europe many of the workers were young transients without roots or a long-term stake in American labor conditions who were often stereotyped as strike breakers or, at best, as unreliable union men. Even most of those who settled, and their numbers increased after 1914, adhered to a conservative realism that made them averse to risking family and livelihood for abstractions such as the Left's vision of a universal brotherhood of workers. On the other hand, unskilled and semiskilled workers, whatever their nationality, shared the same sense of grievance over exploitative working conditions. Many had been exposed to collectivist ideas in the old country and events of the decade before the Great War suggested that sufficiently aggrieved foreign workers could overcome their differences and make common cause against management.[2]

Pittsburgh was the dynamo from which radical energy flowed to the countryside, so the potential danger lay not just in the giant mills and factories that loomed and bellowed smoke near the city. For a hundred miles around lay coal camps and mill towns whose soot and grime and gob piles and waste runoff despoiled the streams and valleys. The immigrant workers in such places where other immigrant institutions such as churches were weak or nonexistent, were susceptible to the appeals of economic and political radicals. Because radicals sometimes seemed the only ones to care, they acted as mediating agents in the process of Americanization and, not coincidentally, in the spread of socialism and anarchism.[3]

When the federal government began its surveillance in Pittsburgh in 1917 it stepped into an ongoing struggle between labor and management. The struggle was not about revolution, although corporate spokesmen liked to say it was, but about industrial unionism, which sought to unite skilled and unskilled workers, foreign and native, into a single force to challenge corporate power in the workplace. A focal point of the trouble was the complex of Westinghouse plants in the Turtle Creek-East Pittsburgh-Braddock area. The application by Westinghouse of the scientific management techniques pioneered by Frederick W. Taylor (1856–1915) was intended to rationalize the shop floor. However, its seemingly endless reorganizations generated a host of worker grievances related to piecework, job reclassification, and pay structure.[4]

Trouble flared in the summer of 1912 against a background of labor unrest stirred by news of the IWW-led Lawrence, Massachusetts textile strike and surging Socialist political strength. After allowing Socialist meetings at the busy corner of Kelly and Homewood for three years, Pittsburgh police suddenly suppressed a rally on Saturday, August 3. Margolis characterized Homewood as "a particularly militant district" and home of "the most revolutionary" Socialist branch in Allegheny County.[5] When red-necktie-clad speakers and demonstrators gathered defiantly at the corner of Kelly and Homewood to exercise free speech, police arrested eleven men and nine women and hauled them off to a night in jail. Among the young women were Celia Lepschutz and Anna Goldberg, who figure in succeeding pages. The next Saturday, August 10, Socialists from all over the area, hundreds of police, and thousands of citizens come to see a free show converged on Kelly and Homewood. In the confrontation that followed, police repeatedly broke up squads of well-organized Socialists and used, as the *Pittsburgh*

Press proudly noted, the department's new motorized paddy wagon to convey forty-four demonstrators to jail.[6] Prominent among the protesters were young, mostly Jewish, women factory operatives along with Croatian and German activists. The city had shown its power, but the Socialists gained a moral and political victory. The use of the police to prevent political discussion aroused public and press sympathy. The next Saturday, the police had to allow the Socialists to rally unmolested near Homewood and Kelly.[7]

Nineteen-fourteen brought hard times to Westinghouse and to labor activists. In June mass layoffs and reductions in piecework rates and the average workweek led to a strike by the recently organized Allegheny Congenial Industrial Union, which later became the American Industrial Union (AIU). Like the IWW the union did not negotiate contracts with management but focused instead on workers' demands. Many of its leaders were skilled machinists. The strike affected fourteen thousand workers and once again young women, three thousand of them pickets led by Bridget Kenny, "the Joan of Arc of the Strikers," served as union shock troops used to discourage men from crossing their lines or company guards from violence against the strikers. The women also took to the streets en masse blowing tin whistles and calling workers still in the plants to come out. Despite such efforts, the strikers went back to work in July with their basic grievances unresolved. For the next two years the AIU shared the open shop floor with the International Association of Machinists (IAM), the AFL-affiliated International Brotherhood of Electrical Workers (IBEW), and a company-sponsored union.[8]

By 1915 the war in Europe had brought Westinghouse a huge order for shells and machine tools causing the company to double its workforce and increase the workweek from forty-eight to fifty-four hours. Similar developments across the industrial East created nearly full employment, a labor shortage, and upward pressure on wages. In September IBEW and IAM organizers joined to demand that Westinghouse increase wages by 20 percent and reduce the workday to eight hours. The company refused, charging the unions were trying to shut down the plants to hurt the Allied cause. Despite the efforts of John L. Lewis and the rest of the organizers, workers voted overwhelmingly to accept the company's terms and there was no strike. But the next year a wave of strikes spread across the munitions and metalworking industries as labor asked for a bigger piece of the pie. At Pittsburgh Westinghouse, the AIU and the AFL-affiliated IBEW vied for the allegiance of the workers.[9]

Near the end of April 1916 the Westinghouse workers led by machinists went on strike demanding an eight-hour day and other concessions. Again young women operatives played a key role and the strikers paraded through the streets with red flags, this time with the intent of shutting down all the plants and mills of "electric valley." On May Day this tactic brought an estimated thirty-six thousand workers out of many plants. With Pittsburgh transit workers simultaneously on strike, it looked like the beginnings of a general strike. When thousands of strikers gathered near the gate to U.S. Steel's J. Edgar Thompson Works in Braddock, they faced an army of heavily armed company guards and coal and iron police. A melee ensued in which three strikers were killed and as many as sixty injured. After Pennsylvania governor Martin G. Brumbaugh sent troops to restore order, the strike quickly ended.[10]

During the strike the one-hundred-member Pittsburgh Manufacturers' Association reorganized into the Employers' Association of Pittsburgh, and its frustrated spokesman Isaac W. Frank told reporters that employers, tired of agitators' demands, would oppose the eight-hour day and work to make Pittsburgh an open labor market. During an interview, he went farther, saying that someone should assassinate Industrial Relations Commissioner Frank P. Walsh, whose pro-union stance infuriated management. In the strike's aftermath local authorities carried out mass arrests of alleged rioters and radical strike leaders. Among those convicted eventually was *Justice* editor Fred H. Merrick, whose three-and-one-half-year jail term effectively removed him from the radical scene during the war and the Red Scare. Also jailed were future Wobblies Rudolph Blum and H. H. Detweiler, who figure later in this narrative, and Anna Goldberg, whom the papers called the girl in the red hat. She had been arrested in the Homewood free speech fight of 1912 and had made news during the stogie workers' strike that year, when a sympathetic reporter told her story under the headline "Girl Socialist Who Spent Night in Police Cell Says She's a Suffragist Too." In the wake of Frank's remark and the convictions of the strike leaders, Pittsburgh labor representatives petitioned the Department of Labor to investigate the abuse of corporate power in Pittsburgh.[11]

Despite industrial defeats and the co-optation of much of the Socialist agenda by the Progressives, a lively, if less than lyrical, Left subculture persisted in the Steel City in 1917. At its center was the Socialist Party of America (SPA). Between 1910 and 1917, the party's strength peaked in western Pennsylvania when Socialists were elected to the mayoralty of New Castle and to lesser positions in Pittsburgh, East Pittsburgh, West Brownsville, Wilmerding, North Versailles, Pitcairn, Turtle Creek, and McKeesport. The SPA claimed two thousand dues-paying members in Pittsburgh and fifteen hundred in nearby McKeesport in 1912. That same year, Socialist presidential candidate Eugene V. Debs ran ahead of Taft and Wilson with 25 percent of the vote in sixteen area steel towns.[12] Surprisingly, for a city where the daily papers were not very sympathetic to labor interests, the SPA had a regular Sunday quarter-page section in the *Pittsburgh Press* just below the "Afro-American" section, which was devoted to its point of view and activities.[13]

Scholars contest whether or not 1912 marked the beginning of its decline,[14] but on the eve of American entry into World War I the SPA stood as the only significant political organization to oppose militarism and American participation, and its membership was growing. At that time in Pittsburgh it could claim a sounding board and chorus of several thousand sympathizers and a hard-core of at least five hundred to one thousand activists. BI and MID files on the activists, by no means complete, show that immigrants and second-generation Americans predominated, most of them skilled workers, salesmen, or lower-level white-collar types. Among the leaders was a smattering of professionals such as optometrist W. H. "Doc" Van Essen, lawyer Jacob Margolis, and newspaper manager James Mering. The files listed only a few women and a single African American, William Scarville, among the hundreds of alleged radicals even though, as noted above, women workers and organizers played important roles in several Pittsburgh-area strikes during the period.[15]

Pittsburgh Socialists maintained a full agenda of public activities. The heart of SPA operations was party headquarters, "New Era Hall," above Frishel's Restaurant at 233–35 Fifth Avenue. Other familiar meeting places included the downtown Labor Temple, Moorehead Hall, the Jewish Labor Lyceum, and, from 1918, the International Socialist Lyceum.[16] Mass meetings were held at the Academy or Lyceum theaters, Kennywood Park, or Summer Hill Grove. There were weekly meetings and occasional open forums, rallies, mass meetings, street demonstrations, picnics, and parades. The Young People's Socialist League (YPSL) operated schools for little comrades on the North Side and in East Liberty. Socialists with the inclination and capital camped together each summer by Conneaut Lake in family-sized tents rented by the party.[17]

Despite this impressive array of group activities and meeting sites the western Pennsylvania SPA was an unstable coalition of groups drawn from disparate neighborhoods, towns, and nationalities. Among the English speakers, the powerful "political" socialists from the Hill District often clashed with factions from the North Side, McKees Rocks, McKeesport, Bentleyville, Monessen, Duquesne, Homestead, and elsewhere. Ethnic social clubs in the region housed the SPA's almost two dozen separate foreign-language branches including, among the more substantial, the Hungarian, Croatian, Italian, Russian, Ukrainian, and Polish.[18]

The Pittsburgh BI's Radical Squad paid only passing attention to the activities of the evolutionary and political SPA "slowcialist" majority that believed it could defeat capitalism incrementally by educating the masses to vote socialist.[19] From 1917 until the SPA foreign language federations went over to the Communist Party in 1919, the radical squad was more interested in the extreme Left, the Industrial Workers of the World (IWW). Federal agents believed that this organization was part of a secret conspiracy behind much of the labor agitation and antiwar activity in the Pittsburgh mill district.

The IWW was born in 1905 in Chicago at a star-studded convention of more than two hundred socialists and trade unionists that included Eugene V. Debs, Mary Harris "Mother" Jones, Daniel DeLeon, William D. Haywood, Algie M. Simons, William E. Trautmann, Father Thomas Hagerty, and Lucy Parsons. The Wobblies, as IWW members came to be called after 1914,[20] were part labor union, part revolutionary movement. They combined elements of homespun radicalism traceable to populists, Knights of Labor, single-taxers, and the like with a belief in the labor theory of value, European syndicalism, and Marxist class struggle. They would defeat the capitalists by organizing the mass of workers at the margins of the economy so long ignored by the conservative, craft-conscious AFL. Migrant farmhands, lumberjacks, sweated immigrants, women, and nonwhites in mills, mines, and shops would come to power if the Wobblies won the day.[21]

By 1908 the idealism and momentary unity of the early IWW had given way to factionalism and disunity that winnowed the organization to its radical core. Essentially reformist elements withdrew or were forced out: the Western Federation of Miners, "political" socialists, Debs, and DeLeon. The victorious leaders, William D. "Big Bill" Haywood, Vincent St. John, and William E. Trautmann, rejected the political approach of the Socialists as nothing more than reform of a system that must be destroyed. For them the only way to true socialism was a working-class revolution. Workers would engage in job action at the point of production (the general strike) to abolish the wage system and create a new workers' commonwealth in the shell of the old society. At least until 1917, the Wobblies welcomed and applauded the Russian Revolution, which seemed to them the opening salvo in the inevitable warfare between capital and labor that would lead toward the victory of social justice.[22]

By 1916 the IWW had fought a host of free speech fights against hostile state and local governments for the right to address "fellow workers" from street corner soapboxes.[23] It participated in more than 150 strikes from coast to coast and its members became prime targets for official harassment and repression. An arrest record was as much a badge of membership as the famous red card.

To the alienated and the downtrodden the Wobblies were heroes who thumbed their noses at authority and pomposity and conferred dignity on those despised by society. And the Wobblies had fun. They carried their message in verse, cartoons, and songs. By 1917 two-inch square stickers, or silent agitators, bearing their "Sab Cat" symbol in red and black appeared in thousands of places where workmen gathered. The Wobblies marched in parades or demonstrated mutely with printed cards stuck in their hatbands. Their tactics were outrageous and spontaneous and yet down to earth. From that time to this the romance of their rebelliousness and egalitarian rhetoric has appealed to many idealists and to those of tender social conscience.[24]

The IWW had its greatest success in the West, but the organization always wanted to reach out to immigrant workers in the East and Salvatore Salerno calculates that more than 40 percent of its members were immigrants.[25] It had enjoyed its first eastern success and considerable public support in the 1909 strike at a U.S. Steel subsidiary, the Pressed Steel Car Company plant at McKees Rocks just down the Ohio from Pittsburgh. Speed-ups and a complicated piecework pay system triggered a walkout that soon turned violent. IWW organizers played a key role in keeping the multiethnic workforce together through their ordeal. When worker Steven Horvath was killed in a confrontation with state troopers, the graveside eulogies were delivered in fifteen different languages. Many more strikers would be injured, but in the end the strikers won and the company restored the old pay system and an IWW local was set up. The strike led to the permanent establishment of the IWW's leading periodical *Solidarity*, which began publication at New Castle.[26] However, the Pittsburgh area IWW membership of four to six thousand in 1909 had fallen to only twenty by 1912. Although a reorganized Pittsburgh IWW in 1912 and 1913 managed partially successful strikes of mostly Jewish female stogie workers in the Hill District, it would never again equal its Pressed Steel Car success in western Pennsylvania.[27]

Cooperation between Socialists and Wobblies during the Lawrence, Massachusetts, textile workers' strike in 1912 seemed to hold the promise of real IWW presence in the East and of a reunited political and industrial Socialist movement. But hopes of unity were dashed at the Socialist Party Convention of that year when conservatives, led by Morris Hillquit and Victor Berger, passed Article II, Sec. 6 of the party constitution, expelling those who opposed political action and countenanced industrial sabotage, as did the IWW. The next year they forced IWW leader Haywood off the SPA executive committee.[28]

The greatest American Socialist, Eugene V. Debs, contributed to the split by denouncing IWW tactics as anarchist and reactionary. To embrace IWW direct action, he charged, was to play into the hands of the capitalists. Such secrecy and stealth would open the Socialist "movement to agents provocateurs," cause mass defections, and leave those who remained "responsible for the deed of every spy or madman."[29]

By 1916 a faction of the IWW leadership led by Bill Haywood recognized that the inflammatory rhetoric and hit-and-run assaults that had worked so well for the western "overalls brigade" had failed in the industrial East and Midwest. Major Wobbly strike efforts in the industrial heartland, at McKees Rocks, Lawrence, Akron, and elsewhere had not brought permanent gains for the workers or permanent IWW organizations. The eastern debacle showed that constructing a workers' commonwealth in the shell of the old society would require the support of the millions of mostly foreign industrial workers in heavy industry. Ideology prevented the IWW from pursuing change through political action, and shock tactics such as free speech fights and sabotage frightened away American workers. Therefore the dominant Haywood faction concluded that the IWW must back away from such tactics and must behave more like a labor union. That meant that, rather than jumping into the middle of a labor-management fight in progress, IWW representatives must first organize on the job and build up a permanent organization and a strike fund prior to launching a job action.[30]

Afterward, instead of moving on to the next battle, Wobblies were to stay and build their union. Mirroring the corporate structure it despised, in 1916 the IWW drew up an organizational chart featuring bureaucratic centralization and emphasizing strict fiscal accountability to Haywood and his staff, now ensconced in their new four-story Chicago headquarters at 1001 West Madison Street. Under the new regime dues were raised and all IWW locals made up of workers in a particular industry became "branches" of one of thirteen national industrial unions. All others, members-at-large and members of mixed locals, were put into branches of a new National Recruiting Union. Under the new system, aided by a tight wartime job market, membership soared from about forty thousand in 1916 to one hundred thousand by 1917. These changes spurred dissatisfaction and defections. In 1917 a disobedient and unreconstructed Elizabeth Gurley Flynn was relieved of organizational duties. Joe Ettor, Carlo Tresca, Arturo Giovannitti, and other effective eastern organizers of immigrant workmen were forced out or resigned in disgust over what seemed to them the IWW's turn toward centralization.[31]

How to react to the Great War was the source of potentially mortal problems for the IWW. In 1914 and 1915 it officially denounced the war as an imperialist adventure but took the view that it could not prevent eventual American participation. While many Socialists and trade unionists organized against American involvement, the IWW officially remained on the sidelines, even though much of the rank and file was openly antiwar. In the fall of 1916 the IWW General Executive Board put out a leaflet that formally condemned nationalism, patriotism, and militarism and called for a "General Strike of all industries" if the U.S. should enter the war. It went on to warn the "capitalist masters" that Wobblies would not fight. They would resist an attempt "to compel us—the disinherited—to participate in a war that can only bring in its wake death and untold misery, privation, and suffering to millions of workers." Beyond such rhetoric, the IWW sponsored no formal antiwar campaign. Although a large faction openly opposed the war and the draft, probably most Wobblies bought Liberty Bonds or performed military service.[32]

Still, the antiwar rhetoric of the organization and the militancy of the antiwar faction was more than enough to cause the mainstream press, lawmen, businessmen, and patriotic groups to call for harsh repression of what they considered the anarchosyndicalist, terrorist IWW. When the United States entered World War I in April 1917, no other group in the country could count as many enemies. The organization that promised to empower marginalized "stiffs" in the West and that had the admiration of middle-class rebels-at-heart and admirers of the lyrical left, was to mainstream Americans, in Paul L. Murphy's words, a band of "rowdy, Rabelaisian itinerants." Mainstream labor leaders such as the AFL's Samuel Gompers shrank from association with the Wobblies. He dismissed the IWW as "never more than a radical fungus on the labor movement." He despised the rival organization for refusing to accommodate to the reality of established capitalism, for organizing the unskilled, and for feeding a public backlash against all labor.[33]

The IWW was not friendless. A few politicians and Wilson Administration officials such as U.S. Commissioner of Industrial Relations Frank P. Walsh and Assistant Secretary of Labor Louis F. Post were its defenders. In the 1916 Mesabi strike Minnesota small businessmen had allied themselves with the Wobblies, but generally Main Street feared and shunned them. Business propagandists used their antics and rhetoric as a convenient cudgel with which to batter the entire labor movement. Nativists regarded the IWW's efforts to organize the "New Immigrants" as a step toward a takeover of the United States by foreign revolutionaries. Even some civil libertarians hesitated to assist the IWW. Was the Wobblies' free speech protected by the First Amendment when they advocated revolution and the destruction of the First Amendment along with the rest of the Constitution?[34] Exposed to the anti-IWW diatribe from so many quarters, the American public could hardly avoid associating the IWW with anarchist violence, public disorder, foreign influences, and revolutionary doctrines. Even before the United States entered the war, local police and politicians had used every means possible to stamp out the IWW. After April 1917, the U.S. Justice Department joined the attack with the intent of crushing it once and for all.

Because its shadowy existence and decentralized structure resisted conventional law enforcement techniques, detectives, informers, and agents provocateurs had long plagued the IWW. Its policies might be formulated at 1001 West Madison, but its movers and shakers were a relatively autonomous irregular army: local ethnic leaders and itinerant organizers and agitators. It drew its wildly fluctuating and (sometimes) dues-paying membership largely from migratory workers in the West and new immigrants from Southern and Eastern Europe in the industrial East. The vast force of floating labor was faceless and marginal and, as an unsympathetic A. Mitchell Palmer told a congressional committee in 1920, "nobody loved them."[35]

To outside observers, the IWW seemed less a union than a transitory movement that sprang up where labor discontent was rife and then vanished when it subsided. Carleton H. Parker may have exaggerated in 1917 when he wrote that the IWW was "incapable of legal death" because it had no formal politico-legal existence, its treasury being "merely the accumulation of strike funds." Still, there was truth in his contention that its appeal was as much social as ideological or economic. Local Wobbly headquarters were "gregarious centers" where "the lodging-house inhabitant or the hobo with his blanket can find light, a stove, and companionship." Where there was prohibition, he added, "the I.W.W. hall has been the only social substitution for the saloon for these people."[36]

Their gregariousness, openness toward strangers, and itinerancy made the Wobblies vulnerable to their enemies. The IWW could not screen new members effectively without betraying its principles, so it was easy to infiltrate. Wobblies came to assume that they were being watched and even that some fellow workers were traitors, but there was little they could do except express their frustration. Bill Haywood did so when he called the detective the "lowest, meanest, most contemptible thing that either creeps or crawls, a thing to loathe and despise . . . [that] breeds and thrives on troubles of his own making."[37] As for government undercover agents, the *One Big Union Monthly* railed that "these hyenas have got to earn their blood money some way, and they do it by staging fake revolts, bomb plots, riots, effectively aided by the thugs employed by private detective agencies."[38] The Wobblies could never be sure which fellow workers were traitors.

The only kind of explosions the I. W. W. causes

"The only kind of explosions the I.W.W. causes." Wobblies respond to
attacks by using "truth" to burst the bubbles produced by bourgeois in-
tellects such as "bull," "con," "bomb plots," "lies," "reward in Heaven,"
"contentment," etc. (*OBUM*, March 1919)

In the spring of 1917, with the IWW on the rise nationally, the Pittsburgh BI
prepared to place local Wobblies under surveillance. The problem was that there
was no visible IWW organization in the area. In mid-May Judge learned from a
conservative Socialist that about 150 radical Socialists were active in the city, who
were "more or less" "anarchists," "I.W.W.s," or "direct actionists." According to
the source, one of the two leaders of this group was sheet metal worker Ben Anderson (Anisman).[39] Over the next four years only a few file entries document activities of the naturalized Russian immigrant Anisman. It is possible that this
shadowy figure was an informer, perhaps for private industry. At various times he
was IWW branch secretary or president and was often present at inner circle

meetings. Information attributed to him in several investigative reports led to the arrest of radicals at Beaver Falls, Pennsylvania, and New York City.[40]

The other leading radical was attorney Jacob Margolis, the "brains" of the movement. He was to be the key to the government's antiradical operation in Pittsburgh. Margolis was a familiar figure to Steel City Socialists. He was above average height, of medium build, 150 pounds with black hair and dark eyes. He was a native Pittsburgher, born in 1886 to Jewish immigrant parents from Russian Poland on Magee Street in the Lower Hill District, just east of downtown. His parents were among the more than thirty thousand Jews who came with the massive influx of Eastern and Southern Europeans to the steel valleys in the three decades before World War I. From Poland, Russia, Latvia, Lithuania, Romania, and Austria-Hungary they came to crowd into streets and row houses in the Hill District, occupied in former days by English, German, and Irish families.[41] One scholar has described the Jewish quarter as a place with "the look, the feel, the noises, and the odors of the ghetto . . . [where the] architecture seemed to sweat humanity at every window and door." Here the settlers carved out economic niches in their new land as peddlers, junk men, stogie makers, and merchants. As they did so they learned about Anglo-American customs, speech, and economic practices and soon became small business proprietors and middlemen between the old country immigrants and the new land's culture.[42]

Margolis followed the typical second-generation path toward assimilation into American culture, but with a decidedly radical twist. Bright, articulate, and ambitious, he saved enough money as a newsboy so that after he finished public school he could attend Washington and Jefferson College. After a year he withdrew, returned to Pittsburgh, and read for the law in the office of James C. Gray. He graduated from Pittsburgh Law School in 1909 and started a practice the following March. From his teens "Jake" was a radical activist and street-corner orator whose well-known anarchist views kept him from being accepted in the legal community. He was not asked to join the Allegheny County Bar Association or admitted to practice in the federal courts.[43]

Margolis called himself an anarchosyndicalist, or a direct-actionist. Like most Wobbly advocates, his ideas were derivative rather than original. Nonetheless his ideological positions were consistent and clearly articulated. For him the only way to realize the Socialist dream was through a two-stage revolution. The first, or negative, stage would destroy capitalist government. The second, or positive, stage would construct a new democratic and decentralized society in the shell of the old. Workers, "the underlying population" possessing the technical expertise to manage production, would build "a new society without capitalists, wage workers, or government" at "the point of production," the workplace.[44]

Like so many radicals of the time, Margolis had no faith in the revolutionary potential of American-born workers who were incurably individualistic and lacked both a revolutionary tradition and class consciousness. Beguiled "by the subtle poison called Democracy" and the myth that "everyone is equal and everyone has the same opportunity of success," they hoped to escape from the employee group into the employing group. Even when their own lives did not improve they stubbornly clung to the illusion that education would lift their children up the economic ladder. The rags-to-riches success of the few lent plausibility to the myth accepted by the many. The truth was, according to Margolis, that when old-stock American workers did advance to the skilled ranks they left behind immigrant workers to receive "all the hard blows of capitalism."[45]

Margolis was willing to take them as clients, but he held American trade unions in contempt for buying into capitalism and opposing real change. He believed in dual unionism, whereby the class-conscious part of the working class would maintain its separate organization, the IWW. Boring from within the mainstream unions such as the craft-oriented AFL or even its industrial affiliate the UMWA would not help to establish the new order. Only the mobilization of the millions of European immigrants left behind by capitalism could bring about the revolution. The immigrants' less individualistic social organizations made them more class conscious than American workers. This, coupled with their lowly status and the brutal working conditions they had to endure, made them potential rebels. If they rose up the radicals could "sweep away capitalism . . . and bring into being a classless society wherein all are workers." The new society would be based on "creation, not possession; achievement, not inherited wealth; voluntary cooperation, not super-imposed authority."[46]

In 1912 Margolis wrote a revealing article for the *International Socialist Review* enthusiastically describing the Homewood "free speech fight" waged by Socialists against Pittsburgh authorities. Here Margolis savored the victory, advertised his own radical credentials, and proclaimed the existence of an organized revolutionary movement in Pittsburgh. To put Pittsburgh on the map, he included photos of IWW leader Haywood addressing a crowd of fifteen thousand at Kennywood Park in support of imprisoned Lawrence strike leaders Joe Ettor and Arturo Giovannitti.[47]

By and large the IWW was nonviolent. However, inspired by the rhetoric of revolution and backed by masses of the disgruntled and marginalized, the disorganized anarchical mob or, worse, the *organized* masses just below the surface threatened to erupt. As one Wobbly put it, "You will understand, of course, that we are a labor union. But, a labor union that is also a revolution and the germ of a new social order."[48] When, as they often did, Wobblies addressed the issue of violence, they might as well have been speaking in tongues. When they advocated sabotage did they mean terrorism or destruction of property or only deliberate work slowdowns and calculated inefficiency? When they called for revolution were they calling for a bloodbath or some nonviolent process of democratization? The rhetorical ambiguity probably reflected real confusion and division with the ranks of the IWW. Certainly as a stratagem violence was a two-edged sword. On the positive side it left enemies guessing, underlined the potential brute power of the lumpen proletariat, and appealed strongly to marginalized and resentful elements of the lower orders. However, by threatening to act outside the law, the IWW frightened the public and gave authorities a rationale for the harsh repression they meted out.[49]

Despite his strong attachment to the IWW program and its revolutionary ends, Margolis categorically rejected violent means. The proper tactics, he insisted, were "passive resistance" and mass demonstrations designed to goad authorities into repressive measures that would backfire and win public sympathy for the IWW. He described the 1912 Homewood free speech fight as a pageant of oppression. The socialist fighters won a major victory when police arrested a band "led by a slender girl, Elizabeth Hobe, who was waving a red flag as they marched . . . [and which] did not stop playing until the players were arrested." Even then, a young drummer made a splendidly theatrical exit; he could be heard beating out the *Marseillaise* from the police van that hauled him off to the lockup. Another victory for the demonstrators was "the beautiful awe inspiring spectacle of thirty mounted policemen filling the street from curb to curb riding through a peaceable crowd pushing them on to the sidewalks and against the buildings." This naked display of force helped to "enlist the cooperation of the workers and enlisted the sympathy of the liberal minded."[50]

Margolis practiced law, advocated free speech, and championed civil liberties as a means to bring about the revolution. "Free Speech," he wrote, "is a valuable asset. To be deprived of it means secret methods must be employed and . . . are hardly ever successful." He wrote that "a great wave of public sympathy is very much more effective than a court decision, and even though the courts of Allegheny county and the state of Pennsylvania decide against the workers, they have not lost, for they have succeeded in arousing a storm of protest and . . . in doing such effective propaganda work by the Free Speech Fight that we cannot estimate its value."[51]

Margolis viewed the legal system as a tool of the capitalist enemy. He expressed his contempt for it when he joined leading anarchists Ben Reitman, Alexander Berkman, Emma Goldman, and Errico Maletesta in contributing to the May 1915 *Mother Earth*. Over his initials, "J. M.," he published "Walter Loan," a satirical short piece. Loan, a Westinghouse worker and Wilkinsburg anarchist, was on trial for two felonies and a misdemeanor in the wounding of a policeman. Margolis characterized the court's treatment of Loan ("Anarchist and defendant. Brave, frank, refined, uncompromising") as a procedurally correct mockery of real justice, which made the defendant its victim. American society was "the painted courtesan—overfed, hypocritical, smug, propertied." Those who sat in judgment he caricatured as "Judge B.—Rednosed, bulging eyes, behind spectacles, bald, Cynical sneer, chewing tobacco and spitting incessantly. Jury of 12 Men, good and true—Mason, Oddfellow, Knight of Malta, Presbyterian, deacon, Jew, one-eyed man, Sunday school superintendent, Nondescripts and commonplace." The Margolis piece was, to say the least, unusual both in venue and the treatment of the subject for an officer of the court.[52]

When Margolis wrote "Walter Loan" the IWW–Socialist Party coalition in Pittsburgh had already shattered. In 1913 "political" or "conservative" SPA leaders expelled from the party four hundred "IWW direct actionists" led by Fred Merrick and Margolis. Merrick's imprisonment in 1916 left "Jake," as many knew him, to lead a radical faction that functioned almost as a subculture of the Socialist subculture. All the while he prospered in a substantial, if unorthodox, law practice devoted to defending and advising labor unions, radicals, and immigrants on an array of legal matters. In 1915 Margolis traveled to Bellaire, Ohio, to represent the IWW's Joe Ettor, who had been arrested for a speech Ohio officials had denounced as an attempt to "levy war, insurrection, and rebellion." Representing Ettor was not unusual, for Margolis was likely to be the first lawyer called if a radical or immigrant had legal trouble within one hundred miles of the Golden Triangle. In 1918 Margolis and his associate James J. Marshall were the first Pittsburgh cooperating attorneys for Roger Baldwin's National Civil Liberties Bureau, the predecessor to the ACLU.[53]

Those close to Margolis in the movement were also bound to him by economic interest and family ties. They included his wife, a naturalized immigrant from the Pale, his mother, brother Ralph or "Ike," brother-in-law Oscar Kaminsky, law clerk Victor Slone or Sloan, and law partner Marshall. This inner circle had its own haunts. One was Margolis's home at 302 Ophelia Street in the Oakland section, where he frequently extended hospitality to leftists of many stripes. Another was his office in Room 507 of the Union Arcade at Fifth and Grant, a radical hangout, mail drop, and distribution point for propaganda. A third was in Room 211 of the McGeagh Building, 607 Webster Avenue.

Margolis had first appeared at the McGeagh Building, which was used for meetings and offices by labor unions until the 1930s, to attend meetings of the International Hotel Workers (later Waiters and Cooks) Union. Shortly afterward, in 1915, he arranged for the IWW to sublet the IHWU rooms for its meetings. In November 1916 he leased Room 211 for the Radical Library Group to house a collection of anarchist and left-wing books and pamphlets. The Radical Library was to be the home of several radical projects: the Rationalist Society, the Keystone Literary Association, the Pittsburgh chapter of English-speaking IWW, the People's Council of America for Peace and Democracy, the Soldier's and Sailor's Soviet, and the Anti-Conscription League.[54]

In the evenings when he was not at his office or the Radical Library or a labor meeting, Margolis sometimes engaged in revolutionary discourse with comrades at one of three downtown cafes near Grant Street: the Bismarck, Piatt, and Budweiser, or while dining at Kramer's Restaurant. Often the conversation and conviviality continued into the wee hours at private clubs or speakeasies or in animated debate under smoke-dimmed stars on the corner of Fifth and Grant.[55]

Margolis was a dynamic, controversial speaker. He was open about his hatreds: government, war, capitalism, political socialism, trade unionism, conscription, and, in 1919, the new Communist movement. Hecklers at radical meetings, nuisance arrests, slights from the bar association, official harassment, and, eventually, disbarment did not silence him. He frequently traveled to radical centers such as New York, Chicago, and Detroit and kept in touch with cosmopolitan left-wing radicals all over the country. In her autobiography, Emma Goldman acknowledged Margolis as "her very able friend" who arranged for her weekly Pittsburgh lectures in 1916 and "her good old comrade" with whom she corresponded from her jail cell in 1919. Margolis was a name-dropper who tended to inflate acquaintance into friendship. He craved national recognition and the approval of leading radicals such as Goldman, Alexander Berkman, and IWW general secretary Vincent St. John.[56]

He never achieved national prominence, perhaps because he seemed unwilling to forsake completely the capitalist world. Despite his denials, he, too, was seduced by the lure of capitalism. He was adept at turning the struggle against capitalism to his own profit and he accepted the trappings and rewards of the system he denounced. He kept his law office first in the ostentatiously capitalist Frick Building at Fifth and Grant and later across the street in the ornate Union (Bank and Trust) Arcade. When he was not occupied with plans to advance the revolution, he was concocting a host of personal money-making schemes. The fact that he was a lawyer made him useful but not fully trusted in radical circles. He was an attorney for the damned but he was not truly one of them. Bill Haywood expressed a common Wobbly sentiment when he called all lawyers "mouthpieces of the capitalist class."[57]

Although he called it an "easy compromise," the contradictions of Margolis's life could not have been so easy. Could a revolutionary really live with his head in the capitalist world and his heart in the revolution to come? His Jewish heritage was another obvious source of personal conflict. His ideology and personal background tied him to persecuted and hated groups: Jews and Wobblies. But he always made it clear that he was not an actual member of the IWW and he was patently uncomfortable with his Jewishness. He trumpeted his atheism and made it a point to speak only English and never Yiddish. Although many of his clients were Eastern Europeans, he claimed ignorance of the Polish and Russian languages. This even though he grew up in an immigrant household, was married to a Jewish immigrant from Poland, and employed a live-in Polish maid.[58]

There were more inconsistencies. Margolis, the tireless propagandist for anarchism, spoke of propaganda as a base form of discourse. His personal tastes ran to the more elegant radicalism of the *Dial, Nation,* and *Liberator.* He looked down on immigrant industrial workers as too ignorant and deluded by hope of economic success to make a revolution or create the ideal commonwealth without the guidance of educated, skilled leaders such as himself. On principle he refused to own real property, but he dressed ostentatiously, earned a sizable income, and owned a "few thousand dollars," bank stock, and a $27,500 life insurance policy. He was, he said, only dealing with "things as they are."[59]

As things were, Margolis had one foot in the legal profession and the other in a movement to destroy it. He had become Americanized, but his heart lay with immigrants who had not. He acted as a mediating agent to assist greenhorn immigrants with the riddles of life in America; and that is why government special agents took such an interest in him. They hoped that through him they could solve the enigma of the radical subculture.

In the spring of 1917, Pittsburgh BI agents shadowed Margolis and instituted a coast-to-coast background check. The New York field office clarified that he was not Jacob Margolis the Russian Jewish cap maker who supported Socialist causes and who was "not a dangerous character."[60] More tantalizing was a June 1916 San Francisco police report. A middle-aged woman who said she was from Chicago calling herself Mrs. Pearl Margolis had stayed at a Clay Street rooming house with a younger woman. A man who visited them, and whose description loosely fit Jacob Margolis, aroused the landlady's suspicions. She then called police and told them that she thought the trio was connected to Alexander Berkman's radical publication, *Blast*.[61] A police check uncovered nothing, but Margolis was in Los Angeles and San Francisco in March and April of 1916 to advise and organize support for labor leaders David Caplan and Matthew Schmidt, who were charged in connection with the 1910 bombing of the *Los Angeles Times*. The Pittsburgh BI evidently knew nothing of this; only that Margolis had boasted that he knew Berkman, who had spent fourteen years in prison near Pittsburgh after his 1892 attempt to assassinate Henry Clay Frick. The report added no real information to Margolis's growing BI dossier, but it fed suspicions that he was a revolutionary with connections.[62]

It was Margolis's antiwar activity that convinced the government to target him for intense surveillance. In May 1917 postal inspectors had intercepted postcards from the Pittsburgh Anti-Conscription League at Room 211 of the McGeagh Building. The cards said, "I am opposed to the killing of human beings and have conscientious scruples against taking human life, and therefore pledge myself not to be conscripted." Judge's informant Manuel Tanzer followed the trail of intercepted postcards first to a waiter at Kramer's Restaurant, then to the Anti-Conscription League's headquarters at the "Radical Literary Society" in the McGeagh Building. On May 22 the Pittsburgh police chief led a raid on the McGeagh Building and SPA headquarters. The police arrested Margolis and other members of the League and confiscated its records, which were then turned over to the BI's Judge. The charges against Margolis were soon dropped for lack of evidence, but now federal agents were very interested in him.

In July an informer provided the BI with a photostat of a draft handbill, dictated by Margolis to his legal clerk-stenographer Victor Slone.[63] It read:

WORKERS AWAKE! The revolutionists in Russia have succeeded in bringing about a New Russia, where there is freedom of speech and press. Here, in America, the so-called land of the free, two of the noblest and finest spirits who escaped from Russian oppression and have come here to fight for the freedom of the worker have been sent to the penitentiary because they dared to raise their voices against the slaughter of working men.

ONLY YOU CAN LIBERATE THEM! LAY DOWN YOUR TOOLS AND FOLD YOUR ARMS! CALL A **** STRIKE! ORGANIZE YOURSELVES AND DONT GO BACK UNTIL

EMMA GOLDMAN AND ALEXANDER BERKMAN ARE FREED FROM THE PENITEN-
TIARY! AROUSE YE SLAVES! THIS IS THE TIME TO SHOW THAT YOU ARE THE BE-
LIEVERS OF THE LIBERTY WHICH HAS BEEN WON IN RUSSIA![64]

Margolis had ordered a total of fifteen thousand of these handbills in Lithuanian, Polish, and Russian. Writing to Bureau Chief Bielaski, SAC Judge, worried
that the handbill might increase already "more or less widespread labor unrest"
among Eastern European workmen, pledged to do everything possible to prevent
its circulation.[65]

Judge then proposed a bold step. Although Pittsburgh currently had no official
IWW local, he told Bielaski that the group led by Margolis was "in thought and action and to all intents and purposes the same as I.W.W.s elsewhere." Rumor had
it that the IWW was planning to organize Pittsburgh steel. It would be a good
idea, Judge thought, to plant a high-level spy close to Margolis, who was intimate
with the Wobblies. An informer, P-45, thought it would be "an easy matter for a
clever person to rope in with this outfit" but that it should be someone from out
of town. In the hierarchy of strike breakers and labor detectives "roper" meant an
informant, a shadower, and a "hooker" was someone who recruited informants.
Such an operative might also be the contact for one or more "missionaries" or labor spies.[66] The roper who was sent for was Louis M. Wendell.

TAMING THE STEEL CITY WOBBLIES, 1917–1918

> In no instance has an agent or employee of the Bureau of Investigation . . . ever
> actively participated in the activities of any radical organization or taken any
> part in the formulating of its principles or platform.
>
> J. Edgar Hoover, May 1920

FROM APRIL TO OCTOBER 1917 a wave of strikes plagued war production throughout the nation and cost industry 6,285,519 workdays. Leading the list were the metal trades, the source of one-fifth of the lost days. Next came shipbuilding and then coal mining. In these industries three-fourths of the strikers belonged to the AFL, but overall one-sixth of the lost workdays came from strikes led by the IWW. Meanwhile the SPA, as the only large national organization outspokenly opposed to the war, became a rallying point for antimilitarists, anti-imperialists, and draft resisters.[1] This made the left-wing Socialists and Wobblies prime targets for federal surveillance.

Within forty-eight hours of coming to Pittsburgh, Wendell had presented himself at SPA headquarters on Fifth Avenue as a radical come to help promote the IWW. Soon thereafter, he called at Margolis's office. The wartime situation that drew streams of workmen to Pittsburgh and the openness and informality of the Socialists must have eased his entry into the radical scene. In such a fluid setting friendships and alliances were formed easily, with few questions asked. Wendell passed the next several weeks "loafing," drinking, and, as it was summer, "bathing" with radical Socialists.[2]

At SPA headquarters Wendell encountered two accomplished and colorful Wobblies, Sam Scarlett and J. A. "Jack" Law.[3] Their presence in Pittsburgh gave weight to rumors that the IWW was ready to begin its long-awaited assault on the citadel of the steel magnates. In 1913 organizer George Speed had blamed U.S. Steel "with its perfected spy system and thug police" for the IWW's decline in western Pennsylvania.[4] Now the IWW seemed ready to renew the struggle.

The newly arrived Scarlett's presence seemed especially ominous. He was a high-level field organizer associated with the most militant IWWism. Born in Kilmarnock, Scotland, in 1883, he emigrated to Canada in 1903 and then turned up in Denver, Colorado, the next year. As Scarlett told it, in 1911 in Sacramento, California, a rousing street-corner speech by soapboxer James P. Thompson, "the rough neck Isaiah of the American Proletariat," converted him to the cause. In agitating and organizing for the IWW, Scarlett proved exceptionally adept. His machinist's skills enabled him to get work almost anywhere and his talent as an outstanding soccer player who loved American football made him a natural leader in the hypermasculine culture of the industrial workplace. He was one of the IWW's fiercest advocates of industrial sabotage and confrontation with management. His message to workers was to abstain from violence but to be willing to use the Scottish on-the-job "ca-canny" (go-slow) sabotage.[5]

Scarlett had been a leader in the northern Minnesota iron ore miners' strike against the corporate owners, principally U.S. Steel, that began in June 1916. More than ten thousand Finnish, Russian, Italian, Croatian, and Romanian strikers had taken part and when the IWW entered the dispute, Sam Scarlett became a principal organizer. After a deputy sheriff and a bystander were killed in strike-related violence, Scarlett and fellow organizers Joseph Schmidt and Carlo Tresca were indicted as accessories to murder.[6] In December the state dropped charges against the three after several miners who had participated in the violence pled guilty to manslaughter. In their farewell speeches to the Mesabi miners, Scarlett and the others had vowed to carry on the fight against big steel. They expected that having planted the seeds of industrial unionism in the iron range, the miners would strike in the summer of 1917. Now in July 1917 here was Scarlett in Pittsburgh intent upon bringing the struggle to the doorstep of the oppressors of the Mesabi.[7]

Unlike the skilled worker and outstanding athlete Scarlett, footloose Wobbly Jack Law went from job to job and always seemed to need money. He was a native Pittsburgher, but for years he had drifted. Between 1913 and 1915 he had been an oil pipeline worker in the Mid-Continent field in Oklahoma, had done "the TANGO in a sawdust joint that serves stew, in the capacity of pot wrestler at the wage of forty and found" in Sweetgrass, Montana, had been in jail, "butt hotel," in Butte, and moved on to Minneapolis. Everywhere he worked hard for the IWW. In the spring and summer of 1913 he was a leader in free speech fights at Denver and at Minot, North Dakota. That same year he set up Tulsa's first IWW local and explored the possibilities of Wobbly unionization all the way to the Texas-Louisiana Gulf Coast. In Sweetgrass he was arrested after he circulated a leaflet among Montana national guardsmen "telling How many men have been Killed by gun me[n] in the last year" and urging them not to report for strike control duty.[8]

As an industrial union organizer Jack Law was distinctly inferior to Scarlett. He was a smooth talker and brave enough in a fight, but he lacked self-discipline and was easily bored by routine administration. In Tulsa, rank-and-file Wobblies had tried to oust him from the leadership of their local. He confessed to Vincent St. John that the men wanted him out for being "to[o] much of a dictator. . . . Their kick is that i am getting stale, and that i was out in a buggy with some woman." Fellow Wobbly Harrison George found him abrasive, saying "he forgets all about tactics when discussing things with another wob. Starts out good but loses control and his temper and his cause all at once."[9]

By 1916 Law had returned to Pittsburgh's North Side and was a salesman for the Jewell Tea & Coffee Company in company towns and camps of the coke and coal region adjacent to the city. The job, he wrote to Bill Haywood, the IWW general secretary–treasurer, gave him access to "a stragetical [sic] point of the coal field" and the steel industry and gave him the opportunity to do "a little for the O. B. U. [One Big Union]." Most of the miners, he noted, were Slavs and Italians so Haywood sent him IWW literature in Polish, Hungarian, and Italian and asked casually, "drop me a line occasionally, and let me know how you are doing." Haywood instructed Law to contact Jacob Margolis (to whom Haywood had sent IWW recruiting materials), the secretary of the Pittsburgh area Vehicle Workers Union, and veteran IWW organizer Joe Ettor in Scranton about the coal mine labor situation.[10]

Until March 1917, personal distractions, caring for a physically handicapped sister and unpaid bills, limited Law's IWW activities. By then he had a new wife, Madeline "Madge" Law, whose name soon turned up on BI lists of dangerous radicals. She was, he told Haywood, "American born, member of the I.W.W., radical Socialist, anarchist." Not only that but "she will fix a fine feed, believe [me] she can cook some." So inspired, Law declared that "at last the spirit has moved me and a couple of other fellow-workers." His plan, "just as soon as I can get my hands on a ten dollar note . . . to have a duplicate [IWW membership] card fixed as mine was stolen . . . [is] to cooperate with anybody or try alone to get the neuculis [sic] of an organization together starting in the coke regions & working toward Pittsburgh." He believed that if we "get the coke workers we will have a powerful club over the mill-men owing to the fact that we have the raw material from both ends."[11]

There in a nutshell was the IWW plan to slay the Pittsburgh steel giant: to organize mostly Italian and Slavic miners in the coal and coke towns in western Pennsylvania and as far away as eastern Ohio and northern West Virginia. Put them together with radicalized Mesabi miners and the IWW could call a general strike to cut off both fuel and ore to the steel mills. Left undefined was the meaning of the "club" against mill owners. Would it be used to drive the owners from the plants or just to wring wage, hour, or workplace concessions from them?

Added evidence that the IWW intended to make a move in Pittsburgh was Wendell's subsequent discovery of two more prominent out-of-town Wobblies, Abner Woodruff and Harrison George. Woodruff, a self-styled philosopher of the movement, first said he intended to organize Ohio farm laborers, but then turned his attention to the coke-producing areas.[12] The eccentric and able George wrote poetry, songs, and fiction, affected a Kansas corncob pipe, and was addicted to health food and colonic irrigation. At first George, who was staying with the Laws and using the name George Gardner, said he was in Pittsburgh to escape the draft. Then he, too, began to talk about reviving the local IWW.[13]

Wendell soon discovered that the most immediate task of federal intelligence in Pittsburgh was to stop the advance of the People's Council of America for Peace and Democracy (PCA).[14] At the end of May 1917, following a mass meeting at New York's Madison Square Garden, Louis P. Lochner and others founded the council. Its declared purposes were to bring about an end to the war "in harmony with the principles outlined by New Russia, namely: no forcible annexations; no punitive indemnities; free development of all nationalities." The PCA supported an internationalist approach to securing world peace and sought "to induce our government to state concretely the terms upon which it is willing to make peace." In domestic policy, the PCA stood for repeal of the conscription, safeguarding labor standards, and protecting civil liberties.[15]

Because it was an umbrella organization of the Left, the PCA has been likened to the Communist Party's popular front of the 1930s. Prominent Socialists and New York City union leaders offered support. Scott Nearing, Morris Hillquit, and James M. Maurer sat on its executive committee, but it also reached out left and right to radical and liberal elements of the New York City and Chicago intelligentsia. Most troubling to conservatives, the PCA took for its model the Petrograd Soviet, based on the belief of many of its members that a soviet might better represent the American people than Congress.[16]

The Allegheny County PCA chapter sprang to life in mid-July 1917 after an evangelizing rally led by traveling organizer Lindley M. Keasby.[17] After Keasby moved on the Pittsburgh area chapter was led by sincere, idealistic, Socialist Joseph R. Mountain. Mountain's day job was as a salesman for Stungo-Radium Rubber; American Tire, Rim, and Rubber; and Dixie Oil,[18] but most of his energy and spare time went to keeping the Pittsburgh chapter together. Wobblies like Scarlett and Law, who had no sympathy for the PCA's essentially political agenda, used it for their own purposes. They stuffed envelopes and gave speeches for the PCA—speeches promoting the IWW agenda of industrial unionism.[19] The fact that Margolis supported the PCA added to its problems. His participation rubbed salt into old Socialist wounds. Conservative or "political" SPA members still had not forgiven him for his role in the party schism of 1913.

Authorities harassed the PCA from the start. On July 26, 1917, coincidentally the day that J. Edgar Hoover began his career at the Justice Department, ex-President Theodore Roosevelt delivered a jingoistic speech calling for 100 percent Americanism before a huge crowd at the Allegheny County Courthouse that included Wendell and his radical comrades. In the afterglow of TR's harangue, Pittsburgh police were in no mood to permit the PCA to rally against conscription with featured speaker Charles E. Ruthenberg, who had just been convicted under the Espionage Act for opposing the draft. The night before the scheduled July 29 rally, the police revoked PCA's permit to use the Lyceum Theater.[20]

At the regular meeting of the SPA English-speaking branch that evening, Scarlett, Margolis, and Law took the floor to urge the Socialists to defy the authorities. Margolis denounced conscription as unconstitutional and urged mass action against it. Jack Law departed from the current IWW party line against free speech fights when he called for volunteers "to make the fight on every corner until they filled the jails." Scarlett followed, ridiculing some of the comrades for their timidity. Members then voted to move the rally beyond the city limits to Summer Hill Grove. They agreed that several hours before the meeting they would mass outside the locked Lyceum Theater. In their hatbands they would display cards advertising the meeting, and once a crowd had gathered all would parade silently to the grove. To deter police attacks, they planned to carry enough American flags "to give it the appearance of a patriotic parade." If the police did interfere they vowed to fight. The next morning Wendell reported the SPA's plan to BI agent Dillon who in turn notified the city police, a North Side commissioner, and, as the grove was outside the jurisdiction of city police, the Allegheny County Detective Bureau. The police promised to stop the parade and the county to observe and report on the meeting.[21]

Meantime dissension threatened the People's Council, much of it caused by Margolis, Scarlett, Law, and their direct action comrades. To Wendell's delight, they attempted to take over the PCA. On August 8 at New Era Hall, they paralyzed the PCA meeting by disputing every motion. They raged against members who had given advance information about PCA speakers to journalists. They demanded that the PCA should sponsor an appearance by Emma Goldman in behalf of radical labor leader Tom Mooney who had been sentenced to die for the deadly 1916 San Francisco Preparedness Day bombing.[22] They were voted down on both propositions because the majority of the thirty or so present feared that "the prestige of the Peoples Council would be injured" by association with the controversial Goldman. The Margolis faction carried on the dispute after the meeting until last call at the Budweiser Cafe. After the saloons closed, Wendell had his second long conversation with Margolis. The first had been on the exemption of aliens from the draft. This time the two men stood on the corner of Fifth and Grant until 1 A.M. talking about syndicalism and the prospects for industrial unionism. Margolis claimed that the AFL was "ruled by a bunch of Grafters" who had lost the support of the Westinghouse workers. He believed that the time was ripe for the IWW to organize them.[23]

At the next SPA meeting after the routine business, Scarlett gave a long speech to the fifty or so assembled promoting direct action over political action. This set off a bitter debate which, in Wendell's judgment, Scarlett won. Jack Law then lectured on the relationship of the master class and the working class. He recited incidents of industrial violence from McKees Rocks to Australia where "riots, burning of homes, docks, steamships, etc." had taken place. Wendell told the BI that Law "was laying the foundation of a reign of riot, destruction and bloodshed in this district." So fired up were the dissidents after the meeting that they repaired to a North Side after-hours club and talked "Science and anarchy" until 5 A.M. Then Wendell, Scarlett, and several others went to Joe Mountain's home and fell into exhausted sleep.[24]

The next afternoon at the PCA picnic at Summer Hill Grove, which went ahead as scheduled, they heard New York attorney Jacob Panken give a speech that Wendell labeled as radical but not actionable under the Espionage Act. Then the academic radical Scott Nearing took the podium. Nearing has been a favorite of scholars of the World War I–era Left, but on this day he disappointed the Pittsburgh Wobblies. Scarlett thought his speech was boring and even Wendell found him very "tame." They divined the gist of Nearing's brief address to be a criticism of the Wilson Administration for not appointing a representative of labor interests to the Council of National Defense. This was hardly a message to arouse those who had no use for the political system anyway. Still, the day was pleasant, the comrades drank and picnicked until 9 P.M. and the collection and sale of refreshments netted about $450 for the PCA.[25]

When they first met, Jack Law had told Wendell that he and Scarlett already had lined up a good nucleus for an IWW branch in Pittsburgh but would wait until they had eight hundred members to apply for a charter. But only two weeks later, on the evening of August 6, Scarlett, Wendell, and three others sat down and prepared a charter petition. In a show of symbolic unity they all went to mail it along with a ten-dollar money order for the application fee. A week later Wendell, Scarlett, longtime Socialist Jane Tait, and a half-dozen others crossed the Allegheny to the North Side for the opening of the Socialists' free speech fight. Then they attended an SPA branch meeting on East Street, where Scarlett pitched the IWW and direct action and invited the comrades to the first meeting of the new IWW branch on August 18. He explained that his mission in Pittsburgh was to make good his pledge to the Mesabi miners that "we had beat the Steel Trust at the point of raw material and that I was going to Pittsburgh to the point of production of finished products [to] organize and beat the Steel Trust again and I asked them if when that time came they would stick and strike at the mines so that the Steel Trust would be completely tied-up. They answered yes POSITIVELY."[26]

For all the talk about hundreds waiting to join the IWW, only eighteen men and two women signed the charter petition. By the time of the first meeting the total was only twenty-five. Along with machinist Scarlett, salesman Law, tinner Anisman, and "inspector" and auto mechanic Wendell were two more machinists, three more salespersons, a toolmaker, a weigh master, a carpenter, a tailor, a pressman, a draftsman, a bricklayer, a brewery worker, a waiter, an embroidery designer, two house painters, and three railroad workers. Scarlett remained upbeat despite the meager turnout. In the Budweiser Cafe after the East Street SPA meeting, he told Wendell that he had lined up twelve Dravo workers for the IWW and that at least seven hundred Italians in Duquesne and Homestead wanted to join. "*Walsh* old boy," he toasted fellow worker Wendell, "after the meeting Saturday night we will send telegrams to the miners in Minnesota and Michigan and tell them that we have laid the kiel [sic] for the I.W.W. Battleship to fight the Steel Trust at this end and warn them to get ready to help us win."[27]

By mid-August the days of talking anarchism, syndicalism, and direct action and the nights of intensive male bonding at downtown saloons had paid off for the BI. "Walsh Old Boy" had gained the confidence of the radicals. He was now the recording and financial secretary and organization committee member for the Pittsburgh English-speaking IWW Recruiting Branch and was trusted to keep the IWW charter and paperwork in his hotel room. He had a pass key to the Radical Library, which he had copied for SAC Judge. Wendell was now in position to be a provocative agent, to help fuel discord within the Pittsburgh Left.[28]

His chance came after an armed mob instigated by Anaconda Copper expelled more than one thousand largely IWW copper miners from Bisbee, Arizona, to the

New Mexico desert.[29] When the Margolis-Scarlett faction urged the PCA to take up the stranded miners' cause, Hill District Socialists, who were in the majority, voted them down. Knowing that the Margolis clique and the Hill District faction had been enemies since the 1913 split of the SPA, Wendell calculated that he could "wreck the People's Council, put the I.W.W. in a position for some time to come where they will have an organized opposition from the Socialists and cause a big dissension among the Socialists of Allegheny County." At the next PCA meeting he would encourage Margolis to push Walter Hirschberg, who was unpopular with Hill Socialists, as the IWW representative, under the rule that "anyone who is an authorized representative of any organization must be seated." The radicals would also demand that the Hill District-dominated PCA propaganda committee that had refused to aid the Bisbee miners should be enlarged from three to five members. Wendell predicted that the fight would disrupt the meeting and might even destroy the Pittsburgh PCA. If not, at the following PCA meeting the newly organized IWW chapter would secretly designate each of its several dozen members official delegates to the PCA. This parliamentary maneuver would make the Wobblies an instant majority that would "stampede the meeting and put on every resolution we desire."[30]

Melodramatically Wendell reported that he needed to convert Margolis "to my ideas, but . . . I must conceal my motives, because he is in perfect accord with the aims and objects of the People's Council and would not injure it in any way." Wendell soon won over Margolis, he claimed because Margolis was "an egoist, so I decided to play this weakness."[31] One suspects the plan to take over the PCA was Margolis's from the first. At the least, given his deep, long-standing enmity toward the Hill District Socialists, it would not have taken much to convince him.[32]

Whoever was responsible, the plan worked. At the next PCA meeting the Margolis faction put forward Hirschberg and proposed enlarging the propaganda committee. The meeting ended in uproar after the propaganda committee chairman resigned and the entire McKeesport delegation and half of the Hill District's representatives walked out. Afterward Wendell, Margolis, Hirschberg, and friends celebrated at Wolfgang Zuber's Bismarck Cafe on Sixth Avenue and plotted their next move, to stack the majority with IWW supporters at the next PCA meeting. After the saloon closed, Wendell and Margolis talked "on general subjects" until 1:30 A.M. on the corner of Fifth and Grant.[33]

When the Pittsburgh IWW General Recruiting Branch met for the first time on Sunday afternoon, August 26, Wendell and Scarlett were a bit under the weather. Until 5 A.M. that morning they had made the rounds with visiting steeplejack and Wobbly organizer George "Spike" Moore. Their headaches could not have been eased by the presence of only fourteen persons at the IWW meeting. The principal business was to plan a mass meeting to raise funds for the Bisbee exiles and call attention to the IWW in Pittsburgh. But the branch, with only $28.75, not enough to pay for mailing fliers, had to limit publicity to the display of banners at the Labor Temple and PCA and SPA headquarters.[34]

At the end of August Sam Scarlett lost his job at Dravo Contracting Company and moved in with Wendell. No longer could he use his lunchtime to proselytize the "slaves." He owed his firing to his new roommate. Scarlett's exposure among the Dravo employees by Wendell prompted Raymond E. Horn, MID and ONI agent and chief detective for the Employers' Association of Pittsburgh, to boast to Van Deman of MID that "the Department of Justice has an excellent arrangement to be notified in advance of everything . . . [the IWW] intends to start in this District."[35]

Unemployment sapped Scarlett's enthusiasm for the IWW's offensive against big steel in Pittsburgh. He began to talk about invitations he had received from Cleveland to organize machinists and from Conamaugh, Pennsylvania, where coal miners supposedly were threatening to bolt the UMWA for the IWW. It was hard to be optimistic when only eighteen persons, including three new members, attended the second meeting of the Pittsburgh IWW branch. A couple of days later organizer Abner Woodruff added to the gloom when he reported that he had failed to get the IWW going in the coke-producing regions. So far it was not much of a revolution in the steel valleys.[36]

Meanwhile, Washington was secretly preparing to put the IWW out of business. Under heavy pressure from western politicians and businessmen, the Justice Department planned to charge the IWW with hindering the war effort and hoped to prove that German money had financed its activities. On August 21, 1917, Attorney General Gregory notified President Wilson that he planned a raid on the Wobblies. That same day Chicago Division Superintendent Hinton Clabaugh, who was to raid IWW headquarters and coordinate the assault nationwide, wired the Pittsburgh BI for the names of all the IWW organizers in the area. Judge responded that he was still assembling the list and characterized the IWW as "not particularly active in this district until recently." Two weeks later, on September 5, BI agents assisted by U.S. marshals and local police raided IWW offices nationwide. This giant dredging operation produced a mass of material including "minute books, correspondence, typewriters, desks, rubber bands, paper clips, and, in Chicago, Ralph Chaplin's love letters, Joe Hill's ashes, and Frank Little's death mask."[37]

In Pittsburgh, SAC Judge, following guidelines from Clabaugh, prepared the search warrant based on the IWW's alleged violation of the Espionage Act by "willfully causing and attempting to cause insubordination, disloyalty, mutiny, and refusal of duty in the military and naval forces . . . while the United States was at war [and] . . . using the mails and postal service for the transmission of mail matter advocating treason, insurrection, and forcible resistance to the laws of the United States concerning the present war." The warrant targeted IWW membership lists, propaganda, literature, constitutions and by-laws, correspondence, and organizational receipts, invoices, records, and accounts.[38]

At 3 P.M. on September 5 special agent Dillon, a U.S. marshal, an IRS inspector, and District Immigration Inspector W. W. Sibray used a janitor's key to enter the Radical Library in the McGeagh Building. After a search they carted away a large volume of evidence, including correspondence, pamphlets, handbills, clerical supplies, items pertaining to the Tom Mooney Defense Fund, single issues of *Blast* and *The Masses*, a "marked map of Pennsylvania," a subscription list to *Solidarity*, and three copies of the weekly paper "taken from a vendor on the street." Two weeks later, for good measure, the G-men raided Wendell's room at Gibson's Hotel and confiscated a half-dozen letters between Haywood and Scarlett and local IWW Jack Shean, rental receipts, a ledger, a day book, a minute book, and a pad of filled-in membership applications. They also seized envelopes, blank postcards, miscellaneous blank forms, letterheads, due books, a rubber date stamp, stamp pad, and "DuLux" Ring Binder. The raids disabled the Pittsburgh IWW, leaving its officers without funds, organizational materials, or even a membership list.[39]

The mountain of "evidence" seized in Pittsburgh contained nothing to prove that the IWW engaged in violence, treason, or had a German connection. Absent were copies of allegedly treasonous publications such as the IWW's suppressed antiwar pamphlet, "Deadly Parallel," Arturo Giovannitti's translation of Emile Pouget's *Sabotage*, or the IWW *Little Red Song Book*.[40] Judge sent the confiscated material to Clabaugh who took two weeks to examine it along with the evidence from other cities. Then, on September 22, he sent a partially coded wire asking Judge to confer with "tremble," U.S. Attorney E. Lowry Humes, and send the names of no more than six of the most active "keeve unman unman," that is, IWW officers and agitators in the Pittsburgh district. Judge, who had no wish to destroy the infant Pittsburgh IWW chapter and with it Wendell's influence inside the Left, replied that "tremble" was out of town and "my judgment evidence insufficient [to] include any local leaders in indictment unless mere possession of literature is considered sufficient."[41] However, soon after, a federal grand jury in Chicago handed down 166 indictments of Wobbly officials on various of five counts under the Espionage Act. On the list were Frank Little, who had been lynched by a mob in July, and Vincent St. John, who had officially left the IWW in 1915.[42] Seven names had Pittsburgh connections: Scarlett, Law, Harrison George, Otto Justh, Grover H. Perry, Alexander Cournos, and George Andreytchine.[43]

At the end of September Bill Haywood and IWW lawyer George Vanderveer urged those who had been indicted to turn themselves in. Melvyn Dubofsky writes that "only an overwhelming belief in their own innocence and an unquestioning faith that the laws they denigrated would protect them" could explain the behavior of the IWW leaders. That may be, but Law, George, and Scarlett followed the lead of Joe Ettor, Carlo Tresca, and Elizabeth Gurley Flynn, who urged those charged to avoid arrest. Law fled south to Charleroi in Washington County with George after BI agents came to his home on the twenty-fifth. Three days later, following Wendell's tip, special agent Dillon took the interurban streetcar to Charleroi where at midnight he and the local police found the two hiding out above a dentist's office.[44]

Sam Scarlett left Pittsburgh to speak in Cleveland a couple of days before the raid, then disappeared. But Wendell and the BI knew exactly where he was. The Scotsman had written to Margolis on September 21 from Akron, where he was staying in a second-floor rear apartment on Howard Street using the name Tom McLean. He said that after the raids on September 5, Haywood had directed him to leave Cleveland for Akron in order to secretly build the IWW among construction and rubber workers. He was to use a new method of organization, one that anticipated later Communist Party methods.[45] Members were not to use names at business meetings and committee reports were to be taken unsigned from a sealed box. Job delegates were to issue due stamps to members who were not to know the names of branch officers. Scarlett boasted that he had already set up committees for Hungarian, Italian, Swedish, and American workers. Optimistic as ever, he gushed that "this method keeps the bosses [sic] agents up in the air continually. New members keep pouring in and the wobblies is the big thing here."[46]

To atone for abandoning his Pittsburgh comrades, Scarlett promised to get Akron workers who supported the IWW "enthused" about working in the Pittsburgh steel mills once frost ended the outdoor construction season. Quoting from *The Little Red Song Book*, he urged Margolis and the other rebels to "hold the fort" in Pittsburgh, for reinforcements were on the way. Wendell copied the letter and forwarded it through channels to Cleveland SAC DeWoody. Soon after, Scarlett was in Akron city jail awaiting transfer to Chicago.[47]

The very day Scarlett's letter came, Wendell learned that a Hungarian IWW branch had been operating secretly on East Street since March in various guises, the most recent being "the Socialist Club of the 23rd Ward." The Hungarian Wobblies were now ready to emerge, and they invited Walsh to speak on industrial unionism and to help them organize foreign workers at Jones and Loughlin Steel for the IWW. Sent to investigate the Hungarian branch, APL volunteer W. A. Beadling learned that they had rented their club room as the German-Hungarian Beneficial Association. He found the place decorated with IWW and SPA charters and foreign language posters. The beat policeman could tell him nothing about the group. The Post Office agreed to make inquiries.[48] This was exciting news to BI agents, for it promised long-sought evidence of a German-IWW connection.

The leader of the Hungarian IWW proved to be Frank A. Schmidt, an immigrant German machinist. Within a week Wendell reported that Secretary Schmidt came from a German military family, claimed to be the nephew of the German war minister, and that reputedly one of his relatives had been with the Austrian archduke at Sarajevo in 1914. Special agents Edgar B. Speer and K. K. McClure searched the East Street German-Hungarian Union and the homes of Schmidt and union head Peter Neizer. All they found was a list of members of the Hungarian IWW branch. This evidence, concluded a disappointed Chief Bielaski, was not enough to "warrant arrest and detention of these alien enemies under the President's proclamation."[49]

But the search broke the back of the Hungarian branch. The agents confiscated books, records, propaganda, credentials, and membership lists so hindering its operation that by January 1918 Wendell pronounced it "inactive and practically extinct." Not only that, but Judge had "hooked" branch secretary Schmidt. Using unspecified incentives, Judge "engaged former secretary of the Hungarian I.W.W. as an informant for this office." Schmidt was told to revive the branch and to keep the BI informed about its activities. The operation hit a snag in April 1918 when members accused Schmidt of stealing nineteen dollars from the branch treasury. Fortunately for the Bureau, dissident Hungarians took their complaint to the English-speaking IWW executive board, which included Wendell. The board sent Margolis to collect the money and Schmidt was soon forgiven and back as secretary.[50]

Enforcement of the draft was a high priority of the Pittsburgh BI, ONI, MID, and APL. The first conscription act required men between twenty-one and thirty to register on June 5, 1917, and when their number came up to report for a pre-induction physical. In July Wendell asked around among the Wobblies for a forged draft card with an exempt classification. Before long fellow worker Jack Shean gave him an "extra card" and said he knew where to get more. Wendell suspected that Margolis and Marshall were the suppliers. Then a tip from city police to the BI led to a young man who had been approached by a Socialist after his draft number was called. The Socialist showed the potential draftee a picture of a skull and crossbones and suggested that if he wanted to save his skin he should see lawyer James J. Marshall in the Union Arcade. At Marshall's office he met a "tall, dark man in a Panama suit," who dispensed tips on how to avoid military service. These ranged from feigning a physical handicap to getting a physician to certify that he was needed at home to care for an ill and totally dependent wife. The description of the man in the Panama suit fit Margolis.[51]

The BI then set out to catch Margolis violating the Espionage Act by sending ten APL volunteers posing as draft dodgers to his office. As it happened Margolis knew the family of the first volunteer. He advised the young man that he could not avoid military service, but, when pressed, allegedly said, "you do not need to take the physical examination if you do not want to for they can only put you in jail and let you out on bond." The BI agents were disappointed. Despite its obvious lack of patriotic fervor, Margolis's counsel had not violated the law. He had only presented the young man with a choice of military service or jail. The other nine APL men who followed were no more successful.[52] Perhaps the sudden parade of middle-class would-be draft dodgers aroused the lawyer's suspicions.

Wendell was more successful. Avoidance of the draft was a hot topic at SPA headquarters. The party's antiwar position was a recruiting tool that made it a magnet for those opposed to the war. Although it is difficult to know a person's heart, the idealism of many of the younger Socialists must have been tempered by the desire for help in avoiding the draft. They had every reason to be concerned. As a *rage militaire* inflamed the public after U.S. entry into the war, crusading editorial writers called upon all able-bodied men, including aliens, to take up arms. Extreme militarism reached a climax on August 18, 1917, when an estimated 250,000 Pittsburghers turned out along a nine-mile line of march to cheer the passage of 3,500 newly mobilized guardsmen. The huzzahs from New Era Hall must have been faint when the "sparkling-eyed boys" paraded by on Fifth Avenue.[53]

The radicals chewed over a variety of schemes to avoid putting on khaki. Carrying phony draft cards was one way. Another was to send physically unfit substitutes to take the pre-induction physical for fit comrades. One doubts that this was done often when easier and more practical ways were at hand. One could, like Victor Slone, a law clerk in Margolis's office, simply fail to register. Slone gambled

that authorities would not check, assuming that anyone connected with the notorious Margolis would be careful not to disobey the draft law. He knew that if they
did his notary license and entry to the bar would show that he was of draft age.
Nine days after he spilled the beans to Wendell he was arrested for draft evasion.[54]

To avoid service, several of Wendell's radical acquaintances simply left town
with no forwarding address when their numbers came up. In one such case, Wendell and Walter Hirschberg abetted the flight of J. W. Johnston, a Wobbly and
Pressed Steel Car Company weigh master. They laid their plans one August night
at the Bismarck cafe, warmed by alcohol and inspired by radical poetry. Wendell
kept Johnston's packed valise in his room until the dodger was able to slip away
from his home and job. Then the government informer delivered the bag to him
on the street and said good-bye as Hirschberg drove the fugitive to Greensburg to
catch a Philadelphia train. In the city of brotherly love Johnston hoped to disappear among other anonymous "floaters."[55]

The American Left has always had to pay the devil his due. Trying to make a
revolution in this capitalist bastion requires money. Moreover, Margolis and the
Wobblies had to cope with the heavy added expenses of defending themselves
against continuous government prosecution and harassment. Their opponents
tried to identify the IWW with the enemies of the country and to bankrupt its
treasury. It was only a short step from that to the conclusion that the IWW was financed by the kaiser. The government's theory of German backing of the IWW
rested more on wishful thinking than on factual evidence. Certainly pro-German
elements and anti-British Irish nationalists favored any organization that would
hinder Allied war production. The Hungarian IWW seemed suspiciously Ger-
manic. Perhaps isolated German spies infiltrated the IWW and other labor organizations, but there was little hard evidence for the German-IWW conspiracy theory put forward by government detectives, including William J. Flynn, who later
succeeded Bielaski at the BI.

In *The Eagle's Eye,* his 1918 propagandistic novel loosely based on the federal
campaign against German spies, Flynn claimed that in 1915 federal detectives had
defeated German efforts to sabotage production by sowing dissension in the
American workforce, and months of labor harmony had followed. Then suddenly
occurred the "outbreak" of the IWW, a group "formed originally by a cracked-
brain, illogical theorist to agitate the doctrine that a worker is entitled to the gross
proceeds of his labor." After languishing for years, in 1916 the IWW "suddenly ac-
quired apparently unlimited money from some source." IWW agitators appeared

in industrial centers nationwide to play the part of imperial Germany. The plan they followed could not have been their own. It had to be the work of "some sane person," presumably a German master spy. Through strikes, sabotage, and anti-war and anticonscription activities, the IWW had done the kaiser's business.[56] Need one say that the BI's own files and the mountain of evidence it seized in the IWW raids do not substantiate Flynn's version of history? When, in pursuit of the German connection, the BI sent Wendell in search of an imagined steamer trunk full of deutsche marks, he returned with scarcely a pfennig. What he brought back was a very American story of Wobblies minding the main chance and turning wartime prosperity to profit.

Wendell found that Pittsburgh radicals supplemented their regular income from rallies, entertainment, and membership dues through a variety of sources and schemes. They had "respectable" backers such as anarchist James Mering, advertising manager of the *Pittsburgh Dispatch*. Mering had entertained Scott Nearing and his wife had publicly refused to join the Red Cross. Still he kept his job and donated an estimated sixty dollars a month to radical causes. Another backer was old-fashioned liberal single-taxer Julian Kennedy, a consulting engineer at Carnegie Steel, who even pleaded the IWW cause to the Pittsburgh Chamber of Commerce. Even Margolis's longtime rival and leader of the political SPA, Dr. William Van Essen, so prospered during the war that he moved to a larger office and became vice president of the Pennsylvania Optometrists' Association.[57]

The Wobblies also derived income from their work among immigrant workers. Only a minority of the immigrants supported radical causes, but those who did were hardworking and willing to sacrifice. Remarkably, in 1918 a coalition of mainly Central and Eastern European radicals raised a hefty sum, $18,500, to acquire what became the International Socialist Lyceum at James and Foreland Streets on the North Side. The site was an ideal point for Socialist agitation. It was in the heart of the East Ohio Street neighborhood "shaped by the needs of single immigrant men who made up the bulk of its inhabitants: there were rooming houses, taverns and cheap cafes, stores selling work clothes, and newsstands stacked with various foreign language papers." Wendell could not figure out where the money came from. He could only account for what little came from staging a political play, "When Peace Comes," at the Moose Temple.[58]

Some radical ventures exploited the immigrants. In December 1917 Margolis and Marshall advertised free legal advice and help with filling out Selective Service questionnaires to prospective draftees in the Jewish *Vorwartes*. At the time Marshall was on a legal advisory board that provided such assistance free. However, by

bringing the men to their offices, Margolis and Marshall could charge a small notary fee and offer to accept "donations." About the same time Margolis signed on
to a more questionable and potentially lucrative scheme, the United States Protective League (USPL). For twelve dollars a year the USPL promised blanket legal
services to immigrants that included a membership certificate, a display placard,
no-fee representation in police and aldermanic courts, legal document preparation, and, for small businessmen, debt collection assistance.[59] The USPL was the
brainchild of the brothers E. A. and J. H. Wheeler, who had organized the first
chapter in Ohio. Although Margolis's brother-in-law Oscar Kaminsky became
nominal president of the Pittsburgh operation, the Wheelers managed the sale of
certificates behind the scenes. They and their salesmen pocketed as much as six
dollars of the cost of each certificate. Margolis's share was one dollar per certificate
plus 10 percent of all debt collections. In March 1918, a conscience-stricken salesman, Julius Fox, resigned in protest and then spread stories of USPL's sharp practices through the Socialist community. Critics charged Margolis and Marshall
with misrepresenting the service and exploiting the very immigrants they claimed
to help. To promote the certificates salesmen were falsely asserting that Margolis
and Marshall could represent purchasers in the federal courts and guarantee them
exemption from military service. Faced with these embarrassing revelations, Margolis and Marshall had to disavow the USPL.[60]

Another money-raising venture was the sale of IWW Industrial Freedom Certificates to help pay for the defense of Haywood and the others awaiting trial in
Chicago and elsewhere.[61] Peddling the $1 and $5 certificates to small businesses on
Pittsburgh's South Side in December 1917 gave Wendell an excuse to look for a tie-
in between the kaiser's agents and the IWW. He found none.

By the end of 1917 there had been much turnover among the founders of the
Pittsburgh IWW General Recruiting Branch. Scarlett and Law were in jail. Two
others, Knud Sandor or Sonder and Jack Shean, had fled to New York City to avoid
being drafted. With a new name and the help of fellow radicals one could disappear in the city's vastness and impersonality. The word was that police seldom
looked for delinquents at IWW headquarters then in St. Mark's Place. That was
why in October 1917 Wendell, Margolis, and several other radicals were at the station to bid goodbye to the hotel waiter Sandor. Beside dodging conscription he
planned to organize Manhattan food service workers for the IWW.[62]

For Sandor, and doubtless other lonely young men in the city, part of the at-
traction of radicalism was the companionship of other men, particularly older
men as mentors and confidants. In his *An American Testament,* revolutionary

Joseph Freeman describes powerful feelings of his youth in the early 1920s as something he had "in common with men of his age and type in all countries and all social classes." Freeman defines these feelings in Freudian terms as the search for a father surrogate and says he sought to fulfill them in the company of Bill Dunne, William Z. Foster, and Charles E. Ruthenberg.[63]

Sandor and Joe Mountain were two young men who sought similar relationships with "Jake" Margolis, longtime Socialist Party leader "Doc" Van Essen, and government spy Wendell. In late 1917 Sandor wrote letters from New York to Wendell, which ended up in the BI files, that shyly convey deep affection and intimacy. Writing as Edward Hansen to "Dear Friend," Sandor discussed an upcoming Greenwich Village "Bal Primitif, . . . similar to those Jake told us about." He wrote awkwardly, "I wish you were here with me. Together we might mutually enjoy ourselves. . . . Alone I do not feel primitive enough to go near the 'joint,' leaving alone to attend. Together I am sure we could be savages for one night." A few weeks later Sandor was failing in his IWW mission and his personal life was a shambles. He had been ill, had spent all of his money, and was in debt. On Christmas Eve he lost his job when "a drunken detective started a fist fight with me at the same time threatening me with arrest." But his comrades and the cause soon revived him. The New York City Finnish, Italian, and Hungarian IWW branches were growing fast. In Arizona and the Pacific Northwest the tide was turning in favor of the IWW. Lumberjacks, "the most down-trodden of all slaves [were] winning the eight hour day and at the same time proving that our theory of striking on the job is correct."[64]

In mid-December Jack Shean followed Sandor to Manhattan, but he did not remain out of sight for long. Ben Anisman found him there in February 1918 and his arrest quickly followed. He would have been easy to spot at over six feet and 190 pounds with a "very small black mustache, dark suit, short blue chinchilla coat, grey soft hat, and tan shoes." His transparent alias, Jacque [sic] Anseh, an anagram of Shean, could not have provided much cover.[65]

In November 1917 in the respected *Atlantic Monthly* Carleton H. Parker exalted the IWW as the barometer of American labor's conditional support for the war and called it a phenomenon of revolt like the Granger movement, the Knights of Labor, the Farmers' Alliance, and the Progressive Party.[66] That was not a very apt description of the Pittsburgh IWW, which by 1918 was thoroughly compromised by the BI. Along with local unknowns and other spies such as Schmidt and perhaps Ben Anisman, Wendell had rushed to fill the vacuum left by the removal of the IWW leadership. Now he occupied a position formerly held by Law and Scarlett. His placement meant that the federal intelligence agencies could be privy to and influence radical plans and activities. Policy in Washington might dictate that the IWW must be destroyed, but to maintain its observation post the Pittsburgh BI needed the local to keep going.

Although Wendell had searched diligently, he found no significant pro-German activity: no violence or plans for violence involving Socialists, Wobblies, or their hangers-on. He did discover organized draft resistance and that strong anti-war feeling was a unifying force among the comrades. His reports sketch a fissured Left that he believed could be neutralized by federal and local authorities. Pittsburgh BI and MID files indicate no threat of revolution from the radical Left as long as it remained divided and as long as the mass of immigrant workers remained divided and disorganized.

4

EXCURSIONS, ALARMS, AND
SLACKERS ABROAD
EXTENDING THE RANGE OF SURVEILLANCE, 1918

> There is quite a deal of hysteria in the country about German spies. If you will
> kindly box up and send me from one to a dozen I will pay you very handsomely
> for your trouble. We are looking for them constantly, but it is a little difficult to
> shoot them until they have been found.
>
> Attorney General Thomas W. Gregory to T. U. Taylor, April 1918

IN 1918, ALTHOUGH THE PEOPLE'S COUNCIL of America was in ruins and
the IWW leadership in jail, draft resistance and radical agitation continued. Wendell remained the key source, but the Pittsburgh intelligence offices added agents
and informers to expand surveillance to cover new dissident groups and areas distant from the city. In March the Germans launched a major offensive on the Western Front. Soon more than one hundred thousand American soldiers a month
crossed the Atlantic to France.[1] The dreaded bloodying of the American army in
the trenches would come, and with it long casualty lists in the papers. A barrage
of government propaganda designed to elicit support for the war had already
helped to create a mind-set that brooked no criticism of allies or the war effort,
that demonized the enemy and the hated German *kultur*. By mid-1918, volunteer
"Four-Minute Men" organized by the federal Committee on Public Information
were parroting an estimated one thousand identical propaganda speeches to up-
wards of eighty thousand people a day in Allegheny County.[2]

The example set by law enforcement officials, abetted by the journalistic and legal establishments, indirectly sanctioned vigilantism, so it was no surprise that
mobs appeared to purge their communities of all but a 100-percent Americanism.
Other factors also contributed to intolerance. Lucrative government contracts or
high-wage war work made patriots of some without loved ones in military service.
Opportunists used the excuse of patriotism to vent jealousy and animosity toward
those from whom they felt alienated or from whom they wanted to take power.
The result was a slow-motion riot by the majority to force not simply consensus,
but unanimity.

Examples of civil liberties outrages are all too familiar to students of the period. Three that might make a typical short list are: a Collinsville, Illinois, mob tortured and then murdered Robert Prager, whose principal offense was being German; at Butte, Montana, arthritic, one-eyed IWW organizer Frank Little was dragged at the end of a rope by an automobile to the edge of town and then lynched; a Minnesota man was arrested after he told women knitting for soldiers that "No soldier ever sees these socks."[3]

The trouble peaked around Pittsburgh in early 1918. One Sunday in February, two hundred North Side boys targeted the newly opened International Socialist Lyceum for an all-day snowball attack and hostile demonstration. They cheered the American flag, yelled "down with foreigners," and jeered at Socialists, anarchists, and Wobblies. Wendell might have had something to do with the attack. He had reported that the Croatian Society Club in the building's basement, which featured a sixty-foot-long bar and bowling alley, was a rendezvous for Germans and Austrians and the prime site of antiwar activity on the North Side.[4]

Wendell had nothing to do with what happened one March evening to well-to-do McKees Rocks builder John Pryzmusalia. He was driven to a rural area, lectured on the "propriety of living here in America," and then stripped, tarred, and feathered. Relatives of doughboys and workers in war plants had first reported Pryzmusalia to the Justice Department for refusing to contribute to the Liberty Loan. When the government did not arrest him a posse intervened.[5] Shortly after Beaver County pastor Frederick Rader denounced the war as unchristian and told his parishioners not to buy Liberty Bonds an armed mob visited his home at night. When Rader still refused to buy a bond or recant, the Rochester "Home Defense Police" arrested him and took him to the sheriff in order, as they claimed, to save his life. U.S. District Attorney Humes took him in charge and indicted him for violating the Sedition Act.[6] Similarly charged was seventy-six-year-old Andy Williams of Altoona, who allegedly said to an acquaintance that his son had "no Damn business in France." Williams awoke in jail the day after sleeping off a drunk and disorderly arrest and was charged with sedition, which must have made his headache worse.[7]

John Wellman, a naturalized Austrian and an open hearth foreman at Mesta Machine, was convicted under the Espionage Act before federal judge W. H. S. Thompson for remarks about President Wilson and the Food Administration. He gave offense by arguing with fellow employees and boasting of a horde of sugar and flour in his basement. Witnesses said he had shouted "To —— with the President: I am as good as he" and added for good measure that "American soldiers were no good and that all they would do [in France] was eat ice cream and candy, and smoke cigarettes." For this, Wellman went to jail.[8] To Socialist John Schellenberger, who had circulated the anticapitalist, antiwar pamphlet, "The Price We Pay," Judge Thompson delivered a lecture. He told Schellenberger, "this is a just war. In America we are governed by the majority and when our representatives to Congress voted that war be declared upon the Imperial German Government it was and is our duty to lend every assistance to the President."[9]

Such expressions did not shield the judge himself from the charge that he was too lenient toward dissidents. He sentenced Schellenberger to only five months in prison. John Kratkus received a mere ten days for his remark that it was foolish to be drafted when one could change his name and move. The judge defended his actions by explaining why he sentenced John Kolar, who had made antigovernment statements and would not buy a Liberty Bond, to only thirty days. It was, the judge remarked, "a personal privilege whether or not a man wanted to buy a Liberty bond." Thompson's approach did not sit well with Humes, who complained that light sentences would encourage patriots to take the law into their own hands.[10] Humes pledged to prosecute all sedition cases vigorously, warning that "if we cannot inspire public confidence through the administration of civil law through the courts, we must expect violence."[11] Yet for all the talk, of the 1,524 Espionage Act prosecutions reported by the attorney general for the period July 1, 1917, to June 30, 1919, only twenty-one (resulting in thirteen convictions) took place in the Western Pennsylvania District.[12]

Humes's public statements reflected the prosecutorial zeal that he would later use to advantage as staff attorney for the Red-hunting Overman Committee of the U.S. Senate. They were also in response to pressure from Washington. In April 1918, head of the Justice Department's War Emergency Division, John Lord O'Brian, warned Attorney General Gregory of growing mob violence. Rumors were spreading that German agents had put ground glass and poison in food, destroyed ammunition, and caused factory fires. The administration should remind the public that "with . . . Government and State officials and a very large body of private citizens organized for the purpose of watching out for offenders against the cause of Government, this country is being policed more thoroughly and successfully than ever before."[13] Instead of following O'Brian's advice, the administration threatened to impose even tougher sentences for seditious remarks.

In May the Allegheny County sheriff met with Humes and county officials to seek ways of controlling loyalty mobs. The sheriff, his ears ringing with the complaints of victims, blamed the epidemic of lawlessness on "misdirected enthusiasm." He thought the mob actions to be baseless and unjust, having originated from gossip "that has been around for several days." Yet with no apparent sense of irony, he concluded that much of the trouble was caused by "the Kaiser's propagandists."[14]

But the vigilantism continued. On May 25, 1918, Pittsburgh hardware store clerk J. J. Albrecht's coworkers partially stripped him, poured two gallons of red paint on "every part of him" including his face and hair, and then turned him out onto busy Penn Avenue. Albrecht's offense, aside from his German name, was his refusal to donate a day's pay to the Red Cross and allegedly saying "To Hell with the Red Cross."[15]

Despite mobs, citizens' groups, and law enforcement agencies it was hard to break the habit of free expression. First to be charged in Pittsburgh under the tough new Sedition Act of 1918 was an unreformed John Pryzmusalia of McKees Rocks. It was claimed that he told stories of American soldiers' cruelty toward German prisoners and referred to the doughboys as "bums." This time more or less official vigilantes or a "posse comitatus" known as the McKees Rocks Patriotic League arrested him and turned him over to authorities.[16]

If the Justice Department did not discourage the vigilantes neither was it very interested in the random targets of the 100-percent Americans. The Radical Squad was after conspiracies, not isolated nonconforming individuals or local scapegoats. For example, the Pittsburgh BI did not pursue a December 1917 complaint from the general secretary of the Washington, Pennsylvania, YWCA demanding a federal investigation of a suspicious character, Mrs. Olaf Ljungstedt. The official feared that this inquisitive, out-of-town woman with her Nordic name and her "brown eyes wide open and a bit strange," who claimed to be digging for genealogical information on the Robinson family, was "either not strong in mind or loyalty to the U.S." Perhaps her interest in genealogical records in the country courthouse was only a ploy to make a plan of the building.[17] In another case, agents did follow up by inquiring of the constable in tiny Republic, Pennsylvania, after a high school teacher wrote to the Secret Service. The teacher reported that an usher at the Capuzzi brothers' movie theater ordered her and her class to sit down and not block the screen when they had stood during the playing of the "Star-Spangled Banner." The agents concluded that the incident resulted from the usher's ignorance and the Philadelphia-bred schoolteacher's unfounded suspicion of the local people.[18]

Of the cases described above, only one miscreant was a Socialist and none, it seems, were German agents. The fact was that the Left quickly mastered the rules of survival. Radicals managed to live with and in spite of the Espionage and Sedi-

tion Acts and still find ways to fight. After U.S. Post Office censors barred IWW
defense literature from the mails, the Wobblies found other ways to move them.
When Chicago actress Phyllis Undell came to the Lyceum in March 1918 as Little
Mary in the road company of "Ten Nights in a Barroom," she brought IWW
official Wendell a half-dozen copies of the suppressed *IWW Defense News Bulletin*.[19] After six-year-old Frieda Truhar recited "I Did Not Raise My Boy To Be A
Soldier" at an antiwar gathering, police questioned her Socialist parents. But she
remembered that the episode did not stop her father's "future anti-war activities. . . . and the socialist Croatians in Pittsburgh continued to push anti-war
leaflets printed in English through letter slots."[20]

Federal censorship had a definite chilling effect on political speech. Knowing
that government spies and agents were in their midst, English-speaking radicals
had to watch their words. Foreign-speaking leftists had more leeway because, particularly early in the war, few agents or informers could understand them. Agents
speculated that the foreign language speakers were preaching revolution and violating the Espionage and Sedition Acts, but they had no proof. So radicals continued to meet, to debate events in Russia, raise money for the Chicago Wobblies and
Tom Mooney, and seek the ever-elusive common ground among the diverse factions of the Left.[21] The de facto ground rules laid down by the Pittsburgh police allowed speech as long as it did not directly criticize the government or the war effort. The evident leniency reflected officialdom's belief that the radical speakers
were not effectively reaching a significant portion of the industrial workforce. But,
as Wendell's reports show, as time passed, the Wobblies seemed to be making
gains among the Eastern and Southern Europeans.[22]

The G-men did not accept these gains as legitimate or agree that the IWW was
becoming another labor union. They took it as an article of faith that the Wobblies
pursued a secret agenda whose purpose must be to subvert the war effort by keeping the workers dissatisfied. In February 1918 Wendell made that case in a report.
He said that IWW leaders were anarchists who intended to take over industries,
but that "the rank and file have not advanced enough to have this philosophy—
they look upon the I.W.W. as a union and have joined it the same as members of
the A.F.L., for the purpose of bettering their economic position." IWW speakers,
he continued, always talked about wages and hours. "They know that if they mix
their philosophy in . . . they could not reach the workers. Therefore it is perfectly
normal that the rank and file would have bought lots of Liberty bonds, joined the
army, etc." But the leopard could not change its spots.[23]

It was in this context that the mass trial of *United States v. Haywood et al.* finally began in Chicago on April Fool's Day 1918. Of the 166 Wobblies originally indicted, 113 went to trial. Zealous federal prosecutors rode roughshod over due process to make a weak circumstantial case from the voluminous records and literature seized in the 1917 raids. The defendants tried to live up to the Wobblies' colorful reputation by lounging, dozing, smoking, and chatting through the long trial. Several, including Scarlett, delivered sample soapbox speeches for the court. Radical journalist John Reed recorded the scene vividly for readers of *The Masses*. However, the way that Reed presented the IWW gave its enemies a theme they would use to great effect; he clothed the Wobblies in the garb of the Russian Bolsheviks, whom he so much admired. This supported right-wing theory that the Bolsheviks were puppets of German kaiserism and the sinister foreign force behind the IWW.[24]

Margolis appeared at the trial in July as a witness for Scarlett and Andreytchine. He testified that Scarlett had never been a member of the Pittsburgh PCA and that when the Scot spoke at a PCA picnic in the summer of 1917 he addressed only economic, not antiwar, issues. Margolis portrayed Andreytchine, whom he had known for years, as a Tolstoyan pacifist opposed to violence as an instrument of social change. Under cross examination Margolis readily admitted he was an IWW sympathizer but made clear that his occupation barred him from membership. The prosecutor's final question, "What is your nationality?" evoked an ambiguous answer. Margolis said "Jewish—really American. I was born here and that is the nationality I claim."[25]

Margolis came back from Chicago disgusted with the trial strategy pursued by Haywood and lead defense counsel Vanderveer. They intended to show that the IWW had never taken a formal position against the war and that many Wobblies were patriotic. Margolis thought such a defense might help Haywood, but not the rank-and-file defendants. Longtime public hostility and official persecution had stripped them of illusions. They expected to be found guilty and valued the trial primarily as a soapbox for the cause. They were not ashamed of opposing the war and wanted to stand their ground and make the capitalists' war the issue.[26]

At the end of the trial in mid-August, the jury took only an hour to find all of the defendants guilty on four counts. Afterward, Judge Kennesaw Mountain Landis threw the book at the Wobs. Haywood and fifteen others, including St. John, who had left the IWW in 1915, got twenty years in Leavenworth. Thirty-three others were sentenced to ten years and thirty-five more to five years. The Pittsburgh Wobs, Scarlett, Law, George, Perry, Cournos, and Andreytchine, all received long sentences.[27]

Through it all the leftists continued to bring speakers to Pittsburgh and to hold formal luncheons, picnics, dances, and open forums. In January 1918 Arturo Giovannitti, bound for Chicago as a defendant in the big IWW trial, paused in Pittsburgh to rally local tailors preparing to strike.[28] Lilith Martin came from Indiana to the International Socialist Lyceum to argue that women industrial workers were as capable as men and that men and women must stand together and demand the restoration of worker control of the workplace.[29] From New York British immigrant Elizabeth Freeman representing the Liberty Defense Union harangued McKeesport leftists and North Side Young Socialists. She called upon American workers to join with their British and German brothers and sisters and to follow the Bolshevik path to end capitalism.[30]

Local radicals remained quite active. Jennie Wommer (Wormer), dubbed by Wendell the district's leading female IWW agitator, sold IWW Freedom Certificates at the Get Together Club's luncheons in the Kaufmann and Baer store.[31] In April, city police merely watched as delegates to the Pennsylvania Young People's Socialist League (YPSL) convention banqueted, cheered the IWW, sang its songs, and criticized the conservative "old" draft-exempt Socialists who supported the American war effort.[32] Similarly unimpeded, one hundred Croatians met to attack capitalism and to praise the Bolsheviks. Quite publicly, the Allegheny City (North Side) Central Labor Committee made May Day a celebration of Karl Marx with one hundred speakers in a babel of languages. The festivities concluded with a ball featuring the folk dances of many nations.[33]

Wendell continued on the track of the elusive sources of IWW funds. In this regard a May 1918 foray to peddle Freedom Certificates at McKees Rocks proved very interesting.[34] In the Bottoms where most of the immigrant workers lived he met radicals Paul Kluvo and Ignatz Klawir who were trying to organize the men to fight back against the tar-and-feather vigilantes. Kluvo was a 1905 immigrant from Russian Poland who had been active in the 1909 Pressed Steel Car strike and had worked on two radical papers: the Polish language *Gorniki Polski* and Fred H. Merrick's *Justice*. Klawir had also been active in the Pressed Steel Car strike and in IWW local 286 at the Rocks. When Wendell encountered him he belonged to the South Slavic Branch of the Pittsburgh SPA and was a steamship agent involved in immigrant transportation, Wendell suspected as a blind for sabotage and propaganda.[35]

Kluvo and Klawir told Wendell that they were unwilling to reorganize an IWW branch because the police would break it up. Instead they proposed to promote the Wobbly agenda of direct action against the government and the war by means of "scientific" sabotage to slow production.[36] It is clear that Wendell did not believe them when they said that they could "pull off things the I.W.W. would never dare to do." When they told him about the Sterling Specialty and Sales Company, however, he was impressed.

Sterling Specialty was a brilliant concept that took advantage of Liberty Bonds, the war economy, and a federal contract in order to finance antiwar and antigovernment activities. By the time Wendell learned of the scheme, Sterling's officers—Kluvo, Klawir, expelled Socialist Party member David Gilchrist, and Wobbly David Young—claimed to have raised $37,500 in stock sales and loans. Much of the money came through the efforts of two German-American brokers, Wuliger and Kopp. The latter, a nervous type, lived with a packed suitcase in his office where daily he bought up to forty Liberty Bonds from foreigners at from two to twenty dollars below their face value. Kluvo and Klawir also encouraged aliens to exchange their Liberty Bonds at par for Sterling Specialty stock. The bonds would then be used as collateral for bank loans to capitalize Sterling.[37]

The idea was to produce and market a patent spot remover and use the profits for the revolution. First it was necessary to get around wartime federal regulations that designated spot remover as a nonessential product and prevented Sterling from buying raw materials for production. The radicals removed that obstacle by applying for and, according to Wendell's reports, receiving a subcontract from Westinghouse to manufacture shell centers in a rented plant on the North Side! This put Sterling on the federal materials priority list and qualified it to buy spot remover ingredients along with the shell components. Wendell noted ruefully that Gilchrist and the others hugely enjoyed putting one over on Uncle Sam and smirked that they were "not very particular" about the kind of shell centers they manufactured. MID and ONI files contain reports on Sterling Specialty, which the ONI suspect card noted was owned by everyone from German reservists to IWWs. The files do not reveal what exactly was done about it.[38]

While the Chicago IWW trial was in progress in April 1918 Wendell's undercover activities took him to Erie at the northern edge of the jurisdiction of the Pittsburgh field office. With forty-nine war plants employing thirty-five thousand workers, the Lake Erie port was a potential target for labor organizers. Wendell went there with Margolis who was bent upon making political hay and a good retainer from the Espionage Act case conviction of Socialist Ralph W. Tillotson. His crime was distributing a typewritten anticonscription statement entitled "Who Is the Real Coward?" at a PCA meeting in August 1917. The case rested on Tillotson's word against that of three government infiltrators. At the end a somnolent jury ranging in age from sixty-three to eighty-one believed the government witnesses over the Socialist son of German immigrants.[39] Tillotson was probably guilty, but publicly he claimed to have been framed by the U.S. attorney and the Erie Democratic machine. The claim was plausible. With anti-German feeling running high, prosecuting the largely German-American Erie SPA, symbolically headquartered in the Turnverein Hall, was bound to be popular. Tillotson appealed but eventually had to serve sixty days in Allegheny County Jail after his conviction at a second trial.[40]

The Tillotson affair brought the radical Left at Erie under the scrutiny of the Pittsburgh BI. After an April reconnaissance, Wendell reported that, excepting a few Finns and Russians, there was no pro-IWW presence at Erie. He thought that the Socialists, who dominated the Left, ought to be watched but allowed to continue as an outlet for expression. Otherwise, frustrated workers might turn to the Socialist Labor Party (SLP) or to the industrial unionism of the IWW.[41] By August 1918 the tone of Wendell's reports caused the BI to look more closely at the situation in Erie. Margolis and other radicals were planning to make the big annual SPA picnic scheduled for August 4 a protest meeting against Tillotson's conviction. On the second, two special agents went to Erie and arranged with the police chief for Russian and Polish interpreters to cover the event.[42]

The picnic was held at McDaniel's Grove and Wendell and Margolis, in town to counsel Tillotson, joined the crowd of fifteen hundred to hear the speeches and gorge on peanuts, popcorn, and ice cream. Two competing orchestras furnished the music: one representing Finnish National Federation political Socialists and the other industrial unionists. Cacophony beat out counterpoint as each tried to drown out the other. The Socialists and the Polish Falcons, who were picnicking nearby, sold whiskey and beer with predictable results. Wendell described the scene as a uniformed soldier lay in a drunken stupor near the speaker's stand while his distraught mother tried to fan him back to life. Margolis spoke after Tillotson from a platform surrounded by red flags and surmounted by a Russian Soviet flag. He portrayed the war as prologue to an inevitable social reconstruction in the United States in which workers would shape the new society through industrial unionism. When Russian and Polish language speakers took the podium Wendell could only guess what they said. The Socialists counted the picnic as a success. The large and enthusiastic turnout had donated enough to cover Margolis's retainer.[43] Before the next scheduled picnic government agents placed major obstacles to Socialist fund raising at McDaniel's Grove. They jailed the announced principal speaker C. William Thompson for soapboxing and prevented the sale of liquor.[44]

Over the next few weeks Wendell made frequent trips to Erie. He was now working with newly hired BI special agent Henry J. Lenon, whose assignment was to coordinate undercover activities and investigate reports of radical activities received from ONI, BI, Erie Manufacturers' Association, Pennsylvania State Constabulary, the state labor bureau, and even a spy who worked for the *Erie Daily Times*. The word was that out-of-town IWW organizers had moved in and set up a branch that already claimed three hundred members. Rumor had it that the Wobs planned to infiltrate the electricians, machinists, and molders at two key war plants: American Brake and Shoe and General Electric. To promote the IWW Wendell brought propaganda literature up from Pittsburgh to Roy Wright, the leader of the new branch. Wright was supposedly a veteran of pro-IWW agitation at the Mexican border.[45] His second in command was veteran Pittsburgh agitator, machinist Tom Loan. Despite a slight stutter and unprepossessing appearance, Loan, the brother of Walter, was blacklisted by employers and "although not guilty of any overt acts has been a constant source of anxiety to his employers . . . [because of] his irresponsible statements and general attitude."[46]

The BI files make clear that agents labored to prevent labor disruption and strikes and to save General Electric from unionization rather than the country from revolution—or perhaps it was to save GE management from having to accept National War Labor Board (NWLB) mediation.[47] A case in point occurred in August 1918 when Lenon interfered with the Department of Labor's attempt to deal with workers' grievances. Mediator P. J. Barber told reporters that skilled workers might strike at many Erie plants because wages had not kept up with living costs. Barber also faulted the companies' inexperienced personnel departments for placing workers in unsuitable jobs, thereby causing a high rate of turnover and strained relations between dissatisfied workers and irritated managers. Barber called for improved working conditions to avert a wave of strikes.[48]

The public never read Barber's findings because the BI prevented its publication. Siding with manufacturing interests against Labor Department mediators, Lenon had previously "asked" Erie newspaper editors not to print "any news relating to labor trouble, the I.W.W., or Socialist activities without consulting this office." When the *Times* editor read the story to him over the phone, Lenon odered it killed and then had ONI agents Rowe and Burgoyne visit the other papers to stop the story. Then Lenon summoned Barber and his boss to read them the riot act. Afterward Lenon reported, "we have every reason to believe that Mr. Barber will hesitate before breaking into print in the future."[49] The BI's prescription for Erie's labor troubles was to urge the local manufacturers' association to step up its infiltration and surveillance of labor groups, especially at GE and American Brake and Shoe, and the police to suppress radical literature.[50]

At the time of World War I most Americans believed in the fundamental fairness of the federal government. Of course many Native Americans and others at the margins held different views. Still, it took time for some radicals to grasp that the United States Justice Department would not deal evenhandedly with them. In September 1918, after Erie police broke up their street meetings, several Socialists invited Lenon to come to their meetings, sit on the speakers' platform, and "if nothing of a seditious nature was uttered . . . tell the politicians and police to keep hands off." Lenon demurred, saying that the BI would not interfere with their activity "in any way unless the law was violated, but [he] advised against any rabid speeches that would stir up feeling at this time." When the Socialists were gone Lenon, "knowing that these speakers would do more harm than good and might interfere with the New Liberty Loan Drive, and to avoid trouble, . . . used a friend" to intervene with the city council. Soon after, he reported that the council had unanimously voted to forbid the mayor from issuing permits for street-corner meetings. Proudly Lenon explained that he accomplished this "without showing my hand."[51]

In October Judge concluded that Erie was taking too much of Wendell's time and so he assigned another undercover man to radical activities there.[52] Surveying the Erie scene one last time, Wendell found the Socialists frustrated and the Wobblies on the rise. The practical suspension of free speech and a city ordinance against distribution of literature, pushed by Lenon, had made it difficult for the SPA to appeal to the voters. The terrible influenza pandemic, just then reaching Erie, further reduced attendance at meetings. Shutting off the safety valve of political action threatened, according to Wendell, to drive Socialists and workers into the arms of the industrial unionists. Already, he warned, the machinists' union was structured as One Big Union. He added, "they're taking every worker regardless of trade or beliefs, unskilled as well as skilled."[53]

Some of the material in BI Erie files deserves mention because its sole purpose was to protect Wendell from exposure. There were many players on the crowded field of radical surveillance: APL operatives, corporate "secret service," ONI agents, MID Plant Protection operatives, Burns and Pinkerton men, and freelance private investigators. All were watching the Left and some, like Wendell, were part of it. His reports routinely went to various agencies and if now, seventy-five years later, they show the Wendell-Walsh connection, they would have revealed it then. One way to shield him was to plant reports highlighting the nefarious and disloyal activities of the radical Walsh. For example, the August focus on the Erie activities of alleged former Wobbly Villistas neatly embellished the July story planted in the *Press* detailing Wendell's own alleged subversive activities at the Mexican border. Lenon also had Wendell shadowed in Erie by an agent Schlaudecker, probably of the APL.[54] Just as Wendell gave the agent the slip, so he and Lenon intended to do the same to anyone with access to BI files who became too curious.

By March 1918 draft delinquency had become a widespread problem. In January Provost Marshal Brigadier General Enoch Crowder had declared war on those who had not answered the call after receiving estimates that there were as many as fifty thousand deserters and three hundred thousand draft delinquents nationwide.[55] Subsequent negotiations between the Justice and War Departments produced an agreement that BI agents would employ APL volunteers to help carry out raids to capture slackers.[56] Early in March Pittsburgh Public Safety Director Charles B. Pritchard ordered a roundup of draft evaders. He had information, undoubtedly from the Justice Department or MID, that hundreds of slackers were living in the city. They were not, he claimed, "the floater type of 'bums' but men who posed as traveling salesmen and who, in fact, in some cases were the sons of families reported to be wealthy."[57]

Beginning on Saturday night, March 2, squads of Pittsburgh's finest, federal agents, and "special police" corralled men on street corners and raided downtown hotels, rooming houses, pool rooms, cafes, and clubs. Those without proper registration cards were taken to Central Police Station where they remained unless friends or family showed up with their cards. The *Dispatch* incorrectly identified the Justice Department spokesman and chief operative in the roundup as special agent Harry [Henry] J. Lenon, who was with the APL but had not yet officially joined the BI.[58]

The evening sweeps continued for the next few days and were extended throughout the city. Squads of eight to ten lawmen would quickly surround men at street corners and detain those without proper registration. The suspects were transported to jail in groups of twelve to be held as suspicious persons. From partial and often conflicting newspaper estimates it is impossible to state the exact numbers of those detained or the ratio of those detained to actual violators. A fair estimate would be that at least one thousand men were held. By March 6 they overflowed all of the lockups in town. At the Central Police Station fifteen men shared a single cell. The warden at Allegheny County Jail reported that of 901 prisoners on hand, 503 were alleged slackers. To prevent further overcrowding he begged that no more be sent. To relieve the crush, officials hurriedly converted an old armory at Penn Avenue and Station Street into a temporary guard house. On March 8, the *Dispatch* reported that 544 slackers were held there. Mayor Edward V. Babcock, who visited the armory that day, pronounced the men well cared for and revealed that a detachment of regular troops had arrived from New York City to guard them. Federal officials promised that many of the slackers would soon be heading south to boot camp.[59]

The announced purpose of the crackdown was to speed delinquents to basic training at Camp Lee, Virginia, but for those who were detained, their "six weeks of Hell" began in jail. When a flying squad of police entered his rooming house, F. Walendowsky, aged twenty-four, defiantly told them that he would be a "slacker as long as he lived" and declared the United States and its president were "no good and should be in Hell." For that, "Special Policeman" James Noonan forced Walendowsky to kiss the American flag in the corridor of the police lockup and then to march up and down carrying it above his head in front of thirty-two detainees huddled in their cells.[60]

Public Safety Director Pritchard repeatedly justified the extraordinary doings on the streets of Pittsburgh by appealing to class resentment. Unpopular community outsiders, the sons of the rich, traveling salesmen, and "floaters" were the supposed targets. Newspaper stories detailed large amounts of cash and fine watches found on those who were arrested. Certainly a few leisure-class dandies were among the prisoners, as were pickpockets, confidence men, loafers, and criminals. When all of these are accounted for, the vast majority seem to have been transient day laborers and industrial workers, part of the horde drawn to Pittsburgh's booming wartime job market. Among them were twenty-seven Mexican nationals, who had to be released when it was discovered that they were not subject to conscription.[61]

The dragnet trapped many other innocent men. One official estimated that in one group of sixty, only fifteen were slackers. The *Press* complained that "many men, far above suspicion, who had neglected to carry their classification cards were forced to undergo the jeering and looking of crowds." The use of mass street-corner arrests made such mistakes and such abuse likely. During the wait for the paddy wagon bystanders would taunt the prisoners with cries of "shoot the slackers at sunrise" or "give them life" imprisonment.[62]

Some of those arrested were too old or too young for the draft. Many others had registered properly, but slow draft boards had not yet provided them with classification cards. Officials from one local draft board admitted that nearly seven hundred registrants remained unclassified. The raids seemed to blur the distinction between law enforcement and criminal acts. During the roundup, two men in civilian clothes were arrested for impersonating federal officials. One forced bystanders to take cover as he fired random shots near the Labor Temple. Another, caught breaking into the B.& O. Station in the wee hours, claimed he was looking for slackers.[63]

Despite the mistakes, city officials defended the raids. Reiterating that any man not carrying a proper draft card would be subject to arrest, Pritchard promised that "whatever criticism was directed at Pittsburgh heretofore as a locality where evasion of the draft was easy, the director is determined that such criticism will not be justifiable any longer."[64] If there was criticism, it did not come from Washington, which soon launched similar raids in other cities. The raids reached their apogee in metropolitan New York from September 3–6, when more than 21,000 men were detained as Selective Service Act violators. Of these, 756 were inducted and another 2,485 found to be delinquent.[65] The alleged abuses committed during the course of the New York raids by soldiers, sailors, and APL volunteers aroused civil libertarians and brought an avalanche of criticism down upon the Justice Department. Federal courts later condemned these warrantless mass arrests, but tardy court opinions had no practical effect on such wartime suspension of constitutional liberties.[66]

Despite their evasive maneuvers, the draft caught up with many Pittsburgh Wobs and Socialists. Like other area draftees, they were sent to Camp Lee, Virginia, where they joined a small population of malcontents and political conscientious objectors. One of the first to go was Jim Marshall, Margolis's law partner, inducted soon after he lost his seat on a draft advisory board for aliens. Pittsburgh Wobbly Walter Hodge reported for induction after his arrest in Cleveland foiled his plan to flee to a Socialist hideout in the Colorado Rockies. Joe Mountain soon followed. Later, after serving time for failure to register in Allegheny County Jail, Victor Slone joined them. Slone had better luck than another of Margolis's law clerks, Meyer B. Teplitz (Tiplitz), who was sent to the notorious conscientious objector disciplinary barracks at Fort Leavenworth, Kansas.[67]

World War I conscientious objectors needed courage and a thick skin. The Selective Service Act of 1917 exempted only members of religious bodies opposed to war. At the end of June 1917 President Wilson narrowed this already limited definition to exclude all but "well recognized sect[s] or organization[s]" and required potential COs to prove their claims before local draft boards. No provision was made for men with nonreligious scruples. Those who were granted CO status had to report to a military base and subject themselves to military control. In 1918, however, Secretary of War Baker broadened CO status to include all men with "personal scruples against war" and urged military authorities to use "tact and consideration" in dealing with them. Antiwar Socialists and Wobblies could now legitimately claim noncombatant status.[68]

Nationwide, between May 1917 and November of 1918, 64,693 men applied for CO status on political or religious grounds. Draft boards accepted the claims of 56,830 of whom approximately 29,000 passed the physical exam. Of these, more than 20,000 were eventually inducted.[69]

The grandest battle plan hinges on the willingness and ability of subordinates to carry it out. As Peterson and Fite demonstrate, despite a relatively humane official policy, training officers subjected COs to sufficient physical and mental abuse to force most to accept combatant status. Political COs had it especially hard, because the public and many officers considered them to be cowards or pro-German.[70]

One should not assume that World War I COs were helpless, unresisting victims of government persecution or that the army was a monolith where everyone marched in rigid mental lockstep with the zealots of the Intelligence Branch. At Camp Lee the officers and ranks, swollen with wartime mobilization, displayed a wide range of political opinions and attitudes toward war and patriotism. If the army harbored paranoid superpatriots, it also included officers, particularly in the medical and morale departments, who looked sympathetically at the objectors.

One beneficiary of liberal attitudes was buck private Jim Marshall. He spent his tour of duty from January 1918 to May 1919 at Camp Lee working on routine legal matters in the camp quartermaster's office and acting the good soldier. Marshall's commanding officer, who had sold insurance before the war and was a reader of Tolstoy, called him "my bolshevik." Marshall admitted the commander was "a damnably decent . . . [boss] for the slave plantations," and "the first white man" he had met in camp.[71]

In letters to Pittsburgh comrades, Marshall ran alternately hot and cold on the war and the prospects for revolution. At one moment he believed the mass conscription of Americans would become "a million iron boots" after the war to trample capitalism. Every common soldier's gripe seemed to herald a general mutiny. In the next he would cry over life without Pittsburgh's chop suey, Welsh rarebit, and "Piels" beer and fret that the war would last forever and the revolution would never come.[72] Evidently he was unaware that civilians had to suffer, too. Pittsburgh restaurants were forbidden by the food administrator from serving Welsh rarebit for the duration.[73] Marshall's claim that after the Armistice he was openly preaching Bolshevism in camp brought a derisive response from the MID.[74] Months of surveillance, wrote the Camp Lee IO, "convince this office that he is but sounding brass and tinkling cymbal . . . a cowardly braggart."[75]

Joe Mountain was a different case. The Socialist and former prime mover of the People's Council of America worked to subvert morale and to counteract the army's pressure on COs to "accept the rifle." For his efforts, the army harassed him until his discharge long after the Armistice. The principal evidence against Mountain came not from government spies at Camp Lee, but from Wendell in Pittsburgh, who was able to keep tabs on him through letters and friends including Margolis.[76]

On February 12, 1918, Mountain left Pittsburgh for Camp Lee on a special train with 430 other draftees. Less than enthusiastic about joining America's great crusade, he found the journey harrowing. He wrote that every seat in the fifteen-car train was taken and fistfights erupted throughout the twenty-eight-hour trip. The influence of the social hygienists and prohibitionists was nowhere to be seen. Mountain estimated that "not more than fifty" of the recruits were sober and everyone seemed to have suitcases filled with whisky and beer.[77]

Upon arriving at Camp Lee, Mountain told the officer in charge of muster that he "was opposed to killing human beings, but was willing to do anything else." He was then assigned to the quartermaster corps and after a week with a pick and shovel was put in charge of a gang of workers. After three weeks he became a "Sanitary Inspector" commanding a truck and three men, including fellow Pittsburgh radical Walter Hodge. The detail collected waste from the base hospitals and camp headquarters.[78] Mountain wrote to Roger Baldwin and to friends in Pennsylvania that he found this work "interesting" and would perform it to the best of his ability, but that in the evenings and during breaks he kept busy networking among the COs and proselytizing against the war.[79] He had been fighting militarism for five years, he wrote, and would fight it as long as he lived or until there was a demilitarized "United States of the World." The tawdriness of camp life reinforced his antimilitarism and gave him a sense of moral superiority. He thought the army "was the worst thing that could happen to the American boy . . . , making him a gambler and a user of the rottenest, profane language I have ever run into."[80]

In spreading antiwar propaganda, Mountain tapped a national radical network. A sympathetic Roger Baldwin, who himself would soon go to jail for refusing military service,[81] was a frequent correspondent. On February 19, Mountain (an eccentric speller) announced his arrival at camp to "Rodger." He reported talking to many conscripts "and have yet to meet a man who is not cursing his luck." He added, "where there are people, I can work and I find this a mighty firtle field."[82] Over the next three months, he maintained an extensive antiwar correspondence that included Baldwin, Scott Nearing, and Crystal Eastman. From them and others he requested antiwar pamphlets and literature. Mail call brought him antiwar books, and periodicals such as the *New York Call, Industrial Worker,* and the *IWW Defense News Bulletin.* In April 1918 he bragged that he was carrying on a "great anti-war propaganda in camp" and that censorship was a joke.[83] In May he gushed that time at camp passed very quickly. "Evenings are taken up by my Comrades[.] there are some thirty socialist[s] that I am in touch with constantly. some of these are still fighting thair clames. others have been recognized and have very interesting stories."[84]

However, in June he admitted that he was losing many COs to combat status. Although officers and noncoms put heavy pressure on them, it was the shame of letting down friends and family that was hardest to resist. Mountain wrote that his heart ached for a young Erie socialist who abandoned CO status after his mother wrote to him hoping "he would not disgrace her and would be a man and fight for his country . . . [and that he] shurly knew how the people would treat her in Erie when the news was passed around."[85] Mountain thought that the weakness of such comrades stemmed from a lack of education, a lack of faith in socialism. He had long ago come to the point "where I did not give a dam[n] for public opinion, so long as I myself felt that I was doing the right thing." Mountain expressed his moral superiority to those who embraced army life when he held up the example of his Pittsburgh comrade and fellow CO, Walter Hodge. When a major said to Hodge "you are not a man, you have not a drop of red blood in your vaines," Hodge replied "those 1400 venerial [*sic*] men you have down . . . are red blooded[,] I suppose they want to fight and kill. I am made of different stuff and am glad of it."[86]

COs who refused to work or disobeyed orders routinely faced court-martial and incarceration in the camp stockade or, worse, might be sent to the Fort Leavenworth Disciplinary Barracks.[87] To avoid that, Mountain did his job and cultivated his superiors. He pushed his men to be productive and at the end of the day rewarded them for their efforts with a joy ride in the country in their garbage truck.[88]

Mountain had the benefit of helpful evaluations from superiors, such as Major Moore, probably a psychiatrist, who commended his work in the base hospital.[89] The doughboys en masse were subjected to IQ tests and psychological estimates of their potential reaction to combat.[90] Moore explained that Mountain "had a bitter experience earlier in life that made him a Socialist, and he does not believe in war for himself. However, he is perfectly willing to help the sorry results of the war to get well, if they can get well." Moore diagnosed Mountain as a "neuropath" unable to stand "the grind of the trenches." Mountain might become a hero and go over the top in one big charge, but unless his chance to be a hero came quickly, front-line combat would make him a "permanent psychopath."[91] Thus shielded by the new social science and sympathetic superiors, Mountain went about his antiwar activities.

In July 1918 Mountain spent a five-day furlough in Pittsburgh with radical friends. A highlight of his visit was a get-together in his honor at Margolis's home on Ophelia Street. Attending were Ben Anisman, Margolis's brother-in-law Oscar Kaminsky, and, of course, their good friend Wendell. Before this appreciative audience, Mountain recounted his success in building an organization at Camp Lee to help COs "get through." According to Wendell, Mountain described a network that included a comrade working at the base library who had planted radical and antiwar books. From the circulation records of this material, the radicals were able to identify disaffected and potentially radical soldiers. Even though he had heard that he was being watched, Mountain remained unafraid. He boasted that he had composed antiwar propaganda "behind the hospital" and, at every turn, had sown discontent among the soldiers. For example, he had told troops that water boys working for civilian contractors on the base made five times as much as a soldier was paid to give his life for democracy. Mountain had also applied what he claimed was the Wobbly "art of sabotage" or "bucking," which sounds very much like a practice not unknown to common soldiers before or since. After a new officer refused the men passes, their deliberate inefficiency had earned the officer a reprimand for his unit's poor performance.[92]

An August 1918 official report gave a different picture of the CO situation at Camp Lee. It noted that fifty-two COs were properly segregated and under the command of "careful and tactful officers who have converted many." One hundred and seven others had been furloughed for farm work. Officers described these men as "sincere, quiet, retiring men for the most part . . . [who] will not become dangerous propagandists even when furloughed to their home communities." Another one hundred, including Mountain, were assigned to the medical corps or the quartermaster department.[93]

A month after Mountain, Walter Hodge arrived home on leave and, in his turn, enjoyed a hero's welcome at New Era Hall. But Hodge was worried. He now kept apart from Mountain in camp because they were being watched. Wendell knew this well enough because he was a principal watcher. Long before, he had warned his BI and MID contacts that Mountain would be a CO and would try to spread discontent in the army. That warning was promptly transmitted through MID head Van Deman to the Camp Lee IO with instructions to report on Mountain's activities. In the following months Wendell submitted frequent reports based upon Mountain's letters to his Pittsburgh comrades. By June 1918 the Camp Lee IO was convinced that Mountain should be court-martialed but he did not have direct evidence. When he tried to bring the radical before a visiting special board of inquiry for objectors, instead of Mountain his commanding officer sent the board a fifteen-word statement: "This soldier is now on duty at the incinerator plant, and his work is satisfactory."[94]

Since June the new MID chief, Brig. Gen. Marlborough Churchill, had pressed the Camp Lee IO to prosecute Mountain under Article 96 of the Articles of War, "owing to the great possibility of serious disturbance if this man is allowed to consummate his plans and continue his agitation by camouflaging [it] by diligent work in the Public Utility Department."[95] The Camp Lee IO then began to intercept Mountain's mail and was alarmed to find the *IWW Defense News Bulletin* and *The Liberator* (Crystal Eastman was sending six free copies a month of the successor to *The Masses*).[96] He was also in touch with the National Civil Liberties Bureau (NCLB), which specialized in protecting COs and was under investigation by MID and BI.[97] Based on this information, in August Mountain's commander was ordered to assign him the "hardest work he had." For a month Mountain performed pick-and-shovel work mending roads. Then he was moved to the segregated CO detachment.[98]

All along Wendell and his BI superiors feared that the army might want to use 836 reports to prosecute Mountain. To avoid that, Wendell looked for other ways of getting the goods on the CO. One way was to goad Mountain to openly defy military regulations from long distance. In June 1918, longtime Pittsburgh SPA leader W. J. "Doc" Van Essen wrote Mountain that Walsh (Wendell) had called him a traitor to the working class because he was "slave driving" men who worked under him to support the war and was collecting fifty-three dollars a month for doing it. Van Essen advised Mountain to disregard such talk and take the softest job he could in the army. Socialism being inevitable, it needed "no martyrs to bring it about—if it could be achieved by propaganda work then it would be here by this time—but it will and is coming in spite of all the bone-heads both inside and outside the Radical ranks."[99] Mountain's reaction is not recorded, but Wendell's ploy failed.

Another of Wendell's schemes was apparently more successful. In September 1918, on the eve of a massive new draft registration of men up to forty-five years of age, federal agents Speer, Burgoyne, and Montgomery arrested Wendell at a Socialist Party meeting at New Era Hall before fifty witnesses. "Prisoner Is Thought I.W.W. Plot Leader, Federal Agents Arrest L. M. Walsh as Chief of Anti-Draft Conspiracy, Here One Year," went the headline on the front page of the second section of the *Gazette-Times*. The G-men told reporters that they had broken up a well-organized antidraft organization in the city in 1917 "that was presumably financed with German money" and sent its leaders, principally Scarlett and Law, to jail. Now opposition was forming to the new draft law and Walsh, having stepped into the shoes of the jailed Wobblies, was its leader. They explained that Walsh was "one of the big men of the I.W.W." He was a dangerous agitator who had kept one step ahead of them as they traced him from coast to coast. They admitted that they still did not have enough to charge him, but would hold him for three days. Then on September 12 they would personally escort him to register for the new draft.[100]

The facts the federal agents withheld from the public were as interesting as those they fabricated. Wendell was not really in jail. He had "framed his own arrest," which was then carried out at Judge's orders. Then agents had put him on a "train to somewhere in Ohio," from where he would return to publicly register in a few days.[101] The charade evidently enhanced Wendell's credibility and stature among the Wobblies. A month later, Jim Marshall wrote from Camp Lee to a Pittsburgh friend, "I hear that Louis [M. Walsh] took a little vacation with my old friend Bob Judge of the Department of Justice and that he is back in town." Indeed he was.[102]

Through September and October 1918 Wendell kept up the flow of accusatory reports against Mountain. Pittsburgh IO Flood, using information supplied by Wendell, wrote to Churchill that Wobblies Mountain and Hodge "are not conscientious objectors, moved by any moral or religious objections to the war, but merely suffering from 'cold feet' and an unwillingness to fight for organized government, which they hate."[103] But he could not prove it.

A few days before the end of the war, Major John L. King, Camp Lee IO, tried to persuade his Boston counterpart Major Fred Moore to plant at least two undercover operatives among eleven thousand draftees due in from Massachusetts on November 11. They were to cover Mountain and Hodge, whose "conviction is earnestly desired in Washington." King explained that the Pittsburgh COs had been too clever for operatives he had placed near them. The assignment would be difficult. An earlier attempt, wrote King, had ended when "our [Justice Department] operative broke down and gave away the whole plan before he even got thru [*sic*] his company commander." The spies would have to claim CO status before they arrived at camp and then go through "six weeks of Hell." Eventually they would have to testify against Mountain and be exposed. Moore turned King down, suggesting diplomatically that such an assignment would take "very good operatives" and that MID headquarters in Washington was the place to find them. But Washington would not provide them either, so the plan died.[104]

The end of the fighting in November 1918 brought no armistice in the government's war on Joe Mountain. In December, MID headquarters sent Mountain's file to BI headquarters to see if there was enough to warrant prosecution. The answer came back no, "bearing in mind our inability to use the confidential informant in Pittsburgh." On January 7, 1919, Mountain signed out on a five-day pass to be spent in New Haven, Connecticut. Under orders to watch Mountain, "notorious as an organizer of conscientious objectors," Northeastern Department IO Moore delegated this task to J. F. Murphy, Jr., of the MID's Plant Protection Section. What ensued was a comedy of errors that sent Murphy on a wild goose chase to a fictitious address, "Wogrami Avenue." Later in January Hodge, in Pittsburgh on a pass, told the comrades that his previous visits and those of Mountain had been reported to the Camp Lee MID. This apparently compromised security upset Pittsburgh MID agents. They were relieved when it turned out that the leak was a "foolish sergeant" at Camp Lee who, when refusing them a pass, told the two COs that they were "under observation[,] . . . that he would get them sooner or later." This incident so angered Wendell that he threatened "to discontinue any further reports on radical agenda at Camp Lee."[105] Flood sided with him, pointedly reminding the MID director that "confidential informant No. 836 is the friend and adviser of the radicals in this district, and is well known throughout the United States as a prominent Socialist. As a matter of fact, he is in the employ of the Government as an expert investigator."[106]

Despite his pique, just as the MID seemed about to give up the investigation of Mountain, Wendell devised a new approach. He remembered that Mountain claimed a monthly allotment for his wife and child but that he was divorced and she had custody of their child. The divorce had become final in June 1917, months before Mountain's induction, and did not require Mountain to pay alimony. So, if he knew the divorce was final, the allotments were fraudulent. Proving that Mountain knew this would be difficult because he was not in court when the decree was handed down.[107]

The demobilization of the Camp Lee MID at the end of March 1919 caused the transfer of Mountain's case to the judge advocate's office with the recommendation for continued investigation. Agents were reminded that "Mountain cannot be kept indefinitely in the Army, [and] we are trying to expedite the investigation as much as possible." Until June 15, 1919, when Mountain was finally discharged, MID sought written proof from his ex-wife that he had known about the divorce when he applied for the allotment. However, fear of punishment for taking the government money caused Edna Mountain to flee from Pittsburgh. The records of the fruitless search for her leave no doubt about the government's motives. If they found her, agents were to assure her "that neither the authorities here [in Pittsburgh] nor at Camp Lee have the remotest intention of prosecuting her for receiving allotments to which she was not entitled." They were after Joe Mountain, "one of a group of agitators . . . [that] has been giving the authorities . . . much concern since his arrival at camp. However, his known activities were not such as to subject him to severe military discipline or punishment."[108]

The Mountain case illustrates the pitfalls of bureaucratic persistence carried to extremes. The files do not document that he performed a single specific act of harm against the war effort at Camp Lee. What Wendell's reports and Mountain's own statements show is that he bragged of spreading propaganda and working to stiffen the resolve of conscientious objectors in his off-duty hours. Every attempt in the camp to catch him at it failed, and once the war had ended it is hard to see what damage Mountain could have done to a war effort that no longer existed. Yet government agents persisted in the allotment fraud investigation.

Along with keeping tabs on Pittsburgh Wobs at distant Camp Lee, Wendell also fingered a "subversive" soldier training at the University of Pittsburgh. Private Jack Lever was in the National Army Training Detachment, a program begun in April 1918 at 157 colleges and universities to train recruits in a range of skills from radiotelegraphy to sheet metal work.[109] Lever, a former IWW organizer, consorted with the Socialists and Wobblies in his off-duty hours. He had knocked about in IWW and machinist and marine transit union circles in Toledo, Philadelphia, and Baltimore before the army. He said with disarming frankness that he had enlisted to spread revolutionary ideas among the troops and to get "the wonderful mechanical and military training" the army offered. He professed to see a great opportunity for IWW agitation in the fact that the soldiers in training at Pitt were "generally dissatisfied with . . . their uniforms and their meals."[110]

Despite his obscure past as a radical and his ludicrous claim that griping about chow and uniforms made soldiers ripe for mutiny, Wendell and MID took Lever seriously. One of his most "dangerous" actions occurred in June 1918 at a Socialist rally at McKeesport's Westmoreland Park. The featured speaker was Elizabeth

Freeman, the former organizing secretary of the PCA. Lever, in full uniform, took part in the collection, literally passing his soldier's hat to net $14.51 for the cause.[111] When his unit prepared to ship overseas Lever promised that he would "carry on a campaign abroad among the soldiers so that when the War is over they may overthrow the Government." In July, when the unit went to Camp Mills, New York, Flood passed the case to the Camp Mills IO, urging him to watch Lever and keep him stateside as long as possible. What happened to Lever after this is not clear, except that he survived and in the summer of 1919 he was a civilian in Philadelphia working for a maritime union.[112]

Wendell's role in the Mountain and Lever cases underscores the strengths and weaknesses of a confidential informer. As a key figure in the government's war against Pittsburgh's draft-dodging radicals he was able to keep Mountain and Hodge in hot water and document the law violations of others. It was he who uncovered Teplitz's and Slone's failure to register, who provided to government officials the details of the antidraft counseling activities of Margolis and Marshall, and who contributed to Marshall's removal from a Pittsburgh legal advisory board for immigrant draftees.[113] Yet to make its cases against Mountain and Lever, the government needed Wendell to testify in court. The decision that his identity must be protected at all costs meant that in effect his handlers had to accept his information on faith and then try to substantiate it by conventional means. Often that proved impossible.[114]

Wendell's value to the government remained high as long as he was tied to Margolis and as long as Margolis was at the center of the radical scene. In November 1918 the radical lawyer appeared to be precisely there. He was the exclusive Pittsburgh area representative of several militant small unions of skilled workers including machinists, pattern makers, molders, tailors, and waiters. He also represented the Russian Bolshevik government in western Pennsylvania and the National Civil Liberties Bureau.[115] Along with his legal work, Margolis kept up his visible and controversial public speaking. He agitated for a cluster of ideas that alarmed government officials. Until late 1918 he preached that the IWW and the Bolsheviks shared identical aims and goals. Workers, he argued, should join the IWW and not the SPA, SLP, or the AFL.[116] Borrowing liberally from Leon Trotsky's *Bolsheviki and World Peace,* at that time serialized in the *Sun* and available at Pittsburgh bookstores, Margolis claimed that once they were truly in power the Bolsheviks would fashion a workers' democracy instead of a proletarian dictatorship.[117]

However, Margolis remained a pacifist. He disagreed when New York anarchist comrades took the position that the war was good because it had opened the way for the Bolsheviks. For his stand they accused him of being for peace at any price.[118] On the vexing issue of whether the Russian workers should resist a German invasion, Margolis argued that nonresistance by the Russians coupled with propagandizing the German workers was the way to secure the revolution. Let the British and Germans continue to bleed each other in their capitalists' war. The eventual exhaustion of both sides would open the way for the inevitable workers' uprising.[119]

BI and MID agents worried more about Margolis's local activism than about his global perspective. They were unhappy to hear him tell industrial workers, after a failed iron molders' strike, that using slowdowns and calculated inefficiencies was better than striking to gain concessions from employers.[120]

When the guns fell silent in France, Pittsburgh radicals had the support of only a minuscule portion of the regional workforce. It was a workforce increasingly beguiled by the diversions of mass culture and the blandishments of emerging welfare capitalism. It was at the same time segmented, fragmented, and isolated according to religion, ethnicity, skill level, and neighborhood or town. In western Pennsylvania the IWW had fared badly among the Italians, most numerous of the immigrant laborers. Margolis could not persuade his Italian anarchist contacts to embrace union activity. When Wendell approached Martha Pesci, an alleged former "paramour" of Carlo Tresca, to raise IWW defense funds, she rebuffed him. She said that Pittsburgh Italians had lost faith when Tresca left the IWW.[121]

Still, in November 1918 radicals dared to hope. They fantasized that their ragged ranks could unite around the promise of the Bolshevik triumph in Russia. They would work together to harness the pent-up discontent in the industrial workforce, their task made easier by the restoration of First Amendment rights and other civil liberties now that the war was over.

PART 2

THE RED SCARE AND AFTER, 1919–1921

5

BOMBS, A NEW MISSION, AND THE USUAL SUSPECTS, 1919

> You jailed us, you clubbed us, you deported us, you murdered us when you
> could. . . . We know the proletariat has the . . . right to protect itself. Since
> their press has been suffocated, their mouths muzzled, we mean to speak for
> them the voice of dynamite, through the mouths of guns.
>
> *Plain Words,* 1919

AFTER THE ARMISTICE in the winter of 1918–1919 a combination of national labor unrest and opportunist Red-baiting inflamed a public opinion already rubbed
raw by war propaganda. Abroad at Versailles, Woodrow Wilson's idealistic peace
plan sank in a morass of European realpolitik while the Bolshevik-led Third International proclaimed the spread of the Communist revolution throughout the industrial world. At home repressive wartime policies toward dissenters encouraged
the desire to "make them pay" as xenophobia intensified. Fueling these attitudes
was an outbreak of strikes that began in the Northwest and then seemed to infect
the whole country. There was much discontent in labor's ranks. Although the war
had ended, government-imposed wartime restrictions on labor remained in effect. Rising retail prices, rising expectations, accumulating unresolved grievances,
and the ex-doughboys' return to the labor market intensified discontent. Workers
felt alienated when their patriotic support for the war produced little tangible reward or recognition. The prospect of exploiting workers' grievances encouraged
Pittsburgh leftists, but even more inspiring was the Bolshevik triumph in Russia.
Now they dared to hope that the socialist revolution was finally at hand.

The guardians of the status quo were duly alarmed. In February and March
1919 a Senate judiciary subcommittee chaired by Lee Overman (D-N.C.) held
wide-ranging hearings on the Bolshevik threat and its possible links to German
propaganda, immigrants, radical feminists, and whatever else made Americans
insecure at the moment. With past and future western Pennsylvania U.S. Attorney, now Major, E. Lowry Humes as lead counsel, the committee heard sensational revelations from anti-Bolshevik witnesses and disturbing opinions from high-

profile American radicals such as John Reed, Louise Bryant, and Albert Rhys Williams.[1] The committee's report, which served as a rough blueprint for the Justice Department's subsequent antiradical campaign, recommended deporting alien radicals, enacting peacetime sedition laws, and making patriotic propaganda to head off a Bolshevik type of revolution in the United States.[2]

The events that inspired radicals and frightened the elites presented the federal intelligence bureaucracy with opportunity and peril. The new radicalism could be a valuable bargaining chip for the agencies as they sought a niche in the postwar government. The political and public relations rewards for conquering radicalism would be handsome, but failure would destroy public confidence and diminish congressional appropriations.

The navy had already officially dropped out of the game. ONI closed its Pittsburgh branch operations and vacated Room 31 of the St. Nicholas Building at the end of January 1919. By May 1919, every intelligence officer in the Fourth Naval District, Philadelphia and Pittsburgh, had been detached or demobilized. The wartime ONI agents found comfortable careers. Arthur Burgoyne Jr. became a city editor of the *Pittsburgh Gazette-Times,* a Republican Party functionary, and an aide to Republican Senator James H. Duff. In March George E. Rowe and Raymond E. Horn (probably joined by Bob Judge who suddenly resigned from the BI at that time) went into the private detective business. Openly trading on their government experience, they took offices in the St. Nicholas Building as the Federal Service Bureau. Warned by the Secret Service that they could not use the official American eagle on their letterhead, still they listed their firm as a government agency in the Pittsburgh City Directory until MID and BI officials complained. The new welfare capitalism and the near collapse of the labor movement in the 1920s hurt the labor espionage business, and Rowe and Horn went into more profitable endeavors. Rowe went on to an advertising career in Chicago and New York while Horn rose to be chief executive of Abbott Laboratories.[3]

At first it appeared that MID would go the way of ONI. After the Armistice, Secretary of War Baker ordered sharp budget and personnel cuts.[4] In January 1919, the MID's acting director announced that the "emergency which required . . . observation of radicals no longer exists." MID was not to conduct "espionage among the civilian population [or] even to inquire into the political or economic beliefs or activities of individuals or groups . . . be [they] Anarchists, Socialists, I.W.W.s, Bolshevists, or members of some special ethnic group." MID personnel were not to attend radical meetings or actively seek information on such individuals or groups.[5]

Four months later a surge of antiradical hysteria emboldened MID brass to lobby to return to domestic counterintelligence by redefining their wartime mission into what Joan Jensen has characterized as counterdissent.[6] On April 28, DMI Churchill rescinded the January policy directive. Henceforth operatives could seek accurate information on radicals and their activities "so far as it may be obtained in a legitimate manner," without exciting antagonism or apprehension or calling attention to themselves. They could collect radical literature and attend public meetings but must "not . . . interrogate individuals in a summary and inquisitorial manner nor . . . institute searches and seizures."[7]

By May 1919 MID, armed with War Plans White, an ambitious contingency plan for domestic counterintelligence, was ready to lobby Congress for a $500,000 appropriation to battle the Red Menace. Still, orders from Washington severely limited its undercover work in Pittsburgh.[8] A branch of the Soldiers and Sailors Soviet or Soldiers, Sailors, and Marines Protective League led by ex–conscientious objector Walter Hodge had sprung up in Pittsburgh. It was believed to have 250 members, mostly enlisted men and veterans pledged to protect the "industrial rights" of workers. Later that summer similar groups would launch strikes in Seattle, Butte, and Toledo. When Hodge resigned as president, Wendell told the MID's Flood that he could "promise the election of an undercover man, preferably an overseas enlisted man, to fill this vacancy." Flood eagerly accepted the offer, but Washington MID did not concur. To place an undercover man in the Soldiers and Sailors Soviet, Churchill wrote, would violate the April 28 guidelines for information gathering. The most Flood could do was send a representative to take notes at SSS meetings. It was just as well. The SSS failed to catch on and only twenty-two persons, among them five ex-doughboys, showed up for the May 14 election.[9]

In seeking a domestic intelligence mission MID bucked political winds that favored giving the Justice Department the primary responsibility. At Justice the Armistice brought a changing of the guard as the war managers returned to the private sector. Attorney General Gregory left in early 1919 and his assistant for radical matters John Lord O'Brian and BI chief Bielaski soon followed. Former Alien Property Custodian A. Mitchell Palmer succeeded Gregory, and O'Brian's former assistant, William E. Allen, replaced Bielaski. These changes in Washington were felt in Pittsburgh. When SAC Bob Judge suddenly resigned in March, Robert B. Spencer, a four-year BI veteran previously assigned to the Chicago and Milwaukee, Wisconsin, field offices, replaced him. Speer now took charge of radical investigations.[10]

The day that Judge resigned, Erie police chief W. F. Detzel fired off an angry letter to the BI complaining that he could not "work with any degree of harmony" with special agent Lenon. Contrasting him to his predecessor, "who always conducted himself as a gentleman," Detzel accused Lenon of repeatedly issuing orders to policemen without consulting him and of speaking of the department brass "in unfriendly terms." A few days later BI officials asked Lenon to resign. They told him that budget cuts required closing the Erie office and that he was at the bottom of the seniority list. He left in April 1919 for a job in labor espionage with American Steel and Wire in Cleveland.[11]

Lenon accepted his firing stoically but had a bit of revenge when Wendell filed a report that blamed Chief Detzel and his men for the dangerous resurgence of the Erie Socialists. Bolshevik propaganda, Wendell claimed, was having "wonderful success" among returned soldiers and trade unionists because the police allowed radical meetings. Maliciously, and perhaps mendaciously, Wendell reported seeing an Erie policeman, "Murrie, badge #35," a devoted Sinn Feiner and Bolshevik sympathizer, standing guard at a Socialist meeting and entertaining the comrades with renditions of the "Red Flag" and "Internationale" on the Jew's harp.[12]

The departure of Judge and Lenon stripped Wendell of his closest BI associates. Still, with Speer as his contact, he remained undercover as both radical agitator and roper. In the latter role he received, consolidated, and transmitted to the Bureau daily reports from various informers identified by code numbers: "101," "201," "300," "51," and "500." Superiors in Washington and Pittsburgh continued to praise his work and to carefully protect his cover.

The federal campaign against the IWW had worked so well, at least in the eastern United States,[13] that it had utterly incapacitated the former Pittsburgh Wobbly leadership. Wendell took advantage of the rudderless state of the IWW to gain influence in the Pittsburgh English-speaking General Recruiting Branch. By early 1919 he had become a key recruiter and administrator. In April he boasted that "the real moving spirits" of the IWW were "McGurty, Murphy, Walsh, and Wickenheiser," a quartet able to effectively prevent the branch from doing anything. The trouble was that Wendell manned a sinking ship; the IWW now attracted few new members. At their headquarters, where in 1917 and 1918 twenty-five or thirty had gathered most evenings, seldom were there more than one or two fellow workers and the secretary.[14] The branch survived mainly on the dues and loyalty of a few of Margolis's increasingly marginalized followers and the government agents.

Early in 1919, Pittsburgh MID and BI reflected little worry about radical activity. More than four thousand area foreign workers, mostly Italians, had gone home

since the Armistice and an average of 125 more applied to leave each day. Returning veterans shied away from manual labor. Therefore, unskilled labor jobs vacated by departing immigrants went begging. In western Pennsylvania coal miners
and skilled workers were much in demand. There seemed little cause for unrest.[15]
At Erie, according to Speer, the situation offered "no occasion for alarm." Since
the Armistice the large concentration of war workers had dispersed, taking with it
many foreign-born and American radicals. In March 1919 the industrial workforce
stood at just over half its wartime peak of thirty-five thousand. Erie's potentially
radical IWW local and the Finnish soviet seemed in decline as the "aggressive
types" of radical agitators went elsewhere.[16]

Yet the Pittsburgh Radical Squad had no firm idea of how many foreign radicals were within its jurisdiction.[17] In one of his last reports from Erie, Lenon had
observed that as long as employers continued to use alien laborers, it would be
very hard for the Bureau to identify the radicals among them.[18] The undeniably
charismatic appeal of Bolshevism in some quarters was evident near the end of
January when John Reed stopped in Erie en route to Chicago to extol the glory of
the USSR and herald the coming world revolution. With scant advance notice or
advertising, Reed's appearance filled Auch's Hall with more than one thousand
people, revealingly described by agent 827 as "men from every race, creed, and col-
or except the African, Chinaman, and Japanese." Written on many faces during
Reed's two-and-one-half-hour speech the spy read "a smile of satisfaction that all
would be well soon, a hope that the revolution would spread to America[; that
they] . . . needed only to rise up and demand what they wished and it might be had
for the asking." All they required was "to spread a little more propaganda, add a
few more thousands to their ranks . . . and then wait for the fateful day to strike."[19]

In March 1919 under Lenin's direction the Third International or Comintern
convened to promote world revolutions along Soviet lines. Both the American
IWW and SLP were invited to attend, but neither did. About this time occurred a
sea change in Radical Squad thinking. Now Speer and Spencer saw danger everywhere. They made much of the fact that fifteen hundred moderate leftists jammed
the Academy Theater on Liberty Avenue for a defense fund benefit for Socialist
Congressman Victor L. Berger. The audience heard "slowcialist" speeches favoring
women's suffrage, the moral influence of mothers, and a gradual revolution to be
achieved through the ballot box. Even though they heard the antiwar Berger denounce the IWW's allegedly violent methods, the agents still professed alarm.[20]

In April 1919, led by chairman W. W. Nooning and paid labor organizer W. P.
Snow and inspired by the Bolshevik example, the Pittsburgh Socialist Party be-

came very active. It drew large crowds to meetings on Sundays at the Academy and weekday evenings at either the International Socialist Labor Lyceum on the North Side or the Jewish Labor Lyceum on the Hill. Its program remained essentially reformist, including support for the Tri-State Cooperative stores, women's suffrage, workman's compensation laws, and the abolition of child labor. But the Socialists did not hide the fact that they took inspiration from radical foreign, especially Bolshevik, socialism. At their meetings they sold Irwin St. John Tucker's *Internationalism* and praised the deeds and courage of the imprisoned Debs and Germany's Spartacist martyrs Rosa Luxemburg and Carl Liebknecht. They welcomed speakers who supported the Soviets and opposed U.S. military intervention in Russia. They listened as one told of atrocities committed by White Russian armies while another praised the Soviets' love of children. Government agents felt helpless to silence the speakers who were careful, as one agent said, not to "preach that bomb and torch stuff." The emotional power of Bolshevik success was made manifest each time the South Slovak orchestra played the "Internationale" and hundreds rose to sing.[21]

The government agents had better cause to worry when more radical leftists filled the Academy for a speech by Oscar Ameringer of Milwaukee on the Russian and German revolutions and on the need for labor solidarity. Ameringer and other speakers called for the release of the American "martyrs," Debs, Mooney, and Haywood. More bad news came from an informer who told of the start of a new Pittsburgh semimonthly, *Izvestia,* aimed at the area's estimated six thousand Russian residents. It was to be a propaganda vehicle for the local "Union of Russian Citizens" who, it was said, had recently gone over en masse to the Bolsheviks.

By April, it seemed to the G-men that radicalism was spreading like the flu through the city neighborhoods and the industrial towns of the three rivers. Reports of Bolshevik meetings came in from East Liberty and the towns of Monessen, Bentleyville, McKees Rocks, Charleroi, Ellsworth, and California. But the BI's own reports show sharp divisions on the Left. The success of the Russian Bolsheviks energized and inspired Pittsburgh radicals without uniting them. There was no consensus on the October 1917 revolution, even among the Russians. Socialists, individualist anarchists, communist-anarchists, and anarchosyndicalists all interpreted events differently.[22]

Wendell and his Pittsburgh superiors continued to view Jacob Margolis as the key to the Left, but Margolis's position was changing. He remained the lawyer to the dangerous classes and a well-known rabble-rouser, but as his activities became known outside the Pittsburgh area, Washington higher-ups began to pressure

Pittsburgh MID and BI offices to rein him in. Then in a series of "open forums" Margolis made himself less useful by publicly distancing himself from the emerging Communist movement. In December 1918, speaking to a Moorehead Hall crowd of 250 that included many Russians, Margolis contrasted the Bolsheviks' success in spreading revolutionary propaganda in Europe with the utter failure of the Socialists or the AFL to do the same here. The IWW, he claimed, was the only true American Bolshevik movement. A week later he made clear that it was only Bolshevik *tactics* that he admired. Adhering to his individualist-anarchist roots, he insisted that the Bolsheviks and Wobblies had very different visions of the workers' utopia. In a talk entitled "The End of Civilization" he blasted "fetishes" such as religion as inhibitors of individual freedom and warned that all dictatorships were wrong, whether they were capitalist or Bolshevik.[23]

Starting on January 26, 1919, Margolis lectured on five successive Sunday evenings at Moorehead Hall under the banner of the Keystone Literary Association "'On Revolution vs. Industrial Organization,' or 'How Are We Going to Build the New Society in the Shell of the Old.'" The project amounted to a philippic against the Bolsheviks, portraying them as political tyrants and betrayers of the true revolution. Word of Margolis's defection spread throughout the Left, jeopardizing many of his contacts and alienating old allies. From her prison cell Emma Goldman wrote angrily to her niece and acting amanuensis Stella Ballantine that as long as the Bolsheviks "are besieged on all sides, hated and despised, maligned and misrepresented, and now to be crushed, my place is with them, and so is that of Jake and all others who have a revolutionary spark left." Pittsburgh radical Celia Lepschutz put it more colorfully, saying that she had once considered Margolis "a tin Jesus, and we insignificant little beings bowed to his omnipotence." But "his glory is waning rapidly, and his disciples are few now." Following an "absolute anti-Bolshevist speech" that brought boos and catcalls from the audience, Wendell fretted that Margolis would lose his Pittsburgh following.[24]

Attendance at Margolis's speeches did dwindle after he broke with Bolshevism, but he was undeterred. One evening he attacked the visible agents of capitalist hegemony—public schools, newspapers, churches, courts, colleges, libraries. These institutions, he raged, kept workers from the knowledge and education that would prepare them to take over industries at the point of production and build the new society. Knowing this, he pointedly refused to endorse the AFL's attempt to organize steelworkers. In his last lecture, Margolis withstood heckling to denounce AFL-style unions as worse than useless to workers. Trade union bosses, he argued, were captives of the industrial system, and boring from within would not work. Therefore the IWW remained the workers' only hope to end unemployment and curb the capitalists' excess profits. The IWW's success would depend on winning over foreign workers because their American-born counterparts lacked class consciousness and were slaves to the "myth that every man's son can be Henry Ford, J. P. Morgan, or the President."[25]

In April 1919 someone injected violence into the struggle. On the twenty-eighth an aide to Red-baiting Seattle mayor Ole Hanson was very lucky when he opened a package return-addressed Gimbel Brothers, New York City. The potentially lethal bomb inside failed to detonate. The device was constructed of acid, fulminate of mercury, and dynamite mixed with lead slugs. A day later a maid employed by Senator Thomas Hardwick (D-Ga.) was not so lucky. She lost her hands when she opened an identical package at his Atlanta apartment. Alerted by the news of the Hardwick bomb, a New York City postal clerk found sixteen more bombs being held for insufficient postage at the Thirty-third Street Post Office. A frantic nationwide search of the postal system turned up a total of thirty bombs addressed to public figures and prevented further explosions and possible injuries.[26]

The bombs were addressed to federal officials, judges, state governors, city mayors, congressmen, senators, a newspaper editor, and capitalists J. P. Morgan and John D. Rockefeller. All had pronounced antiradical sentiments or connections in one way or another to immigration matters. Paul Avrich points out that perhaps the most interesting name on the target list was Rayme W. Finch, one of the most obscure. Since 1917 BI special agent Finch, based in Cleveland and New York City, had tracked a group of Italian anarchists from Ohio Valley coal camps to the East Coast. The group's leader was Luigi Galleani (1861–1931), an alien agitator and propagandist who preached rejection of all authority and extolled the spontaneous, violent, revolutionary act. In July 1918, federal officials, led by Finch, raided and shut down the publication *Cronaca Sovversiva* for articles that attacked militarism and conscription, and they took Galleani into custody. Soon after they let him go, but in February 1919 they rearrested him, intending to deport him.[27]

While the BI puzzled over the source of the letter bombs, the Pittsburgh MID sent three agents, probably from PPS, to look for clues in the exotic McKees Rocks underworld. Amateurishly they identified themselves in their report as agents numbers 1, 2, and 3 and then signed their names.[28] The McKees Rocks police chief showed them around the Bottoms, a slum, as they said, with a population of about ten thousand and "about 300 voters" made up of blacks, Greeks, Poles, Croats, Slavs, and Italians. In a barroom they met the "king" of the Bottoms, a major resident slum lord, who promised them evidence of Bolshevik, IWW, and Socialist activity. He took them on a quick tour of cheap dance halls, cabarets, and speakeasies featuring victrola music and painted women. They were told that a radical society or Bolshevik association met every Sunday morning and some weekday evenings to sing songs against the government, to talk "about denouncing the United States Government and to overthrow the President, Capatilists [sic] and make everyone one class." A man who said he lived above their meeting place added that the Reds did not "believe in God, Jesus or anyone or anything—all they believed in was revolutions, strikes and down with Capitalists and the Government." They were said to be armed and connected to similar groups in Ambridge, Homestead, Braddock, and Aliquippa. Agents 1, 2, and 3 were not convinced. They observed that the "king," their principal informant and interpreter, had recently quarreled with one of the radical leaders.[29]

The letter bomb scare did not interfere with western Pennsylvania's first postwar May Day celebration. At Bentleyville 1,400 immigrant workers stepped smartly to a twelve-piece Russian band, 150 of them flaunting IWW symbols. At Ambridge, Poles, Slavs, Russians, and Croats celebrated together at Ukrainian Hall. Up the Monongahela at Gallatin, Italian anarchists overcame their disdain for an American flag at the head of the parade and marched shoulder-to-shoulder with Socialists and workers. In Pittsburgh, 1,800 Allegheny County Socialists and friends celebrated at the Moose Temple where German, Hungarian, and Croatian singing societies entertained them. They gave generously to the Tom Mooney Defense Fund and applauded speeches condemning capitalism and war. Afterward, in a hall lawfully devoid of red flags, but with many bright red neckties and roses in evidence, young people danced to the music of a Croatian orchestra.[30]

Margolis, ever the optimist, saw in the May Day enthusiasm for labor's cause the prospect of real progress for the IWW. Throughout the month he, Wendell, and other Wobbly spokesmen harangued meetings of immigrant miners throughout the area, hoping to woo them away from the UMWA.[31]

In the wake of the letter bombs, the enthusiastic May Day demonstrations, and a growing clamor in the press against Reds, Pittsburgh authorities acted to show the public that they were still in control. On the night of May 4 someone, almost certainly the city police, wrecked the IWW quarters at Moorehead Hall. The intruders broke into desks and carried off dues books, records, and seventy-five dollars' worth of Wobbly literature. The next day, under police orders, the building's owner locked Wendell, Margolis, and the current branch secretary, E. J. McCurdy, out of the IWW rooms. On May 7 the city's public safety director informed Margolis that the IWW could no longer meet at Moorehead Hall.[32]

None of this seriously impeded Margolis. On May 6 he told associates that he had become the "Official Legal Representative of the Bolsheviki in the Pittsburgh District." Five days later he led an international mass meeting that drew a mostly Russian crowd of six hundred to the Jewish Labor Lyceum. Present were members of the Union of Russian Workers (UORW), among them Mike Bielesta out on bond awaiting deportation. Anticipating government oppression, Margolis used the occasion to warn immigrants that they might soon share Bielesta's plight. The appeal brought $1,250 in Liberty Bonds and $110 in cash to pay bail for those whose arrests were sure to come.[33]

Throughout May while Margolis searched for a new headquarters for the IWW masquerading as "The Mutual Benefit Society," Wobblies met at members' homes and pushed ahead with plans to recruit in "Electric Valley" and nearby towns. There was talk of putting out a weekly bulletin and of competing with the AFL for the support of steelworkers. These efforts brought the combined IWW General Recruiting Union and Metal Workers and Machinists Branch membership to fifty-seven. On the list were twenty-two machinists plus clerks, sheet metal workers, bricklayers, laborers, glass workers, salesmen, draftsmen, stenographers, collectors, and a tailor, a motorman, a carpenter, a woodworker, a photographer, a hotel worker, a miner, an electrician, and auto mechanic Wendell.[34] It was an all-time high, but not much of a revolution.

At the same time Margolis kept busy speaking for the IWW, mainly to immigrant miners and mill workers. One such speech on Sunday, May 18, caused Swissvale police to arrest and fine him for disorderly conduct. Four days later, on the twenty-second, Speer questioned him at the St. Nicholas building about his role in distributing *Freedom* and other out-of-town radical publications.[35]

The next day Margolis received a Ku Klux Klan hate letter. It began with the imperative *"LAST WARNING!"* and informed Margolis that "you was the cause of an extra meeting held by our organization last night," which found that "you are defending those damn curs who pose as I.W.W. and Revolutionary . . . [and] that your speeches do not pertain to labor but deal in radical stuff." To avoid a fate worse than "simply a coat of tar and feathers," Margolis was to stop speaking at "radical meetings along radical lines," to stop working for Reds, and, as an attorney, to watch "just how you defend the radical element." Klan members were "damn sick and tired" of Margolis's "ravings against this government." If the lawyer did not obey they would take him by force from the street, his home, or his office and deal with him so that he might not live to tell the tale. The letter closed by warning "Mr. Jake" to mend his ways or else "the radical element will be looking for another Jew to defend them at their next trial, as we as loyal, red-blooded American Citizens intend to . . . if necessary kill off those who are so depraved as to preach revolution within our borders, and don't forget this, you Jew bastard."[36]

Inexplicably the KKK letter was not placed in Margolis's BI file until January 1920, eighteen months after it was written. At that time Radical Division head J. Edgar Hoover canvassed federal agencies for evidence to support the Allegheny County Bar Association's effort to disbar Margolis. In response the New York City Post Office Bureau of Translations and Radical Publications sent Hoover "an exact copy" of the original that Margolis had sent to the editor of the UORW publication *Workman and Peasant* in May 1919.[37] Margolis had asked the editor of *Workman and Peasant* to print the letter as "splendid evidence that we have made the world 'safe for democracy' and saved civilization." It would show the "reactionary forces let loose by the war" and that "to do anything for the American Worker, and particularly the I. W. W.'s [sic] seems, in this district, to be the most serious crime one could possibly commit."[38]

Margolis was certainly a visible target for a nativist hate group such as the KKK, especially after his arrest at Swissvale. If the letter is authentic, it shows Klan activity in Pittsburgh well before 1921, when national organizer Sam D. Rich set up KKK headquarters in the Jenkins Arcade. Yet the timing of the letter raises suspicion that it might have originated in the BI. It is dated the day after special agents questioned Margolis. At that very time Speer was investigating *Workman and Peasant* looking for an IWW-UORW link. Possibly BI agents concocted the letter for the dual purpose of intimidating Margolis and tracing his ties to the Russian workers.[39] Since he intended to have it published, one would expect Margolis to have mentioned the letter to those close to him, yet Wendell's reports do not mention it. The letter's crude anti-Semitism was a hallmark of the 1920s Klan, but this also existed in the government intelligence services and on the Pittsburgh Radical Squad.[40]

The "last warning" did not faze Margolis. On May 25 he spoke to eight hundred Russians, Poles, Ukrainians, and Lithuanians at Carnegie about their treatment by the United States government. On the twenty-ninth he prepared a petition to the president and secretary of labor complaining that they treated these people as a "dangerous element" and yet would not let them return voluntarily to their homelands. The petition appealed for a halt to arrests and harassment and to allow the immigrants to pay their own way home. As he worked on the petition the IWW (Mutual Benefit Society) settled into its new headquarters in Room 301 of the Apollo Building on Fourth Avenue, two blocks from BI, MID, and ONI offices.[41]

Three days later a series of nearly simultaneous bomb explosions in eight cities permanently altered the relationship between the BI and the militant American Left. Late Monday evening, June 2, bombs exploded in New York, Boston, Newtonville (Massachusetts), Philadelphia, Paterson, Washington, Cleveland, and Pittsburgh. All had to be the work of a single group or, as some thought, of several cooperating radical groups. Reinforcing that assumption were identical fliers found at most of the bomb sites. Entitled *Plain Words,* signed "The Anarchist Fighters," and printed on pink paper, they proclaimed the right of the proletariat to self-protection.[42]

The most politically powerful of the bombs blew away part of the front of Attorney General A. Mitchell Palmer's R Street Northwest townhouse in Washington, leaving him and his family unhurt but deeply shaken. The man who planted the bomb was not so fortunate. He was blown to bits when it went off prematurely. The New York City bomb missed its intended victim, Judge Charles Cooper Knott, who was not home, but it killed a night watchman. Elsewhere the bombs caused property damage and fear, but no injuries.[43]

The two Pittsburgh explosions occurred within five minutes of each other around 11:30 P.M.—one in the fashionable streetcar suburb of Squirrel Hill and the other miles away in the modest Sheraden neighborhood. Both bombs missed the homes of their presumed targets. The Squirrel Hill device was placed on the porch of the Aylesboro Avenue home of Pittsburgh Plate Glass official C. J. Cassady. Cassady was certainly on the wrong side of the class struggle, as was the coal company vice president, whose home next door was also damaged, and as was, for that matter, almost everyone living in the affluent neighborhood. However, police soon decided that the bomb had been meant for federal judge W. H. S. Thompson, who lived two doors from Cassady and had presided at several cases involving aliens, including that of the prominent Italian anarchist, Carlo Tresca.[44]

The second blast occurred at the Glasgow Street residence of railroad dispatcher Herbert E. Joseph, an implausible target. But across the street in a house commensurate with his modest $2,240 annual salary lived U.S. Commissioner for Immigration William W. Sibray, a key official in immigrant deportations.[45] The attempt on Sibray required substantial enterprise and effort. His home was several miles west of downtown near the top of Sheraden Hill. The neighborhood overlooks a panorama that includes Bruno's Island and a stretch of the Ohio River, Pittsburgh's North Side, and, to the east on a clear day, the distant Golden Triangle. One can imagine the assassin's heart pounding with anxiety and the exertion of ascending Glasgow Street sidewalk, so steep that it consists partly of steps. It is easy to understand his failure to find Sibray's house in the dark because only those familiar with the neighborhood would know that the houses on either side of the street were numbered consecutively up the hill instead of the usual even-odd sides.

Police found copies of *Plain Words* at both sites, and on June 3 the *Pittsburgh Press* reprinted its text. The bombs were alike: two-and-one-half-foot-long pipes filled with fulminating dynamite and shrapnel. A total of six homes were damaged, the Cassady and Joseph houses most extensively. No one was injured, but at the Cassady home the explosion hurled a large rock through a window perilously close to a sleeping infant. Every window in Thompson's house shattered and Sibray was thrown from his bed.[46]

The BI had only limited experience with bombing cases. On September 8, 1918, an explosion that killed four persons and injured seventy-five shook the Chicago Post Office Building where the Justice Department had offices and *U.S. v. Haywood et al.* had been tried. Immediately agents blamed the blast on IWW terrorists retaliating for the conviction of their leaders. A mass roundup of Wobblies followed, but the government was never able to convict anyone in the case.[47]

The outrages of June 2 led to a major shake-up at the Justice Department. Quickly Palmer added a new assistant attorney general, Francis P. Garvan, former chief investigator of the Alien Property Bureau. At the same time famous detective and former Secret Service chief William J. Flynn took over as BI director. Second in command with the title of chief was former Treasury Russian specialist Frank Burke. A frightened Congress appropriated $500,000 to enable the BI to deal with the terrorist menace. The BI was now back in the domestic intelligence business in a big way, charged with catching the bombers and smothering foreign left-wing groups.[48]

In mid-June, in order to directly oversee field agents in this mission, J. Edgar Hoover, whose job as attorney in the Alien Enemy Registration Section had been abolished, took over the Radical Division, later the General Intelligence Division (GID), with the title special assistant to the attorney general. In his two years at Justice the twenty-four-year-old had advanced from clerk to attorney. Although the BI never brought the bombers to justice, Hoover's spectacular rise in the Bureau began here.[49]

Hoover, with enormous energy and self-confidence, soon tightened controls over field office radical investigations. With a Washington staff of thirty and about sixty special agents in the field dedicated to antiradical work, he systematized the collection and indexing of information. Although he understood that the public expected results in the bomb cases that provided the political impetus for launching the Radical Division, Hoover saw its primary mission, in keeping with the recommendations of the Overman Committee, as specializing "entirely upon deportation cases."[50]

In the wake of the Pittsburgh explosions gawkers clogged traffic at the Alyesboro Avenue bomb site and authorities mobilized. Mayor Babcock called for "100 percent Americanism" and expressed surprise that his city could house "such cowardly miscreants" as the terrorists. Away from the public eye, SAC Spencer put all of his agents on the bomb case. Having been caught off guard and without a clue as to who planted the bombs, on June 3 Spencer ordered a raid on the Apollo building to arrest the usual suspects, the IWW. According to the papers, when the city and county police broke through the door of room 301, a pistol shot rang out and a bullet just missed a city detective. They quickly overpowered the shooter, Edward John Johnson (Johnston), and took him and several others into custody. Next, following BI instructions, they rounded up other notorious Wobblies, among them Wendell, Louis M. Walsh, taken at his room on Charles Street. The front page of the June 4 *Press* featured a photographic montage composed of fragments from the Sibray and Thompson bombings and front-view mug shots of suspects Walsh, Walter Loan, and Johnson.[51] The arrest of Wendell-Walsh-836 served a double purpose. The three days he spent in jail strengthened his cover and enabled him to discretely question the other suspects.

Counting Wendell, the roundup netted eighteen suspects. Except for three Russian immigrants, "not I.W.W., but found with the suspects, and afterwards released," all were radicals. However, their collective profile was that of revolutionary propagandist, not bomb-throwing terrorist. Most were without violent propensities and well-known to the Radical Squad. Several had criminal records, including Wobbly Walter Loan, a machinist who was arrested at his job in Verona. He had been "implicated" in a 1911 bombing in Wilkinsburg and was the subject of Margolis's short piece in the May 1915 *Mother Earth*. In the 1920s, with his wife Reba, who was at one time the recording secretary of the local IWW, he would join the Communist Party.[52]

Although authorities could not have known, the most truly "dangerous" of the suspects were the two "Austrian" (actually Croatian) Blum brothers who were on parole after serving time for strike and antiwar activities. Their father was a Wobbly and Wendell called their mother, Anna Blum, "one of the most rabid radicals in Pittsburgh." The elder brother John was a carpenter who taught in the Pittsburgh Socialist school on the North Side. Like Loan he had belonged to the Pitts-

From the front page of the *Pittsburgh Press*, June 4, 1919, showing June 2 bomb fragments and, clockwise from top left, suspects Edward Johnson, L. M. Walsh-Wendell-836, and Walter Loan. (Carnegie Library of Pittsburgh)

burgh IWW recruiting branch since it was organized in the summer of 1917.[53] However, the family's most precocious revolutionary was the younger son Rudolph or Rudi, just twenty-one years old. At fifteen he had been a leader of the violent 1916 Westinghouse Electric strike. Speer thought he was more intelligent than his brother John and said he "identified with practically every movement in the district."[54] In the summer of 1919 Rudi Blum would join the Communist Party, where as Ray or Rudy Baker he rose through the CPUSA cadre to direct the party's covert apparatus in the World War II era.[55]

When they first arrested the Wobblies, Pittsburgh police thought they had solved the bombings. Their "star" suspect was the pistol shooter, Irish immigrant Edward Johnson. A police spokesman identified him as an IWW organizer recently arrived from Chicago and said that he matched the general description of a man seen near the Joseph home before the bombing. Johnson had received only passing mention in Wendell's reports before his spectacular arrest. Just six days before the bombings Wendell had nominated him as the Mutual Benefit Society's (IWW's) corresponding secretary, an unpopular job to which he was elected by acclamation.[56]

The thirty-six-year-old Johnson had emigrated from Ireland to Philadelphia in 1907. Without family, money, connections, or education, he became a pipe fitter and sometime day laborer who drifted to Florida and then to Louisiana and Texas. From 1910 to 1914 he lived in Bakersfield, California, where he joined the IWW. His only formal run-in with the law there had been an arrest during one of the many West Coast IWW free-speech fights. Between 1914 and 1918 Johnson had drifted across Canada from Vancouver to Toronto. In December 1918 he had reentered the United States by way of Buffalo, telling immigration inspectors that he would stay only ten days. Soon after, he showed up in Pittsburgh, where he first labored on a railroad work train and then at a slag dump. He also began to spend time with Wendell and the boys at Wobbly headquarters and to make speeches and distribute IWW literature.[57]

When the G-men sorted through the shards of Johnson's life, they found an undisciplined drifter with no history of violence. Such a loner was hard to place in the obviously well-organized conspiracy of June 2, yet one newspaper reported that Johnson had confessed and named two accomplices. Another wrote that although he "remained mute despite quite severe handling" during formal questioning, police had gleaned clues from his demeanor that identified his associates. Police then picked up his alleged accomplices. Brooklyn, New York, pharmacist John Boret (or Borst), the supposed "dope" (a dynamite mixer or bomb maker), was soon released after it was apparent that he had no connection with the bombings. Police thought that in the other subject, E. J. McCurdy (McGurdy, McCurty, McCorty), they had the key to the case.[58]

A police captain described McCurdy as "a clean-cut looking chap and a neat dresser." Evidence found at McCurdy's residence hinted that the plot involved secret operations in neighboring West Virginia. In McCurdy's traveling bag was a large Rand-McNally commercial map of the Mountain State with more than 150 locations marked in dark ink.[59] Pittsburgh police sent the map plus McCurdy's mug shots and Bertillon measurements to West Virginia Governor John J. Cornwell as a warning. Today they remain in his papers, where Cornwell filed them along with a copy of W. Z. Foster's *Syndicalism* in a thick folder labeled "Anarchy and Bolshevism, Threats."[60] No explanation was ever given for the marks on the map. Perhaps the black dots marked commercial contacts. McCurdy was a traveling salesman and the marked places are nearly all small towns and hamlets that would have had a general store.

McCurdy had come from Chicago to Pittsburgh in the fall of 1918 and had hooked up with the local IWW chapter. In November of that year he had met with Margolis, Wendell, Ben Anisman, and other IWW insiders to organize the Workers Defense League, a propaganda operation to promote Bolshevism and the IWW. Ten days later he won unanimous election as secretary of the Pittsburgh IWW branch after being, like Johnson, nominated for the job by Wendell. In February 1919, McCurdy resigned as IWW secretary "again" but remained active in the Moorehead Hall and later Apollo Building meetings and as a Wobbly speaker.[61]

Only days after the bombings, the case against Johnson and McCurdy began to crumble. By June 6, police were saying that the case "was up in the air" and that they did not know who was behind the bombings. Privately the BI concluded that Johnson and McCurdy were innocent. After three days in an Allegheny County Jail cell, Wendell, "one of our operatives, in the confidence of [the] suspects," had no clues. The suspects told him that they knew nothing of the plot, "that it was engineered from the outside, and that in their judgment it was an unfortunate move and would act as a boomerang." Independently MID and BI in Pittsburgh concluded that "no matter where the plot originated, the men arrested here as suspects had no part in the conspiracy." All were released, except for five who were held for deportation. Reports described them as unnaturalized immigrants with radical connections: Irishman Johnson; Hungarian Mike Stefanko, IWW organizer; Russian Frank Broida, anarchist; Russian Mike Bielasta, anarchist; and Bulgarian Dmitir Dobreff, SLP member and IWW agitator.[62]

Police identification photo of E. J. McCurdy, secretary of the Pittsburgh General Recruiting Branch of the IWW and suspect in the June 2, 1919, Pittsburgh bombings. Police found in his effects a large West Virginia map with more than 150 locations marked in dark ink. (West Virginia and Regional History Collection, West Virginia University Libraries)

After being cleared of the bombings, Johnson's difficulties with federal officials only multiplied. During a June 23rd interrogation by Pittsburgh Immigration Inspector Michael F. O'Brien, Johnson admitted that he had sold IWW literature in California in 1914, including the Wobblies' famous *Little Red Song Book*. Based upon that admission, O'Brien recommended Johnson's deportation, even though the United States had not entered the war until 1917 and the statutes Johnson was supposed to have violated had not been passed until 1918. Still, a recent Bureau of Immigration ruling made selling or distributing the IWW song book the equivalent of advocating and teaching the unlawful destruction of property. Under the Alien Act of October 1918, immigrants could be deported for advocating anarchism, syndicalism, or violent revolution or for belonging to organizations that advocated such ideas. After the hearing, Margolis bailed out Johnson with five hundred dollars in Liberty Bonds, probably purchased at a discount from immigrants, but by December 1919, after further proceedings by the Immigration Bureau, Johnson found himself at Ellis Island awaiting deportation.[63]

The bomb attacks on Inspector Sibray and Judge Thompson not only caught the Pittsburgh intelligence community by surprise, they also triggered a public relations flap that threatened undercover operations in the Margolis circle. Weeks earlier, one Dimitri Joanowici had told a *Pittsburgh Leader* reporter that Bolsheviks brazenly held open rallies at the Academy Theater and that their leaders met secretly at Moorehead Hall, almost in the shadow of city and county government offices. Two days after the bomb blasts, under the headline "SLEUTH FORETOLD OF BOMBING" the *Leader* recounted Joanowici's claim that Reds, four million strong, were planning to kick off the revolution by bombing the homes of prominent people all over the country. Next they would cut communications and gain control of cities and towns before the army could mobilize to stop them. The story said that Joanowici had even produced lists of alleged plotters along with their police records. The next day the *New York World* and the *Washington Herald* picked up elements of the story. The version that appeared in the *World* asserted that "government officers and police knew of the nationwide bombing plot and other contemplated activities of the Bolsheviki, I.W.W., and other radicals long ago."[64]

Joanowici claimed to have left undercover work because his superiors in the Plant Protection Section had ignored his warnings about the gathering of "some of the world's most notorious anarchists." He added that "a well-known lawyer figures conspicuously in the Moorehead Hall meetings. There he sells literature of an anarchistic nature, and I understand, makes a large profit."[65] Obviously Joanowici's "well-known lawyer" was Margolis and his "notorious anarchists" included Wendell and the others of their circle.

Joanowici's charges forced the MID's Flood into urgent conferences with Spencer and a defense of his operations to Washington headquarters. To DMI Churchill, he explained that Joanowici was a disgruntled former employee who had been fired because "he was obsessed with the idea that there had been a suppression of evidence in one or two cases in which he was interested, and, like many other operatives, being possessed of only partial information, took issue with his Chief and the policy pursued by his department." Flood pointed out that the newspaper story was short on fact and long on generalities and showed nothing to indicate that Joanowici "had any intimate knowledge of conditions at Moorehead Hall." He assured Churchill that his men cooperated closely with the BI, which had been "in constant touch with all meetings held at Moorehead Hall by the radical leaders." The controversy had not harmed the MID-BI working relationship. MID had fired Joanowici in the first place "partly on account of . . . [his] bungling interference with our undercover man" at the hall, meaning, of course, 836-Walsh-Wendell. It would be best to ignore Joanowici, a publicity seeker with a grudge who knew no secrets.[66]

MID agents did not capture the bombers and the embarrassing Joanowici affair left them in no position to find fault with the Pittsburgh BI operation. However, elsewhere, in their bid for a bigger piece of the domestic intelligence action, they did not hesitate to expose the BI's failings. In late June during a few days of investigation in the Boston area MID operative J. J. McCann claimed to have picked up enough leads on foreign radicals around Boston to "keep 15 men busy for a month." His discoveries ranged from a Bolshevik headquarters right across the street from the "old witch house" in Salem to a Lawrence meeting hall where anarchists met to spit tobacco juice on the flag, sing the "Internationale," and curse the government and its agents. Local authorities did not even bother to "ascertain the names of the local leaders, their meeting places and all that can be learned of the membership so that they will know whom to suspect in case of local outrages." His point was that the BI was too undermanned in the area to manage the situation.[67]

In the immediate wake of the explosions the evidence pointed directly at foreign anarchists, but which ones? Many in the BI fixed their suspicions on the little-known Union of Russian Workers. On June 8 the *New York Times* published a story attributed to an "official source in Washington" that quoted extensively from the UORW constitution and from translations of Russian-language propaganda literature distributed at meetings in New York, San Francisco, Cleveland, Akron, Chicago, and Seattle. The source warned that the UORW was controlled from Russia, that it had at least five hundred propagandists in the country, and that it intended the violent overthrow of the United States government.[68]

Without much solid information the Pittsburgh BI and MID continued to believe that Russians were behind the bombings. Seizing upon the refrain from *Plain Words*, "you have deported us," Spencer reasoned that "the only persons deported here and elsewhere, with a few exceptions, have been Russian agitators." Furthermore, a Russian, Adolph Schnabel, "a very clever anarchist organizer," was about to be deported and Sibray, a target of the June 2 bombers, had issued the order. The MID's Flood took a different route to a similar conclusion. "A reasonable presumption," he thought, "is that if any radical groups in this city had a hand in the plot, we would have had some foreknowledge of the conspiracy." Because the government agents did not, the plot must have been carried out by a radical group about which they knew little. The UORW fit that description. Flood explained that "considerable difficulty has always been experienced in placing operatives within the folds of the Union of Russian Workmen." The G-men knew only what UORW members revealed to government operatives on the outside, the main conduit being through Wendell from Margolis. Jake was "the legal counsel of the Bolsheviki in Pittsburgh, who has a secret working pact with them, and who also frames the Bolshevist resolutions passed at their meetings."[69]

All across the country after the bombings MID, BI, and local and state law enforcement agencies scoured their files and pumped informants. In Pittsburgh the investigative agencies took information-sharing seriously. The Secret Service, which had paid little attention to the "radical element" since 1916, now sought to bring its files up to date by consulting various law enforcement agencies. In the agencies' files are commingled BI, MID, ONI, and Pennsylvania State Constabulary reports. Among them are many from Chicago MID where Major Thomas B. Crockett conducted a vigorous and far-reaching effort. He dispatched undercover men on fishing expeditions to known radical haunts in Chicago, Detroit, Philadelphia, and New York City.[70] They came back without a clear picture of the bomb plot, but with plenty of information to fuel a broad range of guesses by the detectives.

Among the more bizarre were the reports of MID confidential informant and former czarist Russian infantry officer A. F. Akatow.[71] Based on his experience among Russians at a Gary, Indiana, settlement house, Akatow believed the bomb plotters were the Knights of the Red Star, who were controlled by the "Double Trinity," a supposed Boston-based revolutionary cabal composed of Irish, English, and American radicals. He speculated that the Knights of the Red Star were connected to the IWW and UORW in Gary. Akatow probably meant a group that called itself "the Local Detachment of the Order of the Red Star" and claimed to represent "liberating and punitive detachments of the People's army" and "avengers of the persecuted, the wronged, and the oppressed." In March 1919 the Order had circulated a Russian-language "Proclamation to the People" promising to "strike fear and terror into the hearts of our enemies" in Gary, Cleveland, and Chicago.[72] Clearly the Order was not the UORW.

A couple of weeks after the bombings the Cleveland police chief and E. E. Noble, a "volunteer" MID agent and chief of the Loyal American League, successor to the APL, cosponsored an informant's two-week tour of dissident haunts in Philadelphia, New York, Boston, and Chicago. Disappointingly, at IWW and UORW headquarters in Philadelphia he found no prominent radicals, only lowly subalterns and poorly disguised detectives who seemed to fall all over each other. In Manhattan he visited the Rand School, Communist headquarters on 43rd Street, and the 40th Street office of Ludwig C. A. K. Martens, official representative of the Soviet government. He claimed to have hobnobbed with John Reed, Albert Rhys Williams, and Emma Goldman's attorney Harry Weinberger and even to have taken Max Eastman to the theater.[73]

The informant brought back conflicting tales. The bombings were the work of a mysterious Committee of Five led by Emma Goldman. Or they had occurred after Italians at anarchist summit meetings at Chicago and Rockford, Illinois, had failed to persuade other nationalities to join them in avenging their jailed comrades. Afterward "most of the Italians and some of the Russians went straight to Philadelphia from where the bombers were sent to various places." Another source said that the bombings were the work of a Camden, New Jersey, Italian anarchist group who "who took nobody into their confidence."[74]

The common thread running through the various leads was an Italian connection. Witnesses had seen "Italian-looking" men with packages before the explosions near some of the bombing sites. The involvement of Italians was mentioned in many intelligence reports. A gruesome, painstaking forensic investigation of the scattered physical remains and effects of the man killed at the Palmer house, including an Italian-language dictionary, a sandal, a laundry mark, and bits of clothing, pointed to an Italian immigrant. But which Italian? A Philadelphia radical said it was Dominico Felicio. Another source said that it was an associate of John Baldazzi, Wobbly convict and alleged former go-between for Goldman and the Italians, who had engineered the bombings from his cell at Leavenworth.[75]

The most likely source of the terror was the group associated with Luigi Galleani. In early June 1919 the Bureau of Immigration had arrested him and eight of his disciples and prepared to deport them to Italy. On June 24, a day after BI agents questioned them at Boston, the men were deported to Italy. It is not clear why the Justice Department did not prevent it. In July Boston MID and BI agents accompanied by a Washington D.C. police sergeant toured the Italian immigrant neighborhoods of Beverly, Worcester, Lynn, New Bedford, Lowell, Lawrence, and Salem. Then multilingual BI agent Feri Felix Weiss (discussed more in chapter 8) and an Italian-speaking informant, assuming that "Italians, as a race, are very superstitious about burial in a 'potter's field,'" posed as undertakers to spread the word in the neighborhoods that they were looking for Ercole Valdinoci. Their story was that they hoped that he would pay for the burial of a body fished from the East River in New York that might be that of his friend Umberto Calerosi (Colarossi). Colarossi fit the description of the Washington bomber and agents could not locate him or Erico (Ercole) Valdinoci, or Ercole's brother Carlo, a fugitive from a deportation warrant. Later they learned that Colarossi was in jail on June 2, and when they found Ercole Valdinoci in Cambridge he would tell them nothing.[76]

The files present a picture of the BI grasping at straws. Since they knew so little about the various foreign-language anarchist groups, investigators from the famous Flynn and the precocious Hoover down through the chain of command to Wendell were stymied. Although the evidence pointed to Italians, nothing could shake the dominant theory that the Bolsheviks must be the masterminds. On June 20, Director Flynn publicly blamed the blasts on foreigners within the ranks of organized labor and warned that "under the guise of unionism the worst sort of seditious propaganda is being spread." In early July, he told a convention of police chiefs that the bombers were "connected with Russian bolshevism, aided by Hun money and are operating and spreading their propaganda under the guise of labor agitation." He cautioned chiefs not to tolerate the "evil" of "street meetings and meetings where foreign languages are spoken" in their jurisdictions. Given the BI's investigative mind-set, by August what one agent called Finerty's "wonderful story" had become what Hoover described as "the most promising of all" leads.[77]

James Finerty was an obsessively antiradical former plant police chief in Bessemer, Pennsylvania, a hamlet near the Ohio border northwest of Pittsburgh between New Castle and Youngstown. For years he had deluged the New Castle district attorney with reports of foreign workers' subversive doings until at last the plant manager fired him for driving away needed labor. After the June 2 bombings Finerty came to Pittsburgh police captain Clyde Edeburn claiming to have special knowledge of the bombings. He named the man killed at Palmer's residence as Louis Lazbue and supported the assertion with an affidavit of Mrs. Mary Delinka of Carbon, Pennsylvania, near Bessemer. Finerty said she was a $1-a-trick prostitute whose house was frequented by a gang of Slavic, Irish, and Italian anarchists. One of the gang drove a Nash automobile, which could have transported the bombs to the target cities. Another, a bibulous ex–college teacher, openly sympathized with the imprisoned Eugene V. Debs. Finerty had reported the gang as Bolshevik agitators to the Pittsburgh BI in early 1919. Edeburn then took some men to Bessemer to investigate Finerty's story and concluded that "there was not a bit of truth in it and that the Chief was a 'nut' and that he was called 'Squirrel' by the people of Bessemer."[78]

Despite the police report the Washington BI pursued the Finerty lead. The most compelling detail of the chief's story was the alleged tie between Lazbue and a blue steel Smith and Wesson revolver found at the Washington bomb scene. In February, accompanied by a Pennsylvania state trooper, Finerty claimed to have found the thirty-five-year-old Lazbue in possession of a pistol at the Delinka house whose serial number matched that of the gun found on R Street NW. Finerty also claimed witnesses would swear that he had obtained copies of *Plain Words* on May 18, almost two weeks before the bombings. He purportedly confiscated the fliers from under Mary Delinka's bed and took them home to his wife for safekeeping. She then hid them between the mattress and springs of their bed, where they remained until June 4 when, grasping their significance, Finerty announced he would "make some of those fellows jump—I have the goods" and said he would take the evidence to Pittsburgh. En route he showed *Plain Words* to a local grocer and to an illiterate Lowellville, Ohio, jitney driver. The latter, upon being shown "what it said on the paper," asked what it meant and Finerty pointed to "those words" and said "why they are the anarchist fighters."[79]

In August Washington dispatched Philadelphia-based special agent J. F. McDevitt to verify Finerty's fantastic story. McDevitt talked to hucksters, jitney men, and quaint village characters in Struthers, Bessemer, Carbon, Lowellville, and other towns near Youngstown. It turned out that Mrs. "Mary Delinka," born Wagner, was an Austrian immigrant wed to a Polish laborer named John Hamonko. Much to John's distress Mary and radical Peter Serich had carried on an affair for a year and a half. In June Mary and Serich ran away to Detroit and she left a note saying that Serich was wanted by police for the bombings. The cuckolded Hamonko gave the BI a negative assessment of Serich, saying he seldom worked but always had plenty of money and drove a new car. He added that Serich was an atheist and, like Lazbue, was always urging men to join the union.[80]

After spending twelve hours with the Finertys at their East Youngstown home in a "very desirable location" McDevitt assessed the wife as "quiet unassuming [and] middle aged." He sensed "considerable hot air about" Finerty who had a few "sores that needed to be healed." On the other hand the ex-chief was respected by "business and professional men and by children." Favorably impressed with Finerty overall, McDevitt teased the evidence into a plausible scenario. He reasoned that since Lazbue and Serich and ten other suspicious-looking men had been seen together in Carbon on May 27, six days before the explosions, they could have manufactured the bombs locally, dynamite being plentiful in the area, and then used Serich's Nash to transport them. The theory had all the elements the BI was looking for and it all seemed to fit: the revolver; the copies of *Plain Words;* that Hamonko's wife was a "German woman"; that Serich had run to Detroit where the UORW constitution had been printed in 1918; that Lazbue, who was missing, could be the dead Italian bomb planter, and the company towns east of Youngstown the center of the plot.[81]

In early September McDevitt crisscrossed Illinois, Michigan, Ohio, and Pennsylvania to confirm the assumptions about Lazbue. A Pennsylvania state police corporal supported Finerty's story, remembering the encounter with Lazbue and the revolver. A Washington D.C. police sergeant deposed that during their June phone conversation Finerty had recited the Smith and Wesson's correct serial number. But there were discrepancies. The G-man had observed that Finerty tended to lead subjects during interrogation and now suspected that foreigners might have been led to say what they thought the policeman wanted to hear. McDevitt also concluded that Finerty had not written down the revolver's serial number in February when he had allegedly seen it, but only did so just before the BI questioned him. And there was no trace of Lazbue. Even when McDevitt tugged at the emotions of the Elgin Italian community with the story that he represented Lazbue's sister in Italy who needed help to bring her three small children to the United States, no one volunteered any information. Lazbue supposedly was a leather worker, but the agent could find no trace of him in the records of the leather workers' union. Then he learned that Finerty had never brought *Plain Words* to the BI or the police in Pittsburgh.[82]

Still, the BI would not surrender its "best lead." On September 10, McDevitt, with aggrieved husband Hamonko in tow, New York City agent Frank Francisco, and Director Flynn himself rendezvoused in Detroit. They staked out a second-floor apartment above a pool room in an industrial section and then used a uniformed city fireman and the pretext of a fire inspection to enter the place. Sure enough, in a three-room apartment with six beds, they found and took into custody Mary Delinki Hamonko. They then waited and watched until a total of ten male boarders came home. But Serich was not among them.[83]

Through a Polish interpreter Director Flynn questioned Mary and John Hamonko separately. She denied knowledge of bomb making or having given an affidavit to that "crazy policeman" Finerty. When they compared signature samples, her "Marry Dilinki" did not match the Finerty affidavit. She swore that she wanted to stay with Serich and have no more to do with her husband. Then Flynn gave up, ordered McDevitt to get Hamonko out of town in order to protect Mary, and beat a quiet retreat to Washington no nearer to finding the June 2 bombers.[84]

After the Finerty fiasco, the BI rethought the whole case, concluding, according to Hoover, by the "process of elimination" that the bomb plot must have originated at Boston, Philadelphia, or New York. So agents McDevitt and Francisco were detailed to investigate each of those cities in turn. By October 1919 suspicion focused on the Italian Pro-Prensa and Galleani groups. An obvious clue to a Galleanist connection was that the *Plain Words* circular signed by "The Anarchist Fighters" closely resembled the flyer *Go Ahead!* from "The American Anarchists" that had circulated a few months earlier in Massachusetts. Eventually investigators narrowed the identity of the deceased bomber to either Umberto Calerosi [Colarossi] or Carlo Valdinoci. By early 1920 they were sure it was the latter. A BI spy at last infiltrated Galleanist groups in Boston and New York City and provided information that led to the arrest of Roberto Elia and Andrea Salsedo. By March the two had admitted printing *Plain Words*.[85]

In a March 1920 memo Hoover wrote that the solution to the June 1919 bomb plot was "within early sight." The BI had "information startling and remarkable in nature." He would not say more because the case was not quite complete.[86] Seventy-five years later the case remains open. On May 2, 1920, Salsedo plunged to his death from the fourteenth-floor window of the New York City room where he and Elia had been interrogated and allegedly beaten over a two-month period. The BI could not easily explain what had happened. After Salsedo's death federal officials hurriedly deported Elia to Italy. Neither he nor Salsedo had told the BI all that they knew.[87]

Recent scholarship points to the Galleanists as the perpetrators of the May and June 1919 bombings, Carlo Valdinoci as the Palmer house bomber, and a probable tie-in with the Sacco-Vanzetti case. That said, excepting Valdinoci, Elia, Salsedo, and a handful of others, no one can name the score or more who were involved, including the two Pittsburgh bombers.[88]

Excepting the forensics work at Palmer's house, the performance of federal intelligence in these bomb cases was unimpressive. A prodigious effort yielded a mountain of half-digested intelligence, much of it unreliable, from which agents fashioned a number of ultimately false scenarios, most of them focusing on the Russians or the IWW. One reason for this was that the BI files were a shambles. Attorney General Palmer admitted as much in March 1919 when he reported that

The BI's only photo of Carlo Valdinoci, who is believed to have planted and been killed by the June 2, 1919, bomb at Attorney General A. Mitchell Palmer's Washington, D.C.; townhouse. This appropriately murky image was originally cut out from a snapshot of three men sitting in an open automobile. The actual photo was evidently discarded after the file was microfilmed in 1952. (National Archives Microfilm Publication M-1085, roll 508, DJ OG 123280, RG 65)

Washington headquarters suffered from "a chaos in the records and organization of the bureau." After J. Edgar Hoover took over the radical hunt in June 1919 it would take many months to reorganize files and procedures, build a reference library, and acquire expertise in dealing with radicalism. In the meantime, agency advocates pleaded with Congress for money and time, saying justifiably that the BI's efforts were "cumulative" and promising that "the results of its work will be increasingly manifest."[89]

Another problem was intelligence-gathering "noise." In Pittsburgh Wendell and the Radical Squad were evidently too preoccupied with other matters to be aware of Italian anarchist activities in their backyard. They knew that in May 1918 Margolis had represented Galleanists Emilio Coda and Giovanni Scussel in Cleveland at their questioning about smuggling bomb-making materials from the Youngstown-Steubenville area to Chicago. Wendell had reported in detail on special agent and mail bomb target Rayme Finch's long conversation with Margolis on that occasion. Nevertheless, in the summer of 1919 Pittsburgh BI and MID forgot the Finch episode and Margolis's connection with Italian anarchists. Evidently Wendell paid more attention to Finch's statement that the government had spies inside radical organizations than to the anarchists' activities. Neither did he emphasize the fact that area Italian groups had been able to raise ten thousand dollars for Scussel's and Coda's bail.

Pittsburgh police files showed that in the past such groups had been active at Duffy, Finleyville, and Snowden. More recent BI files showed that on May Day there were 150 Italian anarchists active up the Monongahela at Gallatin. They also missed the Galleanists' link to recent violent threats and the relevance of Galleani's 1905 bomb manual *La Salute è in voi! (Health Is In You!)*. Not until August 11, long after the bombings, did the Pittsburgh BI employ, at five dollars a day, its first Italian informer. Not until October did it locate and question Coda, who was working in a western Pennsylvania coal mine.[90]

Tunnel vision and prejudice hampered the search for bombers. The Finerty investigation is an example of the lengths to which the Bureau would go to verify its prejudices. Another guiding assumption of the G-men was that radicalism must express itself through labor agitation. The Galleanists existed outside the Radical Squad's frame of reference because they were quite different from the Russians and Poles and intellectuals who aimed to organize and arouse the masses through propaganda. With little use for mass meetings, soapboxing, or labor organizing, they believed in the propaganda of the deed and in avenging perceived wrongs. By contrast, government agents were predisposed to believe that the propaganda *was* the deed. Assuming IWW-Bolsheviki rhetoric to be the greater danger, they paid the Italians scant notice. By the end of the strike-plagued summer of 1919 protecting capitalism from revolutionary assault took priority over capturing a few bombers. As of September only two BI agents were on the case full-time.

Radicals accused federal agents of staging May-June bombings to stir up hatred and promote public support for a war against them. Vincent St. John, who was in Pittsburgh in July 1919, theorized that "those fake bomb explosions were pulled . . . in order to put the kibosh on everything for a while . . . [as the Wobblies] were just getting their second wind." In its July issue, *One Big Union Monthly* elaborated on that theme. Seven months later, in testimony before the House Rules Committee, attorney Swinburne Hale blamed Justice Department agents for letter bombings of May 1919.[91] The Wobblies' paranoia is understandable, but BI and MID files do not support such a plot. Government investigators wanted to catch the June bombers for reasons of pride, professionalism, and public relations. They had to endure considerable criticism, some of it tinged with sarcasm, for their failure.

Still, the bombings benefitted the government's broader antiradical program and played into the hands of business elites. The explosions provided an excuse for suppressing "radical" labor movements. They gave government detectives a new budget-fattening mission and forestalled personnel cuts.[92] Crying up the dangers of the UORW, the Wobblies, and the Bolsheviks drew public attention away from the BI's failure to arrest the bombers. Yet, as long as the bombers remained unnamed and on the loose, they could well be Russian or Wobbly labor activists or some symbolically malignant combination of revolutionaries within the American labor movement.

The uncertainty helped to enshrine the myth of Communist complicity in the bombings in anticommunist legend. In his McCarthy-era semiofficial *FBI Story*, Don Whitehead opened his chapter on "The New Enemy—Communism," "the most evil, monstrous conspiracy against man since time began," with a dramatic description of the Palmer house bomb blast.[93] Yet the BI investigations showed no Communist involvement in that outrage. The inaccuracy did not deter J. Edgar Hoover from providing a laudatory foreword to Whitehead's book. The director had evidently forgotten the details of his first big case as a Red hunter.

6
THE GREAT STRIKES OF 1919
STEEL AND COAL

> Investigation [of the steel strike] showed that many patriotic members of the AMERICAN FEDERATION OF LABOR have been led into this strike by subtle and pernicious activities of pronounced radicals, such as William Z. Foster. . . . The coal strike likewise attracted the attention of the Department and particularly in the coal fields of West Virginia many agitators connected with the UNION OF RUSSIAN WORKERS were discovered . . . leading astray the earnest labor men of that section.
>
> J. Edgar Hoover, memo, March 1920

AFTER THE "RED SUMMER" OF 1919, which had been marked by a wave of bloody race riots, an epidemic of strikes that included the Boston police force, and the spread of revolution in Europe, the Justice Department still had not caught the May and June bombers. Insecurity verging on hysteria gripped the nation's political and business elites and their allies in the press and religious and education establishments. Even the influential and conservative *New York Times* faulted the Justice Department for lack of progress against radicalism. Many legislators demanded an all-out war on dissent, defining it to include everything from anarchism, communism, and IWWism to most labor strikes.[1] In response, Attorney General Palmer intensified the efforts of his department, a move that thrust to the forefront the Radical Division headed by the up-and-coming J. Edgar Hoover.

In the summer of 1917 Sam Scarlett had bragged that the Pittsburgh Wobblies were laying the keel "for the I.W.W. battleship against the steel trust." In the summer of 1919 the steel trust was about to be attacked, but not by the IWW. The government had destroyed that battleship before it could be launched. The Wobs were in federal prison cut off from the movement and burdened with a difficult legal defense. Some might joke that Leavenworth was the "Oxford of the proletariat," but the lessons of the place were hard and the prisoners' anguish and distraction cry out from the BI's transcriptions of their intercepted correspondence.[2]

Harrison George kept his sense of humor and amused himself by learning shorthand and foreign languages, reading Carl Jung, and bantering by mail with female admirers on the outside. But he spent time in the prison hospital with gastritis and grew increasingly irritated with some of his fellow workers.[3] Sam Scarlett implored correspondents to keep the IWW faith, especially the Mesabi iron miners.[4] Jack Law raged in frustration from behind bars after his wife Madge left their Pittsburgh home to go to Chicago with her new "daddy," a "petty thief and second entry man." He heard that she had peddled most of his prized possessions including his Colt .28 ("betsy"), Kodak camera, and walking stick and that she was "boozing or doping."[5]

Most of Pittsburgh's other prewar IWW activists had been neutralized. Fred Merrick was still in the workhouse for his part in the 1916 Westinghouse strike.[6] Joe Mountain, who was finally out of the army, was busy in June at Philadelphia and New York City raising bail money for Law and Grover Perry from Young Democracy and the ACLU's Albert DeSilver. Returning to Pittsburgh only briefly, in July he wrote to Jack Law that he was in Levittsburg, Ohio, in the "Root Beer Biz." In August he was back in Pittsburgh where he took part in a riot against Pittsburgh Street Railway strike breakers. After that he disappeared from the BI files.[7] That left only Jake Margolis, Wendell, and a skeleton crew of nonentities to carry on the local movement. It would not be easy for the BI to blame the IWW for the troubles in the Pittsburgh area steel and coal industries.

The confrontation between steelworkers and management had been brewing for a long time, at least since the Pressed Steel Car strike of 1909, but it was the Great War that caused a surge of orders that ended layoffs and created a scarcity of labor in mills and mines. When the war shut off the flow of immigrant labor from Europe, management imported blacks from the rural South and offered high wages to attract white workers. The manpower shortage grew more severe after the United States entered the war because conscription drained the labor pool at the same time production demands soared.[8]

While the government was eviscerating the IWW, conservative labor gained unprecedented, if still subordinate, power in Washington. AFL president Samuel Gompers gambled that the Wilson Administration would repay loyal unions for their wartime cooperation, and the actions of the National War Labor Board (NWLB) seemed to fulfill his hopes. Headed by ex-president William Howard Taft and union advocate Frank P. Walsh, the board pushed the steel industry to accept minimum wage–maximum hour regulations and to permit organization of the mills. However, after the Armistice the NWLB, its members divided on the merits of collective bargaining, lost the ability to impose its decisions on unwilling employers.[9]

Labor's wartime gains only hardened the resolve of steel company leaders who, while edging toward welfare capitalism, followed the lead of U.S. Steel chairman Judge Elbert H. Gary, who remained adamantly against unionization and aggressively in favor of the open shop. Between 1916 and 1918 the steel companies increased wages to keep pace with rising prices and offered profit sharing and other welfare benefits, mainly to skilled workers.[10] From their Pittsburgh bastion the companies continued long-standing policies designed to aggressively undermine worker solidarity. First, they continued their systematic program to destroy the culture of craft among steelworkers. They did so, according to John Bodnar, by creating a workforce that was "a segmented mass with deep fissures running along occupational, neighborhood, racial, and cultural lines." All the while they wooed away some of labor's potential allies by investing heavily in the social, cultural, and educational life of Pittsburgh so dear to the aspiring working class and the confident middle class.[11] Less visibly, through control of politics and law enforcement in the steel, coke, and coal towns around Pittsburgh, they made it difficult for union organizers to even speak or hold meetings. Secretly, they increased antilabor espionage activity and used their influence in the national government to lobby agencies such as the BI to smear even the AFL's organizing efforts with red. During the steel strike most of the arrests of strikers by the Justice Department would be based on information supplied by the steel companies.[12]

Preparation for the great strike began on August 1, 1919, when thirty AFL union leaders met in Chicago to form the National Committee for Organizing Iron and Steel Workers. In this association of twenty-four separate steel industry unions each was to keep its autonomy, but all were to contribute money and organizers to a massive unionization effort. Little money ever materialized, but workers signed up in droves around Chicago. By the time the strike began on September 22, AFL organizers had brought the steel unions to life. But they found the going very tough in the Pittsburgh area, the source of 70 percent of the nation's steel. The companies, supported by local governments and police, harassed organizers at every turn. Union men could not hold meetings or speak on street corners in Braddock, Rankin, and McKeesport. While Pennsylvania Governor William C. Sproul turned a deaf ear to union protests, Duquesne's mayor was quoted as saying that "Jesus Christ couldn't speak in this town for the A.F.L." Led by former Wobbly William Z. Foster, who was arrested three times, the AFL had to resort to that old Wobbly tactic, the free speech fight.[13]

The strike proved to be most effective outside Pittsburgh, especially at the Gary, Indiana, mill complex, and it drew more support from foreign than from native-born workers. Historians have identified a number of reasons why American-born workers failed to answer the strike call in 1919—fear of losing their jobs, the seductive power of fringe benefits recently given to skilled workers, fear of competition for skilled jobs from immigrants if the strike led to unionization of the mills, and the historical memory of defeat at Homestead twenty-seven years before. These factors undermined the walkout, but credit for eventual collapse also belongs to a brutal campaign of repression by law enforcement coupled to effective propaganda that painted the strike leaders and many of their followers as Bolsheviks. The belief that the strike was led by revolutionaries was a prominent factor in persuading native-born skilled workers not to come out.[14]

During the war a sense of grievance and inclination to organization had built up among the unorganized Southern and Eastern European immigrants who filled most of the low-wage jobs in steel. Wages rose, but seven-day weeks and twelve-hour shifts persisted. Left stranded by the war in mills and mines were many unattached single men who longed to return to their homes and families in Europe. For them and for the immigrants who had chosen to stay in the United States, the harsh conditions that they could tolerate on temporary work seemed intolerable in a lifelong, dead-end job.[15]

At its peak in early October the strike idled 250,000 to 300,000 men, half the workforce, and sharply curtailed production. That is when the Pittsburgh BI entered the fray on the side of big steel.

As government forces prepared to battle the "ultraradicalism" of the steel strikers, they were in disarray. In August 1919 E. Lowry Humes, who was about to leave the army judge advocate's office and return to his old job as U.S. attorney for western Pennsylvania, complained to BI officials in Washington about Edgar Speer, Wendell's main BI contact and head of the Pittsburgh Radical Squad. Humes had heard that "on different occasions" Speer had condemned him "in the strongest terms." To avoid antagonizing the influential Overman Committee counsel, Washington immediately transferred Speer to Philadelphia.[16] On the whole, Speer preferred not to be in Philadelphia, and Pittsburgh SAC Spencer tried his best to get him back. Spencer admitted that Speer was hasty, impulsive, and a grandstander, but he was also "active, fearless and, with the assistance of a good informant, has done excellent work." Spencer even passed on to Washington an appeal from Speer's wife for her husband's return to Pittsburgh, which was denied.[17]

Meanwhile, before the steel strike began, Wendell as Walsh took part in a violent confrontation associated with a strike of Pittsburgh streetcar motormen and conductors. On August 15, after a long dispute with management, the Street and Electric Railway Employee's local rejected an NWLB proposed pay increase of five cents an hour and struck the Pittsburgh Railways System. Company trustees (the firm was in receivership) had promised twelve cents an hour which would have given workers parity with carmen in Detroit, Cleveland, and comparable cities. The dispute turned violent on August 26, when strike breakers brought in from New York and Philadelphia attempted to operate cars in the Golden Triangle. Several trolleys made it past a gauntlet of angry women who hurled bricks at them as they passed Ophelia on Forbes Avenue on their way downtown. Once there a hostile and growing crowd followed them until someone disabled the lead car by disconnecting it from its overhead power line on Fifth Avenue between Smithfield and Wood. While police, who sympathized with the strikers, stood by, the mob swarmed hurling brickbats, pop bottles, and horseshoes. When the mob was done two strike breakers were injured, two streetcars were wrecked, and Fifth Avenue was littered with broken glass. Although the papers did not identify and the police did not arrest any of the leaders of the mob, Wendell reported that he had "assisted" Wobblies Walter Hodge, Ed Pritchold, John and Rudi Blum, and Joe Mountain in disabling and attacking the cars.[18]

Once the steel strike got underway, the Pittsburgh BI played a central part in discrediting strike leader William Z. Foster. Judge Gary had always emphasized the importance of favorable public opinion to the giant U.S. Steel trust, whose sheer power and size made it a subject of public suspicion.[19] Given a fair hearing of the steelworkers' situation, the public would be sympathetic. As industrial relations specialist Whiting Williams had written to Gary in August 1919, objective observers believed that "Pittsburgh is the center of reactionary capitalism . . . and is likely to see the outbreak of the class war which its employers are doing more to bring on than any others except perhaps those in Lawrence, Mass."[20] To counteract such a view it was vital to convince the public that the strike was the work of foreign revolutionaries. Because the venerable Gompers, who had loyally supported the war and the administration, was unassailable, Foster was the key.[21]

Wendell saw at once that Foster was the AFL's ideological Achilles heel and that Margolis could be used to connect him and the AFL to the IWW. Ten months before the strike he filed a three-page report on Foster, who had just come to Pittsburgh. The report traced Foster's Socialist beginnings, membership in the IWW, his part in the free-speech fights in Spokane, and his contributions to Wobbly, Socialist, and IWW periodicals in the Northwest. It noted his attendance at the 1911 syndicalist conference in France and his embrace of the tactic of sabotage. It covered his involvement with the abortive Syndicalist League, his failed attempt to "decentralize" the IWW, and his departure in 1915 to "bore from within" the AFL.[22]

Subsequently Foster had great success as an AFL organizer of the Chicago meat-packers who had remained oppressed more than a decade after Upton Sinclair had dramatized their plight in *The Jungle*.

Wendell's point was that Foster remained after all these years on good terms and in frequent contact with Wobblies. Foster, he said, had attended the long trial of *U.S. v. Haywood et al.* and had chided the boys at the IWW's Chicago headquarters for their troubles with the Justice Department. If they joined the AFL and bored from within, he said, they would have been safe. Wendell added that since coming to Pittsburgh Foster had met often with one of the Chicago defendants, Otto Justh, alias Joe Klinger, who remained an active Wobbly. Justh thought Foster intended to build a movement within the AFL that "will overthrow the Gompers machine and blossom forth into an organization which will carry with it the philosophy of the I.W.W."[23]

Whatever the merits of Wendell's assessment, there can be no doubt that Foster, a product of the Philadelphia slums and a future American Communist leader, was a dedicated revolutionary.[24] In his 1912 forty-seven-page, red-bound pamphlet *Syndicalism,* Foster had attacked the wage system as exploitive and enslaving and the state as the tool of heartless capitalists.[25] It would take a revolution to destroy the state to make way for the future: a myriad of local shop-based organizations that would administer social and economic affairs in decentralized nonpolitical units. Foster wrote that neither Socialist political action nor labor unions could bring the kind of revolution he advocated. The best the IWW had been able to do was only to "disorganize" the western mines. The vast majority of American workers were politically backward and wedded to retrograde notions such as "a fair wage for a fair day's work" and to moral and legal concepts that perpetuated capitalism and statism. Therefore the dedicated syndicalist minority must carry on a daily, dirty, no-holds-barred war against capitalists. It must use sabotage in all its forms and, in the short run, bloodshed was likely. In the name of achieving power, Foster proclaimed, sentiment must be overcome.[26]

By 1919 Foster had supposedly evolved. According to Gompers, "he . . . declared himself to be so thoroughly changed" as to merit a chance to be "helpful to the bona fide labor movement." Foster's actual position was that conservative trade unions such as the AFL were inherently anticapitalist. There was no need, he argued, to make trade unions anticapitalist by converting their members "to a certain point of view or by the adoption of certain preambles; they *are* that by their very makeup and methods." Some might argue that Foster, the intellectual pilgrim at a way station on his path "from Bryan to Stalin" (the title of his autobiography), was at this moment a true convert to trade unionism. But his career bears testimony to his belief that the ends justified the means, and he later wrote that he was in fact "boring from within" the AFL. In 1920, in his own retrospective account of the steel strike he wrote that because corporate leaders used deception and propaganda to further their cause, so must trade union leaders camouflage their true purposes from the public and even from their own members. Defiantly, he wrote that if the "trade unions instinctively throw dust in the eyes of their enemies, they do it for an altogether worthy purpose."[27]

In the months before the steel strike Foster was in contact with Pittsburgh Wobblies. In early 1919 he heard Margolis lecture on the obstacles to the revolution created by capitalist control of education and information, which prevented workers from educating themselves to take over society. Although he met with Margolis several times, they disagreed on many points. Foster dismissed as visionary the One Big Union idea that Margolis favored and called the Wobblies "impossibilists" whose program amounted to little more than propaganda. Yet he believed that a steel strike could be a radicalizing epiphany for steelworkers. According to Edward Johanningsmeier, for Foster the steel strike had become "the perfect expression of the possibility of working class transcendence."[28]

Margolis, who despite the 1916 purge of radicals there always saw the Westinghouse plant complex as the more fruitful field for industrial unionism, thought from the first that the steel strike must fail because the steel trust was too strong. For him the AFL's partnership with capitalism and its nucleus of American-born workers, "religious and bourgeoisminded," was no vehicle for revolution. Foster would not radicalize the AFL; the union would corrupt him into serving its conservative purposes. That said, Margolis supported a strike. He hoped that in attempting to organize steel the AFL would unintentionally stir up the industry's unskilled, class-conscious foreign workers. Therefore Margolis agreed to encourage Pittsburgh anarchists, Wobblies, and UORW members to back the strike. As he wrote in October 1919, he expected the AFL to betray the steelworkers. Then, he hoped, in their disillusion they would turn to the IWW. He was convinced that "borers from within," meaning Foster, would learn that they could not remake society, that only the IWW represented "the revolutionary aspirations of the class conscious portion of America's working class."[29]

Meanwhile, anti-union forces were hard at work seeking to discredit Foster. In April 1919 *Pittsburgh Labor World* had "exposed" his authorship of *Syndicalism*. As the strike date approached, the BI Radical Squad shadowed him and monitored his mail, addressed to and from "J. G. Brown." Special agent K. K. McClure followed him to Washington D.C. and back on September 8–10 when he traveled with his son-in-law and Mother Jones to an AFL gathering. Hearing that he was living in Pittsburgh with "an anarchistic woman, *not his wife*," agents tried to develop a "white slavery" case against him. That was a dead end for Foster had, in fact, married Esther Abramowitz in 1918. So was trying to make a case of the rumor that he had "juggled the books" of the AFL so that it was no longer possible to identify steelworkers by their former craft unions.[30]

On September 24, two days after the strike began, Director Flynn was in Pittsburgh. In a propagandistic press briefing, he explained that his presence was because of a flood of reports that "I.W.W. leaders and other radicals have been trooping to Pittsburgh in hopes of stirring up rioting and possible bloodshed." Flynn acknowledged that the Bureau had not been able to verify the reports, but he had planted the seed and stated the theme of the government's campaign against the strikers. A few days later Senate Labor and Education Committee chairman William S. Kenyon (R-Ia.) asked BI radical division chief Hoover for background on Foster. Hoover replied with a memo stressing the similarities between Foster's IWW past and present AFL activities. He then summoned Wendell, "836," to Washington, where on Saturday, September 27, he "examined him at great length and had him remain over" to talk about Foster.[31]

While Wendell was in Washington, negotiations began to terminate Speer's Philadelphia exile. On October 2, BI Acting Director Burke, at Hoover's recommendation, decided that all would be forgiven if Speer made "a manly admission of his regret" to District Attorney Humes. There is no record of Speer's apology, but after a "satisfactory talk" with the agent Burke gave him a pay raise and returned him to the Radical Squad. Obvious explanations for the action were that the Radical Squad was stretched to the limit by the steel strike and incipient coal strike and that Wendell and Spencer wanted Speer back. Perhaps Hoover wanted to pay back Humes for leaking Wendell's confidential report on William Z. Foster to a *Philadelphia Ledger* reporter. The Pittsburgh BI, the Carnegie Steel Company, and Humes had the only copies. The reporter would not divulge his source, even under threat of subpoena, but he did say that it was not the steel company. Since Hoover trusted the Pittsburgh field office, Humes must be the culprit.[32]

Another distraction was the Sellins case. On August 26 a five-week-old strike against the Allegheny Coal Company's West Natrona mine had turned violent. During a confrontation on a public highway adjacent to a mine entrance, deputized plant guards, most of them private detectives, shot and killed miner Joseph Starzelski and UMWA organizer Fannie Sellins. It appeared that the deputies might have deliberately targeted the unarmed Sellins. She was in the middle of a crowd of women, children, and workers when she was shot twice, one bullet entering her head from the left and behind. Sellins's was no ordinary strike death, if there is such a thing. She was a forty-seven-year-old widow and onetime St. Louis garment worker who has been compared to the illustrious Mother Jones. From 1913 to 1917 she was at the center of a legal dispute over the right of the UMWA to organize miners who had signed individual employment or "yellow dog" contracts with their employers. In 1914 when she persisted in organizing such workers at Wellsburg a federal judge held her in contempt and she became the first woman to serve time in the Marion County, West Virginia, jail. The issue was eventually decided in the U.S. Supreme Court as *Hitchman Coke and Coal Company v. Mitchell* (1917) in favor of the company and was a heavy blow to unionization. Afterward President Wilson extended an olive branch by pardoning Sellins and since January 1917 she had worked for the UMWA in the Alle-Kiski valley. Punishing her murderers became a union cause célèbre.[33]

On September 26, an Allegheny County coroner's jury ruled that Sheriff Haddock's deputies had killed Sellins in justifiable self-defense and commended him for his "prompt and successful protecting [of] property and persons and in selecting deputies." The jury went on to "criticize and deplore the . . . Alien and Foreign agitators who instill Anarchy and Bolshevist Doctrines into the minds of Un-American and uneducated Aliens." After the verdict, protests and petitions from Sellins's allies and family inundated the White House and congressional offices. On September 30, a UMWA delegation called on Hoover and Flynn in Washington hoping to get a statement from the Justice Department "giving the actual facts . . . and showing that the killing of these two persons . . . was nothing but cold-blooded murder, as they termed it." Hoover dismissed the Sellins case as strictly a local matter but recommended that they ask Senator Kenyon to put the matter on the agenda of his committee's steel strike hearings. After the delegation left, Hoover ordered Spencer to prepare a background investigation for the committee. The treatment accorded the UMWA delegation reinforced the assertion by liberal Protestant Interchurch World Movement investigators that no government entity would act on the workers' behalf.[34]

Under Hoover's orders, for the next two weeks special agent Fred Ames gathered facts, interviewed dozens of witnesses, and produced an impressive 150-page case file that included the conflicting stories told by the mostly foreign strikers and by the deputies and company employees. Almost all of the eyewitness strikers and bystanders said that a man dressed in a gray suit directed the action and fired the shots. In the last paragraph of his summary, Ames noted the disappearance of "Deputy Sheriff Pearson, the man in the gray suit, and the one identified as having shot Fannie Sellins. . . . No account is given as to his apprehension, or alibi."[35] Like a paid assassin, Pearson, if that was his name, had disappeared, and in spite of the dedicated efforts of her adherents no one was ever tried for Fannie Sellins's death.[36]

On October 3, William Z. Foster spent an uncomfortable five hours in Washington before the Senate Labor and Education Subcommittee. In testimony larded with tautologies, equivocations, and evasions, he insisted that he was no longer a radical. Asked to state his political views, Foster refused unless, as he wrote in 1920, "the vulture press, which was bound to misrepresent what I said, was removed from the room." Hoover was an interested spectator and afterward went over inconsistencies in Foster's testimony with committee chair Kenyon and gave him copies of Foster's prosyndicalist articles from 1910 in the IWW's *Solidarity*. Hoover left the hearing convinced that Foster was still closely tied to syndicalism and the IWW.[37]

On October 8, Wendell was again in Washington, just back from New York City, where Hoover had sent him to try to connect with UORW and Soviet groups. Wendell had met with Margolis in New York, where the lawyer was angling to replace Harry Weinberger as Emma Goldman's and Alexander Berkman's legal counsel at their deportation hearings. According to Wendell, Margolis seemed "willing and anxious" to testify on the steel strike and was miffed because Foster had not acknowledged their friendship before the committee. Wendell believed that Margolis would tell "all he knows and would not protect Foster."[38] This initially confused Hoover while he considered Margolis as a witness and pondered a report from Cleveland SAC Bliss Morton that two former Pinkerton detectives had claimed that Margolis had been an informant for Pittsburgh SAC Bob Judge. To answer Hoover's query as to whether Margolis was "working two games at the same time," Spencer deferred to Speer. Carefully choosing his words, Speer said the detectives might have seen Margolis at the St. Nicholas Building because he was often there in behalf of some radical client. Invoking his "personal knowledge of confidential informants" during the last two years, Speer stated categorically that "at no time *then* was Margolis an informant of *this office* [italics added]."[39] Still, the lawyer would be a good witness who "would tell the truth" and discredit Foster.[40]

The BI planned to use Margolis to show that Foster was a secret Wobbly. The Pittsburgh Radical Squad had a letter that tied Foster through Margolis to former

IWW general secretary Vincent St. John. "The Saint" had severed his formal connection to the IWW in 1915, but as a principal theoretician and former leader whose tracts were still sold by the IWW, St. John retained influence in Wobbly circles, and he knew almost all the *U.S. v. Haywood et al.* defendants. In the summer of 1919 while he was in Pittsburgh to raise bail and appeal money for Scarlett, Law, and Perry and other Wobs in Leavenworth, St. John had his mail routed to Margolis's office. When St. John met with Foster, whom he had originally recruited for the IWW, in Pittsburgh in July they made a seemingly innocuous agreement. In return for Foster's good offices in raising money for the incarcerated Wobblies, St. John promised to do what he could to get Wobbly support for Foster's steel organizing. After he left Pittsburgh, St. John wrote to Margolis admonishing him to tell Foster to fight for industrial unionism and against AFL leaders who would divide the steelworkers along craft lines. Once Wendell had secured a copy, the BI pounced on the letter as proof that Foster was still at heart a syndicalist Wobbly.[41]

Moving to exploit that evidence, while the Senate subcommittee was visiting the Pittsburgh strike scene on October 10, Spencer put Margolis forward as a witness during a meeting with Senator Thomas Sterling (R-S.Dak.) at the William Penn Hotel. Spencer had come prepared with a photostat of the St. John–Margolis letter and a list of questions to put to Margolis, thoughtfully prepared by Wendell. Two days later Spencer's subordinate, special agent D. E. Tatom, lunched with committee members Kenyon and Kenneth D. McKellar (D-Tenn.), "a personal friend," to lobby for Margolis as a witness.[42]

When on the morning of October 16 Margolis received a summons to Washington to testify on October 20 Margolis sent Jim Marshall to show Foster the telegram. Foster then proposed to meet Margolis at 5 P.M. at Fifth and Smithfield under Kaufmann's department store clock. Fearing to be seen with Foster at such a public place, Margolis did not go to the clock. Instead, that evening the two rendezvoused in the best spy-novel style at a Central Labor Council meeting at the Labor Temple. As Foster sat near the back of the hall, Margolis slipped into the row behind him. BI informant 101 observed as they "exchanged papers" and whispered. After the meeting as they stood in a dark corner of the lobby Margolis did most of the talking and "seemed very nervous and excited." Eventually they left the building still talking.[43] Agents shadowed Margolis to Washington where his appearance before the Senate committee proved to be all Justice Department officials could have hoped for.

Senator Kenyon opened by telling Margolis the committee wanted "to have a pretty frank talk . . . about general conditions up there [in Pittsburgh] relating to the strike, and . . . whether this strike is really to benefit conditions or remedy conditions, or whether it is part of a movement among the radical element to get control of the American Federation of Labor." What followed was a wide-ranging exploration of Margolis's radicalism and its possible connections to Foster and various left-wing ideas and associations. It began with the elicitation of Margolis's background, which showed his Eastern European Jewish roots and his reputation as an antiwar radical. Margolis treated the hearing as a bully pulpit, sprinkling his answers with examples and references that showcased his wide reading. He volunteered to being an atheist and a relativist, citing Darwin and Herbert Spencer to argue that truth, honor, and virtue were mere beliefs whose content and meaning varied with time and place.[44]

The part of his testimony that drew the most press attention was the colloquy in which Margolis tried to establish his total opposition to violence. The committee members set him up by getting him to say that he would not resist a thief who demanded his coat. Then they sprang the trap.

> The CHAIRMAN, And if a man came into your home and should do violence to your family, would you permit him to do it?
>
> Mr. MARGOLIS, I would permit him to rather than fight him.
>
> The CHAIRMAN, And if a man came in and assaulted your wife, would you try to persuade him not to?
>
> Mr. MARGOLIS, I would try to persuade him not to; yes sir.
>
> The CHAIRMAN, But if you could not persuade him, then you would do nothing?
>
> Mr. MARGOLIS, If I could not persuade him, I would not use violence; I would do nothing.[45]

Margolis explained his philosophy as Tolstoyan anarchism or syndicalist anarchism and made clear that he was not a communist-syndicalist. He admitted knowing Emma Goldman and Alexander Berkman but dismissed their anarchism as "old school," not realistic, and not syndicalist.[46] Disingenuously he denied knowing much about the aims of the UORW, because he could not read its literature, which was in Russian. He admitted that he represented twenty UORW members in deportation proceedings and that he had addressed, in English, twenty or thirty delegates in August 1919 at East Youngstown, Ohio, in order to persuade them to back the steel strike. Under questioning, he admitted to knowing that there were or had been UORW chapters near Pittsburgh at McKees Rocks, Duquesne, and Homestead.[47]

Margolis acknowledged that he knew St. John and various Pittsburgh IWW leaders, specifically including L. M. Walsh, and that he believed in the Wobbly program. He reminded the committee that the IWW did not allow lawyers to be members. Then the questioners turned to establishing that the radical and despised IWW was secretly behind the AFL strike and that Foster was the Wobblies' secret ally. Margolis affirmed that St. John had been in Pittsburgh several times during the summer of 1919 and that Foster and St. John were acquainted. But, rather lamely splitting hairs, he insisted that St. John the mine owner, although "not much of a capitalist," could no longer be a member of the IWW.[48]

Margolis explained that he had first met Foster in 1918. He said Foster had come to hear him speak once and that another time they had spent five hours dining together and then walking and arguing. In August Foster had told Margolis that he doubted if the steel strike would ever take place. He feared that the steel executives would avoid the strike and welcome unionization by the conservative AFL, rather than see the men radicalized into joining the IWW. Asked his opinion of Foster, Margolis told the committee that he found the man an enigma. It seemed that the exigencies of the moment dictated Foster's behavior. One could never be sure what he actually believed or what ideas were "in the back of his head."[49]

Margolis had hoped to raise important civil liberties issues, but the senators turned a deaf ear when he brought up repression of AFL organizers by the authorities. Committee members suggested that it was the flu pandemic that caused local authorities to cancel the strikers' meetings. One senator wondered when the right to hold public meetings had become a civil liberty, anyway?[50] When Chairman Kenyon questioned Margolis about the National Civil Liberties Bureau, it was clear that he did not think that civil liberties included the rights of workers to organize. Margolis defined the NCLB as "an organization to defend persons whose civil liberties had been violated."

The CHAIRMAN, Did it relate to the draft, particularly to the draft?

Mr. MARGOLIS, To civil liberties. They were very insistent upon it. They did not want to get mixed up in any of these draft matters, and it was all a question of civil liberties.

The CHAIRMAN, That would cover the whole thing, civil liberties?

Mr. MARGOLIS, Freedom of speech, freedom of the press, and things of that kind— civil liberties.[51]

From the press accounts of Margolis's testimony one would conclude that he had linked the Bolsheviks to the steel strike, which he had not. *Gazette-Times* reporter Robert M. Ginter wrote that Margolis told "a stealthy tale of extreme radicalism, its sway in Pittsburgh, and its insidious influence in the nation-wide steel strike." It linked the IWW, the Bolsheviks, the UORW and the AFL steel strike leaders. A *Gazette-Times* editorial claimed that Margolis showed that local units of a Soviet society were already striving to create "anarchistic communism" in Pittsburgh, Duquesne, Homestead, and Youngstown. "Incendiaries like Margolis and Foster," the writer hyperbolized, "are left free to carry the red torch among ignorant foreign workers who, thoroughly saturated with the traditions of Russian terrorism, run amok in industrial America." Margolis's testimony ought to shame "parlour Socialists who declaim over the rights of free speech and berate county peace officers for stamping out the sparks of anarchy before they develop into a great conflagration."[52]

The *New York Times* was no more restrained, likening Margolis to a Shaysite rebel of 1786, although a Whiskey Rebel of 1794 might have been more apposite.[53] The *Times* writer hoped that his testimony would serve "to concentrate public attention upon the combination of sinister and revolutionary elements that seek to destroy the American Federation of Labor and all trade unions." In typological foreshadowing of the 1950s, he urged that Margolis be disbarred and that all Bolsheviks be ousted from government. Anti-Wobbly crusader and former Seattle mayor Ole Hanson concurred and demanded that Gompers purge the AFL of Reds. Hanson thought that Margolis, a highly educated man with no sympathy for the country to which he belonged, had "proved" the link between the AFL and Goldman, Berkman, the UORW, IWW, and anarchism.[54]

The Senate Labor and Education Committee's official report, issued in early November, linked Foster and Margolis as twin threats to the republic. Foster, the report said, was connected to St. John and "was closely associated with Mr. Margolis, prominent attorney for the I.W.W.s at Pittsburgh, who has been behind this strike with all his power." The report acknowledged that Margolis was not connected to the strike or the AFL but had rallied the UORW and IWW behind it. He was a "highly educated man, a good speaker and the kind of man who is calculated to do immense harm. He cares not for the country which by law protects him." The widespread misrepresentation of what Margolis said had its intended effect. Months later, H. D. Williams, president of Carnegie Steel, cited Margolis's testimony as powerful evidence of Bolshevik influence in the steel strike.[55]

The steel companies' huge inventories, almost bottomless war chest, and the loss of public support doomed the strike to eventual failure and with it, the effort to bring industrywide collective bargaining to big steel. The strike continued losing momentum until it petered out in January 1920.[56] The defeat was a heavy blow and the strikers were left with little but their heroes, such as Father Adelbert Kazinsky, the Slovak labor priest from Braddock; and their adopted martyr, Fannie Sellins, a copy of whose widely circulated postmortem picture Foster kept on his office wall. As David Brody has written, the association of the steel strike with foreign radicalism during the Red Scare made it politically impossible for the federal government to intervene in a mediating role.[57] Instead the Department of Justice intervened on the side of the steel companies.

The shrewdest analysis of the whole affair was probably Foster's. He pointed out that "the crew of detectives and stool pigeons of the steel companies and the Department of Justice, who had dogged my footsteps for a year past [could not] cite a single word said, a thing done, or a line written by me in the entire campaign which would not measure up to the most rigid trade-union standards."[58] Calling Margolis before the Senate committee had been "a deliberate frame-up against the steel strike." The G-men knew that Margolis had acted independently, but they had enlarged upon his activities "in the hope that his radical reputation would lend color to the plot theory which they were laboring so hard to establish." They had even "elevated unheard of I.W.W.s [L. M. Walsh, Ben Anisman, et al.] into powerful strike leaders and surrounded the most ordinary comings and goings with revolutionary mystery." Margolis had never spoken at a steelworkers' union meeting and his efforts in support of the strike had been entirely on his own. The lawyer was made a scapegoat by the steel trust to show that the strike "was a desperate revolutionary *coup,* engineered by men seeking to destroy our civilization."[59]

Notwithstanding Foster's put-down, unheard-of Wobbly Louis M. Walsh, who was also Special Employee Wendell and agent 836, had done his work well. But it would be left to other Radical Squad members to deal with the coal strike.

In October 1917 coal operators, the UMWA, and the Federal Fuel Administration entered into the so-called Washington Agreement that tied wage increases to higher production. For the rest of the war the miners' union had for the most part kept a no-strike pledge, paid a penalty for wildcat walkouts, and accepted a wage freeze. After the Armistice, operators raised coal prices but wages did not keep pace. In 1919 consumer prices soared while coal companies were said to be squirreling away huge profits, as much as 2,000 percent of 1917 capital stock. Union men were convinced that the operators had set aside the windfall for a war chest to promote the open shop and break the UMWA.[60]

The men nursed a long list of local grievances including irregular work schedules, delayed paydays, dangerous conditions, and what seemed to be management's contempt and insensitivity toward them. Within the UMWA leadership, dissident factions and new President John L. Lewis played political hardball. The dissidents challenged Lewis's shaky control by spurring the rank and file to put forward unrealistic wage and hour demands. They calculated that Lewis's inability to make good on the union's demands would discredit his leadership. Lewis countered by ordering a strike for what he knew to be unattainable goals. Because of the Washington agreement, technically the miners would be striking against the federal government, which would have to oppose the walkout. Let the onus be on the government for breaking the strike.[61]

Meeting in convention in Cleveland in August, UMWA delegates authorized a strike against the nation's unionized coal mines on November 1, 1919. If most of the 425,000 miners left the pits, it would be the largest strike yet, transportation and industrial production must eventually grind to a halt, and homes and businesses throughout the land would feel a big chill in the coming winter. The convention also endorsed the so-called Plumb Plan, which would have nationalized the nation's railroads. To pro-business conservatives the Plumb Plan was the first step to a Bolshevik takeover of the United States.[62]

The operators made avoiding a strike difficult by refusing to negotiate and insisting on adherence to the wartime contract until April 1920. William B. Wilson, a fiercely antiradical former miner, did his best to avert a strike, but his position as the first secretary of the recently established Labor Department was weak and the Washington Agreement put the federal government in the middle between the operators and the miners. The hard line against the UMWA taken by Joseph P. Tumulty, acting for the incapacitated Woodrow Wilson, and his ally Attorney General Palmer insured that the UMWA-operator dispute would be a labor-government battle.[63]

By autumn 1919 a large faction of the miners favored a strike and the rhetoric grew heated. In an open letter to Woodrow Wilson from Charleston, West Virginia, UMWA official Frank Keeney expressed their passion. Let "those who envy the miner his lot, and who rest under the delusion that the miner is over-paid . . . come on and go down in the bowles [sic] of the earth where so many of us die each year. . . . As God reigns we will not see our employers revel in wealth, even though they blind the public. . . and [we will] not face the dreadful ordeal of winter in the mines without a just compensation."[64]

To counteract the miners' bid for public sympathy, the operators followed the example of the steel corporations by propagandizing that the strike was the prelude to revolution. Operator-inspired antilabor articles and editorials fanned public hysteria. An impressionable *New York Tribune* writer came back from West Virginia and interviews with "some of the greatest coal operators in America . . . almost quaking as they spoke." They told him that "thousands of . . . [miners] red-soaked in the doctrines of Bolshevism, clamor for a strike as a means of syndicalizing the coal mines without the aid or consent of the government, and even . . . [for] starting a general red revolution in America."[65]

The coal strike prompted the extension of the Pittsburgh BI field office jurisdiction into the northern West Virginia coal fields. As John C. Hennen points out, in order to realize their vision of the nation as an economic world power, coal, steel, railroad, and timber corporate interests and their political allies used World War I to promote the ideology of industrial Americanization. This was not simply an Anglo-conformist effort to assimilate immigrants, but a way to "implant their principles into the consciousness of a culture and thereby transform ideas into commonly held values that are immune to debate in the political arena." They wanted citizens to believe that loyalty to state and nation were "interchangeable with loyalty to one's employer, teacher, or leader."[66] The intended effect was to frame the field of political thought to exclude all socialisms.

Democratic Governor John J. Cornwell was an enthusiastic agent of industrial Americanization in West Virginia. During the war he was an advocate for the state's compulsory work law, which required able-bodied males except students between sixteen and sixty to work at least thirty-six hours a week. After the war Cornwell tirelessly invoked the specter of Red revolution. In March 1919 he pushed through the legislature the controversial Constabulary Act, which established a state police force. He argued that it would benefit workers by eliminating the notorious mine guard and detective system, but its purpose, it was understood, was to protect corporate property and interests from labor "radicals." In the same session the legislature passed a "Red Flag" law to punish sedition. The May and June bomb attempts on public officials and his receipt of the mysteriously marked McCurdy map from the Pittsburgh police (see chapter 5) reinforced Cornwell's contention that the IWW and Bolsheviks threatened a revolution in the Mountain State. Saying that the Justice Department was fully informed, the governor, for security reasons, was vague on particulars of the threat. He would later claim that his men had intercepted and seized two truckloads of illegal arms from New York intended for revolutionary miners in the Mountain State. Cornwell did not make public the incident until the state's old capitol building burned in January 1921. Then he explained that the confiscated weapons stored secretly in the attic produced "the explosion of the thousands of rounds of ammunition [that] caused much wonderment among the thousands who watched."[67]

Union officers in West Virginia's northern panhandle publicly branded Corn-well's accusations as ill-disguised attempts to smear labor's legitimate aspirations. They charged that the governor's purpose was to fix "a cloud of suspicion upon in-nocent men, enable the guilty to profit, and frighten the public, prejudicing the people against the legitimate activity for the betterment of the working and living conditions of the wage earners of our state." Cornwell replied that he had not meant that West Virginia miners and industrial workers were Bolsheviks, only that IWWs and Bolsheviks were active among them. But he told a businessman that he was "very sincerely of the opinion that the radical leaders who have gotten control of many labor organizations are going to precipitate strikes and industri-al disputes which will savor of local revolutions and will take on more or less a po-litical flavor." A month before the strike was to begin, Cornwell contacted right-wing General Leonard Wood about sending federal troops to West Virginia to stop the revolution.[68]

Like many of his kind in West Virginia, Cornwell, a former lawyer and small businessman from a rural community, felt both blessed and cursed. He was a gate-keeper who owed what power he had to the beneficence of the corporations.[69] Yet those same interests—steel, coal, timber, and railroads—brought cheap foreign labor to the hills, provoking in men like Cornwell deep and irrational fears. The outsiders became scapegoats for the changes wrought by industrialization. Their exotic nationalities, religions, and customs seemed to threaten Anglo-Saxon, male, Protestant, middle-class control.

Given his nativist, anti-union mind-set, Cornwell prepared for the coal strike as though the barbarians were at the gate. Believing that his opposition to the union-ization of Guyan Valley coal fields might lead to his assassination, he dictated a statement to be read by his family and friends in case of his death.[70] He was re-signed to the fact that if organized labor leaders wanted "to remove me, they will find a way to do it. . . . Unless people who believe in law and order and in the right of all as against the privileges of the classes, assert themselves not only our Gov-ernment but our civilization is doomed." He melodramatically volunteered to sac-rifice his life to "help stay the tide of Bolshevism and Anarchy, with which the country is threatened."[71]

On the eve of the strike Cornwell issued an inflammatory letter urging the state's sheriffs and mayors to form local committees of "Public Aid and Safety." The strike would likely bring the state to a halt, then "disorders may follow on a small or possibly, in some places, on a large scale." Possibly the strike would be used "by the criminal and radical element to ply their nefarious trades and to bring about a general social and industrial revolution." Officials should not underestimate how many there are, native and foreign, "who will rejoice at an opportunity to plunge the country into Anarchy."[72]

Cornwell postulated that large quantities of arms and ammunition were stockpiled by revolutionaries in the state and painted a picture of disorder with "hundreds of thousands of men out of employment . . . and the distribution of food stopped, men will not stay in one place and starve while houses and barns are filled only a few miles away. Then it may be necessary to call the people from the peaceful communities to aid in preserving order in the industrial sections."[73]

At least one UMWA official shared the gatekeepers' alarm about the radical advance. In August, at the same time that the BI was secretly tapping John L. Lewis's telephone and investigating the UMWA headquarters operation in Indianapolis, H. E. Peters, UMWA District 17, Subdistrict 4 president, contacted the Justice Department to urge the arrest of foreign miners, allegedly Wobblies, who refused to obey UMWA officials. Peters approached BI special agent John B. Wilson in Wheeling, who advised him to ask state lawmen to use West Virginia's new anti-syndicalist or "Red flag" law against the dissidents. Peters's action took place in the context of friction between American-born and immigrant miners in northern West Virginia, where the UMWA had only recently gained a foothold and where many mines remained nonunion. Some UMWA officials had complained that many of the foreign miners would not accept union discipline. They characterized the immigrants as overly emotional, caught up in local issues, quick to strike, and generally impatient. It is unclear if Peters really thought the foreign miners were radicals or whether, following the mine operators' example, he hoped to use the government to chasten foreign dissidents. What is clear is that by agreeing to keep the BI informed about radical activities in the mines Peters became "hooked."[74]

In 1918 after twelve ships carrying West Virginia coal arrived in South American ports with their cargo on fire Pittsburgh ONI looked into the possibility that incendiary devices had been planted at the mines.[75] Otherwise the intelligence agencies left spying on coal mines with their chronic labor shortages and high turnover rates to the operators' secret service or private detectives. The coal strike would change all that and, given the governor's unbalanced reading of the situation, it was probably better for everyone. If the G-men did not bring evenhanded justice, at least they brought a modicum of professionalism and restraint.

A June 1919 Pennsylvania State Police report from Greensburg had piqued BI interest. It alleged the spread of IWW-Bolshevik-UORW activity in the Monongahela Valley and traced UORW organizers as they advanced from Homestead, site of the great 1892 strike, up the river through Donora, Monessen, Charleroi, Allenport, VanVoorhis, Bentleyville, and Ellsworth. Supposedly the UORW had reached coal camps near Morgantown and Fairmont, West Virginia.[76] These northern West Virginia mines were in many ways connected to Pittsburgh and therefore of interest to the Radical Squad. Clustered near the headwaters of the Monongahela, they tapped the rich Pittsburgh and Sewickley coal seam and were partly owned by western Pennsylvania interests.

On August 14, the *Morgantown Post* reported "on good authority" that IWW organizers were establishing northern West Virginia branches. They held meetings on Sunday, when the miners could attend, to "address them on the doctrine of I.W.W. or the Bolshevists." The paper claimed that the organizers delivered two different messages, first in English and then "in Russian or Slavic so that the large elements to whom radical doctrines most strongly appeal may get the full meaning of the propaganda, and at the same time, Americans may be left in the dark as to its real impact." Indicating that the writer knew that the organizers were actually with the UMWA, he noted that even though UMWA rejected IWWism, "the great mass of the foreign population does not understand the orderly progress toward a better economic state, and grasps at the chemical [chimerical?] prospects held out by radicals who desire to see the whole system of government overthrown."[77]

Soon after the *Post* article, Henry J. Lenon, past and future Pittsburgh Radical Squad special agent, who was then working for American Steel and Wire in Cleveland, visited the area. Lenon reported to Spencer in Pittsburgh that "outside agitators" were misleading honest, hardworking citizen-miners. His outside agitators were UMWA organizers, and seeing they wore sidearms, he proposed a check of their permits. If they were "I.W.W.s in disguise," with forged permits, they could be arrested. In any case, he thought "a good man could frame this bunch of agitators and settle this trouble for the best of all concerned in reasonable time."[78]

The coal strike began on November 1, and when it did, Pittsburgh BI was ready. On October 31 Speer had assembled Radical Squad members at the St. Nicholas Building and assigned eight agents to potential trouble spots in the coal fields of southwestern and west-central Pennsylvania.[79] Discreetly, each agent was to make himself known to local mayors, police chiefs, and state police officers. He was to suppress radical literature and gather information on every "agitator" in his jurisdiction, including citizenship, place of birth, and political affiliations. Speer had six undercover informants lined up to work with the special agents. All belonged to the UMWA and four were fluent in foreign languages. Each special agent was to report to the Pittsburgh office by telephone daily late in the afternoon.[80]

For the first few days things were quiet in western Pennsylvania, except at

Monessen where Fred Ames and his undercover man Michael I. Yankovich discovered a UORW branch. Elsewhere state and local officials, using the usual methods, seemed to have the situation under control. Wendell remained in Pittsburgh and, judging from "LEO" typed above the name of the agent on many field reports, spent his late afternoons receiving and transcribing them.[81]

In the northern West Virginia coal country things were anything but quiet. While frightened operators there were calling for the U.S. cavalry to crush the strikers, one "expert" predicted that the strike would kill more people than World War I.[82] Attorney General Palmer testified in 1920 that he did not have the "slightest fear that any revolutionary movement can succeed in this country, even to the extent of seriously menacing our institutions." The worst that radical agitation could do would be to upset "peace and good order in the country and serve to obstruct progress and delay settlement of the many serious problems." But in the same testimony he called the coal strike the most important of 1919, because it involved nearly half a million miners and "battered at the very foundations of the safety of the American democracy. It threatened not only universal hardship cruel to our own country and dangerous to the world, but it seemed to indicate defiance of law and public welfare on the part of American labor."[83]

At the time Palmer certainly took the coal strike very seriously. As soon as it began he secured a temporary federal injunction against it, which became permanent on November 8. Based on the technical point that the United States had not ratified the Treaty of Versailles, the injunction described the walkout as a violation of "wartime" emergency laws. When the union leaders, as expected, defied the injunction, the Justice Department prepared to step in.[84]

Northern West Virginia would later be attached to the jurisdiction of the Pittsburgh BI, but at first enforcement fell to the U.S. attorney for northern West Virginia, Stuart W. Walker, and BI special agent Ernest W. Lambeth, who were headquartered east of the mountains in Martinsburg. Accompanied by a clerk, on November 3 they set up operations in Fairmont, "the very center of this great coal situation." Located eighty-five miles south of Pittsburgh where the West Fork and Tygart Valley Rivers join to form the Monongahela, the town was the birthplace of the industry giant Consolidated Coal and the headquarters of the Northern West Virginia Coal Operators' Association (NWVCOA). Along with Governor Cornwell, it was the NWVCOA, representing owners in a thirteen-county area that annually produced twenty million tons of coal and employed more than twenty thousand men, that had clamored for federal intervention.[85]

When they arrived, Walker and Lambeth were handed thick intelligence files on UMWA and radical activities containing what an operators' spokesman described as "information collated by persons connected with the Northern West Virginia Coal Operators Association." The association had an elaborate "secret service," with dozens of informers and infiltrators in the region's mines. The NWVCOA spies described the miners as angry and dissatisfied. There was much "kicking" about wages and working conditions, along with militant, perhaps wishful, talk promising union solidarity and worker victory in the ordeal to come. Coal camp orators castigated capitalists and government officials, railed against the "S-bs" in Washington, and spoke darkly of destroying the capitalists and getting their money. Some miners were even heard to say that "the *Bolsheviki* were alright."[86]

The intelligence also showed that miners' collective anger provided a very brittle unity that the sharp ethnic divisions within their ranks could easily shatter. As much by necessity as design the NWVCOA had followed the Pittsburgh steel magnates in creating a bewilderingly multiethnic workforce. On the job they routinely favored native-born workers over foreigners in hiring, firing, job assignments, and coal weighing. They nurtured resentments by discriminating among the various foreign groups, for example, by openly preferring northern Italian laborers over other nationalities. These policies left Austrian (south Slavic), Russian, and Hungarian miners particularly bitter and resentful.[87]

NWVCOA spies were inclined to see radical Wobblies and Bolsheviki behind every tree, but it was true that radical and pro-Bolshevik literature in several languages circulated at some camps. It turned up on porches, in mailboxes, at the mine portal, or even the coal face. Russians, who made up less than 10 percent of the region's immigrant miners, made an enticing target for discipline by example to break the coal strike. There were three Italians and two Austria-Hungarians in the pits for every Russian. The government could jail all of the Russians without crippling the workforce.[88]

There was no doubt that, as a group, the Russian miners were frustrated and restive. Like other immigrant manual laborers of the period they were mostly single men without families in America who intended to stay here only long enough to accumulate enough wealth to improve their lot in the old country. The war had stranded these sojourners. After it ended, thousands had left the Pittsburgh mill district for Italy and other nations. However, the Russians could not go home because the United States did not recognize the Bolshevik regime.[89]

In October, Spencer in Pittsburgh spent much of a day with informers discussing unrest among Russian immigrants. He learned that many believed that the corporations "have so influenced the Government that the Russians are being kept here for the purposes of preventing a labor shortage." Spencer dismissed that as propaganda. When "the ignorant foreigners have . . . [it] spread among them by agitators speaking in their own tongue, it has the same effect . . . as if it were a fact, and . . . [the foreigner] feels he has a real grievance against the Government." The informants added that the high cost of living in America and the denial of passports home were very sensitive points. That American workers had not supported them in the recent steel strike added to the appeal of radicalism and fueled resentment of the AFL among the Russians. Spencer downplayed the importance of the Russians' grievances by invoking a stereotype. He had it on the authority of an International Harvester official that the Russian workman was quiet and peaceable "until he is stirred up by a radical agitator."[90]

In the northern West Virginia mines the Russians were not quiet and peaceable. Homesick Russian men began to act out their frustrations and resentments toward operators and government a month before the big coal strike began. At the end of September 1919, Russians walked off the job at a Farmington mine to protest the hiring of an American to replace a Russian machine operator.[91] They then produced a list of demands that included the dismissal of a weighman, extra pay for overtime, and the replacement of mine committeemen. They were not only angry at management, but also at local UMWA officers, and accused one union man, an African American, of spying for the company.[92]

The protest soon spread to Russians at other mines in the area and then began to affect other nationalities. At one mine, unrest among the Russians led the sheriff and company men to search a boarding house where they turned up copies of the UORW's *Bread and Freedom* and a stash of "Bolsheviki" literature. Although the searchers could not read the Russian language material, the mine superintendent later swore that he recognized the word *Bolsheviki* in the otherwise indecipherable Cyrillic literature. The meeting room of this UORW peoples' house, for that is what they had stumbled into, featured a large table upon which was a red-covered book, pamphlets, pen, ink, and writing paper. Benches lined the walls, which were decorated with lithographs of Lenin, Trotsky, Liebknecht, Emma Goldman, and Debs. A closet contained red and black crepe paper, presumably for use at initiation ceremonies. After that discovery, rumor and alarm spread among coal company officials. Spies reported that Russian miners in one part of the county were meeting secretly in the woods to read aloud out of a red book and, in another, five Russians were plotting together in a room festooned with red and black flags.[93]

In spite of such reports, early in the strike U.S. Attorney Walker publicly downplayed the role of radicalism. He told the papers that it was the high cost of living, not working conditions or unionization, that fueled the unrest. Walker knew that the UORW was not responsible for the strike. As he wrote to Palmer on November 4, the whole difficulty was caused by the actions of twelve to fifteen UMWA "field agitators . . . of good dress and appearance . . . from remote points, like New York, Chicago, and other cities, who are stopping at the best hotels, and whose duties seem to be to go out and each morning go over their respective routes over the interurban lines visiting the various mines keeping the men in line with the strike." However, because such activity violated no law, one could not arrest the union representatives. Neither could it deport the entire foreign labor force. In 1919 alone more than 330,000 immigrants returned to Europe of their own accord.[94] Deporting troublemakers and radical leaders among the mostly Southern and Eastern European coal strikers seemed the best course to follow.

Away from the public eye, Walker, special agent Lambeth, local lawmen, and coal operators nervously prepared to play the radical card. After conferring privately with the NWVCOA officials, and secretly with UMWA official Peters, Walker ordered raids on suspected radical nests in coal camps of three counties: Marion, near Fairmont, Monongalia at Star City, and Taylor at Wendel. Strikers at these places, he declared, "are composed of Bolshevists and anarchists of the worst type, and pretty generally unnaturalized citizens [sic]."[95] The main raids, in Marion County, would target five of a total of fifty-five deep mines "where most of the agitation was taking place, and where local lodges of the I.W.W. and Federation [of Unions] of Russian Workers existed."[96] All the mines had large, unionized, and predominantly immigrant workforces. The largest, employing five or six hundred, also boasted the county's most influential UMWA local.[97]

State and county officials prodded Walker to implement the plan by telling him that many native-born and alien miners stayed on strike only out of fear that they would be killed by the foreigners. His resolve was further strengthened by the NWVCOA, whose leaders he found "imbued with the seriousness of the situation, and absolutely loyal, ready, and willing to make any sacrifice in the interest of the Government." But, they told him, arrests would not be enough unless they were followed by deportations, which "would have a most wholesome effect, if they can be started at once." Walker also passed on the opinion of NWVCOA officials that under Chief Inspector Sibray the Pittsburgh Bureau of Immigration was "too conservative in its investigations and hearings" and would likely slow the deportation process. Better, Walker believed, to have some other immigration inspector take jurisdiction.[98]

Meanwhile, Lambeth, who was to lead the raids, surrendered any vestige of an objective view of the situation by withdrawing what few federal undercover men were in the mines. Now he would rely on telephone briefings from mine managers and written reports from NWVCOA undercover men. Although the strikers showed no sign of violence, he turned the Marion County courthouse in Fairmont into a command center. A local newspaper gushed later that it had been the rendezvous for "an almost unbelievable number of plain clothes scouts." In the sheriff's office next door deputies stockpiled long guns and ammunition and each deputy "put on a new cartridge belt and went around awed by what he had to do."[99] Justice Department political aims and the operators' labor policy were about to combine to bring ruin to the hapless Russian minority in northern West Virginia.

7

THE PALMER RAIDS I
THE UNION OF RUSSIAN WORKERS, 1919

> The Government of the United States had started relentlessly to make war on the horde of "Reds" within its borders whose purpose is to undermine the institutions of America and achieve the government's overthrow by revolutionary means.
>
> *Pittsburgh Press,* November 8, 1919

AT 3:30 A.M. IN THE PRE-DAWN MURK of Sunday, December 21, 1919, the ferry *Immigrant* churned the icy waters of New York harbor carrying 246 men and three women from Ellis Island to the old 5,000-ton troop transport U.S.S. *Buford* anchored off Fort Wadsworth. She would take them to Finland from whence they would travel overland to Soviet Russia. As if to underscore the importance of the event, a navy tug carrying two dozen armed BI men dogged the ferry's wake. Two hundred soldiers waited aboard the *Buford* to guard the prisoners. J. Edgar Hoover visited the ship in person at 4:00 A.M. to see the deportees on their way. At dawn the "Soviet ark" sailed.[1] Although only nine of the deportees were listed as being from Pittsburgh, in fact more than one-third (87) came from the industrial heartland within a 150-mile radius of the Steel City: Youngstown-Akron-Cleveland, Ohio (37); Buffalo, New York (9); Greensburg, Pennsylvania (14); and Fairmont, West Virginia (18).[2] Most of those deported were members of the Union of Russian Workers.

Compared to the widely known and despised IWW, the UORW was mysterious and unknown. Organized in New York City in 1907 by anticzarist Russian émigrés, it had no more than four to seven thousand members nationwide. Its troubles with federal investigators stemmed from revolutionary statements in its official publications. Its *Little Red Book* said oppression of the toilers, peasants, and workers would end only when they rose in class revolution against the rich. Its statement of purpose called upon members to join "the struggle with capitalism and government"; to support the liberation movement in Russia; and

145

to "support revolutionary elements of workers in America."[3] Although it was an anarchist organization, in 1917 the UORW members supported the Russian Bolsheviks and opposed the United States nonrecognition of the Soviets and military intervention in Russia. Based on limited information, government investigators believed that the UORW provided a link between the Russian Bolsheviks and the IWW and constituted a potential conduit to carry the Communist revolution to the United States.

However radical the political views of UORW leaders, few ordinary members took them seriously. Organization headquarters, the People's House at 133 E. 15th Street in Manhattan, was a source of revolutionary literature, but elsewhere the organization was a loose association of "people's houses" scattered across the industrial states. More than revolutionary centers, these were social gathering places for Russian immigrant male laborers excluded from American life by barriers of language, culture, prejudice, and indifference and cut off from family and friends in Russia by war and revolution. The BI in Pittsburgh, lacking Russian-speaking agents or informants, had only limited, secondhand information about the UORW. In May and June 1917 an agent known as P-45, the U.S. attorney's office, and the BI's John R. Dillon had investigated the "Russian Workmen's Association" in Pittsburgh as a conduit for anarchists returning via Vancouver, British Columbia, Japanese merchant ships, and the Siberian Railroad to the motherland. The government's interest was to see if the repatriates would hurt the Allied cause by supporting Russian withdrawal from the war. In passing the reports noted the existence of two UORW chapters in Pittsburgh and others in Duquesne, McKees Rocks, and Homestead with a total of almost three hundred members. The Russian consul told Dillon that anarchists from the group dominated the local committee that administered the Provisional Government's fund to repatriate Russian political refugees. He described the Steel City as "the center for Russian anarchists in this country" and said that more than 150 had already left the city for Russia. Now funds had run out and thirty to forty anarchists were still waiting to go home, presumably to destabilize the regime and force Russia into a separate peace with the Central Powers. The consul urged the Justice Department to suppress two troublemaking Russian-language papers: New York's *Voice of Labor* and Detroit's *Russian Voice*.[4]

In July 1917 BI agents intercepted a letter from W. Losov at IWW's Chicago headquarters inviting the Pittsburgh UORW to send representatives to a gathering of the whole "Russian Revolutionary Colony." The letter buttressed BI speculation that the mysterious UORW was in fact an IWW foreign-language operation.

The letter charged that from the beginning of the Russian Revolution the American government had persecuted Russian immigrants "with the utmost energy." It had interned Russian revolutionaries, "for the most insignificant and trifling reasons." It claimed that Russian Provisional Government representatives were working with the American government for the conscription of the Russian citizens in this country. This information provided good reason for the BI to investigate the UORW, but Pittsburgh had no Russian-speaking agent or informant to infiltrate the group. Wendell had not been of much use in the probe of the Russians. For example, his report on a UORW drama given at Erie consisted of saying "it was clearly shown to me as an anarchist playlet said to depict the oppression under the old regime (Act I) and the flowering of the new Soviet state (Act II)."[5]

The UORW was not simply, as its defenders claimed, a harmless educational association. It was, at least rhetorically, revolutionary. Two key statements in its printed one-page "Fundamental Principles of the Federation" exposed its members to deportation under the 1918 Alien Act. The first said that the class struggle would end only when the "laboring masses, organized as a class . . . establish *by force a social revolution of the whole world of riches*" (italics added). The second predicted that the working class would take power after "having accomplished such a revolution and at the same time having *destroyed all government institutions and power*" (italics added).[6] The UORW was philosophically anarchist, not Communist or Bolshevik, but it was made up of Russians and it certainly *sounded* Bolshevik to nervous Americans. From the Justice Department's perspective, it seemed possible to cripple or destroy the UORW but not, at least for the moment, the true Bolshevik spawn, the Communists.

The UORW had an organizational structure, its people's houses, that was easy to attack. Compared to the groups first proposed as targets by Hoover, the Buffalo, New York, Spanish *El Ariete* and the Paterson, New Jersey, Italian *l'Era Nuova*, which had an estimated total of thirty-six members, the destruction of the UORW with a nationwide membership of four to seven thousand would appear to be a formidable blow against radicalism. In the deportation campaign A. Mitchell Palmer saw a chance to advance his bid for the 1920 presidential nomination.[7]

In the early summer of 1919 the BI had contemplated raids on a variety of New York City radical centers. However, in June the New York state assembly's antiradical Lusk Committee, sponsored by the Union League and led by perfervid Red hunter Archibald Stevenson, made numerous arrests and seized a mass of documents in raids on IWW headquarters, the office of Soviet representative Ludwig C. A. K. Martens, and the left-wing socialist Rand School.[8] Thus preempted,

Hoover and Burke shifted their focus to the UORW and to the secretaries of locals and delegates to the organization's January 1919 convention, "when certain particularly obnoxious resolutions were passed." They would be the targets of a "simultaneous raid throughout the country."[9]

The Department of Labor's Bureau of Immigration, which had requested $500,000 to carry out selective deportations to cripple the Left, lacked the manpower for large-scale investigations. So the Justice Department, which claimed the expertise and manpower to do the job, was to undertake the investigations. The two departments agreed that based on warrants issued and special funds provided by the Immigration Bureau, the BI would investigate, capture, and conduct the preliminary questioning of alien radicals. Then immigration officials would complete the deportation proceedings.[10]

Expelling troublemakers, or cleaning house, was hardly a new policy. While the nation was at war from April 1917 to November 1918, 4,215 aliens had been ordered out of the country. From the Armistice until June 30, 1919, another 2,544, or an average of 318 per month, were deported. Six hundred and sixty-one more were added from July to September. However, as of October 23, 1919, 4,067 of nearly 7,500 official deportees were still in the United States. During the war Secretary Wilson had postponed deportations rather than expose deportees to U-boat torpedoes. Since the Armistice, a backlog of cases had built up and many individuals could not be sent home because there had been no sailings to their country of origin.[11] Bolshevik Russia, with which the United States had no diplomatic relations, was at the top of the list of closed nations. What was new about the proposed UORW deportations was the focus on a single organization and a single nationality and the arrangement for mass transportation on a government ship.

During the war Secretary of Labor Wilson, while supporting the deportation of aliens who advocated the overthrow of the government by force and violence, had refused to expel them for IWW membership and had defended their right to counsel and bail. However, in the fall of 1919 anti-immigrant forces in the press and Congress launched a heavy attack on Wilson's department for "coddling reds" that culminated in a House resolution requiring Wilson to explain his policy. The concurrent resignation of his principal liberal advisor on immigration matters, Frederic C. Howe, added to the storms swirling around the Labor Department caused by the steel and coal strikes and placed Wilson on the defensive. That at least partially explains why he delegated his authority over deportation of alien radicals to Solicitor John W. Abercrombie. The solicitor, although attached to the Department of Labor, had been appointed by the attorney general. For whatever reasons Abercrombie, an Alabama politician and educator, deferred to Palmer and Hoover.[12] So did other key Labor Department officials: Bureau of Immigration chief legal counsel A. W. Parker and Commissioner General of Immigration Anthony Caminetti, the first Italian American elected to Congress, who had been fighting alien radicalism for several years.[13]

The operation to deport alien radicals began in the Pittsburgh mill district in August 1919 when, at the urgent request of Washington, Spencer spent much of a week working up a list of radicals in his jurisdiction who could be deported. The list had only sixteen names, twelve of them Russian, and most already awaiting final deportation orders.[14] Spencer blamed the meager harvest in part on Immigration Inspector Sibray's insistence on constitutional due process in deportation cases. Many of those currently under warrants were free on bail, which the Bureau of Immigration set too low at $500 or $1,000, allowing them to continue their radical activities and to be hailed as "heroes among their associates." Bail in deportation cases should be $10,000.[15]

Spencer also complained that giving radicals access to legal advice before they were questioned complicated the BI's task, because the aliens "seem to have been carefully advised not to make any statements that would make it appear that they have violated any present immigration laws." In May the Immigration Commissioner's office had refused to issue deportation warrants against five Pittsburgh UORW members owing to insufficient evidence "that any of them are active propagandists or have become a menace to the community." In light of that decision, Spencer saw the need for taking into consideration "an alien's associations and general activities . . . even if his words cannot be obtained as evidence of his violation of the present immigration laws."[16] Spencer's proposal to use organizational membership and guilt by association to justify deportation was also, indirectly, a complaint against Jacob Margolis, the main fount of legal advice to radical aliens.

On August 12 Spencer wrote in a confidential memo for Hoover that the IWW and the UORW were "going strong" and that "the deportation of some of the most active members would have a most wholesome effect in this district." However, by late October when BI headquarters ordered Spencer to compile a list of UORW agitators, both he and Speer admitted there were difficulties. Pittsburgh UORW activities since spring had been limited to quiet Sunday gatherings without speakers of about a dozen men at Schenley Park, Highland Park, or Heinz Grove. Erstwhile UORW chapters at Bentleyville and Ellsworth no longer existed.[17] If there was to be a UORW roundup it would have to take place well outside the city.

Then on November 7, during the first week of the coal strike, the Pittsburgh BI received from Washington headquarters a copy of a memo for "J.P.T." from "O.C."[18] The addressee was of course Joseph P. Tumulty, President Wilson's secretary and one of the triumvirate with Colonel Edward M. House and Mrs. Edith Wilson who carried on the presidency while Wilson lay sequestered in the White House recovering from a stroke. The initials of the memo's author are those of Tumulty's close friend Otto Carmichael who was personal secretary to U.S. Steel founder Daniel Gray Reid.[19] Tumulty had lobbied retiring Attorney General Gregory to support Palmer as his successor and like Palmer he held strong antiradical beliefs. One imagines that Tumulty forwarded the O.C. memo to his friend Palmer, who passed it on to Burke, who sent it to Spencer.[20]

The memo promotes a plan, supposedly from U.S. Attorney Humes, to end the coal strike. One cannot know the details of the bureaucratic gamesmanship involving Spencer and Humes and Pittsburgh business interests. It seems likely that federal officials were reacting to pressure from steel and coal company officials to arrest foreign strike militants. There is more than a hint of this in O.C.'s description of Humes as "a very vigorous but prudent man" in possession of enough evidence to issue warrants against two hundred "of the trouble-makers in the Pittsburgh district [who] are aliens under observation." Echoing Spencer's August statement, O.C. asserts that "if these men were removed from their special localities and their un-American agitation [was] stopped it would have a wholesome and immediate effect in the local strike efforts." In an obvious end run around Immigration Inspector Sibray, the memo recommends picking up the aliens "quietly a few at time" and taking them to "New York where the necessary official inquiries will be made." The arrests should be handled without "publicly bagging the offenders and causing gleeful expressions from coal mine owners."[21] To reassure Democratic politicians about the possible effect on labor's support and to rebut members of Wilson's cabinet who opposed the deportation policy,[22] O.C. dismissed the alien agitators as "not especially prominent labor folks" whose appeal to foreign miners "is specially vicious, harmful, and un-national." The arrests would "have a wholesome effect on many agitators as well as workers" and make "the mine workers understand that the government will use more strength than statements and declarations."[23]

The memo reached Spencer with orders to get the names from Humes and to proceed in accordance with Hoover's confidential instructions of August 12. Those instructions ordered the BI field offices to gather evidence to deport alien radicals, including "all information of every nature whether hearsay or otherwise."[24] The "O.C." memo in the Pittsburgh files shows that government officials understood deportation primarily as a device to tame rebellious industrial workers—native and immigrant—not an emergency measure to save the country from revolution.[25]

On November 7, the second anniversary of the Bolshevik Revolution, Hoover's men assisted by police arrested hundreds of Russians in simultaneous raids on UORW people's houses in a number of cities in the Northeast and Midwest. Of the more than six hundred persons taken into custody, only seven were arrested in Pittsburgh. However, membership lists found in the New York City people's house helped to pinpoint a second round of UORW raids, this time in coal country, that would add to the Pittsburgh district total.[26]

Two days after the UORW raids the Sunday *Pittsburgh Press* featured a carefully timed propaganda article by Feri Felix Weiss, a former immigration inspector who was a BI special agent in the Boston field office.[27] Weiss, himself an immigrant who had arrived in 1892 and an advocate of then-fashionable eugenics, argued that the United States should use the same care in admitting foreigners as "with the horses, cows and dogs we import."[28] Ostensibly his article was to reveal the hitherto secret evidence that enabled him to secure the internment of Boston Symphony Orchestra conductor Dr. Karl Muck as an enemy alien in 1918. Muck, a champion of German *kultur* and the music of Wagner, became a marked man when he failed to open BSO concerts with the *Star-Spangled Banner,* but it had been difficult to arrest him. Orchestra management and "society ladies" had raised a "hue and cry." It turned out that "quite a few native Americans of Anglo-Saxon stock were outright pacifists" and that the Eastern "smart set" had an affinity for "Germanism." These blue bloods had favored the "FIDDLE OVER THE FLAG and cared more for the symphony than for democracy."[29]

Weiss explained that another impediment to removing Muck from American society had been the Justice Department's difficulties in coping with the enormous potential for subversion that came with the nation's entry into the war. There had been too few BI special agents and some had proved to be "unreliable," untrained, or else just too lazy to do the hard work of catching subversives. Others were too attached to legalisms and to traditional notions of the rules of evidence to deal effectively with radicalism. In their "palace of slumber" they would not arrest "vermin" like Muck just because he was a citizen of neutral Switzerland. Weiss revealed that the sensational secret evidence that caused Muck's downfall stemmed from the fact that the married, middle-aged conductor was amorously involved with a twenty-year-old, unmarried Boston socialite. Armed with a search warrant, Weiss had seized Muck's love letters literally from the young woman's boudoir.

The *Press* used quotations from them set in front-page boxes to tease readers. In one, calculated to anger Pittsburgh chauvinists, addressed to "My Darling," Muck wrote, "Here I am at Pittsburgh where America's cattle make millions of dollars which they worship. It breaks my soul to think that tonight I have to perform before this ignorant pack of Hunds."

Weiss claimed that the government had been honeycombed with pro-German agents in 1917. He described an in-house BI controversy over the handling of loyalty cases between those favoring strict adherence to the Constitution and criminal statutes and those who believed that the wartime national emergency justified whatever means necessary to punish disloyalty. The pragmatists prevailed and, according to Weiss, being soft on Muck had cost two agents in the Boston field office their jobs. The article unabashedly beat the drum for a national "secret service" or political police that would be unfettered by constitutional and evidentiary restraints.[30]

Weiss's article does not bear the imprimatur or the official authorization of the Department of Justice or the BI, but it has Hoover's stamp all over it. Weiss could not have published the formerly confidential evidence without the tacit consent of Hoover, former attorney in the Alien Enemy Bureau and now Radical Division chief. The Weiss piece should be seen as part of the propagandistic side of Palmer's antiradical campaign that included offering articles and cartoons to newspapers free of charge and postage paid by the Justice Department.[31]

Meanwhile the government prepared for the second round of raids. Although two days after the Weiss article appeared, on November 11, in response to a permanent federal injunction against the coal strike, UMWA leaders revoked their strike order, few men returned to work. On the fourteenth coal operators rejected a settlement endorsed by Federal Fuel Administrator Harry Garfield that would have given miners a 31.6 percent pay raise.[32] On November 13, in anticipation of operators rejecting the proposed settlement, West Virginia Governor Cornwell complained to Palmer that in spite of abundant evidence, U.S. Attorney Walker refused to move against IWW-UORW activity near Fairmont without orders from Washington. The governor assured the attorney general that "if a half dozen of these aliens can be arrested immediately and promptly deported this situation will be smoothed out." That evening at 6:28 Palmer wired Cornwell that additional BI agents were on their way to West Virginia to arrest all alien radicals. Soon after, special agents John Wilson of Wheeling, and Fred Ames, D. E. Tatom, and C. D. Ryan from Pittsburgh arrived to assist Lambeth. Near midnight the UMWA's Peters phoned Lambeth to tell him that Russian miners at key agitation points were planning to "arouse all Russians." Rumors flew that these men had resolved to condemn the United States government and to march on Washington. On the fourteenth, a week after the first national UORW raids, Lambeth, concluding "that the foreign element was at the bottom of the reluctance of the miners to return to work at the principal points of agitation, . . . decided to start to round these radicals up."[33]

For the next few days BI agents directed sheriff's deputies and "special police" in arresting Russian miners and searching their boarding houses. The first day eight were caught. On the second day the lawmen stumbled upon a People's House. Hidden in the woods nearby they found a revolver, some political literature, and a membership list. Then, acting on a mine manager's tip, they picked up seven more Russians, including the president and secretary of the branch. When agents burst in on them the men were "drinking and smoking around a table having a general good time."[34]

Throughout the roundup, none of the Russians resisted, even though they were supposedly bent upon destroying the American way of life. A reporter wrote that although Reds were known to oppose all government, these were "not very blood thirsty about it." Neither were they equipped to shed blood. In all the raids lawmen discovered only a few knives, one pistol, some dynamite caps, and six feet of fuse. This was a negligible haul in a ruggedly individualistic culture where hunting enjoyed exalted status and the use of explosives was a routine part of coal mining. Deputies, armed to the teeth and expecting the worst, marveled at how easy their task had been. One recounted how three men could easily have gotten away. They were going over a hill and were out of gun range. But when he yelled at them they came back, looked puzzled, and said "We no handle pick handle [coal field moonshine]." Few seemed to understand why they were in jail. At first, some even thought it an honor.[35]

There was little honor in the treatment accorded to the Marion County captives. Their plight was not as miserable as that of the UORW suspects in the Hartford, Connecticut, jail where ninety-seven men were held for five months without being charged after a BI raid, but it was bad enough. During November and December as many as eighty men remained incommunicado for days in the overcrowded county jail. At first the prisoners were allowed no visitors, not even attorneys and relatives. Newspaper reporters dug in vain for their names. Even the Salvation Army could not conduct its usual religious services at the jail on account of security imposed by the BI.[36]

When Pittsburgh Immigration Inspector Michael F. O'Brien arrived three days after the raids began for preliminary deportation hearings he found the jail packed with men who had not even been before a justice of the peace. After he sorted things out, to the chagrin of BI agents, he ordered the release of twenty-five. Some, it turned out, were not even Russians. Others had simply been in the wrong place at the wrong time. One "alien radical" turned out to be just back from eighteen months in the U.S. Army. But local officials, reluctant to let the men go, rearrested many under the state red flag law.[37]

Elsewhere in northern West Virginia twelve aliens were arrested near Star City and jailed at Morgantown in connection with miners' defiance of UMWA orders to return to work. The biggest single raid took place on November 25, when agents Lambeth and Tatom and more than thirty heavily armed lawmen invaded the notorious and remote Maryland Coal Company camp at Wendel in Taylor County. In the past a deputy had been killed and a constable badly beaten there and it had been a center of militant union activity for some time. The agents made a house-to-house search under a state warrant to look for prohibition violations, but turned up very little. Intriguingly, at nearly every house they found pistol and rifle bullets but not a single firearm. There were few Russians in the community of four to five hundred and no evidence of the UORW. From Lambeth's report, it is clear that belatedly he realized that mine owners had used the BI to settle a score against an unruly community of foreigners.[38]

By the end of 1919 the raids around Fairmont had turned up more than fifty alleged UORW members but not one proven Wobbly. Investigations at Wendel and Star City had been even less productive. Despite that, as of early December, about one-quarter of the region's Russian coal miners had been arrested and many were still in jail.[39] Arrests continued in northern West Virginia sporadically into 1920, but BI agents found no new IWW or UORW branches.

The government and the coal operators were quick to declare that the arrests had defeated the strikers. Lambeth reported that jailing the Russians had silenced union militants and frightened other miners into submission. A week after the raids began, the NWVCOA reported that coal output in the area had risen from 20 percent to 60 percent of normal. There was no new agitation and operators predicted that those miners still on strike would soon return.[40] Actually, the strike continued until December 10.[41] By then BI agents suspected that UMWA officials and miners had a secret "understanding" that the men would ignore their leaders' orders to return to work.[42] Not until the national union leaders were threatened with jail and accepted a face-saving 14 percent wage increase did the strike end.

The evidence gathered by the BI demonstrates UORW activity in northern

West Virginia. Several months before the raids organizers from New York City and Pittsburgh had made a swing through the camps, but the UORW was not much of a venue for revolution. Only twenty-four men were found to have paid dues into it of between twenty cents and two dollars over a two-month period. The translation of the Russian minutes of the Farmington Branch does not exhibit the stuff of which revolutions are made. The group spent its funds on a rubber stamp and house rent. Its most subversive acts were ordering radical literature from New York, sending a delegate to a UORW conference, and resolving to begin a school with the comrades at a neighboring mine. The whole membership list, including those who evidently did not pay dues, totaled thirty-four.[43] The inventory of radical literature confiscated in the raids also fails to impress. It included books and pamphlets by Vincent St. John, the book, *Russian Songs of Freedom* by Max M. Maisel, *Bread and Freedom,* and miscellaneous Russian-language pamphlets.[44]

The UORW in the coal fields, then, was neither an ignition source for revolution nor a serious factor in prolonging the coal strike. It is better understood as a target of opportunity for a Department of Justice much in need of a public success to silence critics of its failure to act decisively against radicalism.[45] In November 1919 it was not yet clear just how much of a public relations bonanza the raids would prove to be. That would depend on whether or not they paved the way for mass deportations.

The Pittsburgh BI Radical Squad together with Immigration Inspectors Sibray and Michael F. O'Brien processed the UORW Pennsylvania cases originating in Pittsburgh, Erie, and Greensburg and those from Fairmont in West Virginia. Immigration and Naturalization Service case files of most of the Fairmont deportees, released under the Freedom of Information Act, help to explain the government's deportation policies.

The Alien Act of October 16, 1918, authorized the deportation of aliens who were anarchists or "members of or affiliated with any organization that entertains a belief in, teaches, or advocates the overthrow by force or violence of the Government of the United States or of all forms of law, or that entertains or teaches disbelief in or opposition to all organized government . . . or that advocates or teaches the unlawful destruction of property."[46]

According to the BI's interpretation of this law, an alien did not have to engage in radical activity or even hold radical views to be expelled. It was enough to belong to an organization such as the UORW. Regulations required a regional immigration inspector to hold a preliminary inquiry into the case, followed by a formal fact-finding hearing, and to recommend for or against deportation. His recommendation went to the commissioner-general of immigration and finally to the secretary of labor or his acting designate, whose approval sent the alien at government expense to Ellis Island to await transportation out of the country.[47]

Soon the Labor and Justice Departments were at odds over the latter's insistence upon broad construction of membership in the UORW to include passive or inactive members who did not even attend meetings or engage in organization activities. In the case of Russians arrested in northern West Virginia, the BI agents maintained that the presence of an alien's name on a UORW membership list was good and sufficient reason to deport him. Here Justice Department officials were applying the approach that Allan Pinkerton had used with the nineteenth-century Molly Maguires: that mere membership made these men part of the "outer ring of followers . . . unaware of the criminal purposes of their [radical] leaders" but still a danger to the country because of their blind loyalty. The BI also came to the convenient conclusion that deportation of such blind followers was not punishment, only an administrative procedure for the good of the country. Relying on this technicality, Justice Department officials hoped to avoid lengthy proceedings and promote speedy deportations.[48]

Construing deportation as an administrative procedure led logically to the BI's argument that the time, often months, that aliens spent in jail awaiting the outcome of Immigration Bureau proceedings was not "imprisonment . . . [or] deprivation of liberty without 'due process' of law." It was only "detention" and jail was "detention quarters." Yet when it suited their purposes, these same officials portrayed deportation as a criminal proceeding. Attorney General Palmer made this clear when he explained to a House committee that deportation proceedings necessarily have "the nature of a trial, to a degree . . . [and] the accused, if such can be said of a party to administrative proceeding, shall show cause why he should not be deported. That is to say, the burden of proof . . . is not upon the people of the United States, but upon the alien."[49]

Until the spring of 1920 the Bureau of Immigration's top administrators went along with the Justice Department instead of following their generally more humane and cautious approach to deportation cases. Then, with Secretary Wilson's blessing, Acting Secretary of Labor Louis F. Post repudiated the Justice Department's approach and joined the civil liberties pantheon by voiding thousands of deportation warrants against mostly Communist alien radicals arrested in January. But in the UORW cases arising from the November 1919 raids, Post went along with the immigration officials who favored mass deportations and even signed the order to expel his acquaintance and former ally Emma Goldman. Thus it was left to field inspectors, if they were so inclined, to stand up to the political and bureaucratic pressures and give fair treatment to the UORW pariahs. BI agents expected immigration inspectors to join the deportation team and rubber-stamp their findings. However, in the western Pennsylvania–West Virginia cases Inspector Sibray frustrated them by adhering to his own interpretations of procedure and making his own independent decisions.[50]

Like Palmer, Sibray was of Quaker heritage and, like the attorney general, on the night of June 2 was jarred from his bed by a bomb meant to take his life. Like Palmer, he was deeply involved in the UORW deportations. There the comparisons end. Palmer's fashionable R Street NW Washington townhouse was a palace beside Sibray's modest, lower-middle-class, hillside dwelling. Sibray was a plodding but competent veteran civil servant with a strong sense of independence. The fifty-six-year-old Indiana native had been with the Immigration Bureau since 1904 and in the Pittsburgh office since 1906 where he had served both as immigration inspector and Chinese Exclusion Act inspector. His job had not been easy. Superiors volunteered him at no extra pay to be a civil service examiner. For years without a secretary, he typed his own correspondence and made do with spare office furnishings including some borrowed from the Treasury Department. A 1915 federal budget shortfall forced him to take a month's furlough without pay.[51]

As a veteran civil servant committed to meritocratic principles, Sibray was used to following regulations. As a field inspector on his own far from Washington, he was also used to interpreting those regulations in individual cases. As the BI soon discovered, Sibray would not blindly follow the dictates of the Justice Department or of its upstart Pittsburgh operatives, none of whom had more than five years on the job. Neither would he be the tool of coal or steel company officials. He evaluated the key evidence in each case according to his own lights.

In the northern West Virginia UORW cases, Sibray and Pittsburgh BI Radical Squad agents were at odds from the beginning. Part of the problem was a turf war between two agencies with the BI cast as the intruder. An added component was Sibray's sincere, if paternalistic, sympathy for the immigrants. From the first he refused to accept the mere presence of an alien's name in the UORW minute books as sufficient grounds for deportation. This, despite Department of Labor legal findings that supported that interpretation. Instead, Sibray compromised most of the government cases by insisting that the accused must say that he had attended UORW meetings, which, of course, most would not. The inspector's intransigence brought from one BI agent the revealing complaint that "it appears to me that Mr. Sibray leans toward these aliens. If that is not the case, he gives them the benefit of the doubt."[52]

The alien's right to a lawyer during deportation proceedings was another issue. Originally the Immigration Bureau's Rule 22 denied prospective deportees the right to counsel until federal agents had completed their initial interrogation. Then, in March 1919, Secretary of Labor Wilson changed the rule to permit aliens to have counsel from the beginning of proceedings against them. Much to the dismay of BI agents, under the revised rule alien radicals learned from their lawyers to invoke their protection against self-incrimination. This made it harder for the government.[53]

Throughout, Sibray tried to adhere to the rule. The Russians were either represented at their hearings or advised of their right to counsel. Even though he was forced to contend with the presence of BI agents acting as what Palmer called prosecutors for the people, counsel could give advice, cross-examine, and file a statement on behalf of his client. However, at their soonest, the hearings took place only after the men had been in jail several days. Usually before that the BI had managed to interrogate them so as to secure the "government's interest."[54]

Margolis and Marshall represented almost all of the northern West Virginia Russians.[55] Actually Marshall did most of the work, for Margolis was preoccupied with disbarment proceedings against him and a full schedule of speaking engagements. Marshall first tried to bail the men out with the Liberty Bonds Margolis had been collecting, but the war chest was soon empty because there had been so many arrests and because the Justice Department demanded $10,000 bail, ten times the usual amount, in all cases. This, even though none of the Russians stood accused of specific acts of violence, sabotage, or disorder. Palmer defended the high bail as necessary to prevent the aliens from fleeing. More convincing, if unspoken, reasons were the Justice Department's desire to make a public show of large-scale deportations and its commitment to defeat the coal strike.[56]

At every turn Sibray and the BI agents clashed over the proper treatment of the UORW prisoners. A case in point was the quarrel over Sibray's Russian interpreter, Miss A. Liebgardt, a Pittsburgh YWCA community worker. Soon after the November raids, Sibray and Liebgardt took the train down from Pittsburgh to West Virginia with BI agent Fred Ames and his prize informant Michael I. Yankovich, formerly a private in Troop A of the Pennsylvania Constabulary. Yankovich, who spoke Russian, had gone undercover in June for the state police in the Pittsburgh Steel Products plant at Monessen.[57] His mission was to spy on a newly organized UORW chapter. Later, the state withdrew the order to investigate the UORW and Ames, himself a former "cossack," engaged Yankovich to continue undercover work for the BI. During the November raids at Monessen Yankovich found and fingered at least twenty alleged UORW members.[58] When, during the train ride, Yankovich related that he had testified against a number of Russians who had befriended him at Monessen, the social worker Liebgardt, instead of praising him, had arched her brow and uttered only a disapproving, "Oh." In defense of his informant, Ames put his arm around Yankovich and pointedly praised him as "100 percent American." Thereafter, Ames marked Liebgardt. In Fairmont, he and Yankovich carefully observed her behavior with the Russian suspects. She aroused their suspicions when she appealed to Ames in behalf of a prisoner who had asked to keep some of his books in jail. When the agent denied the request, Liebgardt rebuked him by saying that these men deserved education instead of deportation.[59]

The BI agents took the Liebgardt matter to their Washington superiors, who in turn complained to the Labor Department. They charged that she had incorrectly translated answers of UORW detainees to G-men's questions. The basis for the accusation, since none of the agents spoke Russian, was the word of the informer Yankovich, whose ego Liebgardt had so wounded. Sibray was then forced to dismiss her and turn over the interpreting chores at Fairmont to Yankovich and another individual.[60]

By mid-December 1919 the official tally of Russian coal miners and alleged UORW members arrested in the Fairmont area was fifty-eight. Of these, eighteen were eventually deported. It is possible to draw a rough composite of the group from the files of fifteen that were released to the author under the Freedom of Information Act/Privacy Act and for the others from declassified Department of Justice Old German files.

The men in the sample were between twenty-three and forty years old. None had applied for citizenship although one had been in the United States for ten years and all but one had been here at least five years. The majority (nine) had come over near the beginning of the Great War (1913–1914), partly, perhaps, to avoid military service. All said that in Russia they had been landless farmers or peasants. Five were illiterate; two said they could read only a little bit of Russian. None spoke passable English. Most had floated from place to place in the western Pennsylvania–eastern Ohio–northern West Virginia iron and coal triangle from one insecure and dangerous heavy labor job to the next. Although one man had saved $800 and another $200[61] the great majority were very poor. Most had nothing beyond a few dollars' pay coming and what possessions would fit into a trunk or a suitcase.[62]

Although the plan was to deport a mass of alien radicals, established procedures required that each case be handled separately. This led to decisions that do not seem objective or consistent. The confiscated chapter minute and blue dues books found in the effects of most of those who were deported showed them to be members of the UORW; but the same was true for a larger number of detainees who were not deported. A standard attachment to each deportee's file was an English-language copy of the "Fundamental Principles of the Federated Union of Russian Workers" with its arguably revolutionary message. But, as government agents well knew, many of the deportees could not read any language, and the blue dues books that some carried contained no revolutionary statements or description of the purposes of the UORW. The truth was that the government could not prove that these men even knew what the UORW stood for. To make things more difficult, most of the men denied even attending UORW meetings. They told suspiciously similar stories: a stranger, a man from New York, had accosted them; they had made a small donation; and then he had put their names in a book. Collectively they offered three reasons for joining the UORW: 1) to underwrite a school where they could learn to read;[63] 2) to organize against the U.S. government's "blockade" of the Soviet Union so that they could return home;[64] and 3) to socialize with other Russians in this lonely land.[65]

Another standard attachment to dossiers of the deportees who said they could read was what the BI referred to as a UORW publication, "*Novomirsky,* 'Manifesto of Anarchists-Communists.'"[66] In the November 7 raid in Philadelphia, UORW member Matthew Furshtman had been arrested while lecturing at the people's house with a copy of it open on the table in front of him.[67] The use of such evidence illustrates either the BI agents' imperfect knowledge of the Russian Revolution or a cavalier attitude toward evidence. In fact, Novomirsky's "Manifesto," dated 1907, had nothing to do with the Bolsheviks. It had been written in the wake of the failure of an earlier phase of the Russian revolution and had long been available at the New York Public Library.[68] A copy had been among the UORW chapter effects; it did call for revolution; and it ended with this inflamed rhetoric that spoke to the Russian miners:

> Wake up, look around you! See how poor and degraded you are! Remember that you are a man, and that you—erected all the world of wealth! Understand: that the workers of all countries are your brothers, and that you all have one task—to destroy the world of gain and erect a world of freedom for all; there is one means—armed intervention and forcible seizure of all instruments and all products of toil. . . . Woe to the enemies of the laboring class![69]

How could illiterate Russian miners have read this English-language pamphlet?

The sample cases show that the Immigration Bureau did follow a discernible policy in deciding which of the UORW members to deport. Two of the eighteen northern West Virginia deportees were activists and the brains of local UORW branches. David Eelak had been a fugitive since June when he skipped bond, put up by Margolis in Pittsburgh after a deportation proceeding. Eelak readily admitted to giving anarchist speeches in New York City and McKees Rocks, to believing in anarcho-communism, to selling and distributing the UORW publication, *Bread and Freedom,* and to being an enthusiastic student of anarchy.[70] The other activist, Peter Novikoff, had joined the UORW at Monessen and proudly told government officials that he was an anarchist-communist and "an anarchist pure and simple." Not even his lawyer Marshall could think of any legal reason to oppose deporting Novikoff.[71]

Three others were not considered dangerous but were local UORW officers or had been found with radical literature and admitted to subscribing to radical ideologies. Artemy Pauluk carried a grudge against the United States government. In 1918 he had been drafted illegally and forced to serve in the U.S. Army. Pauluk was the recording secretary of the Farmington, West Virginia, UORW chapter and had distributed UORW publications.[72] Evan Elko said that he could not read, but when he was arrested he possessed radical pamphlets as well as dynamite caps and six feet of fuse. Andrew Lopitsky claimed he did not understand anarchism but said he was trying to learn and to become a communist and an anarchist. He complained bitterly about the hardships of life in the United States and about the absence of educational opportunities for poor Russians like himself.[73] One may question the wisdom and justice of the 1918 immigration law and yet grant that these five men, Eelak, Novikoff, Pauluk, Elko, and Lopitsky, fell within its scope. They were not simply passive holders of UORW membership books but promoters of its aims.

The same cannot be said of the other deportees. Their names were in the UORW minute books and they were technically members.[74] That said, there is little to suggest that they understood anarchism or that they had spoken or acted at all for the UORW. Why then were they deported? The simplest answer is that they were marginal members even within the outcast Russian miners' community. Several were in their late thirties or ill and therefore of limited use as laborers in heavy industry.[75] One had spent nine months at Woodville Insane Asylum near Pittsburgh after a breakdown that he blamed on the stresses of steel mill work. He told the government men that he was still sick "all the time." Sibray ordered him out of the country before he had another breakdown and became a public charge.[76] Another man suffered from rheumatism.[77] Still another had an alcohol problem.[78] The immigration inspectors characterized others as being of the "ignorant peasant" or of the "undesirable" type.[79] From a political standpoint, and it was certainly a stretch, one could argue that these men might be dangerous to the country as blind followers of charismatic leaders.[80] That was equally true of many who were allowed to stay.

The Pittsburgh immigration inspectors' distaste for the UORW deportations is clear from their "Summary and Evaluation" of most of the deportees. This section of each file constituted the inspector's formal recommendation to Commissioner-General Caminetti. Here both Sibray and O'Brien expressed their doubts. Typical was Sibray's comment on Vasil Kozlov: "If it is the policy of the Department to deport for the sole reason of membership in the Union of Russian Workmen, then this alien should be deported. Otherwise, the warrant should be canceled and he should be permitted to remain in the United States."[81]

Sibray and O'Brien tried to show compassion in their recommendations. Hindsight shows that Bolshevik Russia in 1919 was a terrible place for an anarchist, but that was not at all clear in America at the time. Many of the Fairmont deportees wanted to go home. They even sang as they began the journey to Ellis Island. For some, their plight there could have hardly been more bleak than it was here—without family and in failing health in the harsh world of the industrial Appalachians. It is important to make that point, because many accounts of the 1919 deportations focus on the well-known Goldman and Berkman and dismiss their 247 shipmates as either a faceless rabble or an equally anonymous company of innocent victims. An influential example of overgeneralization was the powerful and passionate attack on the injustice of the Palmer raids by Zechariah Chafee, Jr. He wrote that "the men deported on the 'Buford' were torn from their families, who still remain in America."[82]

But that was true of only a small fraction of those deported on the *Buford*. In a widely reported incident, the families of a dozen of the deportees tried to storm the Ellis Island ferry to join their men for the trip to Russia. Yet when Chafee's contemporary, the liberal Constantine Panunzio, examined the files of two hundred of the *Buford's* passengers, he found that only thirteen had left families here.[83] If Chafee is correct for less than 10 percent of the total, he is totally incorrect for the contingent from northern West Virginia. Throughout the deportation process, officials from Abercrombie down to field inspectors like Sibray conscientiously sought to avoid breaking up families. They knew that the 1918 Alien Act did not provide for the repatriation of wives and children of "Bolsheviks." That helps to explain why every one of the men in the sample was either single, or married with a family in Russia. In each dossier, a penciled notation on Caminetti's "Memorandum for the Acting Secretary," the documentary basis for the deportation warrant, records the marital status and location of the subject's family.

On December 19, 1919, just before the deportees were about to leave the Marion County jail for Ellis Island, Sibray removed four men from the list when he learned that they had wives and children here who, if left behind, would likely become destitute. Then he ordered that these men should be granted bail while their cases were pending. His action saved the men from deportation but provided little relief for their families. Since none could raise even nominal bail they remained in jail for another month until they were at last released on their own recognizance.[84]

Most of the UORW deportees did not want to remain in the United States. As one of their lawyers, Swinburne Hale, explained, many wanted to go back to Russia, as long as it was Soviet and not the Russia of Admiral Alexander Kolchak, leader of the Whites. Hale's analysis squares with the testimony of the men in the sample under consideration here. Ten said either that they wanted to return to family and friends or else that they had no objection to going to Russia. Several added that they joined the UORW in the first place to speed their return. The Pittsburgh immigration inspectors weighed that in their recommendations.[85]

Despite the Justice Department's powerful campaign against the UORW, it was never certain that the deportations would take place until the *Buford* actually sailed. When it did, many were surprised. Just a week before the ship weighed anchor, Margolis was in Fairmont holding forth to local reporters. He characterized the realities of peasant life in czarist Russia as black bread, corrupt priests, no education, and a government remote from the people. He even granted that the jailed Russian miners were better off than their brothers had been in czarist times, but in America, too, he said, the government was remote and meant nothing in their daily lives. He pictured the average Russian detainee as a simple man who dug coal, lived his life, sang his folk songs, and tried to be happy. Margolis portrayed the UORW as a harmless, nonviolent ethnic organization. He said it meant the same to Russian immigrants in West Virginia as West Virginia societies in New York and Washington meant to homesick ex-Mountaineers in those places. He called attention to the fact that fewer than half of those picked up in the raids had turned out to be UORW members. Government agents, he sniped, could not tell Poles from Russians, and he added sarcastically that if there had been bomb throwers in the area, the BI had not found them.[86]

As late as December 15, 1919, Margolis predicted, based on the findings of Sibray, that no more than five of the prisoners would actually be deported. Just two days later Caminetti and Abercrombie signed 250 deportation warrants. The Justice Department then moved with great haste to get the deportees out of the country before opponents could mount a legal challenge. Of the thirty-eight who remained in the Marion County jail, fourteen were to be deported and the rest to be released. Last-minute changes, noted above, spared four men from deportation, but eight others were added, making a total of eighteen.[87]

On December 19, the Russians started for Ellis Island in a special car attached to the 5:20 P.M. Pittsburgh train. Guarding them were the local sheriff and U.S. deputy marshals. The established community showed no sympathy for these men whom it did not know. Only their immigrant friends and retailers near the jail who had profited from their incarceration mourned their departure. They reached New York the next day, and the sheriff who escorted them felt the tingle of celebrity as newsreel cameras focused on him as he marched his prisoners to the Ellis Island ferry. It hardly could have been coincidental that on the same day the *Fairmont Times* published the first in a series of articles entitled "Our Poisonous Immigration Cancer," by Feri Felix Weiss, that prolific scourge of the un-Americans and propagandist for the Justice Department.[88]

Two days later the *Buford* sailed. Its two best-known passengers were Emma Goldman and Alexander Berkman. She was the fifty-two-year-old anarchist writer-lecturer and icon of radical feminism and labor militancy since the 1880s. Her writings, some thought, had motivated Leon Czolgosz to assassinate President William McKinley. Berkman was her longtime associate and sometime lover who had spent fourteen years in Pennsylvania's Western Penitentiary for his attempt on the life of steel magnate Henry Clay Frick in 1892. Both Goldman and Berkman had been jailed during the Great War for their opposition to conscription. Hoover believed that these two, the "Red Queen" and her lover, were part of the secret inner circle of conspirators who were intent upon overthrowing the United States government.[89]

With two or three exceptions, the other deportees hardly fit Palmer's description: "the worst offenders of the Russian anarchist group." Some had been arrested as long ago as 1917, but the largest contingent was the fruit of the November UORW raids. Although about fifty were deported for their personal beliefs in anarchy and revolution, the offense of a far greater number, more than 180, was UORW membership.[90] Large as this number seems, it represented less than a third of the six hundred warrants originally issued for UORW members and only a small fraction of its estimated four to seven thousand total membership.[91]

In the northern West Virginia coal fields harsh words and hard feelings followed the deportations. UMWA local officials, led by H. E. Peters, had abetted operators and G-men in purging the Russians. In general, American miners had stood by indifferently and even approved of the arrest of their fellow workers. An incident that took place the day the *Buford* sailed illustrates the division in the ranks. According to an NWVCOA spy, the trouble began at the area's largest mine when American UMWA officer Edward Myers encountered UORW member Nick Neckrash at the company store. Neckrash had not been deported, but he had been arrested in November for allegedly saying to a deputy sheriff, "God damn this country, I want to go back to Russia." When Myers needled Neckrash by reminding him that as they spoke the deportees were on their way to Russia, Neckrash spat back, "fuck this Government." Later that day, the UMWA local met to elect officers and Myers was nominated for vice president. Neckrash then arose to denounce him as a government agent who should be expelled from the union. Myers, he said, had helped a mine official and government men arrest "our people."[92]

UORW advocates were not alone in expressing their disgust with the deportations. Sibray, in the western Pennsylvania portion of the *Annual Report of the Commissioner of Immigration* (1920), minced no words. He complained that efforts to Americanize immigrants had mostly ceased after 1914 and that "these ignorant Russian workers were . . . cast adrift [in the United States] with no effort on the part of our own people to teach and inculcate in them the spirit of Americanism." Their families were in Russia and "they had not been here long enough to learn to speak English and their only associates were their own people." When the UORW organizers approached them, they enthusiastically joined, but the majority "insisted that their only thought was to have the ports opened and be permitted to return to their native land."[93]

Assistant Secretary of Labor Louis F. Post was an old single-taxer and longtime friend of radicals of various stripes. Writing in 1923, he portrayed the UORW deportees as victims of a "deportations delirium" and the Red Scare as "a gigantic and cruel hoax." He blamed the delirium on the Department of Justice; "the detectives and those who employed them, filled the newspapers with lurid accounts of what the 'Reds' had done and were planning to do and produced a small scale 'reign of terror.'"[94]

At the Justice Department Hoover saw things very differently. He asserted in an internal Department of Justice memo that "all of the persons leaving on the 'Buford' were admitted anarchists and their activities have been proven in each case, showing in many cases their active identification with the coal strike or the steel strike."[95] In the attorney general's *Annual Report,* he pointed proudly to the voyage of the "Soviet Ark" as ridding the country of Goldman, Berkman, Adolph Schnabel, editor Peter Bianki of *Bread and Freedom,* "and other leading agitators . . . who had for many months been the cause of a considerable amount of the industrial and economic unrest."[96] He would not be able to say, however, that the second wave of Palmer raids, aimed at the Communists, was as successful.

THE PALMER RAIDS II

> Undoubtedly these raids are the most stupid thing yet done by the adminis-
> tration. To hold the belief that 2,000 people can ever overthrow this country
> is seeing spooks in the worst form.
>
> Jacob Margolis, quoted in the *New York Call*, Jan. 4, 1920

THE *BUFORD* WAS STILL ROLLING IN HEAVY SEAS in the Bay of Biscay on
January 2 when Palmer ordered raids in thirty-three cities in twenty-three states
coast to coast. The successful assault on the UORW boded well for phase two
aimed at the meeting places of the Communist Party of America (CPA) and the
Communist Labor Party (CLP). Eastern European immigrants made up an estimated 75 percent of their membership, enough to fill up a fleet of "Soviet arks."
On the authority of three thousand blank warrants signed by Solicitor Abercrombie, the dragnet netted thousands of aliens. As in the earlier IWW and
UORW operations, agents confiscated tons of printed matter including books,
pamphlets, membership lists, and financial records. Smaller strikes followed the
initial raids over the next three months.[1]

In May 1919, a great schism in the Socialist Party had led the party's right
wing to expel the pro-Bolshevik Left. It was a Pyrrhic victory for the Right, which
retained the Socialist name, headquarters, and records but lost two-thirds of the
members, including the entire Detroit party and the foreign language federations. These thousands of former Socialists now became the nucleus of the CPA
and the smaller CLP, both of which emerged in September 1919.[2]

Considering strength of numbers and the nature of its membership, at the
beginning of 1920 the Communist parties were more of a threat to other left-
wing organizations than to American capitalism and democracy. The larger of
the several estimates Theodore Draper gives for Communist Party membership
at the end of 1919 is just under twenty-seven thousand, all but three thousand

drawn from the former Socialist foreign language federations. The Communist Labor Party could claim perhaps ten thousand members.

Numbers did not tell the whole story. At the Overman Committee hearings in early 1919 Red hunter Archibald Stevenson addressed the question of the true danger of Communism. "Taking the great body of the American people," inquired a senator, "were they not too level headed to be influenced by this outfit?" Stevenson had a ready answer: "We must remember Senator, that the American people—and by that I mean really American people—are not present in very large numbers in our industrial centers. They [the Communists] have made a great impression on the foreign element." The theory, subscribed to by many on the Right, was that a small minority could bring down the country by exploiting foreign laborers' susceptibility to subversive foreign ideas. But for all of the breast-beating by politicians and the press about the danger, the BI files do not show the Pittsburgh mill district was especially receptive to Communism at this time. The steel and coal corporations presented a strong obstacle to all workers' movements. Then, too, the successive federal campaigns against the Wobblies, PCA, and the UORW had decimated what from the first was an anemic left wing.[3]

The first signs of a Communist movement in the Steel Valley showed up soon after the bombings, on June 8, 1919, when the SPA met at the International Socialist Lyceum to debate its future. The comrades considered two courses: conservative political action and Bolshevik direct action. When a conservative speaker called for the expulsion of the direct actionists, he was hooted down. Wendell described the split as between the predominately American-born who wanted to adhere to political socialism and the majority of the foreign-born who demanded their own party. The acrimony accompanying the discussion signaled that the time for parting had come. The conservatives discussed calling themselves the National Labor Party. The other party, as yet without a name, would include communists, anarchists, and syndicalists.[4]

By October the Radical Squad had firm evidence of Communist handbills and other propaganda circulating among American Bridge Company workers. Soon after, H. H. Detweiler, a leader in the 1916 Westinghouse strike, received a charter for a Pittsburgh English-speaking branch from the CPA's Blue Island Avenue headquarters in Chicago. There was soon a second branch, the South Slavonic.[5]

Wendell was present on November 2 when the Pittsburgh Communists met for the first time at the International Socialist Lyceum along with delegates from twenty-one former Socialist foreign-language federations. In what amounted to a central committee meeting, they agreed that each federation would incorporate as a separate party branch with the expectation of meeting officially as Communists in about two weeks. By November 11, 1919, twenty-two ex-Socialist branches had joined the party and agreed to surrender their SPA charters and records to their federation comrades who did not. They then booked CPA executive secretary Charles E. Ruthenberg to speak at a mass meeting on Sunday, November 23, and planned a New Year's Eve ball.[6]

Communism took hold at Erie in late October when Detroit-based organizer D. A. Batt called upon Socialists there to switch to the CPA. With the Espionage and Sedition Acts no longer in force, citizen Communists knew that their activities did not violate existing federal law.[7] Defiantly, Batt began his speech by saying, "for the benefit of the Government Agents and Authorities who are watching this meeting" and looking for alien radicals, "unfortunately I am an American citizen and am not proud to admit it." Even though he held no formal office in the Erie party, BI agents believed that former Socialist Ralph Tillotson, the devil they knew, was its prime mover.[8]

By the end of November Wendell and Spencer were calling the Communists the area's most dangerous radical group and rated it "fairly strong," as it consisted of about two hundred active members in its English and Russian branches. Agents were seeing much Communist propaganda literature and hearing of new party branches in neighboring Westmoreland, Beaver, and Cambria counties. Still, *foreign* Communists did not seem to be the greatest danger. On November 14, at Hoover's request, Spencer sent a list of "all agitators in the district" known to the Radical Squad. Belying Hoover's claim that 90 percent of radicals were aliens, there were only twenty-six aliens, just over half of whom were Communists, on the list of sixty-one names. The majority of "dangerous agitators" were citizens.[9]

According to a summary written later by Henry J. Lenon, the Pittsburgh agents had difficulty in understanding the aliens' role in the growing Communist movement because "we were . . . baffled and oft times did not know whether we were dealing with Anarchists, Union of Russian Workers, Socialists, Communists, or the Communist Labor Party." The agents believed that "many of the aliens were reading everything issued by the different organizations and interrogation showed that in many cases they too were puzzled in the stages of formation of the different organizations." For months the Radical Squad wondered why it appeared that nearly all the new Communists were aliens and former Socialists. Why would an alien join a political party when he could not vote and did not intend to become a citizen? Eventually, fatefully and incorrectly, the agents concluded that there must be little real difference in any of these left-wing factions. Call themselves what they would, subscribers to Marxist principles and the Third International were all revolutionaries.[10]

The first evidence in the Pittsburgh files of the impending government attack on the CPA was in mid-December, when Spencer sent to Washington thirty-three affidavits naming local alien Communists. Then, on December 31, 1919, in preparation for a massive dragnet, Solicitor Abercrombie, acting for the secretary of labor, reinstated the original Immigration Bureau "Rule 22," which denied alien suspects the right to legal representation until they had been thoroughly questioned by federal agents. On Friday evening, January 2, 1920, the great nationwide sweep netted, according to Hoover's conservative estimate, 2,500 alien Communists. To facilitate the roundup, Washington had instructed Bureau informants inside the CPA to make sure that party meetings were held as scheduled that evening. When he learned of it later, this order prompted federal judge George W. Anderson to charge that the BI partially "owned and operated" the Communist parties, a charge Hoover strenuously denied.[11]

The Pittsburgh roundup was a decidedly modest affair.[12] Special agents Speer, McClure, and Morgan with police and "special police" made scattered arrests in the Downtown, North Side, and South Side sections of the city and in the nearby communities of East Pittsburgh, McKees Rocks, Conway, Wilmerding, Rankin, Rochester, and Vestaburg. The next morning, according to the *Press*, even though they had only served twelve warrants, they had rounded up thirty-nine alien Communists. Two days later, Spencer reported that only twenty-two of these were still in custody, including two who had been arrested days before the raids. The papers printed only eight names. As usual in these dragnet operations, when the innocent were sorted from the "guilty," many were let go.[13]

Perhaps personnel problems associated with the Pittsburgh Radical Squad contributed to the relatively small number of Communist arrests. The steel and coal strikes, the UORW, and then the Communist raids required the deployment of agents hither and yon from Erie to West Virginia and points in between. Then, on January 3, the day after the Communist Party raids began, special agent Speer quit the BI on short notice.[14] A few days later, SAC Spencer proposed as his replacement, to "work along radical lines," Henry J. Lenon, the former special agent at Erie who had been let go eight months earlier. Spencer touted Lenon as "entirely trustworthy, active, fearless, and a good detail man ... well known to ************ [FBI censored, L. M. Wendell] and myself." He had talked the matter over with Wendell, and they agreed that "a better man could not be found to look after radical details." He added, "owing to the great value of said informant it has always been my policy to have him become known to as few Agents as possible."[15]

Since his dismissal Lenon had kept in touch with the Pittsburgh BI while working as a steel company detective in Cleveland. He was antiradical to the extreme—anti-alien, anti-union, anti-Semitic, and anti-feminist—yet hardly the beau ideal of a special agent. He was middle-aged, with a sixth-grade education, unschooled in the law or foreign languages. A complaint from the Erie police chief about his arrogant meddling in department affairs was already in his file. Moreover, he wanted seven dollars per day, which was more than other Pittsburgh Radical Squad agents made.[16]

Pointing out that it would require a special appointment to meet Lenon's salary demands, J. T. Suter proposed having someone else take over the radical work. Spencer replied that no one in the Pittsburgh office and few agents anywhere were suited to such a "rough and dangerous" assignment. If the agent did not have "enthusiasm and fondness for reading and study . . . to absorb the philosophy of radical teachings," he would miss "the most important points in radical investigations and interrogations." Pointedly, Spencer added that "************ [L. M. Wendell] . . . went over this matter very thoroughly with Mr. Hoover. In fact it was *** [FBI censored, 836] who first suggested Mr. Lenon's appointment to me . . . and I do not think a better man could be found to fill the position." On January 13 Hoover used a "RADICAL-Confidential" memo to urge the immediate appointment of Lenon and to inform the BI director that he had discussed Speer's "successor with *** [836] as it is absolutely essential for the efficiency of the office to have someone agreeable to *** [836] and with whom *** [836] can work." A week later Lenon took over the Pittsburgh Radical Squad.[17]

Despite the ongoing distractions, on January 6, three days after the first raid, federal agents struck McKeesport and Lyndora[18] and arrested more Communists. By the end of January Sibray had conducted deportation hearings for more than forty accused Communists. Nationally the BI won an important legal-administrative victory in its quest for mass deportation authority when, in the case of Massachusetts CPA member Englebert Preis, Secretary of Labor William B. Wilson ruled that party membership was sufficient cause for deportation.[19]

In February the search for Communists in and around Pittsburgh continued. Spencer's men, relying on stoolies, raided the North Side Russian CPA where they confiscated the charter and a group photograph with the members conveniently numbered for identification.[20] Next they struck at Slovenian Hall and the alleys of the Lawrenceville section to arrest members of a Croatian singing society believed to be a Communist front. A phony tip led to a raid on the back room of a Reeds-dale Avenue motion picture theater that turned out to be only a former Socialist Party hangout. In March Lenon, Ames, Yankovich, Beadling, and other agents went to Erie and brought back ten Communist suspects, mostly Lithuanians. The Russian Communists there eluded them by frequently moving their meeting place.[21] In April, agents Ames and Yankovich returned to northern West Virginia, the site of their November triumph. This time they were after the CPA, not the UORW, and the hunting was not so good. Raids on three coal camps netted eleven alleged CPA members, seven of them holding party cards.[22]

By the end of April 1920 the Communist roundup in Pittsburgh had just about run its course. Spencer's periodic progress reports give the details. By mid-March arrests totaled 110, of whom Sibray had processed 44 and recommended expulsion for 37. Ten fugitives remained at large and eight warrants had not yet been received. In the western Pennsylvania district, then, the Palmer CPA raids were less productive than the UORW ones. Spencer had observed in January that the CPA was much more dangerous than the UORW. The Communists in custody, he said, were "smart, evasive, and shifty."[23]

Just who were the Pittsburgh alien Communists taken in the Palmer raids? The files suggest that most were small fish—industrial workers and members of the former SPA foreign language federations. As in the UORW cases, typically the evidence against them was the presence of their names on membership or CPA dues lists. None were leaders of the Communist movement.[24] However, unlike the UORW detainees, most of them had families here and did not wish to return to Europe.[25]

The record of one alleged Communist, Mike Mesich (or Mesick) of Wendel, West Virginia, survives in the ACLU archives. Ames had arrested the twenty-eight-year-old immigrant Croatian at the Maryland Coal Company's mine on April 3. On the slimmest evidence he claimed Mesich was the secretary of the local CP. The miner admitted giving $1.25 to a party organizer who made one or two visits to the Wendel camp in January but denied attending any meetings or even knowing what Communism was. To prove him a liar, Ames produced Communist literature said to have been found in his boarding house and a postal clerk who said Mesich had sent a money order for more than $100 to CPA headquarters in Chicago.[26]

Neither proof was very persuasive. The Communist material could have belonged to any of the several boarders. Under questioning Ames admitted that he had written Mesich's name on a copy of *The Communist Manifesto* found at the house "for identification purposes." The postal clerk insisted that she remembered Mesich sending the money order months earlier even though she had never spoken to him before or since. She admitted that near paydays she handled up to two dozen money orders a day. It seemed odd then that she could not associate a single name in her transaction records with a specific face, except Mesich's. To cloud the issue further, when it was pointed out that Mesich's signature on his pay slips did not match the signature on the money order form, the clerk admitted that she had signed the form as she did for many foreign miners. Despite the shaky case and the fact that Mesich had a wife and children in Wendel, Sibray, who was much tougher on CPAs that he had been on UORWs, recommended deportation.[27]

The Palmer raids did not destroy the CPA or reveal all of its facets. Pittsburgh BI agents had struck at the Lithuanian, Polish, South Slavic, Croatian, Hungarian, and one of several Russian branches, but they had not learned the identities of the leaders of many Communist foreign-language branches. They still lacked inside informants.[28] Since it had become difficult to obtain from the Labor Department the unsigned or John Doe warrants that had been the basis for the January raids, Spencer proposed another way to get at these groups. Agents should arrest everyone found at their meeting places and then afterward apply for warrants for those believed to be Communists.

Justice and Labor Department authorities had crafted a legal fig leaf to cover just such arrests. Agents would forward the names of aliens they found at Communist nests and detained to Sibray, with whom Spencer had patched things up. Sibray would then wire the commissioner-general of immigration who would telegraph the warrants to Pittsburgh. However, the policy did not work very well. Agents were unsure whether to seek the warrants through Sibray in Pittsburgh or Hoover in Washington or directly from the Labor Department. Before long the route did not matter because the large volume of arrests nationally overwhelmed the Washington bureaucracy. The confusion and paperwork delays were so bad that at no time during the Red Scare could the Labor or Justice Departments say exactly how many aliens had been arrested. In March 1920, responding to a query from Hoover, who did not know either, Caminetti guessed that about 50 percent of the 6,396 deportation warrants that had been issued since July 1, 1919, produced arrests. A month later Post took a different approach. He offered Hoover precise figures for the numbers deported, released, or undergoing legal processing, but he could not tell how many deportation warrants had actually been issued or the arrest total. That Post misstated the number deported on the *Buford* as 241 casts doubt on his other figures.[29]

An obstacle to filling another Soviet ark was the Labor Department's policy, absent unusually compelling reasons, of setting bail for the alien Communists at $1,000 instead of the $10,000 advocated by the Justice Department. High bail had kept the UORW prisoners in custody during their deportation processing. Although some accounts say that $10,000 bail was usually imposed in the CPA cases, Sibray routinely imposed the lower amount; thus many of the Communists were back on the streets soon after arrest.[30]

The January raids stunned Pittsburgh radicals into temporary inactivity and forced them to consider new tactics and organization. Almost at once Chicago headquarters ordered the Communists to prepare to go underground. Secret groups of ten headed by an organizer who alone had contact with the party apparatus were to replace the old visible and vulnerable branches. Branches were to destroy dues books and membership cards and frequently change meeting places. Party members were to steel themselves for persecution and jail.[31]

Despite the federal campaign against them, in February the English-speaking CPA members risked an open meeting on Pittsburgh's North Side to discuss what to do. Party member Wendell, as Walsh, took the floor to urge the comrades to renounce the Communists and return to the IWW. From its beginning, he argued, the CPA had been a gathering place for "temperamental, hysterical radicals" and it could never be an effective industrial organization. The government had already crushed the Communists, he claimed, so feeding naive workers Communist propaganda could only endanger them. The IWW remained labor's best hope. It was all right to help arrested Communists with their legal defense, but that was all. A week later Wendell's North Side Central Branch voted to quit the CPA for the IWW. However, the important foreign language federations would not go along, thereby remaining as opaque to the BI as ever.[32]

Wendell's stance on the CPA altered his position among Pittsburgh radicals and ultimately, one imagines, reduced his value to the government. After he opted out of the CPA the Pittsburgh IWW shrank to insignificance, causing changes in the Radical Squad culture. Agents Ames and Yankovich were able to develop sources inside some foreign-language CPA branches and challenge the Lenon-Wendell duo as its "stars."

One can only guess why the shrewd and calculating Wendell chose to distance himself from the Communists. Perhaps party membership was too dangerous. Party leader Ruthenberg would certainly recognize the radical "Walsh" as a detective. Then, too, his expertise was in industrial espionage and his major contacts were the American-born Socialists and Wobblies. If the Communists continued to be dominated by Russian and Eastern European elements, he could never be part of its elite.

Still, the resourceful Wendell had a plan. The BI had brought him to Pittsburgh in 1917 so that he could gather information at the center of Margolis's radical network. Margolis's office, the McGeagh Building, New Era Hall, and the third floor of Moorehead Hall had been listening posts where Wendell could consort with leftists of all kinds. Now he hoped to establish a new vantage point, the International Socialist Lyceum, which he would promote as a center for Communists, Wobblies, and associated radicals. To accomplish this he joined a cabal of Wobblies and Communists to wrest control of the ISL governing board from the "reactionaries," meaning political Socialists. After the Socialist schism in the summer of 1919, the building's stock had been divided between the Communists and the Socialists. In March 1920, Wendell persuaded fellow Wobblies Ed Frank and Ed Solomon to join him in investing $100 apiece to acquire twenty shares of ISL stock, which entitled them to seats on the governing board. The trio then colluded with Communist board members to drive out conservative Socialists, "thus giving ownership to IWWs and Communists, and making it one of the best rendezvous for the ultra-radicals."[33]

Wendell's intrigue did not accomplish what he had hoped, for two reasons. First, federal harassment forced the Communists to disperse into small, secret, underground groups and prevented the ISL from becoming the radical rendezvous that Wendell envisioned. Second, the Red Scare was increasingly unpopular and support for BI undercover work was softening.

On March 15, 1920, Hoover produced a long memorandum on the work of his radical division from its inception on August 1, 1919. He pointed to what he had accomplished with a Washington staff of thirty clerks, stenographers, and assistants, and the sixty-one special agents in the field who were assigned full time to radical work. He enumerated their successes, including the discovery that Foster was boring from within the AFL and the "subtle and pernicious activities" of the UORW in the West Virginia coal fields. He credited his division for the absence of terrorist acts since its creation. He described in detail his "editorial card system" that now contained eighty thousand entries and reduced the time required to search radical subjects at the BI from a minimum of two hours to a maximum of two minutes. The cards, arranged by name, subject, organization, and geographical area, included every individual who was reported to the BI. His staff was also monitoring hundreds of radical publications, domestic and foreign.[34] But now there were questions as to whether Congress ought to fund these operations.

Opposition to the Palmer-Hoover anti-Red project from responsible legal, business, and government circles had solidified. As early as January, Secretary of Labor Wilson expressed doubt about the propriety and legality of the Communist raids but did little to stop them. In March, confronted with a huge backlog of undecided cases, Wilson took a month's leave of absence to care for his ill wife and mother and placed Assistant Secretary of Labor Louis F. Post in charge of deportations. Post quickly determined that mere Communist Party membership was not enough to justify deportation. The reestablishment of procedural due process encouraged civil libertarians to come forward with objections. By April, when Wilson returned, Post had canceled several thousand deportation warrants, dismissed charges against most subjects, and released many others on three months' probation.[35]

Post was not acting without important support. Fearing it would lead to the end of cheap foreign labor, Charles Schwab of Bethlehem Steel and T. Coleman DuPont of the chemical and munitions giant publicly decried the Red Scare. In weekly radical reports in February and March, Spencer chronicled the fears of Pittsburgh industrialists that "common labor was very much in demand and hard to get" and that a mass exodus of immigrants returning to Europe "will produce a shortage of labor in this district breaking all records." Concurrently, Boston federal judge George W. Anderson, a close friend of former attorney general Gregory and therefore no friend of Palmer, publicly castigated the actions of federal agents during the Palmer raids. Anderson's remarks came after he heard their testimony in *Colyer et al. v. Skiffington,* involving eighteen alien Communists seeking writs of habeas corpus.[36]

After Anderson's blast, in May came a blistering attack in the form of a sixty-seven-page pamphlet, *Report Upon the Illegal Practices of the United States Department of Justice.* It began as a brief prepared by Post's lawyer Jackson Ralston to answer Justice Department charges. Expanded and edited to pamphlet form and signed by twelve respected, nationally known lawyers including Zecharia Chafee, Jr., Felix Frankfurter, and Swinburne Hale, it became must reading for jurists. It cited the Justice Department for a host of constitutional violations ranging from cruel and unusual punishment to the use of agents provocateurs to wrongful spending of federal appropriations on anti-Red propaganda. Hoover's response, very much in character, was to privately impugn Frankfurter's loyalty and covertly aid attempts to have Chafee dismissed from the Harvard faculty.[37]

The former Wall Street lawyer Hale had become Hoover's nemesis. He was an old-stock Yankee and former MID intelligence officer with AEF whose ancestors had fought in every American war starting with the Revolution. A Harvard alumnus, he had voted for Theodore Roosevelt in 1912 and for Woodrow Wilson in 1916. In 1920 he was living in Greenwich Village where he consorted with writers and artists and flirted momentarily with socialism. Hale, who had opposed the UORW deportations and argued against Hoover in the Preis case, now represented Communists facing deportation. His credentials as a patriot gave weight to his opinions, which were, to say the least, very liberal. Naturally Hoover ordered him investigated only to discover that Hale was "a perfectly harmless nut, and a liberal rather than a radical, whose only concern for the radicals seems to be that they get free speech."[38]

A beneficiary of the growing sensitivity to aliens' rights was Edward Johnson, who had been arrested at IWW headquarters in Pittsburgh on June 3, 1919, in connection with the bomb attacks on Judge Thompson and Inspector Sibray. Cleared of the bombings, he had been ordered deported (see chapter 5). In January 1920, while Johnson remained at Ellis Island, NCLB (ACLU) attorneys, no doubt prodded by Margolis, applied to the U.S. District Court in New York for a writ of habeas corpus on Johnson's behalf. The lawyers, Charles Recht, an expert on deportation law, and ACLU founding father Albert DeSilver, challenged the government's claim that Johnson, who had supported himself in the United States and Canada for many years, was likely to become a public charge. They also challenged the assertion that he had taught or advocated the destruction of property. Recht assailed the fairness of the June 1919 hearing before Inspector O'Brien where Johnson had admitted to selling *The Little Red Song Book*. According to the transcript, when asked whether he sold song books in 1914 as a part of his IWW activities, Johnson answered, "I reckon I sold song books, too."[39] Then:

Q. "Do you know how many song books you have sold?"
A. "No."
Q. "Would you have sold as many as 100?"
A. "I might have sold 6 and I might have sold 2. They are not very good sellers."
Q. "Have you ever sold these books in any other city?"
A. "No, I never sold song books in any other city, not that I know of, I may have."[40]

After reviewing the arguments, Judge J. C. Knox granted a rehearing, noting that the government had offered in evidence a 1918 edition of the song book, which the judge found to be politically harmless. The 1914 edition was, perhaps, seditious, but Johnson's testimony was weak evidence that he had distributed any edition. That meant that the government must show that Johnson distributed the 1914 IWW song book, which it could not do. So government lawyers tried to delay the rehearing while Johnson's lawyers sought to bail him out. In response federal officials delayed as long they could and then pressured bondsmen not to put up bail for "Reds." This prompted DeSilver to appeal to a sympathetic Louis Post, who responded in writing that the Department of Labor did not wish to detain aliens for long periods and absolutely would not criticize companies that wrote bail bonds for persons who held unpopular ideas.[41] After Hoover did not reply to a Bureau of Immigration request to have Pittsburgh BI agents testify against Johnson, the government dropped the case, Judge Knox ordered Johnson's release, and Post canceled his deportation warrant.[42]

In Pittsburgh, even after Post began to cancel warrants, Spencer remained confident that most of his cases would stand up to the new legal dicta. The first wave of cancellations had included only five Pittsburgh aliens. However, the anti–Red Scare movement reached Pittsburgh in March 1920 when the recently established American Civil Liberties Union (ACLU) sponsored a rally featuring Union Theological Seminary professor and future ACLU chair Harry F. Ward. Ward criticized the *Buford* deportations and claimed that the government had railroaded the UORW men without a fair hearing. A few days later, the Rev. Dr. Luther Freeman, rector of Emory Episcopal Church, who had introduced Ward, was "invited" to the BI headquarters where Spencer and Lenon "interrogated him at length." If their purpose was to intimidate Freeman they failed. He agreed to bring Ward to the BI office for an interview the next time he was in town. The minister defended his longtime friend's effort to secure fair play for the deportees, "these innocent and misguided people." Spencer reported that Freeman was "biased against capital and feels that labor is not getting a square deal. He admits to having read considerable I.W.W. and other Radical literature." For a time Freeman had Spencer and Lenon on the defensive. They "spent considerable time" justifying the government's deportation of "Reds" and "trying to convince Rev. Freeman that he had not looked into the matter thoroughly and had read only one side of the question." The agents believed that the clergyman "left the office with a more thorough knowledge of the subject and a favorable impression" of their work.[43]

On April 11 the ACLU sponsored a rally at the Jewish Labor Lyceum in the Hill District. The key speaker in a group that included William Z. Foster and James H. Mauer was former assistant U.S. attorney general B. B. McGinnis. McGinnis, in what BI observers agreed was a legal and not especially rabble-rousing speech, called the suppression of civil liberties "Kaiserism" and denounced those who would wrap themselves in the flag to suppress dissidents. The BI already regarded the ACLU as an object of "interest." Since March 1920 Wendell had been drawing up a brief on the civil liberties group on assignment from Hoover's aide George Ruch. Late that month he went to New York, evidently in connection with the ACLU probe. Thereafter minutes of the ACLU's meetings in New York were a regular feature of the Pittsburgh Weekly Radical Reports.[44]

In the meantime the Palmer-Hoover antiradical campaign was foundering. The alliance between the Labor and Justice Departments was shattered. Since April Secretary of Labor Wilson had fully supported and even extended Post's policies. A congressional investigation of Post had failed to link him to the IWW. Post was a disciple of the late Henry George and a leader of what remained of the Single Tax movement, but he was no revolutionary. Then Hoover and Palmer turned to congressional allies to discredit and impeach Post. The scheme backfired when Post eloquently defended himself at a House Rules Committee hearing on May 7–8, just after Palmer's dire predictions of a violent Red May Day uprising had not come true.[45] By summer the tables were turned and it was Palmer who was before the House, with young Hoover at his side, defending his department against charges of wholesale civil liberties abuses.[46]

With the Red Scare on the wane, in the early summer of 1920 the Pittsburgh BI turned its attention to more immediate matters. In June and July Spencer's men were acting as an auxiliary detective force to assist the corporations in the control of their workers by "concentrating on the outlaw railroad strike."[47] After the strike ended, Spencer experienced firsthand the new judicial climate that was hostile to the BI practices that had made a mockery of civil rights.

On July 26, following Judge Anderson's ruling in *Coyler* that neither CPA nor CLP membership in and of itself was a deportable offense, Spencer suffered through a difficult meeting with Federal District Judge Charles P. Orr in chambers. Anticipating that radical matters would be the subject, Spencer had sent the judge documents on the Red menace, including a "book" by Wendell on Communism and a copy of the June *Communist*, one of two "official" publications identically titled and put out by competing communist factions. But these did not move the judge, who informed an unhappy Spencer that there was nothing new in them and that in his opinion "the Communists in this country on the point of numbers were negligible in comparison with patriotic Americans and he did not think they were such a menace as many people believed."[48] The judge even questioned whether the Communists really advocated the overthrow of the government by force and violence. Spencer countered by reading aloud from party documents that the "function of the United Communist Party is systematically to familiarize the working class with the necessity of armed insurrection as the only means through which the capitalist government and capitalist system can be overthrown." His Honor then literally laid down the law to Spencer. Arrests without warrants by BI agents during slacker raids and the Palmer raids, Orr said, had violated the fundamental rights of the people. If BI agents continued to make such arrests in western Pennsylvania he would cite them for contempt of court.[49]

An unrepentant Spencer wrote to Hoover that he might have expected that Orr, who had opposed the slacker raids, "which sent to the Front a large number of men who otherwise would have evaded their duty to their country, would fail to grasp the menace of the radical movement and consequently failed to judge the agents of the government in a manner which would allow them to exercise some discretion in meeting emergencies." Spencer acknowledged that his men would have to obey the court, "except in those cases where we can get the local authorities to act or warrants can be secured from the immigration authorities before arrests can be made."[50]

Judge Orr's pronouncement was a timely indication of shifting political winds in Washington that would severely curtail official federal domestic surveillance. Effective July 31, 1920, the force of field agents assigned to radical work and the number of paid informants was cut to the bone. Thirty-nine undercover men in eighteen cities were dismissed. Only four, P-132, P-134, Z-111, and K-92, remained officially on the payroll. The number of Radical Squad field agents was reduced from over sixty to seventeen.[51] In Pittsburgh, Lenon and Michael Yankovich, now a special agent, were to share the Radical Squad duties. The order to Pittsburgh does not mention Wendell or 836. Neither does it contain a standard clause in letters to other cities requesting confirmation that all paid informants have been let go.[52] The evidence shows that 836 was still in Pittsburgh. What is not clear is who was paying him.

The decline of public anti-Red hysteria was apparent in September. On the sixteenth a truck bomb was detonated outside the Wall Street offices of J. P. Morgan, killing thirty-three persons and injuring more than three hundred. Afterward public officials in many places were inundated with bomb or assassination threats, most of them hoaxes. What the *General Intelligence Bulletin* called a "peculiar effect" of the blast occurred in Brooklyn where thousands of persons "skipped their noon day meal and crowded the neighborhood" near the Customs House "in expectation of seeing an explosion." Nothing happened and the *Bulletin* thought that the "joke was on them." In reality it was the Palmer-Hoover Red hunt that was no longer taken seriously.[53]

In October and November 1920 Wendell found himself involved in a bizarre

The IWW view of capitalist Wall Street, "The Monster which causes most of our Sufferings," by controlling commerce and industry, education, the law, politics, religion, and natural resources. The timing of this cartoon was unfortunate, less than two months before the deadly September 1920 bomb explosion outside the headquarters of J. P. Morgan. (*OBUM*, July 1920)

bank robbery scheme with one Konon Parchmenko. Wendell had mentioned Parchmenko, who represented himself as an official agent of the Soviets, as a source on Pittsburgh Russian aliens in a few reports since 1918. The Russian was observed to travel often to New York City and he received his mail at Margolis's office.[54]

In 1920 Parchmenko told Wendell that many Russians in the area, including UORW members, did not support the Soviets. Since the November 1919 raids, the UORW had gone underground and was now training anarchists to return to Russia to bedevil the Bolsheviks. But Parchmenko said that he belonged to a terrorist group that was neither the UORW nor Communist. Ultimately the members wanted to return to Russia to overthrow the Bolshevik regime, but first they planned to steal money and spread terror in the United States by assassinating capitalists and officials.[55]

In October, in line with the aim of expropriating capital, Parchmenko invited Wendell to help him rob a bank at a location he would only say was somewhere between Youngstown and New Castle near the Ohio-Pennsylvania border. Wendell, who worked as an auto mechanic, was to drive the getaway car. Parchmenko would not identify the other holdup men except to say one was from New York City and the other from Cleveland and to hint that they were from the same group that had set off the deadly September Wall Street truck bomb.[56]

What was the BI to do? It wanted to stop the bank holdup, but Wendell could hardly go to the police. He could not take part in the robbery, but, at the same time, the Bureau wanted to learn as much as possible about Parchmenko's confederates. So Wendell strung Parchmenko along, saying he would participate. Then on November 8 Parchmenko notified Wendell the robbery would take place in just two days and they must leave Pittsburgh the next day to set things up. To stall, Wendell claimed to be ill and under a doctor's care. He told Parchmenko to come to his house the next morning when, perhaps, he would be better.[57]

Wendell then met with Spencer and others until 4:30 A.M. the next morning. A private detective who knew the New Castle-Youngstown area guessed that the target bank was at Bessemer, Pennsylvania (see chapter 5). Then Spencer ordered his men to pick up Parchmenko at home on the pretext of questioning him about his connections with several recently deported radicals. So as not to reveal Wendell's true identity and the BI's involvement with anarchist criminals, Spencer arranged to have a third party warn Bessemer officials about the possible robbery. The agents did not find Parchmenko at home that morning and he never showed up at Wendell's; he had disappeared.[58]

The oddest aspect of this strange incident in November 1920 is that the plan for the robbery seems to have been ripped from the pages of the December 10, 1919, *Pittsburgh Post*. That story, headlined "READS LIKE WILDEST FICTION," described how Philadelphia-based undercover private detective Stephen A. Marczewski had joined three alien IWWs from Monessen in a nighttime assault upon the bank in Orwell, Ohio. The detective helped to plan the robbery and even drilled into the bank safe. He also alerted a sheriff's posse, which was waiting with loaded magazine revolvers and riot guns. In the shoot-out that ensued the lawmen killed two of the robbers, but the driver of the large, black getaway car escaped. The detective Marczewski worked for the notoriously antilabor Railway and Industrial Protection Association (RAI), which was the source of the story. The *Post* editor afterward told an Interchurch World Movement investigator that RAI made blaming the robbery on the IWW a condition of giving the *Post* an exclusive.[59]

Parchmenko's plan, as far as it goes, parallels the *Post* story. The alien radicals are stealing money in order to return, rich, to their homelands. They use an automobile to commit robbery in a rural area where law enforcement is weak and they are not known. And, of course, an undercover detective is one of the gang. According to Wendell, Parchmenko even claimed to have been involved in an earlier bank robbery in which two holdup men were killed.[60]

The bank affair, like the *Post* story, reeks of planted melodramatic fiction. The question is, whose fiction? Was Parchmenko an RAI operative recycling an old ploy to lure the radical Walsh into a criminal act? Was he a radical testing Wendell's revolutionary fervor or trying to force Wendell to reveal his identity as an informer? Was he a terrorist attracted to Wendell's powerful car and radical persona?[61] What did Parchmenko conclude when Wendell feigned illness and why does he disappear from the BI files after this incident?[62]

The major staff reductions, decline in the use of undercover informants, and changing political climate did not end BI surveillance. They did create the need to do more with less, meaning increased reliance on fixed procedures and centralized functions. In 1920 and 1921 the GID's editorial card file of radicals grew to more than one hundred thousand entries. From the required field office weekly radical reports, Hoover's staff compiled the *General Intelligence Bulletin* to give the field offices a national overview of radical activities. The project suffered somewhat from distribution problems and because field offices often failed to submit the material on time. Pittsburgh offered excuses for tardiness ranging from a lack of time because of an all-consuming investigation of five thousand syndicalist publications seized by the Pittsburgh police to Lenon's carbuncle that kept him from work for a week.[63]

The weekly radical reports document changes in the Pittsburgh Left and in the Bureau's response to it as the Red Scare faded in 1920 and 1921. The Radical Squad expanded its monitoring activities beyond the SPA, IWW, UORW, CPA, and CLP of 1919 to include the International Bible Association, Czechoslovak and Jugoslav nationalist groups, the Socialist Labor Party, the Sinn Fein and the "anti-Sinn Fein," and the UMWA.[64] There were also special sections each week devoted to "Hebrew," "Negro," and especially Japanese activities. Reports on blacks covered Marcus Garvey's Black Star Line and Universal Negro Improvement Association, the NAACP, and Communist attempts in 1921 to distribute in Pittsburgh black neighborhoods thousands of pamphlets on the "Tulsa Massacre," the bloody and fiery rampage of white mobs through the African American section of that Oklahoma city.[65] The minutes of the ACLU's weekly executive meetings in New York City, which were a regular feature of the radical reports to Hoover from the Pittsburgh BI, provided the only mention, much less criticism, of KKK and American Legion violence to be found.[66]

The weekly reports show that a narrow, countersubversive, 100 percent Americanism informed the work of the Pittsburgh radical squad. Lenon especially operated on the paranoid assumption that he was responsible to protect Americans from cultural subversion by an imagined Marxist-Jewish-feminist conspiracy. In April 1921 he reported on *Women*,[67] a novel about a woman who lived in a ménage à trois and who "found justification in her actions." Lenon fretted that much subversive literature was now "in the form of novels that tended to break down the moral attitude of the readers, more particularly if they happen to be young women." If it were "a purely sordid, licentious or obscene book it could, of course, be stopped, but instead of that, taking paragraph by paragraph, there is nothing in it either licentious or obscene, but there is constant repetition of justification." Lenon then embarked on a fantastic tirade railing that "the Jews are always avaricious in the acquisition of anything, displaying this particularly in the acquisition of learning or knowledge through our public institutions where they can acquire it free." Jews were being the most thoroughly affected by this novel and by the Bolshevik movement in general. He warned that the "same avariciousness of the race will . . . become more prominent with the success of the Soviet Regime" because Jews "are practically the only race or set there who are studying the Russian language." In New York many were taking Russian language classes at the Rand

School. "As a race, the Jews are not only ardent adherents of Soviet Russia, but they believe so thoroughly in its eventual success that they are laying their plans in education and otherwise to be leaders in the hoped-for commercial development that will follow."[68]

In September Lenon returned to an anti-Semitic theme when he castigated Pittsburgh officials for suppressing Henry Ford's *Dearborn Independent*, then featuring the notorious and scurrilous "Protocols of the Elders of Zion." He wrote that "many of the citizens of Pittsburgh who travel the down town section daily could not understand why the Police Department interfered with the men selling the INDEPENDENT and at the same time permitted a Hebrew to conduct a stand on this curb . . . to sell the [Socialist] New York Call. The action . . . can probably be explained . . . as a cheap ploy for Hebrew votes."[69]

Part of the explanation for Lenon's resort to fantasies of conspiracy lies in his growing difficulty in obtaining inside intelligence about the Communists. This, in turn, was caused by Wendell's continuing attachment to the increasingly irrelevant IWW. The rise of the Communists only added to the woes of the IWW, which was already reeling from vigilante attacks, government prosecution and infiltration, and internal dissension. Communism appealed powerfully to some Wobblies as an effective centrally controlled and disciplined organization that could pragmatically combine direct and political action to achieve the revolution. Sooner or later, Bill Haywood, Robert Minor, Charles Ashleigh, Harrison George, Sam Scarlett, George Andreytchine, Rudolph Blum, and others would forsake their fellow workers for new comrades. Margolis's ally from the stogie workers' strike, Fred Merrick, became the western Pennsylvania party chairman.[70]

But Communism repelled many others. Men like Margolis, a Wobbly in all but name, and Ralph Chaplin, author of "Solidarity Forever,"[71] perceived that adherence to Communism would destroy the decentralized democracy, local autonomy, and spontaneity of the IWW that they cherished. IWW historian Fred Thompson recalled that in 1919 the Communists replaced the Wobs as the "new bogeyman" in the press. This was not good news for the IWW, since no small part of its appeal and influence depended on its radical mystique. By stealing the Wobblies' perversely glamorous Public Enemy Number One image, the Communists helped to finish what the government and the corporations had begun.[72]

In June 1920, the local IWW experienced a brief revival; a sort of rally before the death rattle. There was talk of establishing a headquarters at the International Socialist Lyceum and of bringing in George Speed as a resident organizer to get the movement going in Bessemer, Braddock, and McKees Rocks. But Speed did not take up residence and thereafter the Wobblies could scarcely scrape together a quorum for routine business. It did not help their cause that H. H. Detweiler, who remained by default secretary of the local branch, appeared drunk and disorderly at the ISL on several occasions.[73]

By the end of 1921 the collapse of the Pittsburgh IWW was so nearly complete that not even government informers could keep it alive. By April Wendell evidently had left Pittsburgh for good.[74] He would not surface again in the public record until the mid-1930s, when he turned up in Detroit specializing in "industrial investigation [of] sabotage, parts theft, and wild cat strikes" for auto manufacturers. From 1935 to 1947 he was two-thirds of the firm of Wendell, Walsh, and Brown, Public Relations Counsel, whose principals were listed in the Detroit city directories as Leo M. Walsh, Michael W. Wendell, and L. M. Wendell. In 1940, he volunteered for MID service. What role, if any, he played in World War II is not recorded.[75]

Initially, three obstacles had interfered with the Pittsburgh BI's investigation of the Communists. First, the campaign by civil liberties groups and others against the Palmer raids and deportations hindered the G-men from interrogating suspected radicals or searching for their records and literature. Second, the Communists' legal defense became more sophisticated. Finally, they went underground.[76] Nonetheless, by the end of 1921 Pittsburgh agents gained a considerable understanding of the Communist structure. Their big break was the arrest of United Communist Party organizer Joe Martinovich, who led them to a cache of literature and branch records.[77] Soon afterward they were able to insert an informant to supply detailed reports of the party's activities in Pittsburgh, Cleveland, and Detroit. The source was good enough that by June 1921 acting SAC C. D. McKean could estimate with some confidence that total Communist Party membership in the Pittsburgh district stood at between 5,900 and 6,500.[78]

However, as Spencer had predicted after his meeting with Judge Orr in 1920, the Bureau's role was mainly passive observation. It was left to local authorities to keep the lid on the Steel Valley, and keep the lid on they did. Lenon reported that "compared to other cities, the active 'Reds' in Pittsburgh are but a mere handful." Despite the fact that many Russians were sympathetic toward radicalism, "there is no well developed Russian organization, due to the vigilance of authorities . . . [Communist Party activities] are carried on in great secrecy. In New York and Detroit, Communist speakers hold meetings without fear of molestation," allowing their followers to work openly, whereas Pittsburgh Communist leaders had little opportunity even to come in contact with their followers. Even though Communists were active in traditional radical labor hot spots such as Homestead, Duquesne, Braddock, and McKees Rocks, local officials and company security forces had things under control.[79]

By 1921 the opponents of the Red Scare had the upper hand. From January 19 until March 21 Senator Thomas Walsh of Montana conducted hearings into the excesses of the January 1920 raids. Attorney General Palmer and the GID's Hoover responded to a tough grilling with evasion and equivocation. Both denied responsibility.[80] The war emergency and the Red Scare were finally over and control of labor had reverted to its pre-war custodians. Yet as Richard G. Powers notes, the framework for generations of national debate over Communism had been laid. Anticommunists now passionately but incorrectly believed that "the entire left was somehow part of a Communist plot to subvert the country." On the other side liberals and leftists across the spectrum saw anticommunism as an "unconstitutional conspiracy against them."[81]

9
"DEPORTING" MARGOLIS, 1919–1921

> Don't you think it would be a good thing for the United States to find an island
> somewhere and put all the people on it that think as you do?
>
> Sen. Wesley L. Jones to Jacob Margolis (Margolis Senate Testimony, October 1919)

THE ALLEGHENY COUNTY BAR ASSOCIATION (ACBA) had never clasped Jacob Margolis to its bosom. Because law school admissions quotas and accredita-
tion standards were not yet common, the genteel sons of old money who preferred
the dark-paneled and lucrative respectability of corporate law to the more crass
commercial pursuits of their forebears had no way to keep Margolis from practicing law.[1] Still, they made clear to the rabble-rousing former newsboy that he was
unwelcome by pointedly not inviting him to join the ACBA.

From 1917 to 1919 Margolis was the object of several attempted sanctions. The
first came in February 1918 when an ACBA investigating committee summoned
him and his partner Marshall to answer a complaint in a "letter from Washington," about their handling of questionnaires for potential draftees. In a closed-
door, hour-long hearing Margolis rejected the charges as "all bosh" and the ACBA
dropped the matter. Margolis suspected that the Justice Department was behind
the complaint and from that moment believed that the BI was out to get him. He
told Wendell, "I myself, personally would not be a bit surprised to be disbarred at
any time, but until I am disbarred, I am going to continue my business the same
old way."[2]

In July 1918, one hundred attorneys formed the Allegheny County Lawyers
League of Patriotism in order to "furnish speakers to refute the misstatements circulated by enemies of the government." League spokesman J. W. Kinnear, in a
thinly veiled reference to Margolis, "intimated" to the *Gazette-Times* "that there
may be members of the bar who are not as loyal as they should be," in which case
the new organization "may be needed to assist the government in dealing with
their cases."[3]

In November 1918 the MID in Washington was prepared to charge Margolis with illegally collecting fees for filing draft exemptions for Russian aliens. However, it reconsidered after Pittsburgh IO Edward H. Flood reminded DMI Churchill that "Margolis has been under constant observation by our confidential agent for many months, and all his activities and utterances are promptly reported to this office." The crux of the matter was that "Margolis is the source of much valuable information regarding the radical labor and socialistic activities in this district" and that "for this reason we have refrained from taking any action . . . on his violations of the Espionage Act . . . [because] we could scarcely obtain . . . conviction . . . without betraying the identity of our informant." In December 1918 Treasury Department agents tried to catch him evading income taxes. Bragging to associates that he would "be damned" if he would give his money to militarism, he promised that if the IRS came to call he would destroy checks and conceal his income.[4] After Wendell reported these remarks IRS agents did come to call, but they could not find enough to warrant prosecution.

Ten months later, in October 1919, the ACBA, with the full support of the BI and the MID, suddenly began disbarment proceedings. After newspapers all over the country reported on Margolis's appearance before the Senate Committee on Labor and Education (chapter 6), an embarrassed Pittsburgh legal establishment reacted. On October 21, member A. D. Fording complained in writing to the ACBA that Margolis had betrayed his oath as an officer of the court to support the United States Constitution. Margolis denied to reporters that he had said anything against the Constitution, but a week later, after reviewing the transcript of his Senate testimony, the ACBA proceeded against him.[5]

Having arranged for Margolis to testify in Washington in the first place and even having prepared the questions he was asked, government agents now orchestrated his professional downfall. From September 1919 they shadowed him. They lurked outside his office in the Union Arcade; followed him when he walked home; and watched his house until the lights went out. In October, when he went to Capitol Hill to testify, they tailed him from Harper's Ferry to the Capitol and observed him until he boarded the return train to Pittsburgh.[6]

In his fight to retain his right to practice law, Margolis turned to the National Civil Liberties Bureau (NCLB) for which he and Marshall were the Pittsburgh corresponding attorneys. The civil liberties group offered discreet encouragement but no formal help. When Margolis asked Roger Baldwin to publish the ACBA complaint against him along with his reply to it, Baldwin wrote a "Dear Jake" letter, saying that he and DeSilver considered the complaint "exceedingly interesting" but "not the kind of thing that we could publish. *It does not deal with an issue of civil liberty which we could get across to the folks we reach* [italics added]. . . . We are limited in our resources and can publish only what we figure is of immediate interest to our constituency."[7] One can hardly credit Baldwin's statement. The ACBA's contention that Margolis's political beliefs disqualified him from practicing law under the United States Constitution seemed made to order for a legal test. Were lawyers now to face disbarment for their political actions outside the courtroom? What, precisely, was the constituency that Baldwin and DeSilver feared to displease? Was Margolis too radical for the emergent ACLU's liberal financial backers? Did Baldwin think that Margolis was a government informer?

Margolis engaged S. S. Robertson, George Bradshaw, and L. N. Porter to defend him. Porter, who was the best known of the trio, was the brother and law partner of Republican congressman Stephen Geyer Porter and their office was in the same building as the federal intelligence agencies. John C. Bane and Arthur Scully represented the bar association. In preliminary legal maneuvers, January–April 1920, Scully and Bane had the advantage. Scully, a former MID major who served in France under Van Deman, had access to confidential government material on Margolis, much of it conveniently preassembled by the BI. When J. Edgar Hoover assigned an assistant to collate the evidence, it was with the reminder that the standards of proof required for disbarment were far less rigorous than those required in a criminal case. Therefore although the government files did not contain enough to convict Margolis of, say, violating the Espionage Act, they held much that "could easily be construed as unethical coming from an attorney" to support disbarment. Hoover also directed Spencer to give Scully "whatever you think proper and which will not disclose the identity of our informants."[8]

With typical thoroughness, Hoover cast a wide net for evidence. He asked the New York field office to try to get Margolis's correspondence with Emma Goldman from her confidant Stella Ballantine. He also queried the Post Office Bureau of Translators and Radical Publications. In response, postal official R. A. Bowen admitted that his group did not "run strong on Margolies," because it did not monitor the Pittsburgh foreign-language papers. He recollected English-language newspaper stories about Margolis in the *New York World* but when he could not get the newspaper staff to produce them, he was puzzled. Why was the usually responsible *World* "behaving so peculiarly toward this entire matter of the Department of Justice action toward radicals?" Hoover also canvassed field offices in the East and Midwest that had little that was new except a transcript of a November 1919 Margolis speech given at Emma Goldman's appearance in Detroit during her final United States speaking tour.[9]

While federal officials built their case against him, Margolis embarked on a speaking tour of the industrial Midwest that furnished them with more "evidence." His Senate appearance and work for the UORW deportees had made him an instant celebrity of the Left and brought out large crowds. At Wicker Park Hall in Chicago, in the anointing presence of anarchist icon Lucy Parsons, widow of one of the Haymarket martyrs, he shouted down Communist hecklers who were incensed by his reference to the Soviet leaders as dictators. At Detroit he and Agnes Inglis agreed to look after the personal belongings of alien Communists being held for deportation. He joined Helen Todd and Robert Minor in raising $1,000 for the families left behind when the *Buford* sailed. Speaking to six hundred at Arena Gardens, he was careful not to say anything that would violate the Michigan syndicalism law. That, however, did not prevent him from blasting, on the one hand, the Pittsburgh steel barons for suppressing free speech and failing to educate workers and, on the other, the mass of workers for their apathy.[10]

At Akron a GAR Hall crowd estimated by detectives at four to five thousand paid twenty-five cents each to hear Margolis. He used the occasion to catalog the sins of respectable lawyers and to single out Akron's attorneys for setting exorbitant fees to avoid representing poor immigrants and workers. He castigated federal officials for breaking their promise not to use the Lever Act to break the coal strike. It being Washington's birthday, he spoke on the Constitution and, evidently influenced by Algie M. Simons's *Social Forces in American History* (1911), portrayed the Founders as the authors of a secret document designed to protect capitalists.[11]

In March Margolis was again in Detroit and before an audience sprinkled with detectives and stenographers hanging on his every word. He also turned up in Washington at the Labor Department to lobby for his Russian clients threatened with deportation. There he reportedly met with a representative of the Interchurch World Movement, which had published a report damning the actions of corporations and law enforcement officials in the steel strike. His speeches and rallies became grist for the disbarment mill. Reports of them would be included in the ACBA brief and BI eyewitnesses would travel to Pittsburgh to describe them at Margolis's hearing.[12]

The public phase of Margolis's disbarment got underway on April 29, 1920, before a three-judge panel in Common Pleas Court. The first day's newspaper coverage was intense. The *Press* gave the story a page-one headline: "TESTIMONY SENSATIONAL IN MARGOLIS DISBARMENT CASE." "Wanted Germany to Rule in America Is Charge" was the lead. The "sensational" testimony referred to was that of Doctors Alfred J. Buka and Charles T. Brickman. They told of a 1917 meeting of a professional men's discussion group, the University Circle, at which Margolis had said that he "would as lief be under the Kaiser and the German government as our present government."[13]

A heavy-handed federal presence was evident throughout the four-day hearing. The ACBA attorneys relied on Justice Department evidence, principally from ex–Radical Squad lead agent Edgar Speer. He went over material, based largely on Wendell's reports, that the BI had accumulated since 1917 to portray Margolis as a Wobbly and the IWW as a dangerous revolutionary organization. Fred Ames described Margolis's involvement with David Eelack, the UORW activist who had fled Pittsburgh to avoid deportation only to be arrested near Fairmont, West Virginia, and then deported on the *Buford*. Two Detroit BI men detailed the radical aspects of Margolis's speeches there. Two IRS agents told of his refusal to pay taxes, without explaining that the IRS had insufficient evidence to prosecute. U.S. Attorney Humes contributed damaging hearsay when he gave his version of a 1917 private conversation with Margolis about the basic principles of law, in the course of which "Jake" had expressed opposition to conscription on philosophical grounds.[14]

Several nonfederal witnesses also appeared for the ACBA. An SPA member recounted that the party had expelled Margolis in 1913 for his radicalism. The Pittsburgh police superintendent described Margolis's connection to the Radical Library and the Anti-Conscription League. City assistant district attorney John D. Meyer recalled a long-ago "private conversation" in 1908 or 1909 with young law student Margolis. Radical even then, Margolis had said that he did not believe "in any government at all." A West Virginia mine superintendent, a Monongahela policeman, the Charleroi postmaster, and a Pittsburgh printer each tied Margolis to some or other political agitation between 1917 and 1920. The ACBA lawyers hammered at the points that, as one headline had it, "MARGOLIS DEEP IN RED'S WORK" and that he did not subscribe to mainstream American values and assumptions. They offered as their prime example his shocking admission at the Senate hearing of atheism and an unwillingness as a pacifist even to defend his wife from a violent attacker in their home.[15]

After a two-week recess the hearing resumed on May 12, with Margolis testifying in his own defense. What else could he do but admit that he was an atheist and, with qualifications unnoticed by the newspapers, a communist, syndicalist, and anarchist? He owned to speeches against the Russian blockade, conscription, and the deportations of UORW and Communist Party members, but he refined the testimony as to what he said to IRS agents in 1918. It was not that he was "an I.W.W. and a Bolshevist, and I don't care who knows it," but rather "I upheld the I.W.W. and the Bolshevists and that this fact was quite well known." He would not divulge his income except to admit that he had not filed a return since the enactment of the federal income tax in 1913. It was true, he said, that he had represented IWW members, but not that he was a propagandist for the organization. He struggled to explain his pro-German remarks at the 1917 University Circle meeting. He explained that the meeting occurred before the United States entered the war and had featured a hypothetical discussion of a book about a fictitious German landing in New York. From his own hypothetical remarks his accusers Buka and Brickman had cobbled together bits and pieces to falsely claim that he favored a German occupation of the United States. He also hedged slightly his assertion that he would not defend his wife from an attacker, while reiterating his opposition to all violence. At the end, he demanded to know what law he had broken.[16]

In his defense Margolis's lawyers called only three witnesses. The first, attorney Gilbert Zehner, testified that Margolis was a longtime pacifist deeply opposed to violence. The second, lawyer Samuel J. Horovitz, who had attended the now famous University Circle meeting, swore that Margolis had not made the statements attributed to him by Buka and Brickman. The last witness was George Weinstein, secretary of the local SPA, who explained that Margolis had always fervently opposed violence and that he had spoken out against the Soviet's use of force in Russia.[17]

On May 13, both sides presented their final arguments. To the ACBA's lengthy indictment the Margolis team offered a simple defense. George Bradshaw said the bar association lawyers had failed "to distinguish between what we think of Mr. Margolis's opinions and his right to think as he pleases. We have an absolute . . . right to think as we please on matters political and religious as long as we obey the law." The Constitution protected his right to hold and express unpopular opinions and he had broken no law. Ergo, no grounds existed for his disbarment. Tellingly, Bradshaw asked why the government had not tried and convicted Margolis during the war under the Espionage Act.[18]

Even if they knew, ACBA lawyers Scully and Bane could not reveal that prosecuting Margolis would have jeopardized Wendell's cover and that of other government informants and closed the government's clearest window into the Pittsburgh Left. So, eliding sensitive matters, they laid out their case on narrow technical grounds. Speaking first, Scully said, "we care not for his opinions. The sole question is whether or not this respondent violated his oath of office and has he misconducted himself so as to justify disbarment." Neither did they care that Margolis was an atheist. Yet their reason for raising that issue was to show that Margolis "was not a theist. . . . If he were not an atheist he could not be an I.W.W., nor anarchist, nor a communist." The ACBA objected to Margolis's actions, not his opinions or ideas. The radical lawyer deserved disbarment, for "the everyday life of Mr. Margolis has been an overt act." Then Attorney Bane spoke, asking rhetorically, "Has the time come when an attorney of the bar can be a Red, an Anarchist, and still continue to be a minister in the halls of justice? God forbid it! The bar must be kept clean, and we dare not permit a member of our body to preach sedition, to espouse the teachings of the I.W.W., and the communist anarchists and to counsel the overthrow of our government."[19]

So ended the public phase of the disbarment. Then the ACBA lawyers retired for a few days to prepare a brief for the panel of judges. The product was a 192-page compilation of arguments, testimony, and documents that testified to, if nothing else, the extent of the government's long-standing interest in Margolis and its desire to punish him. Mainly drawing upon the testimony of Speer and materials seized or intercepted by the BI, the brief systematically indicted Margolis as an anarchist, a syndicalist, a communist, an atheist, and a pacifist. It offered evidence that he had distributed Louis Fraina's *Revolutionary Age*, predecessor to the CPA's *The Communist*. It tied him to the IWW, showed that he had written pieces for *Mother Earth, One Big Union Monthly,* and *Bread and Freedom,* and established that he had supported and represented members of the UORW. Speer's (or Wendell's) speculations on issues that were not clearly linked by a chain of evidence to Margolis filled several pages. He expounded on the IWW as the "Russian Workers of the World," the "red radicalism" of the Third International, and upon William Z. Foster's *Syndicalism*. He concluded that Margolis had joined with Pittsburgh "riff raff," such as L. M. Wendell, in recruiting for the IWW. The brief also tapped BI sources to show that Margolis had been an active speaker for radical causes and had consorted with some of the country's most dangerous agitators. Emma Goldman's book on "sex anarchy" was in the Radical Library and she had introduced him at Detroit as "old friend." It was also revealed that Margolis had once given a warm introduction to Mary Harris "Mother" Jones when she spoke at a Tom Mooney Defense Fund meeting in Pittsburgh.[20]

In an adversarial process one does not expect an unbiased presentation from either side and that was certainly the case with the brief against Margolis. For example, the brief includes the complete text of the cover letter, intercepted by the BI, that Margolis sent to *Bread and Freedom* with the "final Warning" from the Ku

Klux Klan (see chapter 5). Quoted are snippets from the Klan letter, such as its reference to Margolis's "'speeches at radical meetings' and 'ravings against the government' and 'activities in behalf of the reds.'" But the brief does not mention that these statements are from the Ku Klux Klan! The brief even reprints the announcement of his five lectures on "Revolution and Industrial Organization" of January and February 1919 (see chapter 5), with no hint that those lectures attacked the Bolsheviks. It also incorporates material from Margolis's articles in *One Big Union Monthly* but fails to mention that at the time the *Monthly* was outspokenly opposed to Communist influences within the IWW.[21]

The chain of reasoning to justify disbarment was that Margolis violated his attorney's oath; that the court had the right to disbar attorneys for bad behavior; and that, like deportation, disbarment was not punishment. To lend weight to their argument the ACBA lawyers invoked Justice Oliver Wendell Holmes's famous "clear and present danger" doctrine enunciated in *United States v. Schenck* (March 1919), one of several Espionage Act cases that came before the Supreme Court. Margolis's words had endangered the public welfare, they argued. Disbarment being rare and for overtly political reasons even rarer, the ACBA attorneys had to dig deeply for disbarment precedents. They found three; all of them far-fetched and ironic. In the first a lawyer had taken part in lynching a black man. In the second a lawyer had joined an Oregon mob that tortured three Wobblies and drove them out of Coos County.[22] The third and from Margolis's perspective the most apt citation, from 1793, described a lawyer who abetted a slave revolt in Santo Domingo.[23] The purpose of these precedents evidently was to convince the court that Margolis's radical words amounted to participation in bloody, violent acts.

The ACBA denied that the first Amendment protected Margolis. Had not the Supreme Court in *United States ex rel. Turner v. Williams* approved deporting an anarchist whose speeches advocating a general strike "contemplated the ultimate realization of that ideal by the use of force, or that his speeches were incitements to that end?" In its final salvo, the ACBA thundered, "if an alien, who owed no affirmative duty to this government could be deported in these circumstances, can Margolis under the evidence in this record be permitted to continue to hold his office as attorney?" Margolis had educated himself to be disloyal. "By extensive reading of red literature and long association with anarchists and terrorists whose dominating passion is the lust of plunder, his mind has become poisoned, and he has lost his capacity for true and loyal attachment to our institutions; and, for that reason, he is not fit to hold his office of attorney."[24]

To the ACBA's citation of the pre–Red Scare Holmes of *Schenck,* Margolis answered with Holmes's more recent opinion on free speech from his dissent in *Abrams v. United States* (November 1919). Following the Great Dissenter, Margolis argued that ideas expressed in words could never harm a government. All the ACBA had proved was that Margolis talked, "Yes, beyond a doubt; and that we talked in doubtful company. That we talked to miscellaneous assortments of the sons of men; Russians, Lithuanians, Poles, Italians, Bohemians, Parthians and Medes, Elamites and the dwellers of Mesopotamia." But it was absurd that "grown-up people should be afraid of the wretched nonsense talked by the extreme socialist or anarchistic spouters." That only showed "how very little the average man knows his fellow men of the working classes." But "we whose job it is to deal with them every day . . . get no scares of revolution, although we are perhaps kept stepping lively to meet the inevitable changes in economic conditions which it would be ridiculous to say the working people are creating. How delightfully simple the economic problem would be if it were only a question of more or less wages."[25]

Sarcastically, Margolis pled guilty to keeping bad company, particularly the Wobblies and "those dreadful Russians." But he had not supported the Soviets; and, if he had, what did it matter? Proving that his ability to see the future was imperfect, he predicted that Soviet rule in Russia would be shortlived; he looked "everyday for news that Trotsky and the soviet have both gone sky-wards." Returning to more relevant matters, he reiterated that he had broken no law. He asserted that being a lawyer placed no special limitation on one's freedom of speech and attacked the disbarment proceedings as a violation of due process. The real value of the effort to expel him from the bar was to generate publicity to help "us to know something of how the foreigner is handled and why he does not love us." Roger Baldwin wrote approvingly that Margolis's answer to the ACBA "makes mighty good reading." Indeed, as an intellectual exercise, the use of Holmes as well as jurists Charles Evans Hughes and George W. Anderson[26] seemed to give Margolis the edge in the theoretical argument. But argument was likely to change few minds in this case and Margolis's resort to sarcasm shows that he knew it.

Between June and September while the judges pondered his professional fate, Margolis continued to agitate for the IWW cause. On the Fourth of July he gave the funeral oration for longtime Wobbly Otto Justh and then delivered the principal speech at the IWW picnic at Heinz Grove.[27]

On September 15, 1920, the judges ordered the disbarment of Margolis. They wrote that he had forfeited his position by failing to loyally support his government and by doing "his utmost to breed unrest among the lawless and the vicious, and to incite them to acts of violence and disloyalty. In all this he has been persistent, and he has shown no signs of repentance."[28]

For the BI the victory was sweet, coming at a time when the anti-Red movement was faltering and government legal victories against radicals had become rare. SAC Spencer immediately telegraphed the news to Washington. The next day Wendell, communicating as 836 directly with George Ruch, sent clippings from the evening dailies. More clippings and the welcome news that Margolis was also to be disbarred from Orphan's court were added to the week's radical report to Hoover. MID also celebrated the government's victory. ACBA attorney and former MID Major Scully sent a "secret and confidential" message to MID headquarters with documents from the case, including the brief against Margolis. Included was a thank-you for Pittsburgh IO Flood and "his confidential informant . . . for their assistance." Attorney General Palmer deemed the event worthy of mention in his *Annual Report,* where he commended "the disbarment of Jacob Margolis by Pennsylvania State Authorities."[29]

Mainstream press reaction generally supported the court's decision but, of course, the Left was outraged. A perceptive critique was Swinburne Hale's in *The Nation.* Hale detected the influence of all-powerful U.S. Steel, charging that the corporation had pressured the Allegheny County legal community to have Margolis "deported." He believed that in its decision the court had failed to grasp that Margolis or "any lawyer could have such a faith in the possible reconstruction of society, and, at the same time, support the Constitution and live according to its laws." Hale alluded suspiciously to the Justice Department's extraordinarily detailed knowledge of Margolis's affairs as "an interesting sidelight on the criminal espionage which has come to be part of American institutions."[30]

Margolis sent a copy of the court's opinion to the NCLB, which had now become the ACLU, proposing that it would make "excellent propaganda material." He warned that "if this case is allowed to stand it may be used as a precedent and no lawyer with opinions contrary to the accepted order will be admitted to practise [*sic*] or defend the workers who may have difficulty with their employers." The ACLU's DeSilver was sympathetic and found the court's reasoning "quite beyond me." How, he wondered, could the judges say that Margolis's beliefs had nothing to do with his disbarment and at the same time base their decision on those beliefs? Sympathetic though he might be, DeSilver declined to commit the ACLU to publicizing the case. He brushed off Margolis with "we're awfully glad to have it [the court's opinion] for our permanent records in any event."[31]

DeSilver advised Margolis to appeal and he did so, taking the case to the Pennsylvania Supreme Court of Appeals, which in October 1920 issued a writ of supercedes from the high court temporarily restoring him to the practice of law. This small, temporary victory, according to BI informant 1096, set Margolis to ridiculing the judges and the ACBA. Supposedly he boasted, "believe me boys, that can of beans that they opened on Wall Street has made all of these 'birds' sit up and take notice." Margolis's pleasure in propounding the notion that the appeals court would be intimidated by the Wall Street blast of September 16 is surely out of character for a pacifist. If he did utter those words, he soon rued them. The ACBA, citing the need for a speedy trial, persuaded the court to move the case up on its docket, leading him to complain of being railroaded.[32]

While the Socialists and the IWW Metal and Machine Workers locals tapped their treasuries to pay for his appeal, an unrepentant Margolis carried on his radical activities. Informers reported that he was selling the English-language printing of Alexander Berkman's prison memoirs out of his office. When Bill Haywood was scheduled to speak in Pittsburgh, Margolis petitioned the public safety director on his behalf. But after the city granted the permit, the radicals grew suspicious, fearing a setup to arrest the famous Wobbly cum Communist. So instead of leading a rally when he came to town, Haywood spent the evening at Kramer's Restaurant and riding around in an automobile with Margolis, an unidentified woman, and Wobbly L. M. Wendell.[33]

In February 1921 the state supreme court upheld Margolis's disbarment. The *Gazette-Times* probably spoke for respectable Pittsburghers when it wrote: "It was not necessary that this fellow should have sallied forth with torch and gun in furtherance of a plot to overthrow the Government . . . by force in order to merit disbarment. His offense was in affiliating himself with revolutionary societies contrary to his oath under the constitution. The *sine qua non* of his right to practice was his devotion to the constitution of the United States, specifically to his obligation to support the laws." The editorial writer, like the court, skipped over the important technicality that, despite more than two years' close surveillance, the government had been unable to even indict Margolis for criminal acts. What justified disbarment was that although "as a private citizen he may hold such views as to Government as he chooses, as an officer of the Courts he is bound to maintain the Government. He was proved recreant to his oath."[34]

Soon after the state supreme court turned down his appeal, Margolis ran into BI agents Lenon and Yankovich. The disbarred lawyer told them that he expected it. "I told my attorneys when the proceedings were started I never had a chance . . .

I never was optimistic." But it bothered him, that he was "charged with having advocated force and violence [and] you know and every man in your Department knows that I never did use that argument. I believe in non-resistance. My friends insist that I am not a Bolshevist on that account." Their conversation soon turned to Roustam Bek, a Russian-born former British general staff officer with whom Margolis had refused to share a speaker's platform in Detroit because he was collecting funds for *military* medical relief in Russia. After Margolis's partner Jim Marshall asked Lenon what he knew about Bek, Margolis paid rueful tribute to BI intelligence: "Oh say, I'm surprised at you asking these fellows a question like that. Leave it to them if there is anything to know in any part of this country about anyone within its borders they will find it. They will dig it up somewhere."[35]

From 1921 Margolis's career went into eclipse. As the IWW faded to quaint insignificance, he refused to join the Communists. In February 1921 Wobbly George Speed, who had been run out of Pittsburgh by U.S. Steel in 1913 and was fresh from a year at Leavenworth for an Espionage Act violation, asked him for the names of coal and steel radicals who could organize the mills and mines for the IWW. In March, visiting Communist organizer Floyd Ramp feigned disbelief that "Margolis persists in being an Anarchist when he is a well educated person, and should know that the change in the capitalist system cannot be achieved by peaceful means." Ramp could not convert the stubborn lawyer to Communism. Soon after, Margolis introduced visiting radical speaker Jack Mooney, brother of the imprisoned Tom. Mooney praised Sid Hatfield of Matewan as the nation's best police chief for standing up to Baldwin-Felts in southern West Virginia. Then he drew an appreciative laugh from Margolis when he said that all lawyers were grafters. But the audience and the collection were small.[36]

Margolis continued to speak to an ever-dwindling audience. When he addressed a small gathering at the International Socialist Lyceum on the French Commune he sounded an almost elegiac note. The older generation, he lamented, would never change. Therefore the only hope for the future revolution lay with educating the young "along economic lines." Although he was no longer in the radical vanguard, at the end of April 1921 Pittsburgh police still took the trouble to break up a meeting where he was to speak. Later that month he presided at the appearance of attorney Elmer Smith, who had represented the Wobbly defendants after their Centralia, Washington, battle with American Legionnaires. But the "mass meeting" drew only sixty-three people and raised only $23.55.[37]

Marshall's law practice floundered without Margolis, who was thought to be the brains, despite the fact that he remained about the only Pittsburgh lawyer willing to defend radical immigrants. Given a choice, radical defendants wanted stronger, proven counsel. Typical was Steve Zonoff, who turned down Marshall for New York lawyer Isaac Schorr of Nelles, DeSilver, and Schorr, "one of the men who went after Palmer," not one of his victims.[38]

After 1921 one gets only brief glimpses of Jacob Margolis, once Pittsburgh's most prominent radical. Between 1922 and 1926 he spent some time in Milwaukee and Detroit. In the Motor City he worked for the *Detroit Jewish Chronicle*. During this time he tried over and over to regain admission to the bar. In 1927 he finally succeeded and maintained a Pittsburgh office until 1940. His punishment did not alter his attitude toward "our predatory, privileged social order," as he explained to Emma Goldman when they resumed their long-interrupted correspondence in the late 1920s. He confided that "its greed, cowardice, and stupidity fill me with the same indignation and disgust I felt twenty years ago." Neither did the Pittsburgh establishment forgive him his apostasy. The "utility corporations, bankers, and industrialists" still avoided him "as studiously as they did in those days when I vociferously damned their whole idiotic social order." Still the anarchist, he could not abide the American Communists and the Russian Bolsheviks. So it was ironic that he continued to draw clientele from the Left, including the Communist Industrial Labor Defense organization. Soon after resuming his law practice Margolis defended Salvatore Accorsi, who was accused of the August 22, 1927, killing of a state policeman near Cheswick, Pennsylvania, during a protest of the execution of Sacco and Vanzetti.[39]

The last references to Margolis in anarchist sources occur in the mid-1930s and show that the embers of radicalism still glowed in him.[40] In 1934 he wrote to Goldman, recently back from exile and in New York City, hoping to arrange for her to lecture once again in Pittsburgh. He eagerly looked forward to their first contact since that terrible year 1919 and, he promised,"we shall talk and talk and talk some more."[41] After all, that is what he had always done.

EPILOGUE

Everywhere I saw that Government is a thing made of men, that Government has blood and bones, it is many mouths whispering into many ears, sending telegrams, aiming rifles, writing orders, saying yes and no.

Carl Sandburg, "Government," 1917

By the early 1920s the Wilsonian welfare state was only a memory. Neither big business nor the trade unions had been totally satisfied with the effects of the government's wartime intervention, which each believed the other had used to unfair advantage. This, even though business had by far the greater power in Washington and conservative labor had only taken a bite of the apple of statism. When the adversaries renewed their struggle in the private sector during the Harding administration, business won victory after victory until, after more than a decade of defeats, epitomized by Irving Bernstein as labor's lean years, industrial unionism, pragmatic and bureaucratic, became a major political component of the New Deal coalition.[1]

Much more than it did the trade union bosses, the Great War and the Red Scare left some liberals feeling persecuted and distrustful of the state. The government's all too ready sacrifice of individual rights to the establishment conception of the common good elevated civil liberties to a national issue and created a political constituency, symbolized by the ACLU, that was committed to protecting unpopular individuals and opinions through enforcement of the Bill of Rights and constitutional rule of law.[2]

Of the Pittsburgh IWW's agitations for a revolution to bring into being a new society in the shell of the old there remained hardly a trace in the 1920s. The labor movement was in steep decline and the steel citadel still stood against unions. The Communists now were the region's principal revolutionaries. But when organizer Steve Nelson settled in the North Side on East Ohio Street in 1923 the local party was small and ethnically fragmented. What support the Reds could claim was mostly in the soft coal towns and camps in the hinterlands and among the electrical workers at Westinghouse.[3]

Even if the government-corporate assault of the Left from 1917–1921 temporarily stifled the industrial workers' class-conscious subculture of resistance, it did not destroy it. That industrial workers tended to be cautious but not conservative is suggested by Progressive pro-labor presidential candidate Bob LaFollette's strong showing in the Pittsburgh area in 1924.[4]

A furious 1920s nativist reaction against foreigners and radicals fueled the Sacco-Vanzetti controversy, the rise of the Ku Klux Klan, and the political aspect of Protestant fundamentalism. The Johnson-Reed Act of 1924 addressed the politics of immigration by effectively closing the country to southern and eastern Europeans by means of discriminatory quotas. The need for marginal, temporary workers remained, but now increasingly it would be filled from depressed rural areas of the United States and the Americas, particularly Mexico. In the Pittsburgh mill district these factors worked to stabilize and Americanize the eastern and southern European immigrant population and to weaken the ethnic barriers that had so divided workers in the past.[5]

The end of the Red Scare and the ascendance of Republican normalcy and corporate welfare capitalism sharply curtailed the domestic intelligence agencies' wartime power, influence, and budgets. The BI suffered reductions, endured heavy political flack, and had to give up the use of officially employed spies. The number of special agents, which had peaked in 1920 at 579, fell to about 300 by 1925. In 1924, William J. Burns, who had succeeded Flynn as Bureau chief in the Harding administration, resigned in a hail of charges of incompetence and corruption. By the mid-1920s press talk of "atrocities" committed by the Justice Department during the war and the Red Scare was common.[6]

It would be misleading, however, to read the BI's post–Red Scare troubles as a significant victory for civil libertarians and left-liberals. Truly embarrassed and disgusted though they may have been by the heavy-handed federal repression and corruption of the Palmer raids and the Flynn and Burns regimes, mainstream Democrats and Republicans showed no remorse about the suppression of aliens and radicals. In 1927 wartime Justice Department official John Lord O'Brian, a Republican, testily refused to write for the *American Mercury* on "the atrocities of the Dept. of Justice during the war, particularly of the sort recounted in Chafee's 'Freedom of Speech.'" Instead he defended Justice Department officials as "both conscientious and assiduous in seeking to prevent arbitrary action during the War." The wartime attorney general, Wilsonian Democrat Thomas W. Gregory, continued to insist that his greatest accomplishment was the "handling of the alien enemy population . . . during the war."[7]

The appointment by reformist attorney general Harlan Fisk Stone of young J.

Edgar Hoover to head the BI in 1924 underscored the ambiguity that so often marked the Progressives' attitude toward government power. Hoover reformed, modernized, and increased the professionalism of the Bureau. He rationalized and centralized agent selection and training and embraced scientific detection methods in order to create the familiar image of the clean-cut, buttoned-down, apolitical, automaton G-man. On the record he followed Stone's orders to refrain from domestic spying while off the record maintaining the establishment's comfort level by keeping and adding to already extensive "Communist and ultra-radical" files, by monitoring and collecting radical publications, and by receiving reports from a network of anticommunist and often anti-union forces.[8]

The performance of the World War I–era domestic intelligence agencies in Pittsburgh presents a disturbing picture. Visibly staffed at the top with aspirants to the corporate elite and invisibly below with anti-union detectives, at times in the Pittsburgh mill district the agencies seemed little more than an appendage of big steel labor control that operated behind a veil of secrecy, disinformation, and propaganda. Not even suspicious Interchurch World Movement steel strike investigators fully grasped the magnitude of the Justice Department's covert activities.[9] Voluminous government files attest to a Herculean effort to uncover conspiracies against the nation. But those same files suggest that poorly educated agents blinded by a narrow, if sincere, patriotism, were too ready to mistake words for actions.

One cannot say that the Pittsburgh G-men were particularly effective investigators. They helped to break the IWW and to disbar Margolis, but they could not make a case against Joe Mountain, solve the 1919 bombings, or develop compelling evidence against UORW or Communist alien suspects. From Hoover down, the agents viewed complex political movements simplistically by relying on imperfectly understood captured documents and "experts" such as Wendell. For all his emphasis on scientific and rational crime-solving Hoover seems just as historically illiterate as his early private detective associates.[10]

One should not inflate the part played by the surveillance agencies among the host of internal and external factors that explain the decline of the American Left.[11] But BI, MID, and ONI did contribute by helping to silence and isolate its pacifist and Tolstoyan anarchist elements represented by Margolis, by pruning away the Wobblies who represented, however imperfectly, its native roots and workplace democracy, by driving the Communists underground, and by contributing to myths that distorted the common perception.

Far more than at crime solving, the early BI proved effective at bureaucratic empire building and defensive tactics. It quickly learned to magnify the importance of the easily solved cases in order to divert public attention away from the tough ones. The BI Pittsburgh-area "Old German" files contain less about hard-to-find covert German activity than about the easily detected IWW agitation. Hoover's Radical Division was created in the expectation that it would solve the 1919 terrorist bombings. When it could not it launched a sensational campaign against the UORW and then the CPA. Federal agents in Pittsburgh cannot have believed that either the IWW or the UORW posed a serious threat to the American way of life. But these groups made appealing targets because they existed at the margins of American society, lacked significant political constituencies, and were useful to the nation's elites as scapegoats.

The experience of 1917–1921 institutionalized the nature, assumptions, and rules of government's war against the Left as it would be waged in succeeding generations. To argue that McCarthyism was the product of "habitual fear of the domestic socialist menace—a great, bloated, red-herring," largely created by antilabor detectives, oversimplifies a complex issue and offers an overly benign view of the revolutionary Left.[12] Still, if the World War I welfare state provided a model for the New Deal welfare state, so did the period 1917–1921 shape the official response to Reds in later generations. The span of years from the first Red Scare to the cold war was shorter than the one separating the Vietnam escalation from the 1990s. Just as the fears and passions aroused by Vietnam still haunt American politics, so the misconceptions, passions, ideologies, organizations, and many of the persons associated with seeing Reds in the era of the Great War haunted post–World War II America.

NOTES
INDEX

NOTES

ACRONYMS

ACBA	Allegheny County Bar Association
ACLU	American Civil Liberties Union
AFL	American Federation of Labor
AIU	American Industrial Union
APL	American Protective League
BI	Bureau of Investigation
BSF	Bureau Section File (National Archives)
CLP	Communist Labor Party
CO	Conscientious Objector
CPA	Communist Party of America
CPUSA	Communist Party of the United States of America
DJ	Department of Justice
DMI	Director, Military Intelligence
DNI	Director, Naval Intelligence
EGP	*The Emma Goldman Papers, A Microfilm Edition*
FOIA/PA	Freedom of Information Act/Privacy Act
GID	General Intelligence Division of the Department of Justice
IAM	International Association of Machinists
IBEW	International Brotherhood of Electrical Workers
IO	Intelligence Officer (Military Intelligence Division)
ISR	*International Socialist Review*
IWW	Industrial Workers of the World
JAH	*Journal of American History*
LC	Library of Congress
MID	Military Intelligence Division (sometimes Branch or Section), U.S. Army
NA	National Archives (Washington D.C.)
NA(p)	Mid-Atlantic Region, National Archives (Philadelphia)
NCLB	National Civil Liberties Bureau
NWLB	National War Labor Board
NWVCOA	Northern West Virginia Coal Operators Association
NYT	*New York Times*
OBUM	*One Big Union Monthly*
OG	Old German Files (National Archives)
ONI	Office of Naval Intelligence, U.S. Navy
PCA	People's Council of America for Democracy and Peace
PPS	Plant Protection Section (of MID)
PWW	*Papers of Woodrow Wilson*
PU	Princeton University
rep.	report of agent
RG	Record Group (National Archives)
SAC	Special Agent-in-Charge, Bureau of Investigation
SCPC	Swarthmore College Peace Collection
SPA	Socialist Party of America
UCP	United Communist Party
UMWA	United Mine Workers of America

UORW   Union of Russian Workers
WIB   War Industries Board
WVRC   West Virginia and Regional History Collection
WSU   Wayne State University
WVU   West Virginia University

INTRODUCTION

1. See for example Robert B. Spencer to Frank Burke, Mar. 13, 1910, DJ OG 215915, RG 65, NA. For Pittsburgh's relation to its hinterlands, see Edward K. Muller, "Metropolis and Region: A Framework for Enquiry Into Western Pennsylvania," in Samuel P. Hays, ed., *City at the Point: Essays on the Social History of Pittsburgh* (Pittsburgh: University of Pittsburgh Press, 1989), 182–84.

2. A sketch of Pittsburgh municipal reformers is in Paul Kleppner, "Government, Parties, and Voters in Pittsburgh," in Hays, *City at the Point*, 167–68.

3. The poles on the timing and causes of the decline of Socialism are represented by Daniel Bell, *Marxian Socialism in the United States* (Ithaca: Cornell University Press, 1996), and James Weinstein, *The Decline of Socialism in America, 1912–1925* (New York: Vintage Books, 1967).

4. Frederic C. Howe, *The Confessions of a Reformer* (New York: Charles Scribner's Sons, 1925), 266–72.

5. Joseph A. McCartin, "Labor's 'Great War': American Workers, Unions, and the State, 1916–1920" (Ph.D. diss., State University of New York at Binghamton, 1990), xii–xv; David Montgomery, *The Fall of the House of Labor; The Workplace, the State, and American Labor Activism, 1865–1925* (Cambridge: Cambridge University Press, 1987), 373–76.

6. A recent treatment is Ronald Schaffer, *America in the Great War: The Rise of the National Welfare State* (New York: Oxford University Press, 1991).

7. Stephen Skowronek, *Building the New American State: The Expansion of National Administrative Capacities, 1877–1920* (Cambridge: Cambridge University Press, 1982), 198–200.

8. John F. McClymer, "The Pittsburgh Survey, 1907–1914: Forging an Ideology in the Steel District," *Pennsylvania History* 41 (Apr. 1974): 171.

9. E. Thompson, *The Making of the English Working Class* (New York: Vintage Books, 1966), 61–62, 484–86.

10. A summary overview is in U.S. Congress, Senate Select Committee to Study Governmental Operations with Respect to Intelligence Activities, "The Evolution and Organization of the Federal Intelligence Function, A Brief Overview (1776–1975)," *Final Report Intelligence Activities*, Book VI, Sen. Rep. 755, 94th Cong., 2d sess., S. 13133–38 (hereinafter, Church Committee Report); Frank J. Donner, *The Age of Surveillance: The Aims and Methods of America's Political Intelligence System* (New York: Vintage Books, 1981).

1. THE G-MEN: VIRTUE MADE VISIBLE (AND INVISIBLE)

1. Don Whitehead, *The FBI Story* (New York: Random House, 1956), 13–16. The activities of the Secret Service are recorded in Daily Reports of U.S. Secret Service Agents, 1875–1936, Microfilm Publication T-915, RG 87, NA. Rolls 683 and 684 cover the Pittsburgh operation, 1916–1920.

2. Max Lowenthal, *The Federal Bureau of Investigation* (New York: William Sloane Associates, Inc., 1950), 3–9; Joan Jensen, *The Price of Vigilance* (New York: Rand McNally and Co., 1968), 12–13.

3. Mark T. Connelly, *The Response to Prostitution in the Progressive Era* (Chapel Hill: University of North Carolina Press, 1980), 48–63; Marlene D. Beckman, "The White Slave Traffic Act: The Historical Impact of a Criminal Law Policy on Women," *Georgetown Law Journal* 72 (Feb. 1984): 1118–19, 1123–24.

4. Lowenthal, *Federal Bureau of Investigation*, 14–21; Whitehead, *FBI Story*, 23–25; Howe, *Confessions*, 266–72.

5. "German Plotters Fear Him," *Literary Digest*, Sept. 29, 1917: 61–64; *NYT*, Feb. 20, 1964.

6. Classified State Department documents were found during a warrantless search of the office of the left-wing magazine in 1945, *NYT*, Apr. 6, 1961; *Washington Post*, Apr. 7, 1961.

7. Alan Rogers, "Passports and Politics: The Courts and the Cold War," *The Historian* 47 (Aug. 1985): 500–02. For her hero status to the Right see Andre Visson, "Watchdog of the State Department," *Inde-*

pendent Woman 30 (Aug. 1951): 225–26, 234; *NYT,* Nov. 5, 1966; *Washington Post,* Nov. 5, 1966; *Collier's,* July 11, 1953.

8. Whitehead, *FBI Story,* 12–25, 32; "German Plotters Fear Him," *Literary Digest,* Sept. 29, 1917: 61–63; Church Committee Report, VI, 74–75, 94–95; Jensen, *Price of Vigilance,* 12–15.

9. *Literary Digest,* Sept. 29, 1917: 61–63.

10. Joan M. Jensen, *Army Surveillance in America, 1775–1980* (New Haven: Yale University Press, 1991), 111–51; Ralph E. Weber, ed., *The Memoranda: Major General Ralph H. Van Deman, USA Ret. 1865–1952, Father of U.S. Military Intelligence* (Wilmington, Del.: Scholarly Resources, Inc., 1988), xviii; MID, Plant Files–Western Pennsylvania, PPS, RG 165, NA (Suitland).

11. Jeffrey M. Dorwart, *Conflict of Duty: The U.S. Navy's Intelligence Dilemma, 1919–1945* (Annapolis: Naval Institute Press, 1983), 5–7; Dorwart, *The Office of Naval Intelligence: The Birth of America's First Intelligence Agency, 1865–1918* (Annapolis: Naval Institute Press, 1979), 12–95, 106–12. Elite surnames among Welles's recruits included Lorillard, Pulitzer, Loew, Legare, Van Antwerp, Vanderbilt, Waterbury, and Eddy.

12. *NYT,* Nov. 18, 1955, July 18, 1960; "Numerical List General (Secret)" [1918], ONI Entry 121, RG 38, NA; Dorwart, *Office of Naval Intelligence,* 118, and *Conflict of Duty,* 16; "Activities of Naval Contract and Plant Division-Scope of Work-Policies-Recommendations [1918]," ONI Entry 230, Box 1; George E. Rowe to DNI [1918], ONI Entry 161, Box 1, both RG 38, NA(p); J. Cutler Andrews, *Pittsburgh's "Post-Gazette"* (Boston: Chapman and Grimes, 1936), 231, 270.

13. The standard work remains Jensen, *The Price of Vigilance.*

14. Paul L. Murphy, *World War I and the Origin of Civil Liberties in the United States* (New York: W. W. Norton & Co., 1979), 74–85.

15. Church Committee Report, 95–97.

16. David Brody, *Labor in Crisis: The Steel Strike of 1919* (Philadelphia: J. B. Lippincott Company, 1965), 48–50.

17. See Employers' Association letterhead, Horn to Van Deman, Aug. 24, 1917, MID 10110-253, RG 165, NA.

18. J. Bernard Hogg, "Public Reaction to Pinkertonism and the Labor Question," *Pennsylvania History* 11 (July 1944): 171–72.

19. Thomas J. Tunney, *Throttled! The Detection of German Anarchist Bomb Plotters* (Boston: Small, Maynard & Company, 1919), *passim;* Frank Donner, *Protectors of Privilege: Red Squads and Police Repression in Urban America* (Berkeley: University of California Press, 1990), 31–35; Weber, ed., *Van Deman,* 34.

20. Richard G. Powers, *Secrecy and Power: The Life of J. Edgar Hoover* (New York: Free Press, 1987), 45; Donner, *Protectors of Privilege,* 24; Frank Morn, *The Eye That Never Sleeps: A History of the Pinkerton National Detective Agency* (Bloomington: Indiana University Press, 1982), 168–77. Rhodri Jeffreys-Jones, "Profit Over Class: A Study in American Industrial Espionage," *American Studies* 6 (Dec. 1972): 235–36. Sidney Howard estimated that Pinkerton, Burns, and Thiel combined, the three largest agencies, had 135,000 employees, 100 offices, and 10,000 local branches, *Labor Spy* (New York: Republic Publishing Company, 1924), 17.

21. Morn, *Eye That Never Sleeps,* 169, 166–67.

22. Dennis Porter, *The Pursuit of Crime: Art and Ideology in Detective Fiction* (New Haven: Yale University Press, 1981); Martin Priestman, *Detective Fiction and Literature: The Figure on the Carpet* (New York: St. Martin's Press, 1991); Stephen Knight, *Form and Ideology in Crime Fiction* (Bloomington: Indiana University Press, 1980).

23. Porter, *The Pursuit of Crime,* 120–21, 124; Michel Foucault, *Discipline and Punish: The Birth of the Prison,* trans. Alan Sheridan (New York: Vintage Books, 1979), especially 170–231.

24. The Mollys were a breakaway lodge of the Ancient Order of Hibernians among Pennsylvania Irish-American anthracite miners that used terrorism against mine operators. See Donner, *Protectors of Privilege* 10, 10n; Morn, *Eye That Never Sleeps,* 178.

25. William J. Flynn, *The Eagle's Eye: A True Story of the Imperial German Government's Spies and Intrigues in America from Facts Furnished by William J. Flynn* [novelized by Courtney Riley Cooper] (New York: Prospect Press, Inc., 1918); Flynn, *The Barrel Mystery* (New York: The James A. McCann Company, 1919).

26. Arthur Hornblow, *The Argyle Case* [founded on the play by Harriet Ford and Harvey J. O'Higgins, written with the cooperation of William J. Burns] (New York: Harper and Brothers, 1913), 150.

27. Quoted in Louis Filler, *Randolph Bourne* (Washington: American Council on Public Affairs, 1943), 28–29.

28. Howard, *Labor Spy*, 111.

29. For detective recruitment techniques see ibid., 88–105.

30. For discussions of the reliability and importance of labor espionage see Jeffreys-Jones, "Profit Over Class," 240–48; Gary M. Fink, *The Fulton Bag and Cotton Mills Strike of 1914–1915* (Ithaca: ILS Press, 1993), 68, 75, 91–94, 101–10, 116–26, 133–39; Thompson, *Making of the English Working Class*, 484–94. The quotation is from Jeffreys-Jones, "Profit Over Class," 247.

31. The National Archives has four boxes of rejected applications for special agent ("A-C," 1917) in the surviving headquarters records of the APL in RG 65.

32. Whitehead, *FBI Story*, 13–14, 55–74.

33. Jacob Spolansky, *The Communist Trail in America* (New York: Macmillan Company, 1951), 6–11.

34. Bielaski to Judge (copy), Jan. 19, 1915; Judge, Application for Appointment to Position of Special Agent of the Department of Justice, Oct. 10, 1913, FBI 67-96008, FIOA/PA.

35. Ibid.; Bielaski to Judge, Aug. 12, 1916; note in file dated Jan. 18, 1915, both FBI 67-96008, FOIA/PA.

36. Judge to Bielaski, Feb. 3, 7, 1915, FBI 67-96008, FIOA/PA; Pittsburgh City Directories; Henry J. Lenon, Application for Appointment, June 25, 1918, FBI 67-69, FOIA/PA.

37. Speer, Application for Appointment, July 19, 1917, FBI 67-9973; Bielaski to Judge, Jan. 16, 1915, FBI 67-96008, both FOIA/PA.

38. Speer, Application for Appointment, July 19, 1917; Special Agent ************* [FBI-censored] to Bielaski, Aug. 28, 1917; Bielaski to Judge, Sept. 7, 1917, all FBI 67-9973, FOIA/PA.

39. Ames, Applications for Appointment, Apr. 15, 1921, Nov. 9, 1923, FBI 67-1592, FOIA/PA.

40. Ames, Applications for Appointment, Apr. 15, 1921, Nov. 9, 1923; C. J. Morgan [Pittsburgh Steel Company, Monessen, Penn.], "To Whom it May Concern," Sept. 10, 1915; C. Ward Eicher [District Attorney Westmoreland County, Penn.], "To Whom it May Concern," Sept. 10, 1915; E. Lowry Humes to W. H. Moran, Jan. 4, 1918; Alexander D. McConnell to Moran, Jan. 11, 1918, all FBI 67-1592, FOIA/PA.

41. Lenon, Applications for Appointment, June 25, 1918, Nov. 29, 1923; Lenon to William J. Burns, Apr. 11, 1924, all FBI 67-68, FOIA/PA.

42. Lenon, Applications for Appointment, June 25, 1918, Nov. 29, 1923, both FBI 67-68, FOIA/PA; *Pittsburgh Post-Gazette*, Sept. 28, 1935.

43. Judge's references include former BI chief Stanley Finch, West Virginia newspaper magnate H. C. Ogden, and Pittsburgh Immigration Bureau commissioner W. W. Sibray. Speer named Judge, West Virginia University President Frank B. Trotter, and the city editor of the *Pittsburgh Sun*. Ames gave the Pennsylvania State Constabulary superintendent, a judge, several attorneys, steel and coal company officials, and "any person in Western Penna. holding an official position pertaining to police duty." Lenon listed police officials, private detectives, and steel and coal company executives. See Applications for Appointment, Judge, Oct. 10, 1913, FBI 67-96008; Speer, July 19, 1917, FBI 67-9973; Ames, Apr. 15, 1921, Nov. 9, 1923, FBI 67-1592; Lenon, June 25, 1918, Nov. 29, 1923, FBI 67-68, all FOIA/PA.

44. Applications for Appointment, Lenon, June 25, 1918, Nov. 29, 1923, FBI 67-68; Ames, Apr. 15, 1921, Nov. 9, 1923, FBI 67-1592; Judge, Oct. 10, 1913, FBI 67-96008; Speer, July 19, 1917, FBI 67-9973, all FOIA/PA.

45. Travel and trial and grand jury appearances occupied the rest. Evaluation of Lenon by R. B. Spencer, May 15, 1923, FBI 67-68, FOIA/PA.

46. [George E. Rowe], Activities of Naval Contract and Plant Division-Scope of Work-Policies-Recommendations [1918], ONI Box 1, Reports of Plant Inspections and Related Records, 1918, Entry 230, RG 38, NA(p).

47. F. S. Owen, rep., Sept. 3, 1918, DJ OG 237322, RG 65, NA.

48. Owen, reps., Aug. 14, Sept. 3, 1918; Samuel E. Morison to the President of the United States, Aug. 31, 1918; Attorney General to Henry Cabot Lodge, Sept. 4, 1918; Bielaski to G. E. Kelleher, Sept. 5, 1918; same to John Lord O'Brian, Oct. 5, 1918; Kelleher to Bielaski (Personal and Confidential), Sept. 24, 1918, all in DJ OG 237322, RG 65, NA; *NYT*, Dec. 27, 1948.

49. Howard, *Labor Spy,* 3–13.

50. The Bureau kept sensitive information on confidential informants in a special file, which, if it still exists, remains classified. Curt Gentry, *J. Edgar Hoover: The Man and the Secrets* (New York: Plume, 1992), 45–46.

51. J. Edgar Hoover, Memorandum Upon the Work of the Radical Division, Aug. 1, 1919–Mar. 15, 1920; letters, Hoover to the various SACs, July 26 or 27, 1920, all DJ OG 374217, RG 65, NA.

52. Jeffreys-Jones, "Profit Over Class," 239–40.

53. L. W. Boyce to Capt. Fitzhugh Burns, Sept. 27, 1918; memo, Burns to DMI, Sept. 28, 1918; Brig. Gen. Marlborough Churchill to Bielaski, Oct. 11, 1918, all MID 10110-932; J. Darby to Col. Ralph Van Deman, Mar. 21, 1918, MID 10110-311, all RG 165, NA.

54. Wrisley Brown to Bielaski, Oct. 11, 1918, MID 10110-311, RG 165, NA.

55. Burns to DMI, Sept. 28, 1918, MID 10110-932, RG 165, NA.

56. Judge, rep., July 20, 1917, DJ OG 18179, RG 65, NA; Wendell, rep., July 23, Aug. 21, 1917, MID 10110-199, RG 165, NA. He later roomed at several places on Pittsburgh's North Side, 836, rep., May 15–19, 1919, BI OG 215915, RG 65, NA.

57. The details of Wendell's cover story are from *Pittsburgh Gazette-Times* and *Pittsburgh Sun* stories of Sept. 10, 1918; Norman E. Caulfield, "Mexican Labor and the State in the Twentieth Century: Conflict and Accommodation" (Ph.D. diss., University of Houston, 1990), 74–128.

58. Bielaski to Judge, 18th Pennsylvania Infantry, Camp Stewart, El Paso, Texas, Aug. 12, 1916, FBI 67-96008; Speer, "Application for Appointment . . . Special Agent," July 19, 1917, FBI 67-9973, both FOIA/PA; Jensen, *Army Surveillance,* 128–29, 160–61.

59. Wendell, rep., July 29, 1917, DJ OG 18179, RG 65, NA; *Cleveland Plain Dealer,* July 22, 1917; Oakley C. Johnson, *The Day Is Coming: The Life and Work of Charles E. Ruthenberg, 1882–1927* (New York: International Publishers, 1957), 118–21. For "Wendell" see the Detroit Public Library local genealogy files.

60. Wendell, rep., Sept. 2, 1917, MID 10110-199, RG 165, NA. Beginning in September 1917 some reports used "836." "Wendell" appeared for the last time in March 1918. See reports for Sept. 16, Dec. 12, 1917, MID 10110-199, RG 165, NA and Mar. 18, 1918, DJ OG 67-40, RG 65, NA.

61. Bielaski to Judge, Mar. 24, 1917, FBI 67-96008, FOIA/PA; Lenon, rep., Aug. 20, 1918, DJ OG 291921 RG 65, NA; memo, GFR [George F. Ruch] for Hoover, March 22, 1920, BI 18197, RG 65, NA.

62. *Pittsburgh Press,* June 4, 1919; *Pittsburgh Gazette-Times,* Sept. 10, 1918; Wendell, rep., Sept. 3, 1917, MID 10110-199, RG 165, NA.

63. Gentry, *Hoover,* 80–81, 140; Spencer to Hoover (confidential), Aug. 12, 1919, DJ OG 215915, RG 65, NA; Powers, *Secrecy and Power,* 96–101. For references to protecting the identity of 836 see Flood to DMI, July 3, Nov. 5, 9, 1918, MID 10110-199, RG 165, NA; Bielaski to Enoch Crowder, Oct. 5, 1918, DJ OG 18197, RG 65, NA.

2. THE WORLD WAR I–ERA PITTSBURGH LEFT

1. Richard J. Oestreicher, *Solidarity and Fragmentation: Working People and Class Consciousness in Detroit, 1875–1900* (Urbana: University of Illinois Press, 1986), xv.

2. Richard J. Oestreicher, "Working-Class Formation, Development, and Consciousness in Pittsburgh, 1790–1960," in Hays, *City at the Point,* 129–34.

3. John Bodnar, *The Transplanted: A History of Immigrants in Urban America* (Bloomington: Indiana University Press, 1987), 91–92, 99–104, 107–08.

4. Montgomery, *House of Labor,* 317; Charles J. McCollester, "Turtle Creek Fights Taylorism: The Westinghouse Strike of 1914," *Labor's Heritage* 4 (summer 1992): 4–9.

5. Jacob Margolis, "The Streets of Pittsburgh," *International Socialist Review* 13 (Oct. 1912): 314; Montgomery, *House of Labor,* 317.

6. *Pittsburgh Press,* Aug. 4, 5, 11, 1912. The newspaper listed the names of 44 persons arrested, 37 men and 7 women. Their average age (n=43) was 31.7 years. Most (32) were in their twenties and thirties. The youngest (2) were 17; three were over 60; the eldest was 80. Most had Pittsburgh addresses, but others were from New Kensington, Wilmerding, Chartiers Township, Homestead, Wilkinsburg, Turtle Creek, and East Pittsburgh.

7. Montgomery, *House of Labor,* 318; *Pittsburgh Press,* Aug. 16, 25, 1912.

8. Montgomery, *House of Labor*, 319–23; McCollister, "Turtle Creek," 10–16; Dispute Case File 33–37, Federal Mediation and Conciliation Service, 1913–1948, RG 280, NA.

9. Montgomery, *House of Labor*, 320–21; Melvyn Dubofsky and Warren Van Tine, *John L. Lewis, A Biography* (New York: Quadrangle/The New York Times Book Co., Inc., 1977), 28–29; *NYT,* Sept. 19, 24, 1915.

10. Montgomery, *House of Labor*, 321–27; Dante Barton, "The Pittsburgh Strikes," *International Socialist Review* 16 (June 1916): 712–16; Dispute Case File 33–202, Federal Mediation and Conciliation Service, 1913–1948, RG 280, NA.

11. Montgomery, *House of Labor*, 321–26, 329; *Pittsburgh Dispatch*, Apr. 27, 1916; *Pittsburgh Post*, May 1–9, 1916; *Pittsburgh Press*, Aug. 5, 1912. An analysis of early-twentieth-century radical union leadership at Westinghouse is Ronald W. Schatz, *The Electrical Workers: A History of Labor at General Electric and Westinghouse, 1923–60* (Urbana: University of Illinois Press, 1983), 83–93.

12. Michael Nash, *Conflict and Accommodation: Coal Miners, Steel Workers, and Socialism, 1890–1920* (Westport, Conn.: Greenwood Press, 1982), 114–17; Oestreicher, "Working-Class in Pittsburgh," 134.

13. Among Pittsburgh's seven commercial newspapers the *Press* and *Dispatch* were rated less unsympathetic than the others to labor organizations. Interchurch World Movement, *Public Opinion and the Steel Strike: Supplementary Reports of the Investigators to the Commission of Inquiry* (New York: Da Capo Press, 1970 [1921]), 90–93 (hereinafter, *Public Opinion and the Steel Strike).*

14. A recent summary of the scholarly debate is Michael Kazin, "The Agony and Romance of the American Left," *The American Historical Review* 100 (Dec. 1995): esp. 1488, 1494–96.

15. Two of the women, Madeleine Law and Reba Loan, were married to radicals. A third, Julia Tait, was a veteran Socialist agitator. Vaughan to Military Intelligence Branch, Aug. 20, 1918, MID 10902-3, RG 165, NA; 836, rep., Mar. 16, 1919; Robert B. Spencer to Burke, Nov. 14, 1919, both DJ OG 215915, RG 65, NA. For Scarville see Steve Nelson, James R. Barrett, and Rob Ruck, *Steve Nelson: American Radical* (Pittsburgh: University of Pittsburgh Press, 1981), 25.

16. The Jewish Labor Lyceum was at Miller and Reed on the Hill; and the International Socialist Lyceum was at James and Foreland on the North Side.

17. *International Socialist Review* 18 (Nov.–Dec. 1917): 316; ibid. (July 1917): 58.

18. Wendell, rep., Sept. 27, 1917, DJ OG 67-40; 836, rep., May 2, 1919, DJ OG 360208; Speer, rep., Mar. 18, 1919, DJ OG 215915, all RG 65, NA; and 836, rep., Feb. 12, 1918, MID 10110-199, RG 165, NA.

19. David Shannon, *The Socialist Party in America* (New York: Macmillan Company, 1955), 18–19, 118.

20. An extensive discussion of the term *Wobbly* is in Archie Green, *Wobblies, Pile Butts, and Other Heroes* (Urbana: University of Illinois Press, 1993), 97–138.

21. Melvyn Dubofsky, *We Shall Be All: A History of the Industrial Workers of the World* (Chicago: Quadrangle Books, 1969), 76–87.

22. Ibid., 91–145.

23. See Philip S. Foner, ed., *Fellow Workers and Friends: I.W.W. Free Speech Fights as Told by Participants* (Westport, Conn.: Greenwood Press, 1981).

24. For the IWW as not merely an economic but a sociocultural movement that owed as much to European as American influences, see Salvatore Salerno, *Red November, Black November* (Albany: State University of New York Press, 1989), 1–4, 7–10, 32–34, 114, 130, 151. The key to most sources on the IWW is Dione Miles, *Something in Common—An IWW Bibliography* (Detroit: Wayne State University Press, 1986).

25. Salerno, *Red November, Black November,* 10.

26. Dubofsky, *We Shall Be All,* 202–08; John N. Ingham, "A Strike in the Progressive Era: McKees Rocks, 1909," *The Pennsylvania Magazine of History and Biography* 90 (1966): 355–73; Paul U. Kellogg, "The McKees Rocks Strike," *The Survey* 22 (Aug. 7, 1909): 656–65.

27. Patrick Lynch, "Pittsburgh, the I.W.W., and the Stogie Workers," in Joseph R. Conlin, ed., *At the Point of Production: The Local History of the I.W.W.* (Westport, Conn.: Greenwood Press, 1981), 80–82; Charles I. Cooper, "Stogy Makers and the I.W.W. in Pittsburgh," *The Survey* 31 (Nov. 29, 1913): 214; Ida Cohen Selavan, "Jewish Wage Earners in Pittsburgh, 1890–1930," *American Jewish Historical Quarterly* 65 (March 1976): 272–85. On the industry see Elizabeth Beardsley Butler, *Women and the Trades, Pittsburgh 1907–1908*, vol. 1 of *The Pittsburgh Survey* (New York: Russell Sage Foundation, 1909), 74–97.

28. Paul F. Brissenden, *The I.W.W.: A Study of American Syndicalism* (New York: Russell and Russell, 1920), 278–82.

29. Nick Salvatore, *Eugene V. Debs: Citizen and Socialist* (Urbana: University of Illinois Press, 1982), 253–55.

30. Philip S. Foner, *History of the Labor Movement in the United States* (New York: International Publishers, 1965), vol. 4, 549–54; Dubofsky, *We Shall Be All*, 221–22.

31. Dubovsky, *We Shall Be All*, 344–46, 349–50.

32. Ibid., 351–59.

33. Murphy, *World War I*, 141; Samuel Gompers, *Seventy Years of Life and Labor: An Autobiography*, ed. Nick Salvatore (Ithaca: ILR Press, 1984), 126.

34. Dubofsky, *We Shall Be All*, 429; Murphy, *World War I*, 139–41.

35. The IWW claimed thirty-one thousand members in 1908 of whom about ten thousand paid dues. Dubofsky, *We Shall Be All*, 131; U.S. Congress, House Committee on Rules, "Attorney General A. Mitchell Palmer on Charges Made Against Department of Justice by Louis F. Post and Others, June 1–2, 1920," *Investigation of Charges Against the Department of Justice* (66th Cong., 2d sess., 1920) (hereinafter, "Palmer on Charges by Post"), 21.

36. Carleton H. Parker, "The I.W.W.," *Atlantic Monthly* 120 (Nov. 1917): 659.

37. Clabaugh to Bielaski, Sept. 14, 1917, DJ OG 336190, RG 65, NA.

38. "Stools and Fools," *One Big Union Monthly* [hereinafter, *OBUM*] 2 (Aug. 1920): 12.

39. Roger B. Skelly, rep., May 14, 1917, DJ OG 18197, RG 65, NA.

40. Bielaski to Judge, Mar. 24, 1917, FBI 67-96008, FOIA/PA; Skelly, rep., May 14, 1917, DJ OG 18197; Wendell, reps., Aug. 23, Oct. 8, 1917, DJ OG 67–40, all RG 65, NA; same, rep., Jan. 16, 1918, MID 10110-199, RG 165, NA; G. W. Fowler, rep., June 4, 1918; 836, reps., Feb. 3, Apr. 6, 19, May 5, Aug. 22, 1919; R. B. Spencer to Frank Burke, Nov. 14, 1919, all DJ OG 215915; Lenon, weekly rep., Feb. 19, 1921, DJ BSF 202600-1768, all RG 65, NA.

41. F. E. Haynes to J. Edgar Hoover, Jan. 19, 1920, DJ OG 18197, RG 65, NA; Myrna Silverman, *Strategies of Social Mobility: Family, Kinship and Ethnicity Within Jewish Families in Pittsburgh* (New York: AMS Press, 1989), 28–29.

42. Silverman, *Strategies*, 30–38.

43. *Pittsburgh Press*, May 12, 1920; U.S. Congress, Senate Committee on Labor and Education, S. Res. 202, 66th Cong., 1st sess., *Investigation of Strike in Steel Industries* (1919), vol. 2 (hereinafter, Margolis Senate Testimony), 817–19; "Answer of Jacob Margolis to the Petition of the Allegheny Bar Association . . ." in Court of Common Pleas, No. 2068, January Term, 1920, vol. 139, roll 20, ACLU, PU.

44. Jacob Margolis, "Delusion of War," *OBUM* 2 (Feb. 1920): 29.

45. Jacob Margolis, "The Orthodox Wobbly and the Borer from Within," *OBUM* 1 (Oct. 1919): 27–28.

46. Ibid.

47. Margolis, "The Streets of Pittsburgh," 313–20.

48. Abner Woodruff, "A Letter to the Professor," *OBUM* 1 (Oct. 1919): 2.

49. In Stewart Bird, Dan Georgakis, and Deborah Shaffer, eds., *Solidarity Forever: An Oral History of the IWW* (Chicago: Lakeview Press, 1985), 6, 10, 39, 42–43, 191–92, 194–95, Bill Haywood, Art Shields, Jack Miller, Joseph Murphy, and others offer conflicting interpretations of sabotage.

50. Margolis, "The Streets of Pittsburgh," 316–18.

51. Ibid.

52. *Mother Earth* 10 (May 1915): 113–15, reprinted in Arthur M. Scully and John C. Bane, "Brief in Support of the Petition of the Allegheny County Bar Association *in re* Jacob Margolis" in the Court of Common Pleas of Allegheny County, Penn., No. 2068, January Term, 1920, 122–24 (hereinafter, ACBA Brief) (copy in MID 10110-100, Box 2759, file 5, RG 165, NA).

53. Lynch, "Pittsburgh, the I.W.W., and the Stogie Workers," 81–82, 85–91; Samuel Walker, *In Defense of American Liberties: A History of the ACLU* (New York: Oxford University Press, 1990), 16–29, 37–45; Roy T. Wortman, *From Syndicalism to Trade Unionism: The IWW in Ohio, 1905–1950* (New York: Garland Publishing, 1985), 58.

54. Memo for JEH [J. Edgar Hoover], Jan. 19, 1920, DJ OG 18197, RG 65, NA; ACBA Brief, 127–31.

55. Wendell, reps., Aug. 7, 8, 1917; 836, rep., June 17, 1918, all in MID 10110-199, RG 165, NA.

56. Emma Goldman, *Living My Life* (Garden City, N.Y.: Garden City Publishing Company, 1931), 569, 688. Their 1919 correspondence has evidently not survived, but Candace Falk, Ronald J. Zborsky, and Daniel Comford, eds., *The Emma Goldman Papers: A Microfilm Edition* (Alexandria, Vir.: Chadwyck-Healey, 1990 (hereinafter, *EGP*), rolls 8–10, contain sixty-five letters between the two, January 1915–December 1916.

57. IRS agents estimated Margolis's income at $7,000–10,000 in 1919. 836, rep., Aug. 12–14, 1918, DJ OG 18197, RG 65, NA; Salvatore, *Debs*, 253.

58. Margolis Senate Testimony, 830. The 1920 census lists the "mother tongue" of both his parents and his wife (who came from Vilna as a little girl) as Jewish (Yiddish).

59. Margolis Senate Testimony, 834, 857; 836, rep., Aug. 12–14, 1918, DJ OG 18197, RG 65, NA.

60. Bielaski to Judge, June 15, 1917; Judge, rep., June 28, 1917; J. F. Kropidlowski, rep., July 10–17, 1917, all DJ OG 18197, RG 65, NA. Margolis had at least four contemporary namesakes: Polish immigrant Jacob Margolis (1879–1967), who settled near Pittsburgh in New Kensington, founded a Jewish congregation, and was a longtime furniture store owner; Polish immigrant Jacob H. Margolis (1887–1940), who prospered in the garment business and was a philanthropist in Dayton, Ohio; Jacob Margolis (1876–?), a Detroit salesman who applied for a passport to Cuba in 1920; and Jacob Margolis, Socialist and organizer for the cap-makers union, who applied for permission to go to Canada in 1917. *Pittsburgh Press*, Feb. 10, 1967; *Dayton Daily News*, Oct. 19, 1940; F. E. Haynes, Memo for Hoover, Jan. 19, 1920; J. F. Kropidlowski, rep., July 12, 1917, both DJ OG 18197, RG 65, NA.

61. See Richard Drinnon, *"Blast*, San Francisco, 1916–1917," in *The American Radical Press, 1880–1960*, ed. Joseph R. Conlin (Westport, Conn.: Greenwood Press, 1974), II: 400–06.

62. Goldman to Margolis, Mar. [?] 23, Apr. 3, 6, 11, 1916, reel 9, EGP; Don S. Rathbun, rep., June 25, 1917, DJ OG 18197, RG 65, NA.

63. According to Judge the only other person present when Margolis dictated the handbill to Slone was the informant. Ben Anisman's name on the invoices for antiwar material suggests that it was he who took the copy to the printer and provided a copy for the BI. Arthur S. Burgoyne, rep., May 28, 1917; Judge to Bielaski, July 19, 1917, DJ OG 18197, RG 65; Wendell, rep., Aug. 23, 1917, MID 10110-199, RG 165, NA.

64. Photostat in DJ OG 18197, RG 65, NA.

65. Judge to Bielaski, July 19, 1917, DJ OG 18197, RG 65, NA.

66. Ibid.; draft report of Senate Committee on Education and Labor, 22, folder 5, C-314, LaFollette Family Papers, LC; Jeffreys-Jones, "Profit Over Class," 242. P-45 was an informant, perhaps the notary Fred Golden, employed by the Pittsburgh police, the Department of Justice, the Secret Service, and other agencies. Report of Operative-in-charge, Jan. 19, 1917, Daily Reports of U.S. Secret Service Agents, 1875–1936, Microfilm Publication T-915, Roll 683, RG 87, NA.

3. TAMING THE STEEL CITY WOBBLIES, 1917–1918

1. Montgomery, *House of Labor*, 370–72; Weinstein, *Decline of Socialism*, 146–59.

2. Wendell, rep., July 25, 1917, MID 10110-199, RG 165, NA.

3. Wendell, reps., July 22, 23, 1917; 836, rep., Sept. 12–16, 1917, all MID 10110-199, RG 165, NA.

4. Lynch, "Pittsburgh, the I.W.W. and the Stogie Workers," 81.

5. Donald H. Avery, "British-born 'Radicals' in North America, 1900–1941: The Case of Sam Scarlett," *Bulletin of Canadian Ethnic Studies* 10 (1978): 66–71; trial transcript, July 1, 1918, *U.S. v. Haywood et al.*, 5772–74, 5777, 5796, 5800, 5802, Box 120, IWW Collection, Archives of Labor History and Urban Affairs, Wayne State University, Detroit, Mich. (hereinafter, IWW, WSU).

6. Foner, *History of the Labor Movement*, vol. 4, 493–514; Harrison George, *The I.W.W. Trial* (Chicago: IWW Publishing, 1918), 41–43; Mary Heaton Vorse, *A Footnote to Folly* (New York: Arno, 1980), 132–49; Dorothy Gallagher, *All the Right Enemies: The Life and Murder of Carlo Tresca* (New Brunswick: Rutgers University Press, 1988), 55–62.

7. Dubofsky, *We Shall Be All*, 319–33.

8. Law to Vincent St. John, Dec. 12, 18, 1913; St. John to Law, Feb. 26, 1914; Law to St. John, [n.d. but between June 25 and Sept. 17], Aug. 24, Sept. 1, 7, 17, 1914, Oct. [?] 1915, all Government Exhibit #475 in *U.S. v. Haywood et al.*, Box 120, IWW, WSU; Foner, *Fellow Workers and Friends*, 152, 158, 160, 164.

9. Law to St. John, Mar. 10, 1914, *U.S. v. Haywood et al.*, Box 120, IWW, WSU; George to St. John, July 22, 1919, DJ OG 364089, RG 65, NA.

10. Law to Haywood, Jan. 24, 1916; Haywood to Law, Jan. 24, Feb. 23, 1916, *U.S. v. Haywood et al.,* Box 120, IWW, WSU.

11. Spencer to Frank Burke, Nov. 14, 1919, DJ OG 215915, RG 65, NA; Law to Haywood, Feb. 21, 1916, Mar. 3, 11, 1917; same to Ben Williams, Apr. 24, 1916, all *U.S. v. Haywood et al.,* Box 120, IWW, WSU.

12. Wendell, rep., July 26, 1917, MID 10110-199, RG 165, NA.

13. Al[exander] Richmond, *A Long View From the Left: Memoirs of an American Revolutionary* (Boston: Houghton Mifflin, 1973), 276–77, 289; Harvey Klehr, John Earl Haynes, and Fridrikh Igorevich Firsov, *The Secret World of American Communism* (New Haven: Yale University Press, 1995), 37–40; Wendell, rep., Sept. 28, 1917, MID 10110-253, RG 165; Judge, rep., Sept. 27, 1917, DJ OG 67–40, RG 65, both NA.

14. The PCA was founded in the New York area in 1914 to keep the United States out of the war by Rebecca Shelley and Leila Faye Secor, backed by Mrs. Henry Villard and Oswald Garrison Villard. Before 1917 it had various names: American Neutral Conference Committee; First American Conference for Democracy and Terms of Peace; Emergency Peace Federation; National Conference of Labor, Socialist, and Radical Movements. See Statement of Emily Greene Balch, June 8, 1940, People's Council of America for Peace and Democracy Papers, Roll C3.1, Swarthmore College Peace Collection (hereinafter, SCPC), Swarthmore, Penn.

15. "Appeal for members," The People's Council, n.d. [July 1917], PCA, Roll C3.1, SCPC, Swarthmore, Penn.

16. C. Roland Marchand, *The American Peace Movement and Social Reform, 1898–1918* (Princeton: Princeton University Press, 1972), 294–304, 306–14; H. C. Peterson and Gilbert C. Fite, *Opponents of War, 1917–1918* (Madison: University of Wisconsin Press, 1957), 74–79; Peggy Lamson, *Roger Baldwin, Founder of the American Civil Liberties Union* (Boston: Houghton Mifflin Co., 1976), 73; Wendell, reps., July 22, 23, 1917, MID 10110-199, RG 165, NA.

17. Keasby, a single-tax advocate and economics and political science professor, lost his job at the University of Texas because of PCA activity. Minutes, July 19, 1917, meeting, PCA, Roll C3.1, SCPC, Swarthmore, Penn.

18. Mountain to Roger Baldwin, July 14, 1917, ACLU, PU; memo, W. H. Waldron, IO 80th Division, "*re* Joseph Mountain," Apr. 29, 1918, MID 10902-3/10; W. Walter Vaughan to Chief, Military Intelligence Branch, Aug. 17, 1918, MID 10902-3/34, both RG 165, NA.

19. Wendell, reps., July 26, 27, 28, 1917, MID 10110-199, RG 165, NA.

20. Wendell, reps., July 26, 27, 28, 1917, MID 10110-199, RG 165, NA.

21. Wendell, rep., July 28, 1917; Dillon, rep., July 29, 1917, both MID 10110-199, RG 165, NA.

22. Mooney and Warren K. Billings were convicted on perjured evidence. Although he was not executed, Mooney was perhaps a more authentic martyr of the Left than Sacco and Vanzetti. His death sentence was commuted by President Wilson, but he remained behind bars until California governor Culbert Olsen pardoned him in 1939.

23. Wendell, rep., Aug. 8, 1917, MID 10110-199, RG 165, NA.

24. Wendell, rep., Aug. 11, 1917, MID 10110-199, RG 165, NA.

25. Wendell, rep., Aug. 12, 1917, MID 10110-199, RG 165, NA.

26. Wendell, reps., Aug. 6, 14, 1917, MID 10110-199, RG 165, NA.

27. Wendell, reps., Aug. 11, 14, 1917, MID 10110-199, RG 165, NA.

28. Wendell, reps., Aug. 15, 23, 1917, MID 10110-199; Horn to Van Deman, Aug. 10, 1917, MID 10110-253, all RG 165, NA.

29. Dubofsky, *We Shall Be All,* 384–90; David M. Kennedy, *Over Here: The First World War and American Society* (New York: Oxford University Press, 1980): 263–64.

30. Wendell, rep., Aug. 15, 1917, MID 10110-199, RG 165, NA.

31. Ibid.

32. Ibid.

33. Ibid.

34. Wendell, reps., Aug 25, 26, 27, 1917, MID 10110-199, RG 165, NA.

35. Walter Loan to Scarlett, July 21, 1919, DJ OG 364089, RG 65, NA; Wendell, rep., Aug. 22, 1917, MID 10110-199; Horn to Van Deman, Aug. 24, 1917, MID 10110-253, both RG 165, NA. The directors of the Employers' Association of Pittsburgh included officials of Mesta Machine, Union Switch and Signal, Westinghouse Air Brake, and other prominent manufacturing companies.

36. Wendell, reps., Aug. 28, 29, Sept. 2, 1917, MID 10110-199, RG 165, NA.

37. Dubofsky, *We Shall Be All*, 406; Judge, rep., Aug. 21, 1917, MID 10110-199, RG 165, NA; Peter Carlson, *Roughneck: The Life and Times of Big Bill Haywood* (New York: W. W. Norton and Co., 1983), 253.

38. Search Warrant signed by Roger Knox, Sept. 5, 1917, Box 99, IWW, WSU.

39. "List of items taken . . . ," Box 99, IWW, WSU; Dillon, reps., Sept. 5, 8, 1917, MID 10110-199, RG 165, NA; Jack Shean to Haywood, Sept. 24, 1917; Haywood to Shean, Sept. 27, 1917, Box 99, IWW, WSU.

40. Carlson, *Roughneck*, 256, 278.

41. Judge, rep., Sept. 22, 1917, DJ OG 67–40, RG 65, NA.

42. Dubofsky, *We Shall Be All*, 407–08; Judge, rep., Sept. 27, 1917, DJ OG 67–40, RG 65, NA.

43. Justh, Perry, Cournos, and Andreytchine had not been involved with the Pittsburgh IWW in 1917–1918. They were arrested for activities elsewhere. Justh moved to Pittsburgh soon after the government dropped the charges against him. Perry was arrested in Salt Lake City after being active among the copper miners at Bisbee. He was a veteran of industrial action at Pittsburgh and a close friend of Pittsburgh radicals Walter and Reba Loan. Cournos was the son of Ukrainian immigrants and grew up in Philadelphia. He was the half-brother of writer John Cournos, whose novel *The Mask* won acclaim in the early 1920s. His family moved to Pittsburgh during the war. Andreytchine, who later fled to the USSR with Bill Haywood, was an ally and friend of Margolis.

44. Dubofsky, *We Shall Be All*, 408; Judge, rep., Sept. 28, 1917; Dillon, rep., Sept. 28, 1917; Wendell, rep., Sept 28, 1917, all DJ OG 67-40, RG 65, NA.

45. Wendell, rep., Sept. 2, 1917, MID 10110-199, RG 165, NA; Haywood to Shean, Sept. 27, 1917, Box 99, IWW, WSU; Dillon, rep., Sept. 24, 1917, DJ OG 67-40, RG 65, NA. Compare, for example, "Special Instructions for Efficient Party Apparatus," District 13, April 1933, from the Soviet Archives, reprinted in Klehr et al., *Secret World of American Communism*, 37–40.

46. Dillon, rep., Sept. 24, 1917, DJ OG 67-40, RG 65, NA.

47. Ibid.; Trial Transcript, *U.S. v. Haywood et al.*, 5802, IWW, WSU.

48. Wendell, rep., Sept. 26, 1917, MID 10110-199, RG 165, NA; W. A. Beadling, rep., Sept. 27, 1917; Judge, rep., Sept. 29, 1917, both DJ OG 67-40, RG 65 NA.

49. Wendell, rep., Oct. 6, 1917; Judge, rep., Nov. 17, 1917, both DJ OG 67-40, RG 65, NA.

50. Judge, reps., Jan. 14, 23, 1918, DJ OG 67-40; 836, rep., Apr. 1, 1918, DJ OG 215915, both RG 65, NA.

51. Wendell, reps., July 25, 26, 27, 28, 30, 31, 1917, MID 10110-199, RG 165 NA; Skelly, rep., July 25, 1917; 836, memo for JEH, Jan. 19, 1920, all DJ OG 18197, RG 65, NA.

52. Judge, rep., July 30, 1917, MID 10110-100, RG 165, NA.

53. *Pittsburgh Gazette-Times*, Aug. 19, 1917.

54. Ibid., Sept. 1, 1917; Wendell, rep., July 26, 27, 1917, Aug. 21, 1917, MID 10110-199, RG 165, NA; Weinstein, *Decline of Socialism*, 132–42.

55. Wendell, reps., Aug. 17, 20, 21, 1917, MID 10110-199, RG 165, NA.

56. Flynn, *The Eagle's Eye*, 328–41.

57. 836, rep., Apr. 19, June 7, 1918, MID 10110-199; Van Essen to Mountain, June 23, 1918, MID 10902-3, all RG 165, NA.

58. Wendell, reps., Dec. 6, 1917, DJ OG 67-40, RG 65, NA. Freda Truhar Brewster, "A Personal View of the Early Left in Pittsburgh, 1907–1923," *Western Pennsylvania Magazine of History and Biography* 69 (1986): 348, 355; Nelson et al., *Steve Nelson*, 21.

59. Wendell, rep., Dec. 20–23, 1917, DJ OG 18197, RG 65; 836, rep., Mar. 9, 1918, MID 10110-199, RG 165, both NA.

60. 836, rep., Mar. 14–17, 1918, DJ OG 18197, RG 65, NA. In 1912 teen-aged Fox was arrested in the Hill District for protesting police restrictions on free speech in connection with the IWW-led stogie workers' strike. *Pittsburgh Press*, Aug. 11, 1912.

61. Purchasing certificates in December 1917 were Margolis, Shean, Ben Anisman, William Schulters, James Mering, and Jennie Wommer. Wendell, rep., Dec. 10, 1917, DJ OG 67-40; same, rep., Dec. 17–20, 1917, DJ OG 105989, both RG 65, NA.

62. O. W. Fowler, rep., June 4, 1918, DJ OG 215915; Wendell, rep., Sept. 28, 1917, DJ OG 67-40, RG 65, NA; Wendell, reps., Aug. 8, 14, 21, 22, 23, 26, 27, Sept. 2, 3, Oct. 8, 16, 1917, all MID 10110-199, RG 165, NA.

63. Joseph Freeman, *An American Testament: A Narrative of Rebels and Romantics* (New York: Ferrar and Rinehart, Inc., 1936), 300–02.

64. E. Hansen [Knud Sandor] to Walsh [Wendell], Oct. 13, 1917 (copy) in Wendell, rep., Oct. 17, 1917, MID 10110-199, RG 165, NA; same to same, Dec. 28, 1917 (copy) in Dillon, rep., Jan. 12, 1918, DJ OG 67-40, RG 65, NA; same to same, Mar. 8, 1918, ONI, 21020-4, Entry 78A, Box 64, RG 38, NA.

65. Wendell, rep., Dec. 17–20, 1917, DJ OG 67-40, RG 65, NA.

66. Parker, "The I.W.W.," 651–62.

4. EXCURSIONS, ALARMS, AND SLACKERS ABROAD: EXTENDING THE RANGE OF SURVEILLANCE, 1918

1. David F. Trask, *The AEF and Coalition Warmaking, 1917–1918* (Lawrence: University Press of Kansas, 1993), 42, 53, 59, 65–66.

2. *Pittsburgh Sun,* Sept. 27, 1918.

3. Murphy, *World War I,* 128–32; Schaffer, *America in the Great War,* 15–26, offers lists of civil liberties violations by mobs and state and local governments. See Thomas A. Lawrence, "Eclipse of Liberty: Civil Liberties in the United States During the First World War," *Wayne Law Review* 21 (1974): 33–112.

4. Wendell, rep., Feb. 12, 1918, MID 10110-199, RG 165, NA.

5. *Pittsburgh Gazette-Times,* Mar. 7, 1918.

6. *Pittsburgh Telegram,* May 3, 1918; *Pittsburgh Sun,* May 3, 1918 (clip file, Penn.), vol. 61, ACLU, PU.

7. *Altoona Times,* Aug. 28, 1918 (clip file, Penn.), vol. 61, ACLU, PU.

8. *Pittsburgh Sun,* Feb. 29, May 17, 1918 (clip file, Penn.), vol. 61, ACLU, PU.

9. *Pittsburgh Dispatch,* May 18, 1918 (clip file, Penn.), vol. 61, ACLU, PU.

10. *Pittsburgh Post,* May 26, 1918 (clip file, Penn.), vol. 61, ACLU, PU.

11. *Pittsburgh Gazette-Times,* May 28, 1918 (clip file, Penn.), vol. 61, ACLU, PU.

12. *Annual Report of the Attorney General of the United States for the Year 1918,* 156, 220; *Annual Report of the Attorney General of the United States for the Year 1919,* 120, 184; *Annual Report of the Attorney General of the United States for the Year 1920,* 201, 329.

13. O'Brian to Gregory, Apr. 18, 1918, in Arthur S. Link, ed., *Papers of Woodrow Wilson* (Princeton, Princeton University Press, 1966–1994) (hereinafter, *PWW*), 47: 363–65.

14. *Pittsburgh Gazette-Times,* May 15, 1918.

15. Ibid., May 25, 1918.

16. Charges against Pryzmusalia were later dropped. *Pittsburgh Press,* June 8, Dec. 14, 1918.

17. Beatrice C. E. Henessy, Dec. 3, 1917, DJ OG 104292, RG 65, NA.

18. Judge, rep., Jan. 25, 1918, DJ OG 104366, RG 65, NA.

19. 836, rep., Mar. 14–17, 1918, ONI 21020–4, Box 62, Entry 78A, RG 38, NA; Dubofsky, *We Shall Be All,* 429.

20. Brewster, "A Personal View of the Early Left," 356. The BI files contain an English translation of the program of a February 12, 1921, concert-dance-performance-party sponsored by the Jugoslav Workers that featured two Tamburic orchestras and a "Declamation" by Miss Freda Truha [*sic*] of Pittsburgh's North Side. Lenon, supplemental rep., Feb. 10, 1921, DJ BSF 202600-1768, RG 65, NA.

21. 836, rep., June 7, 1918, MID 10110-199, RG 165, NA.

22. 836, rep., Apr. 28, 1918, MID 10110-199, RG 165, NA.

23. 836, rep., Feb. 2, 1918, MID 10110-199, RG 165, NA.

24. Dubofsky, *We Shall Be All,* 423–37.

25. Trial transcript, July 7, 1918, *U.S. v. Haywood et al.,* 6515–30, IWW, WSU.

26. 836, rep., July 8–9, 1918, DJ OG 18197, RG 65, NA.

27. Dubofsky, *We Shall Be All,* 425–33, 436–37; Patrick Renshaw, *The Wobblies: The Story of Syndicalism in the United States* (New York: Doubleday and Company, 1967), 169–94; Philip A. Taft, "The Federal Trials of the IWW," *Labor History* 3 (winter 1962): 66–76.

28. Wendell, rep., Jan. 18, 1918, DJ OG 67-40, RG 65, NA.

29. 836, rep., June 11, 1918, MID 10110-199, RG 165, NA.

30. 836, reps., June 22, 23, 1918, MID 10110-199, RG 165, NA.

31. 836, rep., June 14, 1918, MID 10110-199, RG 165, NA.

32. 836, rep., Apr. 27–28, 1918, MID 10110-199, RG 165, NA.

33. 836, rep., Apr. 29, 1918, DJ OG 215915, RG 65, NA.

34. Ingham, "A Strike in the Progressive Era," 353–77.

35. Spencer to Burke, Nov. 14, 1919; Speer, rep., Mar. 18, 1919, both DJ OG 215915, RG 65, NA; Ingham, "A Strike in the Progressive Era," 368.

36. 836, reps., May 13, June 20, 1918, MID 10110-199, RG 165, NA.

37. 836, rep., May 13, 1918, MID 10110-199, RG 165, NA.

38. 836, rep., June 20, 1918, MID 10110-199, RG 165, NA; "Sterling Specialty Sales Co.," Aug. 13, 1918, ONI 21020-39A-9, RG 38 NA.

39. *New York Call,* Apr. 15, June 24, 1918, Mar. 7, 1919; *Newark Leader,* June 1, 1918; *Pittsburgh Press,* Mar. 27, June 19, 1918, all (clip file) ACLU, PU; J. C. Rider, rep., Aug. 2, 1918, DJ OG 291921, RG 65, NA; Van Essen to Mountain, June 23, 1918, MID 10902-3, RG 165, NA.

40. *New York Call,* Apr. 15, 1918, Mar. 7, 1919; 836, rep., Apr. 6–11, 1918, DJ OG 291921, RG 65, NA; 836, rep., Apr. 19, 1918, MID 10110-199, RG 165, NA. Wendell estimated that 75 percent of Erie Socialists were German immigrants or their descendants.

41. 836, rep., Apr. 6–11, 1918, DJ OG 291921, RG 65, NA.

42. Spencer, rep., Aug. 2, 1918, DJ OG 291921, RG 65, NA.

43. 836, rep., Aug. 3–6, 1918, DJ OG 291921, RG 65, NA.

44. George E. Rowe to DNI, Sept. 6, 1918, ONI 21020-133, Entry 78A, Box 64, RG 38, NA.

45. Wright's participation in Wendell's Mexican border cover story suggests that he might have been a BI spy. Lenon, rep., Aug 20, 1918, DJ OG 291921, RG 65, NA.

46. Flood to APL, July 31, 1918, MID, PPS, Box 3, Entry 127, RG 165, NA.

47. For GE and Erie see Montgomery, *House of Labor,* 446–47.

48. Lenon, rep., Aug. 14, 1918, DJ OG 291921, RG 65, NA.

49. Ibid.

50. Lenon, rep., Aug. 20, 1918, DJ OG 291921, RG 65, NA.

51. Lenon, rep., Sept. 14, 1918, DJ OG 291921, RG 65, NA.

52. Judge to Bielaski, Oct. 19, 1918, DJ OG 291921, RG 65, NA.

53. 836, rep., Oct. 26–29, 1918, DJ OG 291921, RG 65, NA.

54. Lenon, rep., Aug. 20, 1918, DJ OG 291921, RG 65, NA.

55. From July 1917 to June 1920 the Justice Department prosecuted almost 47,000 draft evasion cases, 122 of them in western Pennsylvania. *Annual Report of the Attorney General of the United States for the Year 1918,* 156, 220; *Annual Report of the Attorney General of the United States for the Year 1919,* 120, 184; *Annual Report of the Attorney General of the United States for the Year 1920,* 201, 329.

56. Jensen, *Price of Vigilance,* 188–92; Kennedy, *Over Here,* 165–66.

57. *Pittsburgh Gazette-Times,* Mar. 5, 1918.

58. *Pittsburgh Dispatch,* Mar. 4, 1918; *Pittsburgh Gazette-Times,* Mar. 4, 1918; Jensen, *Price of Vigilance,* 188–218; *Pittsburgh Dispatch,* Mar. 8, 1918; Lenon, Applications for Appointment, June 25, 1918, Nov. 29, 1923, FBI 67-68, FOIA/PA.

59. *Pittsburgh Gazette-Times,* Mar. 4, 1918; *Pittsburgh Dispatch,* Mar. 6, 8, 1918.

60. Ibid. Mar. 4, 1918.

61. Ibid., Mar. 5, 6, 8, 1918.

62. Ibid., Mar. 4, 1918; *Pittsburgh Press,* Mar. 6, 1918; *Pittsburgh Gazette-Times,* Mar. 6, 1918.

63. *Pittsburgh Press,* Mar. 7, 1918; *Pittsburgh Gazette-Times,* Mar. 7, 1918; *Pittsburgh Dispatch,* Mar. 4, 1918.

64. *Pittsburgh Dispatch,* Mar. 6, 1918.

65. Estimates of the number of men detained vary. I have used BI-APL numbers. E. H. Rushmore to Directors, APL, Dec. 13, 1918, American Protective League Correspondence (New York) Entry 12, Box 7, RG 65, NA.

66. Jensen, *Price of Vigilance,* 194–210; Schaffer, *America in the Great War,* 17.

67. Wendell, rep., Nov. 5–7, 1917, MID 10100-199, RG 165, NA; same, rep., Nov. 19, 1917, DJ OG 18197; same, rep., Nov. 27, 1917, DJ OG 105989; 836, rep., Mar. 1–3, 1918, DJ 06 36412, all RG 65, NA; Mountain to Baldwin, Aug. 21, 1918, ACLU, PU.

68. Peterson and Fite, *Opponents of War,* 122–25.

69. Ibid., 123.

70. Ibid., 125–38.

71. See Marshall to Jimmie [Mering], Oct. 21, 1918 (photostat); 836, rep., Nov. 5, 1918, both MID 10110-199, RG 165, NA.

72. Marshall to Margolis, Oct. 21, 1918 (photostat); Speer, rep., Oct. 25, 1918, both MID 10110-199, RG 165, NA.

73. Also forbidden were club sandwiches, liver and bacon mixed grills, and, unless the customer requested it, bread and butter. *Pittsburgh Dispatch,* Oct. 25, 1918.

74. Acting Director, MID, to IO Camp Lee, Mar. 7, 1919, MID 10110-199; Churchill to W. E. Allen, Apr. 29, 1919, both RG 165, NA.

75. IO, Camp Lee to Director MID, Mar. 18, 1919, MID 10110-199, RG 165, NA. The biblical reference is *Corinthians* I:13.

76. Speer, rep., Oct. 25, 1918, MID 10110-199, RG 165, NA.

77. Mountain to Earl Snook, n.d. [ca. Mar. 15, 1918] (copy); 836, rep., July 15–17, 1918, both MID 10902-3, RG 165, NA.

78. Mountain to Snook, n.d. [ca. Mar. 15, 1918] (copy); 836, rep., July 15–17, 1918, both MID 10902-3, RG 165, NA.

79. 836, rep., Apr. 17, 1918, MID 10110-199; Judge to Bielaski, Mar. 18, 1918, MID 10902-3, both RG 165, NA.

80. Mountain to Snook, n.d. [ca. Mar. 15, 1918], MID 10902-3, RG 165, NA.

81. Lamson, *Baldwin,* 84–114; Walker, *In Defense of American Liberties,* 39–42.

82. Mountain to Baldwin, Feb. 19, 1918, vol. 8, Camp Lee, ACLU, PU.

83. 836, rep., Apr. 17, 1918, MID 10110-199, RG 165, NA.

84. Mountain to Baldwin, May 1, 1918, vol. 8, Camp Lee, ACLU, PU.

85. Same to same, June 15, 1918, ibid.

86. Ibid.

87. Peterson and Fite, *Opponents of War,* 259–64.

88. 836, rep., July 15–17, 1918, MID 10902-3, RG 165, NA.

89. Ibid.

90. Schaffer, *America in the Great War,* 135–39, 199–212.

91. In vol. 8, Camp Lee, ACLU, PU.

92. 836, July 15–17, 1918, MID 10902-3, RG 165, NA.

93. Memo for Lt. Col. Masteller from Office of the Chief of Staff, War Department, Subject I.W.W. and Conscientious Objectors at Camp Lee, Aug. 20, 1918, MID 10902-3, RG 165, NA.

94. 836, rep., Aug. 29, 1918, MID 10110-597; Horn to Van Deman, Feb. 12, 1918; Van Deman to IO, 80th Division, Feb. 25, 1918; W. Walter Vaughan to Chief, Military Intelligence Section, June 15, 1918, all MID 10902-3, RG 165, NA.

95. Churchill to IO, Camp Lee, June 20, 1918, MID 10902-3, RG 165, NA.

96. Spingarn to Churchill, July 2, 1918; Vaughan to Chief, MID, June 23, 1918; Crystal Eastman to Mountain, June 20, 1918 (true copy), all MID 10902-3, RG 165, NA.

97. For the beginnings of the NCLB as the Conscientious Objector branch of the American Union Against Militarism (AUAM) see Charles L. Markmann, *The Noblest Cry: A History of the American Civil Liberties Union* (New York: St. Martin's Press, 1965), 16–26; Lamson, *Baldwin,* 72–74. For its troubles with the federal government during the war see Walker, *Defense of American Liberties,* 37–39.

98. Mountain to Baldwin, Aug. 21, 1918, vol. 8, Camp Lee, ACLU, PU; Vaughan to Churchill, Sept. 24, 1918, MID 10902-3, RG 165, NA.

99. Van Essen to Joe [Mountain], June 23, 1918, MID 10902-3, RG 165, NA.

100. *Pittsburgh Gazette-Times,* Sept. 10, 1918.

101. Burgoyne to Ray [Horn?], Sept. 10, 1918, ONI 21020-133, Entry 78A, Box 64, RG 38, NA.

102. Marshall to Mering, Oct. 21, 1918, MID 10110-199, RG 165, NA.

103. The others were Leonard Finklehor and Fred Roth. Flood to DMI, Sept. 19, 1918, MID 10902-3, RG 165, NA.

104. King to IO, Northeastern Dept., Nov. 1, 1918; Moore to King, Nov. 7, 1918; King to Churchill, Nov. 11, 1918, all MID 10902-3, RG 165, NA.

105. Albert N. Pike to Capt. Pratt, Dec. 5, 1918; Telegram, Dunn to Moore, Jan. 8, 1919; J. F. Murphy, Jr., to Moore, Jan. 13, 1919; Moore to Churchill, Jan. 15, 1919, all MID 10902-3; 836, rep., Jan. 19, 1919; Dunn to Flood, Feb. 14, 1919; King to Dir., MID, Feb. 20, 1919; Flood to Acting DMI, Jan. 24, 1919, all MID 10110-597, all RG 165, NA.

106. Flood to Acting DMI, Feb. 17, 1919, MID 10110-597, RG 165, NA.

107. King to DMI, Feb. 25, 1919; Flood to Acting DMI, Jan. 17, 1919, Mar. 4, 1919; Capt. O. Metzerott to Capt. Hathaway, Mar. 7, 1919, all MID 10902-3, RG 165, NA.

108. King to Acting DMI, Mar. 27, 1919; Flood to Acting DMI, Mar. 28, 1919; same to IO Northeastern Department, Apr. 3, 1919; Murphy to Boston Office, Apr. 8, 1919, all MID 10902-3, RG 165, NA.

109. Carol S. Gruber, *Mars and Minerva* (Baton Rouge: Louisiana State University Press, 1975), 214.

110. 836, rep., June 9, 1918, MID 10110-199, RG 165, NA.

111. 836, rep., June 22, 1918, MID 10110-199, RG 165, NA. For Freeman see Marchand, *American Peace Movement*, 321.

112. 836, rep., June 9, 22, 1918; Flood to Churchill, July 3, 1918; Flood to IO-MID, Camp Mills, NY, July 20, 1918, all MID 10110-199, RG 165, NA; Ben Fletcher to "Capt." Jack Lever, July 20, 1919, DJ OG 364089, RG 65, NA.

113. Wendell, rep., Dec. 20, 1917; Bielaski to Judge, Jan. 2, 1918; same to Maj. Gen. E. H. Crowder, Jan. 5, 1918, all DJ OG 18197, RG 65, NA.

114. E.g., "Anything which would disclose the identity of our informant, or even subject him to suspicion by the radical workers with whom he associates would be nothing short of calamitous." Flood to Churchill, July 3, 1918, MID 10110-199, RG 165, NA; "Mr. Wendell is a confidential employee and it is desired his connection with this service not be disclosed." Bielaski to Maj. Gen. E. H. Crowder, Jan. 5, 1918, DJ 18197, RG 65, NA; "It does not appear that sufficient evidence is at hand on which to base a criminal prosecution against these men, bearing in mind our inability to use the confidential informant at Pittsburgh." Albert N. Pike to Capt. Pratt, Dec. 5, 1918, MID 101902-3, RG 165, NA.

115. Baldwin to Mountain, June 19, 1918, on NCLB stationery lists Margolis and Marshall as the Bureau's Pittsburgh attorneys. MID 10902-3, RG 165, NA; 836, rep. May 6, 1918, DJ OG 18197, RG 65, NA.

116. Wendell, reps., Feb. 6, 12, 1918, MID 10110-199, RG 165, NA; 836, rep., Feb. 21–24, 1918, DJ OG 18197, RG 65, NA.

117. Wendell, rep., Feb. 6, 1918, MID 10110-199, RG 165, NA.

118. Wendell, rep., Jan. 7–9, 1918, DJ OG 67-34, RG 65, NA.

119. 836, rep., Feb. 28–Mar. 3, 1918, DJ OG 18197, RG 65, NA.

120. 836, rep., June 17–19, 1918, DJ OG 18197, RG 65, NA.

121. 836, rep., June 20, 1918, MID 10110-199, RG 165, NA.

5. BOMBS, A NEW MISSION, AND THE USUAL SUSPECTS, 1919

1. U.S. Congress, Senate Subcommittee of the Judiciary, *Hearings on Bolshevik Propaganda*, S. Res. 439 and 469, 65th Cong., 3d sess., 1919, 6 (hereinafter, *Bolshevik Propaganda Hearings); Burke to Spencer, Aug. 22, 1919, DJ 67-9973, FOIA/PA.

2. Robert K. Murray, *Red Scare: A Study in National Hysteria, 1919–1920* (Minneapolis: University of Minnesota Press, 1955), 94–98.

3. F. W. Hoffmann to DNI, Jan. 14, 1919, 21104-6; Arthur MacArthur to same, May 24, 1919, 21104-3-A, both Entry 78A, RG 38, NA; rep., Mar. 7, 1919, Daily Reports of U.S. Secret Service Agents, 1875–1936, Microfilm Publication T-915, Roll 684, RG 87, NA; Anon., "False Representation of Government Agency with Intent to Deceive," July 12, 1919; Burke to Spencer, July 25, 1919; Spencer to Burke, July 30, 1919, all DJ OG 369439, RG 65, NA; *Pittsburgh Post-Gazette*, Jan. 19, 1955; *NYT*, Apr. 17, 1952, July 18, 1960.

4. Jensen, *Army Surveillance*, 180–83.

5. Col. John M. Dunn to IO, Old Hickory Powder Plant, Nashville, Tenn., Jan. 29, 1919, MID 10110-199, RG 165, NA.

6. Jensen, *Army Surveillance*, 177.

7. Churchill to all Intelligence Officers, Apr. 28, 1919, MID 10110-199, RG 165, NA.

8. Jensen, *Army Surveillance*, 178–83. Actually, Pittsburgh MID had been receiving 836-Wendell undercover reports ever since the Armistice.

9. Fred W. Thompson and Patrick Murfin, *I.W.W.: Its First Seventy Years* (Chicago: Industrial Workers of the World, 1976), 128; Flood to Churchill, May 5, 15, 1919; Churchill to Flood, May 10, 1919, both MID 10110-199, RG 165, NA.

10. Judge to W. E. Allen, Mar. 8, 1919; Allen to Judge, Mar. 11, 1919; Memo for E. A. Tamm [author deleted by FBI], Mar. 12, 1941; Memo, C. D. DeLoach for Mr. Mohr, Jan. 25, 1962, all FBI 67-96008, FOIA/PA.

11. Detzel to Judge, Mar. 7, 1919; Allen to Lenon, Mar. 17, 1919; Lenon to Allen, Mar. 24, Apr. 1, 1919; Spencer to Allen, Apr. 7, 1919; same to Frank Burke, Jan. 15, 1920, all FBI 67-68, FOIA/PA.

12. 836, rep., Mar. 19–22, 1919, DJ OG 291921, RG 65, NA.

13. George, *The I.W.W. Trial*, 59; Speer, rep., Feb. 12, 1919, DJ OG 215915, RG 65, NA.

14. 836, rep., Apr. 19, 1919, DJ OG 215915, RG 65, NA.

15. Flood to DMI, Mar. 3, 1919, MID 10110-199, RG 165, NA.

16. Speer to Allen, Mar. 6, 1919, DJ OG 291921, RG 65, NA.

17. Ibid.

18. Rider, rep., Mar. 3, 1919, DJ OG 291921, RG 65, NA.

19. 836, rep., *In re* Jack Reed, Bolsheviki meeting, Jan. 23–24, 1919, ONI 21020-133, Entry 78A, Box 64, RG 38, NA.

20. D. White, rep., Mar. 2, 1919, DJ OG 215915, RG 65, NA.

21. Lenon, rep., Mar. 23, 1919; 836, reps., Mar. 23, 25, 30, Apr. 4, 6, 8, 9–13, 1919, all DJ OG 215915, RG 65, NA.

22. 836, rep., Mar. 9, 1919; Willman, rep., Mar. 17, 1919; Speer, rep., Mar. 3, 1919, all DJ OG 215915, RG 65, NA; 836, rep., Jan. 22, 1919, DJ OG 343013, RG 65, NA; Flood to DMI, Mar. 17, 1919, MID 10110-199, RG 165, NA.

23. 836, reps., Dec. 6–8, 12–17, 1918, DJ OG 18197, RG 65, NA.

24. ACBA Brief, 80–81; 836, rep., Jan. 16, 1919, DJ OG 343013, RG 65, NA; Goldman's letter of Mar. 18, 1919, quoted in Alice Wexler, *Emma Goldman, An Intimate Life* (New York: Pantheon Books, 1984), 259; Lepschutz to Grover Perry, July 19, 1919, DJ OG 364089, RG 65, NA; 836, rep., Jan. 27–Feb. 2, 1919, DJ OG 18197, RG 65, NA.

25. 836, rep., Feb. 9, 1919, DJ OG 215915; same, reps., Feb 17–24, Feb. 24–Mar. 3, 1919, DJ OG 18197, all RG 65, NA.

26. Paul Avrich, *Sacco and Vanzetti: The Anarchist Background* (Princeton: Princeton University Press, 1991), 140–47.

27. Ibid., 147, 118–26, 122–26, 134–36; Mari Jo Buhle, Paul Buhle, and Dan Georgakis, *Encyclopedia of the American Left* (New York: Garland Publishing Co., 1990), 251–52.

28. Harry Rider, Edward Patrick, and M. J. Madigan, rep., May 20, 1919, MID 10110-199, RG 165, NA.

29. Ibid.

30. 836, rep., May 2, 1919; 101, rep., May 2, 1919; Speer, rep., May 3, 1919, all DJ OG 215915; 836, reps., May 2, 1919, DJ OG 360208 and 346058, both RG 65, NA.

31. 836, rep., May 2, 1919; Speer, rep., May 27, 1919, both DJ OG 360280, RG 65, NA.

32. 836, rep., May 5–11, 1919, DJ OG 291921, RG 65, NA.

33. 836, rep., May 7, 1919; Speer, rep., May 9, 1919, both DJ OG 18197, RG 65, NA. City officials allowed the meeting over BI objections. 836, rep., May 11, 1919, DJ OG 215915, RG 65, NA.

34. 836, rep., May 5, 19–26, 1919, DJ OG 215915, RG 65, NA.

35. Spencer to Allen, May 22, 1919, DJ OG 215915; D. E. Tatom, rep., May 22, 1919, DJ OG 18197, both RG 65, NA.

36. *Last Warning!*, DJ OG 18197, RG 65, NA.

37. Robert A. B[owen] to Hoover, Jan. 24, 1920, DJ OG 18197, RG 65, NA.

38. Jacob Margolies [*sic*] to Editor, *Workman and Peasant*, May 23, 1919, DJ OG 18197, RG 65, NA. Margolis never used that spelling and would not have signed his name that way. Copying errors of the Post Office translator-censor could account for this inaccuracy.

39. Emerson H. Loucks, *The Ku Klux Klan in Pennsylvania: A Study in Nativism* (New York and Har-

risburg: Telegraph Press, 1936), 25; Speer, rep., May 9, 1919; Tatom, rep., May 22, 1919, both DJ OG 18197, RG 65, NA.

40. The weekly Pittsburgh radical reports do not mention the KKK. As late as 1923 the army had no policy on KKK activities on military bases. It finally took notice, "not because it is believed that the K.K.K. is in itself an organization that would endanger the government, but, because of its secret nature." See Edward R. Stone to Assistant Chief of Staff, War Department, General Staff, Aug. 30, 1923; memo for Stone from Frank Moorman (secret), Sept. 6, 1923, both MID 10261-161, RG 165, NA.

41. 101, rep., May 26, 1919, DJ OG 343013; 836, rep., May 29, 1919, DJ OG 364083, both RG 65, NA.

42. *NYT,* June 3, 4, 1919.

43. Ibid.

44. *Pittsburgh Press* and *Pittsburgh Gazette-Times,* both June 3, 4, 1919.

45. *Pittsburgh Press,* June 3, 1919; William W. Sibray, employment record, U.S. Office of Personnel Management, FOIA/PA.

46. *Pittsburgh Press; Pittsburgh Gazette-Times; Pittsburgh Sun; Pittsburgh Dispatch; Fairmont* [West Virginia] *Times,* all June 3, 4, 1919.

47. Lowenthal, *Federal Bureau of Investigation,* 67–68; *Pittsburgh Gazette-Times,* Sept. 9, 1918.

48. Powers, *Secrecy and Power,* 63–64.

49. Ibid., 57–58, 67.

50. Hoover, Memorandum Upon the Work of the Radical Division, Aug. 1 to Oct. 19, 1919, DJ OG 374217, RG 65, NA.

51. *Pittsburgh Press; Pittsburgh Sun; Pittsburgh Dispatch,* all June 3, 4, 5, 1919; Flood to Churchill, June 12, 1919, MID 10110-1286, RG 165, NA.

52. Flood to Churchill, June 12, 1919, MID 10110-1286; Wendell, rep., Sept. 2, 1917, MID 10110-199, both RG 165, NA; Judge to Clabaugh, Nov. 10, 1917, DJ OG 67-40, RG 65; 836, reps., Feb. 9, Apr. 6, 1919, DJ OG 215915; Ames, weekly radical rep., Aug. 20, 1921, DJ BSF 202600-1768, all RG 65, NA; *Mother Earth* 10 (May 1915): 113–15.

53. Speer, List of . . . Radicals, Feb. 12, 1919, DJ OG 215915, RG 65, NA; 836, reps., Aug. 14, Oct. 2, 1917, Apr. 27–28, 1918, MID 10110-199, RG 165, NA; agent-in-charge (western Penn.) to Clabaugh, Nov. 10, 1917; 836, reps., Dec. 10, 1917, Mar. 3, 1918, all DJ OG 67-40, RG 65, NA.

54. *Pittsburgh Dispatch* and *Pittsburgh Post,* Apr. 22–May 17, 1916; Speer, List of . . . Radicals, Feb. 12, 1919, DJ OG 215915, RG 65, NA. On Blum the Communist-Socialist schoolteacher see Brewster, "A Personal View of the Early Left," 355.

55. Klehr et al., *Secret World of American Communism,* 59–60, 83–95, 99–103, 119–26, 128, 147–50, 205–15, 202, 204, 225, 230–32. See Nelson et al., *Steve Nelson,* 28, 42, 51, 125; In *Men Without Faces: The Communist Conspiracy in the U.S.A.* (New York: Harper and Brothers, 1948), 18–19, Louis F. Budenz claimed that Baker's real name was Heinz Zimmerman.

56. *Pittsburgh Press,* June 5, 1919; *Pittsburgh Dispatch,* June 5, 1919; 836, rep., May 26, 1919, DJ OG 343013, RG 65, NA.

57. BI —— [INS censored], rep., June 6–7, 1919; U.S. Dept. of Labor, Immigration Service, Arrest Warrant, June 23, 1918, DJ INS File 54616/246, FOIA/PA; Hearing Transcript, John Johnson, June 26, 1919, DJ INS 54616/246.

58. *Pittsburgh Press,* June 5, 1919; *Pittsburgh Dispatch,* June 5, 1919; Flood to Churchill, June 12, 1919, MID 10110-1286, RG 165, NA.

59. *Pittsburgh Press,* June 5, 1919; *Pittsburgh Dispatch,* June 5, 1919; *NYT,* June 6, 1919; *New York Call,* June 6, 1919; *New York World,* June 5, 1919.

60. J. J. Cornwell Papers, A. & M. 952, WVRC, WVU.

61. 836, reps., Nov. 14, 21–24, 1918, MID 10110-199, RG 165; same, rep., Feb. 25, 1919, DJ OG 215915, RG 65, all NA.

62. *Pittsburgh Press,* June 6, 1919; Flood to Churchill, June 12, 1919, MID 10110-1286, RG 165, NA.

63. Arrest Warrant, June 23, 1918; M. F. O'Brien, record of hearing and remarks, June 23, 1918; Sibray to Commissioner-General of Immigration, June 25, 1918; receipt for $500 from Jacob Margolis, June 25, 1918; Caminetti, memo, Sept. 6, 1918; same to Bureau of Investigation, Nov. 17, 1918; John W. Abercrombie to the Secretary of State, Nov. 17, 1918; Warrant-Deportation, Nov. 17, 1918; Caminetti to

Hoover, Dec. 9, 1918; Sibray to Caminetti, Dec. 30, 1918, Jan. 14, 1920, all DJ, INS 54616/264, FOIA/PA.

64. *Pittsburgh Leader,* June 4, 1919; *New York World,* June 5, 1919; *Washington Herald,* June 5, 1919, clippings in MID 10110-1286, RG 165, NA.

65. *Pittsburgh Leader,* June 4, 1919.

66. Flood to DMI, June 9, 1919, MID 10110-1286 RG 165, NA; J. W. Payne to Edmund Leigh, Apr. 7, 1919, MID, Pittsburgh Plant Protection Correspondence, Entry 127, RG 165 NA.

67. J. J. McCann, "Dynamite Plot of June 2"; Henry A. Frothingham to DMI, June 28, 1919, both MID 10110-1282, RG 165, NA.

68. *NYT,* June 8, 1919.

69. Flood to Churchill, June 14, 1919, MID 10110-1286, RG 165, NA.

70. Reps., June 3–15, Daily Reports of U.S. Secret Service Agents, 1875–1936, Microfilm Publication T-915, Roll 684, RG 87, NA; Crockett to Frank Smith, June 18, 1919; same to Bliss Morton, June 20, 1919; John B. Campbell to DMI, June 24 and 25, 1919; Crockett to DMI, July 24, 1919, all MID 10110-1282, RG 165, NA.

71. A.k.a. Andrew Anthony (his identification as an informant), A. Petrovich (his pen name in Russian periodicals), and Mitra (his code alias in the Tsarist Russian Intelligence Service). D. C. Van Buren, rep., June 12, 1919; same, memo for Crockett, June 17, 1919, both MID 10110-1282, RG 165, NA.

72. Crockett to DMI, June 7, 8, 9, 1919; Morton to Van Buren, June 7, 1919, MID, 10110-1282; Crockett to DMI, July 3, 1919; copy (English translation), Proclamation, n.d. [June 1919], both MID 10110-1283; C. M. Brown, Anarchist Bomb Plot, June 28, 1919, MID 10110-1282, all RG 165, NA.

73. Campbell to DMI, June 5, 1919; rep. of operative, June 17–30, 1919, MID 10110-1282, RG 165, NA.

74. Rep. of operative, June 17–30, 1919, MID 10110-1282, RG 165, NA.

75. Hoover, Confidential Report on the Radical Section, Sept. 30, 1919, DJ OG 374217, RG 65, NA; Noble to Crockett, July 1, 1919; MID Chicago, rep. of operative, June 17–30, 1919, both MID 10110-1282, RG 165, NA; Avrich, *Sacco and Vanzetti,* 149; [?], memo, Oct. 17, 1919, DJ OG 364089, RG 65, NA.

76. Avrich, *Sacco and Vanzetti,* 135–36, 168, 171; J. McCann to Sgt. Burlingame, Washington D.C. Police, July 7, 1919, MID 10110-1282, RG 165, NA.

77. *Washington Post,* June 20, July 3, 1919; *Pittsburgh Press,* June 10, 1919; Hoover, Confidential Report on the Radical Section, Sept. 30, 1919, DJ OG 374217; J. F. McDevitt, rep., Aug. 30, 1919, DJ OG 360086, both RG 65, NA.

78. McDevitt, rep., Aug. 30, 1919, DJ OG 360086, RG 65, NA; Speer, rep., Feb. 12, 1919; Speer, List of . . . Radicals, Feb. 12, 1919, all DJ OG 215915, RG 65, NA; rep., June 10, 1919, Daily Reports of U.S. Secret Service Agents, 1875–1936, Microfilm Publication T-915, Roll 684, RG 87, NA.

79. J. F. McDevitt, rep., Aug. 30, 1919, DJ OG 360086, RG 65, NA.

80. Ibid.

81. Ibid.

82. Ibid.; McDevitt, reps., Sept. 2, 6, 8, 1919, DJ OG 360086, RG 65, NA.

83. McDevitt, Sept. 10, 1919, DJ OG 360086, RG 65, NA.

84. Ibid.

85. Hoover, Confidential Reports on the Radical Section, Sept. 30, Oct. 19, 1919, DJ OG 374217, RG 65, NA; Avrich, *Sacco and Vanzetti,* 179–84.

86. Hoover, Memo Upon the Work of the Radical Division, Aug. 1, 1919–Mar. 15, 1920, DJ OG 374217, RG 65, NA.

87. Avrich, *Sacco and Vanzetti,* 191–95. In September 1920 the identification of Valdinoci as the bomber seemed in doubt. A former Boston BI agent "in private secret service among the Mexicans and Italians" reported that Valdinoci had been seen in Mexico near the American border in May 1919 and, incredibly, again in Tampico a year later. If the report were true, Valdinoci could not have been killed in June 1919. Hoover enlisted the State Department to locate the fugitive, but there was no verification of the alleged sighting. M. J. Davis, rep., Sept. 4, 1920; Hoover to W. H. Hurley, Oct. 1, 1920; Hurley to Hoover, Nov. 1, 1920, all DJ OG 123280, RG 65, NA.

88. Avrich, *Sacco and Vanzetti,* 157–59, 170–72. The word of the Italian anarchists seems suspect because the factions had scores to settle with each other. Witness the Galleanists' campaign in the 1920s and 1930s to discredit Carlo Tresca. Gallagher, *The Right Enemies,* 75–91.

89. *Annual Report of the Attorney General of the United States for the Year 1920* (Washington: USGPO, 1920), 15–17.

90. Gentry, *Hoover*, 138; Avrich, *Sacco and Vanzetti*, 53–54, 98–99, 104–21, 168–69; 836, rep., Apr. 29–May 1, 1918, DJ OG 18197; 101, rep., May 2, 1919, DJ OG 215915; Spencer to BI, Aug. 11, 23, 1919, DJ OG 215915, all RG 65, NA; reps., June 5, July 19, 1919, Daily Reports of U.S. Secret Service Agents, 1875–1936, Microfilm Publication T-915, Roll 684, RG 87, NA.

91. St. John to Perry, June 26, 1919, DJ OG 364089, RG 65, NA; *OBUM* 1 (July 1919): 5; Testimony of Swinburne Hale, U.S. Congress, House Committee on Rules, *Hearings on Rule Making in Order of the Consideration of S. 3317.* H. Res. 438, 66th Cong., 2d sess., 1920 (hereinafter, Hale Testimony, Sedition), 111–12.

92. Thompson, *Making of the English Working Class*, 485.

93. Whitehead, *FBI Story*, 39–41.

6. THE GREAT STRIKES OF 1919: STEEL AND COAL

1. Powers, *Secrecy and Power*, 77; Whitehead, *FBI Story*, 46.

2. Wendell, rep., Aug. 14, 1917, MID 10110-199, RG 165, NA; Fred Hardy to Harrison George, Aug. 29, 1919; Perry to J. H. McCarty, Aug. 17, 1919; same to Clara Ford, June 24, 1919; same to St. John, July 13, 1919; Ford to Perry, June 30, July 15, 1919; Law to Otto Christiansen, June 30, 1919; St. John to Perry, Aug. 13, 1919; Law to St. John, Aug. 9, 1919; "Lydia" [a sister] to Cournos, Oct. 9, 1919, all DJ OG 364089, RG 65, NA.

3. George to Eleanor Wentworth, June 22, 1919; same to Mary Gallagher, Oct. 7, Nov. 21, Dec. 10, 1919; same to St. John, July 30, 1919; Wentworth to George, July 17, Aug. 8, 1919; Abner Woodruff to same, July 27, 1919, all DJ OG 364089, RG 65, NA.

4. Scarlett to Finnish Club of Biwabik, Minnesota, June 13, 1919; same to Walter Loan, July 23, 1919; Margaret Roy to Scarlett, June 13, 1919, all DJ OG 364089, RG 65, NA.

5. Law to Joe Gordon, Jr., July 3, 1919; same to Mrs. N. B. Potts, July 4, 1919; same to J. J. Doyle, July 10, 1919; same to Mountain, Aug. 10, 1919; St. John to Law, July 15, 1919; Madge Law to same, Aug. 27, 1919, all DJ OG 364089, RG 65, NA. Grover Perry wrote proletarian poetry for diversion but grew bitter and melancholy as he worried about his wife and children and suffered from tuberculosis. Alex Cournos could think of little but parole to visit his dying mother in Pittsburgh.

6. Mary Ethel McAuley to Manuel Roy, Nov. 1, 1919, DJ OG 364089, RG 65, NA.

7. Mountain to Law, June 26, July 21, 1919; Hodge to same, June 26, 1919; Speed to same, July 1, 1919; St. John to Scarlett, July 20, 1919, all DJ OG 364089, RG 65; 836, rep., Aug. 25–31, 1919, DJ OG 36412, RG 65; Capt. Fred Adams to IO, Pittsburgh, June 25, 1919, MID 10902-3, RG 165, all NA.

8. Brody, *Labor in Crisis*, 45–52.

9. Ibid., 50–58; Valerie Jean Conner, *The National War Labor Board: Stability, Social Justice and the Voluntary State in World War I* (Chapel Hill: University of North Carolina Press, 1983), 126–41, 158–59; David Brody, *Steelworkers in America: The Nonunion Era* (Cambridge: Harvard University Press, 1960), 180–81.

10. Brody, *Labor in Crisis*, 48–50, 71.

11. Bodnar is quoted and John Couvares is paraphrased in Edward Johanningsmeier, *Forging American Communism: The Life of William Z. Foster* (Princeton: Princeton University Press, 1994), 120.

12. Interchurch World Movement, *Report on the Steel Strike* (New York: Harcourt, Brace and Howe, 1920), 221–25.

13. Brody, *Labor in Crisis*, 63–69, 94, 153; Johanningsmeier, *Forging Communism*, 120–23.

14. Robert Asher, "Painful Memories: The Historical Consciousness of Steelworkers and the Steel Strike of 1919," *Pennsylvania History* 45 (1978): 61–62; Interchurch World Movement, *Public Opinion and the Steel Strike, passim;* Johanningsmeier, *Forging Communism*, 129–30; Brody, *Labor in Crisis*, 112–13.

15. Brody, *Labor in Crisis*, 39–47; Samuel Yellen, *American Labor Struggles* (New York: Harcourt, Brace and Company, 1936), 252–60.

16. Burke to Spencer, Aug. 22, 1919; Spencer to Burke, Aug. 25, 1919, both FBI 67-9973, FOIA/PA.

17. Spencer to Burke, Aug. 25, 1919; same to same, Sept. 12, 1919; Burke to Spencer, Sept. 18, 1919, all FBI 67-9973, FOIA/PA.

18. 836, rep., Aug. 25–31, 1919, DJ OG 36412, RG 65, NA; *Pittsburgh Post* and *Pittsburgh Dispatch*, Aug. 13–27, 1919.

19. Robert K. Murray, "Communism and the Great Steel Strike of 1919," *Mississippi Valley Historical Review* 38 (Dec. 1951): 450–51; Brody, *Steelworkers in America*, 156–58.

20. Whiting Williams to E. H. Gary, Aug. 19, 1919 (carbon), General Correspondence, Series I, Folder 1, Whiting Williams Papers, MS 3580, Western Reserve Historical Society, Cleveland, Ohio.

21. Schaffer, *America in the Great War*, 67–69; Whitehead, *FBI Story*, 30.

22. 836, rep., Nov. 5, 1918, MID 10110-935, RG 165, NA.

23. Ibid.

24. Johanningsmeier, *Forging Communism*, is the most recent biography of the shadowy Foster. A hagiographic study is Arthur Zipser, *Working Class Giant: The Life of William Z. Foster* (New York: International Publishers, 1981). Foster produced two autobiographies: *From Bryan to Stalin* (1937) and *Pages from a Worker's Life* (1939).

25. Earl C. Ford, whose name appears with Foster's on the title page, evidently paid for its publication.

26. William Z. Foster and Earl Ford, *Syndicalism* (Chicago: William Z. Foster, 1912), 1–9, 14–15, 20, 26–28, 36, 44–47.

27. Gompers, *Seventy Years of Life and Labor*, 211; William Z. Foster, *The Great Steel Strike* (New York: B. W. Heubsch, Inc., 1920), 259; Brody, *Steelworkers in America*, 245–46; Brody, *Labor in Crisis*, 143–44; Johanningsmeier, *Forging Communism*, 137–40.

28. 836, rep., Feb. 9, 1919, DJ OG 215915, RG 65, NA; Johanningsmeier, *Forging Communism*, 86, 139.

29. Margolis Senate Testimony, 864; Margolis, "The Orthodox Wobbly and the Borer from Within," 28–29; rep., June 6, 1919, Daily Reports of U.S. Secret Service Agents, 1875–1936, Microfilm Publication T-915, roll 684, RG 87, NA.

30. Interchurch World Movement, *Public Opinion and the Steel Strike*, 160–61; Hoover, Confidential Memo on William Z. Foster, Sept. 12, 1919, DJ OG 374217, RG 65, NA; Johanningsmeier, *Forging American Communism*, 52.

31. *Washington Times*, Sept. 25, 1919 (clip), DJ OG 352037; Hoover, Confidential Report on Radical Section for the Week Ending Oct. 3, 1919, DJ OG 374217, both RG 65, NA.

32. Confidential Report on Radical Section for the Week Ending Oct. 3, 1919, DJ OG 374217, RG 65, NA; Burke to Spencer, Oct. 2, 9, 21, 1919; Spencer to Burke, Oct. 6, 9, 14, 1919, all FBI 67-9973, FOIA/PA.

33. James Cassedy, "A Bond of Sympathy: The Life and Tragic Death of Fannie Sellins," *Labor's Heritage* 4 (winter 1992): 34–47.

34. Coroner's Inquest, DJ OG 374675; Hoover, Confidential Report on Radical Section for the Week Ending Oct. 3, 1919, DJ OG 374217, both RG 65, NA; Interchurch World Movement, *Report on the Steel Strike*, 244.

35. Ames, reps., Oct. 1–11, 1919, DJ OG 374675, RG 65, NA.

36. In 1924 three deputies were indicted but one of them could not be located and there never was a trial. Cassedy, "A Bond of Sympathy," 46.

37. *NYT*, Oct. 4, 1919; Johanningsmeier, *Forging Communism*, 142–43; Foster, *Steel Strike*, 153; Hoover, Confidential Report on Radical Section for the Week Ending Oct. 3, 1919, DJ OG 374217, RG 65, NA.

38. Hoover, Memo of Conference with Confidential Informant 836 (Strictly Confidential), Oct. 8, 1919, DJ OG 374217, RG 65, NA. A list of Foster's *Solidarity* articles is in "Palmer on Charges by Post," 170–71.

39. The italicized words leave open the possibility that Margolis worked for the government. Hoover, Confidential Report on Radical Section for the Week Ending Oct. 3, 1919, DJ OG 374217; 836, rep., Aug. 11–17, 1919; Burke to Morton, Sept. 29, Oct. 1, 1919; Flynn to Morton, Oct. 14, 1919; Morton to Burke, Oct. 17, 1919; Hoover to Spencer, Oct. 23, 1919; Hoover to Burke, Oct. 24, 1919; Speer to Spencer, Oct. 24, 1919; Hoover to "Mr. Russell," Oct. 28, 1919; Speer to Burke, Oct. 27, 1919, all DJ OG 18197, RG 65, NA.

40. Burke to Morton, Oct. 10, 1919; Morton to Burke, Oct. 17, 1919; Hoover to Spencer, Oct. 23, 1919; Speer to Burke, Oct. 27, 1919; Spencer to Burke, attn. JEH, Oct. 11, 1919, all DJ OG 18179, RG 65, NA.

41. St. John to Law, July 14, 1919; same to Scarlett, July 21, 1919, DJ OG 386089, RG 65, NA; Johanningsmeier, *Forging Communism*, 42; "Palmer on Charges by Post," 171.

42. Spencer to Burke, attn. J[ohn] E[dgar] H[oover], Oct. 11, 1919, DJ OG 18197, RG 65, NA.

43. 101 to 836, Oct. 16, 1919; Spencer to Burke, Oct. 17, 1919; Memo, JEH to Mr. [Ahern?], Oct. 18, 1919; M. E. Tucker, rep., Oct. 19–20, 1919; H. Alden, rep., Oct. 20, 1919, all DJ OG 18197, RG 65, NA.

44. Margolis Senate Testimony, 817–19, 859, 871–72.

45. Ibid., 820.

46. Ibid., 819–23.

47. Ibid., 829–33.

48. Ibid., 851, 864–67.

49. Ibid., 825–28, 862–64.

50. Ibid., 859–60.

51. Ibid., 855–56.

52. *Pittsburgh Gazette-Times*, Oct. 21, 1919.

53. Revolutionary War veteran Daniel Shays led a rebellion of financially strapped western Massachusetts farmers against the state government. Washington County, Pennsylvania, was the Whiskey Rebellion's epicenter.

54. *NYT*, Oct. 22, Nov. 9, 1919.

55. *Pittsburgh Press*, Nov. 8, 1919. The committee proposed a federal board to settle disputes involving the public interest. Interchurch World Movement, *Report on the Steel Strike*, 32–33.

56. Not until the New Deal in the 1930s did the United Steel Workers emerge as a powerful industrial union. Brody, *Labor in Crisis*, 179–87.

57. Brody, *Steel Workers in America*, 248–49.

58. Foster, *Steel Strike*, 153.

59. Ibid., 154–55.

60. Statement of William G. McAdoo, *Fairmont Times*, Nov. 28, 1919. Federal Fuel Administrator Harry Garfield agreed that miners' wages did not keep pace with the cost of living or operator profits. Dubofsky and Van Tine, *Lewis*, 58.

61. Dubofsky and Van Tine, *Lewis*, 48–51, 52–54.

62. Keith Dix, *What's a Coal Miner to Do? The Mechanization of Coal Mining* (Pittsburgh: University of Pittsburgh Press, 1988), 157–58; *NYT*, Sept. 23, 1919.

63. John M. Blum, *Joe Tumulty and the Wilson Era* (Boston: Houghton Mifflin Co., 1951), 191, 219–23; W. Anthony Gengarelly, "Secretary William B. Wilson and the Red Scare, 1919–1920," *Pennsylvania History* 46 (Oct. 1980): 311–17.

64. C. F. Keeney to Woodrow Wilson, Nov. 3, 1919, DJ OG 303770, RG 65, NA; *Fairmont Times*, Nov. 28, 1919.

65. Quoted in the *Literary Digest*, Nov. 8, 1919, 1. A *New York Tribune* "investigator" after visiting the Kanawha district coal fields told readers that miners did not need or deserve a raise. Unlike city dwellers, they could lease a comfortable five-room house with a garden plot for virtually nothing; receive cheap, abundant electricity and winter fuel; and buy high-quality goods from the company store at low prices. *Literary Digest*, Dec. 20, 1919, 69–70.

66. John C. Hennen, *The Americanization of West Virginia: Creating A Modern Industrial State, 1916–1925* (Lexington: University Press of Kentucky, 1996), 4, 41.

67. John J. Cornwell, *A Mountain Trail* (Philadelphia: Dorrance and Company, 1939), 60–61.

68. Burt Mead and W. L. Cumberlidge to Cornwell, June 29, 1919; Cornwell to Mead and Cumberlidge, July 1, 1919; same to William Rogers, July 23, 1919; same to J. D. Steele, Sept. 14, 1919; Newton D. Baker to Cornwell, Sept. 29, 1919; Leonard Wood to Cornwell (telegram), Sept. 30, 1919; Cornwell to Wood (telegram), Sept. 30, 1919, all J. J. Cornwell Papers, A. & M. 952, WVRC, WVU.

69. Cornwell was a country lawyer, newspaper publisher, and bank president. For the concept of Appalachian gatekeepers see John Gaventa, *Power and Powerlessness: Quiescence and Rebellion in an Appalachian Valley* (Urbana: University of Illinois Press, 1980), 130–31, 258–59.

70. In 1918 Cornwell confronted five thousand armed miners at Lens Creek who were marching on the state capital to tell them that they were breaking the law. Cornwell, *A Mountain Trail*, 57–59.

71. Untitled signed statement dictated to Margaret I. Keller, Sept. 26, 1919, Cornwell Papers, A. & M. 952, WVRC, WVU.

72. Cornwell to "The Sheriffs of the Respective Counties and the Mayors of the Various Municipalities," Oct. 30, 1919, A.& M. 952, WVRC, WVU.

73. Ibid.

74. Dubofsky and Van Tine, *Lewis*, 55; Wilson, rep., Aug. 14, 1919, DJ OG 328353, RG 65, NA; Nash, *Conflict and Accommodation*, 95–96. By 1919 thirty-five states and several cities had red flag legislation making it a misdemeanor to display the symbol of rebellion. Murray, *Red Scare*, 231–34; Wilson, rep., Aug. 14, 1919, DJ OG 328353, RG 65, NA.

75. Roger Welles to Rowe, Sept. 25, 1918, ONI, Entry 230, Box 1, RG 38, NA(p). Hennen, *Americanization of West Virginia*, 58–59, discusses coal operators' entry into the South American market.

76. J. F. Donohue to Commanding Officer, Troop A, Pennsylvania State Police, June 14, 1919, DJ OG 215915, RG 65, NA.

77. *Morgantown Post*, Aug. 14, 1919.

78. Lenon, rep., Aug. 20, 1919, DJ OG 303770, RG 65, NA.

79. The agents and their assignments were: D. E. Tatom, Monongahela City; E. G. Black, Washington; W. A. Beadling, Brownsville; L. E. Van Vleck, Tarentum; E. J. Wheeler, Uniontown; W. W. Wright, Connellsville; Fred Ames, Greensburg; and J. C. Rider, Johnstown. Speer to Burke, Oct. 31, 1919, DJ OG 303770, RG 65, NA.

80. Ibid.

81. Irwin Marcus, Eileen Cooper, and Beth O'Leary, "The Coal Strike of 1919 in Indiana County," *Pennsylvania History* 56 (July 1989): 177–95, and "The Coral Episode of the Coal Strike of 1919," *The Western Pennsylvania Magazine of History and Biography* 114 (Oct. 1990): 543–61; Rider, reps., Nov. 1, 6, 8, 12, 1919; Tatom, rep., Nov. 4, 1919, all DJ OG 303770, RG 65, NA.

82. *Fairmont Times*, Nov. 1–6, 1919. In mid-November Speer had to send Van Vleck and Beadling to Erie to look for Communists. In December he and Ames arrested ten UORW members there. Beadling, rep., Nov. 14–19, 1919; Ames, reps., Dec. 6, 7, 1919, all DJ OG 291921, RG 65, NA.

83. "Palmer on Charges by Post," 19, 25.

84. Murray, *Red Scare*, 154–56.

85. Walker to Attorney General, Nov. 4, 1919; statement of Brooks Fleming, Nov. 3, 1919, both DJ OG 303770, RG 65, NA.

86. Statement of Brooks Fleming, Nov. 3, 1919; #32 (Bower), Sept. 4, 1919; #40 (Grant Town), Sept. 11, 14, 1919; #35 (Clarksburg), Aug. 22, 1919, all DJ OG 303770, RG 65, NA; #37, Oct. 25, 1919, C. E. Smith Papers, A. & M. 1606, WVRC, WVU; ? [#40] (Grant Town), Oct. 10, 1919; #39 (Pitcairn), Oct. 3, 1919; #32 (Bower), Oct. 8, 1919, all DJ OG 328353, RG 65, NA.

87. Agents 40 and 36 were prone to interpret all ethnic griping as IWW and Bolshevik agitation. The imprecise phrase *a dirty bunch* recurs in many reports. [#35?] (Clarksburg), Aug. 22, 1919; #40 (Grant Town), Sept. 11, 14, 1919; #36 (Farmington), Sept. 15, 1919, all DJ OG 303770, RG 65, NA.

88. #36 (Farmington), Sept. 11, 15, 1919, DJ OG 303770, RG 65, NA; J. B. Wilson to C. E. Smith, Oct. 16, 1919; C. H. Charlton to Smith, Oct. 21, 1919, both C. E. Smith Papers, A. & M. 1606, WVRC, WVU. Some 280 of 3,041 foreign miners in Marion County (Fairmont) were Russian. West Virginia Department of Mines, *Annual Report . . . 1919* (Charleston: Tribune Publishing Co., 1920), 246–47.

89. Ewa Morawska, "The Sociology and Historiography of Immigration," in *Immigration Reconsidered: History, Sociology, and Politics*, ed. Virginia Yans-McLaughlin (New York: Oxford University Press, 1990), 195.

90. Spencer's informers were a Polish-born anarchist and a Russian-born interpreter. Spencer to Burke, Oct. 8, 1919, DJ OG 215915, RG 65, NA.

91. In the wake of a 1915 flash rebellion of Croatian and Italian strikers at the same mine that killed a constable and seriously injured the county sheriff, more than one hundred men were held for several months in the same jail that now housed the Russians. The justice system eventually sent thirty-three miners to the state penitentiary, many with life sentences for first-degree murder. Charles H. McCormick, "The Death of Constable Riggs: Ethnic Conflict in Marion County in the World War I Era," *West Virginia History* 52 (1993): 33–59.

92. Unsigned NWVCOA undercover report, Sept. 29, 1919, DJ OG 328353, RG 65, NA.

93. Statement of J. C. Edwards, Dec. 1, 1919, DJ Bureau of Immigration 54709/591, Andrew Lopitsky, FOIA/PA; #40 (Grant Town), Oct. 10, 1919, DJ OG 303770, RG 65, NA.

94. *Fairmont Times*, Nov. 5, 1919; Walker to Palmer, Nov. 4, 1919, DJ OG 303770, RG 65, NA; U.S. De-

partment of Labor, Bureau of Immigration, *Annual Report of the Commissioner General to the Secretary of Labor for the Fiscal Year Ended June 30, 1920* (Washington: USGPO, 1920), 35, 110.

95. On Aug. 22, Peters wired and then phoned special agent John B. Wilson for a meeting about radicals. He met secretly with Walker on Nov. 3 and endorsed the proposed deportations. Later he told the BI that a few foreigners kept the strike going at Scotts Run. Wilson, rep., Aug. 23, 1919, DJ OG 328353; Walker to Palmer, Nov. 4, 1919, DJ OG 303770; Lambeth, rep., Nov. 8–14, 1919, DJ OG 303770 all RG 65, NA. For the struggle within the UMWA between Lewis and traditionally independent locals, see Alan Jay Singer, "Which Side Are You On? Ideological Conflict in the United Mine Workers of America, 1919–1928" (Ph.D. diss., Rutgers University, 1982); Arthur C. Everling, "Tactics Over Strategy in the United Mine Workers of America: International Politics and the Question of the Nationalization of the Mines, 1908–1923" (Ph.D. diss., Pennsylvania State University, 1976).

96. Taken together, these mines employed more than 25 percent of the county's miners and were the site of almost 60 percent of its mine fatalities, 1918–1920, and ninety of the ninety-five injuries reported to the state Department of Mines in 1919–1920. Lambeth, rep., Nov. 8–14, 1919, Dec. 23, 1919, DJ OG 303770, RG 65, NA; West Virginia Department of Mines, *Annual Report . . . 1920* (Charleston: Tribune Publishing Co., 1921), 356–57.

97. Lambeth, rep., Nov. 29–Dec. 6, 1919, DJ OG 303770, RG 65, NA.

98. Lambeth, rep., Nov. 8–14, 1919, Dec. 23, 1919; Walker to Attorney General, Nov. 4, 1919, all DJ OG 303770, RG 65, NA.

99. Lambeth, rep., Nov. 8–14, 1919, DJ OG 303770, RG 65, NA; [Fairmont] *West Virginian,* Nov. 17, 1919.

7. THE PALMER RAIDS I: THE UNION OF RUSSIAN WORKERS, 1919

1. Material in this paragraph is drawn from C. J. Scully, rep., Dec. 22, 1919, DJ OG 341761, RG 65, NA; Murray, *Red Scare,* 207–09; Powers, *Secrecy and Power,* 87–89; Alexander Berkman, "The Log of the Transport Buford," *Liberator* (Apr. 1920), n.p. (clip file), ACLU, PU; Emma Goldman, "The Voyage of the Buford," *The American Mercury* 33 (July 1931): 276–86; Louis F. Post, *Deportations Delirium of Nineteen-Twenty: A Personal Narrative of an Historic Official Experience* (Chicago: Charles H. Kerr and Company, 1923), 1–11.

2. Kate Holladay Claghorn, *The Immigrant's Day in Court* (New York: Harper & Brothers Publishers, 1923 [Arno Press reprint, 1969]), 361, 374. New York City (59) and Hartford (52) sent the largest contingents.

3. Ibid., 368–70.

4. Dillon, rep., May 25, 1917, MID 10110-33, RG 165, NA. Judge to Bielaski, May 12, 1917; Judge, reps., June 6, 9, 26, 29, 1917; R. E. Skelly, rep., June 21, 1917, all DJ OG 369489, RG 65, NA.

5. Judge, rep., July 3, 1917, MID 10110-33, RG 165, NA; Bielaski to Judge, Mar. 24, 1917, FBI 67-96008, FOIA/PA; 836, rep., Mar. 19–22, 1919, DJ OG 291921, RG 65, NA.

6. Typed copy attached to various Immigration Bureau deportation files, e.g., that of Konstantin Skorokod, DJ, Bureau of Immigration, 54709/588, FOIA/PA.

7. Powers, *Secrecy and Power,* 74–76; Stanley Coben, *A. Mitchell Palmer: Politician* (New York: Columbia University Press, 1963), 217–20.

8. Murray, *Red Scare,* 98–104; Coben, *Palmer,* 219.

9. Hoover, Report of the Radical Section for the Week Ending Sept. 12, 1919, DJ OG 374217, RG 65, NA.

10. Powers, *Secrecy and Power,* 67, 71–72, 75–76.

11. JEH, Memo for Francis Garvan, Oct. 24, 1919, DJ OG 341761, RG 65, NA: William B. Wilson, "Deportation of Aliens," *American City* 20 (April 1919): 313.

12. Gengarelly, "William B. Wilson and the Red Scare, 1919–1920," 311–12, 316–20; William Preston, Jr., *Aliens and Dissenters: Federal Suppression of Radicals, 1903–1933* (New York: Harper and Row, 1963), 101–03.

13. Paul L. Murphy, "Normalcy, Intolerance, and the American Character," *The Virginia Quarterly Review* 40 (summer 1964): 450. On ONI's "Secret General Numerical List of Agents" (undated but 1918), the name A. B. Caminetti appears as #253. ONI, Entry 121, RG 38, NA.

14. The list included former bombing suspects John Johnson and Frank Broida. Spencer, rep., July 12, 1919; same to Suter, attn. Ruch; "List of Radicals . . . ," both June 13, 1919, all DJ OG 341761, RG 65, NA.

15. Spencer to Suter, attn. Ruch, June 13, 1919, DJ OG 341761, RG 65, NA.

16. Ibid.; Assistant Commissioner of Immigration to Sibray, May 20, 1919, DJ OG 369489, RG 65, NA.

17. Spencer to Hoover (confidential), Aug. 12, 1919, DJ OG 215915; Chief to Spencer, Oct. 24, 1919; Speer to Burke (ref. Hoover), Nov. 1, 1919; 836, rep., Aug. 24, 1919, all DJ OG 369489, all RG 65, NA.

18. Photostat, n.d., attached to Flynn to Spencer, Nov. 7, 1919, DJ OG 215915, RG 65, NA.

19. William McAdoo thought that the Tumulty-Carmichael friendship placed Tumulty too close "to the interests." Edward M. House Diary, June 11, 1914, PWW (31), 274. Carmichael was a former *New York World* and *Detroit Free Press* Washington reporter who occasionally wrote to Tumulty at the White House, usually on Waldorf Astoria letterhead on subjects ranging from federal appointments to labor and immigration matters to the Sinn Fein. Otto Carmichael to JPT, Jan. 25, 1915, ser. 4, folder 2043, Oct. 4, 1915, ser. 4, folder 1339, and May 6, 1917, folder 64B, ser. 4, all Woodrow Wilson Papers, LC.

20. Coben, *Palmer*, 153, 196–98; Blum, *Tumulty and the Wilson Era*, 187–88; Murray, *Red Scare*, 204–05.

21. O.C. to J.T., n.d., DJ OG 215915, RG 65, NA.

22. In the Wilson Cabinet the antiradical hard-liners were Burleson, Lansing, and Palmer. Those more sympathetic to labor were Daniels, Lane, Houston, and especially Labor Secretary Wilson. Murray, *Red Scare*, 201–05.

23. O.C. to J.T., n.d, DJ OG 215915, RG 65, NA.

24. Flynn to Spencer, Nov. 7, 1919, DJ OG 215915, RG 65, NA. For the August 12 instructions see Powers, *Secrecy and Power*, 74–75; Donner, *The Age of Surveillance*, 34.

25. Coben, *Palmer*, 186–95.

26. Powers, *Secrecy and Power*, 77–78; Spencer to Burke, Nov. 11, 1919, DJ OG 215915, RG 65, NA.

27. *Pittsburgh Press*, Nov. 9, 1919.

28. James J. Badal, "The Strange Case of Dr. Karl Muck, Who Was Torpedoed by the *Star-spangled Banner* During World War I," *High Fidelity* 20 (Oct. 1970): 55–60; Feri Felix Weiss, *The Sieve or Revelations of the Man Mill: Being the Truth About American Immigration* (Boston: The Page Company, 1921), 195. His obituary is in *NYT*, Feb. 6, 1927.

29. *Pittsburgh Press*, Nov. 9, 1919.

30. Ibid.

31. Murray, *Red Scare*, 220.

32. Dubofsky and Van Tine, *Lewis*, 54–58.

33. Palmer to Cornwell (telegram), Nov. 13, 1919, J. J. Cornwell Papers, WVRC, WVU; Lambeth, rep., Nov. 8–14, 1919, DJ OG 303770, RG 65, NA.

34. [Fairmont] *West Virginian*, Nov. 19, 20, 1919.

35. Ibid., Nov. 20, 1919.

36. Ibid., Nov. 17, 20, 1919.

37. Ibid., Nov. 17–21, 1919; *Fairmont Times*, Nov. 18–21, 1919, Apr. 20–21, 1920; Lambeth, reps., Nov. 6–14, 15–21, 1919, DJ OG 303770, RG 65, NA; Ames, rep. on Orteof Schatabnoy (Sahtabnog), and twenty-seven others, Nov. 19, 1919; Tatom, rep., Dec. 2, 1919, both OG DJ 380398, RG 65, NA; Claghorn, *Immigrant's Day in Court*, 404.

38. Lambeth, reps., Nov. 15–21, 22–28, Dec. 23, 1919; same to Burke, Nov. 20, 1919; Wilson, rep., Nov. 14–18, 1919, all DJ OG 303770; Tatom, rep., Nov. 25, 1919, DJ OG 328353, all RG 65, NA.

39. Lambeth, rep., Dec. 6–10, 1919, DJ OG 303770; same, reps., Nov. 15–21, Dec. 23, 1919; same to Burke, Nov. 20, 1919; Tatom, rep., Nov. 22, 1919; Wilson, rep., Nov. 18, 1919, all DJ OG 328353, RG 65, NA.

40. [Fairmont] *West Virginian*, Nov. 19, 20, 1919.

41. On November 30 the militant UMWA local at the Grant Town mine, where a number of Russians had been arrested, voted 220-77 to continue the strike. Lambeth, rep., Nov. 29–Dec. 6, 1919, Dec. 24, 1919, DJ OG 303770, RG 65, NA.

42. Spencer to Burke, Dec. 3, 1919, DJ OG 303770, RG 65, NA.

43. "From the Minute Book of the Union of Russian Workers of the city of Farmington, West Va. and List of Members of the Russian Worker's Union" (trans., S. L. Willmon), Nov. 22, 1919, Orteof Sahtabnog, DJ Bureau of Immigration 54709/586, FOIA/PA.

44. Lambeth, reps., Nov. 15–21, Dec. 23, 1919; same to Burke, Nov. 20, 1919; Tatom, rep., Nov. 22, 1919; Wilson, rep., Nov. 18, 1919, all DJ OG 328353, RG 65, NA.

45. Powers, *Secrecy and Power*, 77.

46. Constantine M. Panunzio, *The Deportation Cases of 1919–1920* (New York: Commission on the Church and Social Service, Federated Council of the Churches of Christ in America, 1921 [Da Capo Press reprint]), 99–100.

47. Under proper procedure a complete deportation file would include: 1) affidavit of probable cause by the BI special agent; 2) copy of the original arrest warrant; 3) record of preliminary examination given the alien at the time of arrest; 4) complete official transcript of all proceedings, including the hearing conducted by the Immigration inspector; 5) summary and findings of the immigration inspector; 6) summary and findings of the commissioner-general of immigration; 7) actual evidence or record of evidence in the case; 8) record of bail, if granted; 9) brief submitted by the alien's attorney; 10) letters from alien's friends and employers; 10) memo from secretary of labor or his designate of final decision. Panunzio, *Deportation Cases*, 11–12.

48. Ibid., 77–78, 90–91; "Palmer on Charges by Post," 55; Powers, *Secrecy and Power*, 70.

49. "Palmer on Charges by Post," 13, 59.

50. Post complimented Sibray in *Deportations Delirium of Nineteen-Twenty*, saying that the "Inspector in Charge [of Immigration in Pittsburgh], a competent and undelirious official, procured Department of Labor warrants for about 40 of [the 85] West Virginia prisoners and caused the others, about 45, to be released" (115). Post failed to mention that Sibray acted four months before he did, and at a time when anti-Red hysteria was at its peak.

51. Sibray, who had a normal school degree, had worked for the Government Printing Office, Pension Office, and Bureau of the Census before joining the Immigration Bureau. His eventual reward was promotion to assistant commissioner for immigration in 1923. He died in 1924. See William W. Sibray, Employment Record, U.S Office of Personnel Management, FOIA/PA.

52. The complaints against Sibray were contained in a three-page, single-spaced letter, "Special Agent" to Walker, Dec. 2, 1919. Lambeth sent the letter to Acting Director Burke on Dec. 3. DJ OG 378383, RG 65, NA.

53. Preston, *Aliens and Dissenters*, 212–13.

54. For example, agents Ryan and Ames interrogated Ortib [Orteof] Schatabnoy [Sahtabnog], on Nov. 18, 1919, two weeks before his hearing with counsel. Ryan, rep., Nov. 18, 1919; Ames, rep., Nov. 19, 1919, both DJ OG 380398, RG 65, NA; "Palmer on Charges by Post," 39, 54–57.

55. Lebed and Noik were not represented and Elko was represented by his brother, another alien. On the aliens' troubles in seeking legal help in deportation cases, see Claghorn, *Immigrant's Day in Court*, 354–55.

56. He cited the case of Ruger Baccini, who was believed to be the Paterson June 2 bomber, as an example. "Palmer on Charges by Post," 25, 27, 36.

57. Sgt. John F. Donohue, rep., June 19, 1919, DJ OG 215915, RG 65, NA.

58. ? [D. E. Tatom] to Stuart Walker, Dec. 2, 1919, DJ OG 378383, RG 65 NA. Claghorn, *Immigrant's Day in Court*, 404–14, summarizes his testimony in many of the deportation cases, referring to him as "Y."

59. Special Agent to Walker, Dec. 2, 1919, DJ OG 378383, RG 65, NA.

60. Ibid. Liebgardt's replacement was S. I. Willmon, whom Kate Claghorn dismissed as a person of no reputation. Claghorn, *Immigrant's Day in Court*, 412.

61. The data above were compiled from the following Immigration Bureau case files released to the author under FOIA/PA: Belusoff, Basil (54709/592); Colbus, Sam (54709/593); Eelak, David (54606/221); Elko, Evan (54709/602); Kozlov, Vasil (54709/601); Krishtop, Theodore (54709/598); Lebed, Arhip (54709/605); Lopitsky, Andrew (54709/591); Losioff, Prokopy (54709/600); Noik, Yakim (54709/594); Novokoff, Peter (54709/590); Paulik, Artemy (54709/605); Sahtabnog, Orteof

(54709/586); Skorokod, Konstantin (54709/588); and Yankum, William (54709/594). The three others, about whom there is little information, were Krassnoff, Tihon; Tabenko, Parfem; and Volch, George. Lambeth, reps., Dec. 6–10, 26 1919, DJ OG 303770, RG 65, NA; *NYT*, Dec. 23, 1919.

62. According to Post, *Deportations Delirium*, 6, the 249 men and women on the *Buford* left behind $45,470.39 in postal savings banks, bank accounts, uncollected wages, personal debts, and Liberty Bonds, an average of $182.61.

63. Paulik.

64. Lopitsky.

65. U.S. Department of Labor, *Annual Report. . . Commissioner of Immigration* (1920), 383.

66. Published by the Federation of Unions of Russian Workers of the United States and Canada, New York, 1919 (21).

67. "Palmer on Charges by Post," 39.

68. Possibly the agents confused Novomirsky's "Manifesto" with *Novyi Mir*, the press organ of the Russian branch of the Socialist Party. For *Novyi Mir*, see Theodore Draper, *The Roots of American Communism* (Chicago: Elephant Paperbacks, Ivan R. Dee, Publisher, 1989), 82–83, 162–63.

69. Novomirsky, "Manifesto," 21.

70. File 54606/221.

71. File 54709/590.

72. File 54709/605.

73. File 54709/602.

74. Colbus, Belusoff, Lebed, Kozlov, Yankum, Noik, Krishtop, Losioff, and Lopitsky.

75. Colbus was forty. Belusoff and Lebed were thirty-eight. Several others were in their midthirties.

76. Losioff.

77. Colbus.

78. Belusoff blamed befuddlement from the effects of "pick-handle" (coal field moonshine) for his decision to join the UORW.

79. Kozlov.

80. Yankum, Noik, and Krishto.

81. Hearing, Dec. 1, 1919, 54709/601, FOIA/PA.

82. Zecharia Chafee, Jr., *Freedom of Speech* (New York: Harcourt, Brace and Company, 1920), 249; Winthrop D. Lane, "The Buford Widows," *The Survey* (Jan. 10, 1920): 391–92.

83. Murray, *Red Scare*, 207; Panunzio, *Deportation Cases*, 89–91.

84. *Fairmont Times*, Dec. 19, 1919, Jan. 21, 1920; [Fairmont] *West Virginian*, Dec. 20, 1919. The four were Fona Velko, Ludwig Kerenski, Tony Uglick, and Theodore Forenchko, miners at three Jameson Company mines.

85. Hale Testimony, Sedition, 101–02. Panunzio found that of the 118 *Buford* deportees who expressed a point of view, 50 (42 percent) wanted to leave and 21 (18 percent) were indifferent. *Deportation Cases*, 72.

86. [Fairmont] *West Virginian*, Dec. 15, 1919.

87. Lambeth, reps., Nov. 29–Dec. 5; Dec. 6–10, 1919, both DJ OG 303770, RG 65, NA.

88. *Fairmont Times*, Dec. 21–28, 1919; [Fairmont] *West Virginian*, Dec. 23, 1919.

89. Powers, *Secrecy and Power*, 80–85, 91; Goldman entry in Buhle et al., eds., *Encyclopedia of the American Left*, 275–77.

90. "Palmer on Charges by Post," 26. Fourteen were deported for nonpolitical reasons. Nine were said likely to become public charges, three to be guilty of moral turpitude, one of being a procurer, and one of illegal entry into the country. Post, *Deportations Delirium*, 25–26.

91. Claghorn, *Immigrant's Day in Court*, 361. Maria Woroby in "Russian Americans," Buhle et al., eds., *Encyclopedia of the American Left*, 662, gives the figure ten thousand, most of whom joined after 1917.

92. Affidavits of Edward Myers and Bud Walker, Jan. 5, 1920; statement of Sheriff John Glover in Lambeth, rep., Jan. 9, 1920, DJ OG 328353, RG 65, NA.

93. U.S. Department of Labor, *Annual Report. . . Commissioner of Immigration* (1920), 383. In FY 1919–1920 the Immigration Bureau recorded 621,576 arrivals and 428,062 departures. Ibid., 35.

94. Post, *Deportations Delirium*, 79, xii.

95. Hoover, Memorandum Upon the Activities of the Radical Division of the Department of Justice, May 1, 1920, DJ OG 374761, RG 65, NA.

96. U.S. Department of Justice, *Annual Report of the Attorney General* (1920), 175.

8. THE PALMER RAIDS II: THE COMMUNISTS AND THE END OF THE RED SCARE, 1920–1921

1. Berkman, "The Log of the Transport Buford," n.p.; Draper, *Roots of American Communism*, 190; Murray, *Red Scare*, 210–22. Estimates vary for the number arrested from January to March 1920 from 10,000 (Preston, *Aliens and Dissenters*, 221; David H. Williams, "The Bureau of Investigation and Its Critics, 1919–1921: The Origins of Federal Political Surveillance," *Journal of American History* 68 [Dec. 1981]: 561), to Murray's and Post's more conservative 4,000. In *Deportations Delirium* Post says that he found about 5,000 outstanding warrants for Dec. 29, 1919–June 30, 1920, which yielded about 3,000 arrests, 556 deportation orders, and 2,202 cancellations of warrants (159, 166–67). Perhaps about 6,000 persons were detained. Powers, *Secrecy and Power*, 104.

2. Draper, *Roots of American Communism*, 15–16, 179–88; Bell, *Marxian Socialism*, 111–12.

3. Draper, *Roots of American Communism*, 188–90; *Bolshevik Propaganda Hearings*, 13; Spencer to Burke, Dec. 13, 1919, DJ OG 379615, RG 65, NA.

4. Speer, reps., June 8, 30, 1919, DJ OG 215915, RG 65, NA.

5. Speer, rep., Oct. 20, 1919, DJ OG 215915; 836, rep., Oct. 21, 1919, DJ OG 379615, both RG 65, NA.

6. 836, reps., Oct. 24–Nov. 2, Nov. 11–16, 1919, DJ OG 379615; Spencer to Burke, Nov. 29, 1919, DJ OG 215915, all RG 65, NA.

7. A federal judge threw out the Department of Justice test case against the Spanish anarchist *El Ariete* group under a long-unused Civil War conspiracy law, leaving the BI without a peacetime sedition statute. Hoover, Memo Upon the Work of the Radical Division, Aug. 1, 1919–Mar. 15, 1920, DJ OG 374217, RG 65, NA.

8. Thomas F. Rice, rep., Oct. 25, 1919; E. J. Wheeler, rep., Oct. 26, 1919; both DJ OG 379615; Spencer to Burke, Nov. 29, 1919, DJ OG 215915, all RG 65, NA.

9. Spencer to Burke, Nov. 14, 29, 1919, DJ OG 215915, RG 65, NA.

10. Lenon, rep., May 3, 1920; Rider to Burke, June 23, 1920, both DJ OG 379615; Lenon to Spencer, May 14, 1921, DJ BSF 202600-1768, all RG 65, NA.

11. Spencer to Burke, Dec. 13, 16, 1919, DJ OG 379615, RG 65, NA; Powers, *Secrecy and Power*, 102–03; Preston, *Aliens and Dissenters*, 217; Hoover, Memo Upon the Activities of the Radical Division, May 1, 1920, DJ OG 374217, RG 65, NA.

12. Despite the assertion of Louis F. Post that Pittsburgh was a "central point in the January raiding," the files for January–March 1920 show that only a small fraction of those taken nationally were arrested in western Pennsylvania and northern West Virginia. Post, *Deportations Delirium*, 115–16; Spencer to Burke, Mar. 17, 1920, DJ OG 379615, RG 65, NA; Preston, *Aliens and Dissenters*, 221; Williams, "The Bureau . . . and its Critics," 561; Murray, *Red Scare*, 213–16; David Williams, "'Sowing the Wind': The Deportation Raids of 1920 in New Hampshire," *Historical New Hampshire* 34 (spring 1979): 1.

13. Spencer to Burke, Jan. 3 (3 telegrams), 5, 1919, DJ OG 379615, RG 65, NA; *Pittsburgh Press*, Jan. 3, 4, 1920.

14. Spencer to Burke, Nov. 29, 1919, DJ OG 215915, RG 65, NA. Speer officially quit January 15 after two weeks' leave with pay. Speer to Burke, Dec. 16, 31, 1919; Burke to Speer, Dec. 19, 1919, Jan. 2, 1920, both FBI 67-9973, FOIA/PA. His son's obituary in the *Post-Gazette*, Oct. 15, 1979, says that Speer worked for the *Post* and *Gazette-Times* until 1927 when the family moved to Philadelphia.

15. Spencer to Burke, Jan. 6, 1920, FBI 67-68, FOIA/PA. In Lenon's file the FBI blanked out all occurrences of what I have deduced from the context and number of blanked spaces to be "L. M. Wendell" and "836."

16. Lenon, Application for Appointment, June 25, 1918; Spencer to Burke, Jan. 6, 9, 1920; Howard Sutherland to Guy D. Goff, Sept. 29, 1921; Ephraim F. Morgan to Howard Sutherland, Sept. 27, 1921; John M. Morin to Harry M. Daugherty, Sept. 26, 1921, all FBI 67-68, FOIA/PA.

17. Burke to Spencer, Jan. 7, 1920; Lenon to William J. Burns, Apr. 11, 1924; Hoover, Memos for Burke, Jan. 13, 19, 1920; telegram, Spencer to Burke, Jan. 20, 1920, all FBI 67-68, FOIA/PA.

18. For Lyndora, near Butler, during the steel strike see Vorse, *Folly*, 282.

19. Spencer to Burke, Jan. 7, 17, 27, 1920, DJ OG 379615, RG 65, NA; Powers, *Secrecy and Power,* 113–14.

20. Microfilm images of both the charter and the badly faded photograph are in the file. Beadling, rep., Feb. 2–9, 1920, DJ OG 379615, RG 65, NA.

21. Louis Grendiski, rep., Feb. 29, 1920; Lenon, rep., Feb. 29–Mar. 3, 1920; Beadling, reps., Feb. 2–9, 28, Mar. 3–10, 9, 1920; Yankovich, rep., Mar. 8, 1920; Lenon, rep., Mar. 7, 8, 9, 1920, all DJ OG 379614, RG 65, NA.

22. Spencer to Burke, Apr. 3, 1920, DJ OG 215915, RG 65, NA.

23. Same to same, Jan. 17, 27, Mar. 17, 1920; same to Suter, Feb. 13, 1920, all DJ OG 379615, RG 65, NA; *Pittsburgh Press,* Jan. 4, 1920.

24. Hundreds of canceled deportation warrants for Communist Party members are in supplemental memoranda compiled by the GID in 1920. More than 250 are in DJ OG 341761, RG 65, NA. Examples of Pittsburghers who would have been deported without Post's intervention include John Kuzbit, a Socialist who paid twenty-five cents in dues to the Communist Party not knowing that it was no longer the SPA (Supplemental Memo #22); John Topolcsanyi, arrested three to four weeks after he joined and who admitted to knowledge of party principles (Supplemental Memo #22); Mike Salimouchik, who paid dues to the party (Supplemental Memo #10); Pete Siniawsky [Siniaiwsky], who was found with a paid-up membership card (Supplemental Memo #22).

25. Hale Testimony, Sedition, 101–02.

26. Nelles to Louis Budenz, Aug. 16, 1920; Hearing for Mike Mesich, Apr. 19–21, 1920, both in vol. 139, reel 20 (1920), ACLU, PU.

27. Hearing for Mike Mesich, Apr. 19–21, vol. 139, roll 20 (1920), ACLU, PU. Tipped by his lawyer that he would be deported, Mesich fled Wendel in February 1921. Ames, rep., Feb. 5, 1921, DJ BSF 202600-963, RG 65, NA.

28. Spencer to Burke, Apr. 3, 1920, DJ OG 215915, RG 65, NA.

29. Same to same, Jan. 5, 1920; Burke to Spencer, Jan. 6, 1920, both DJ OG 379615; Caminetti to Hoover, Mar. 17, 1920; Post to Hoover, Apr. 26, 1920, both DJ OG 341761, all RG 65, NA.

30. *Pittsburgh Press,* Jan. 3, 4, 1920; Burke to Spencer, Jan. 6, 1920; Spencer to Burke, Jan. 14, 17, 1920, both DJ OG 379615, RG 65, NA.

31. Same to same, Jan. 24, 1920, DJ OG 215915, RG 65, NA; Draper, *Roots of American Communism,* 205–06.

32. 836, reps., Feb. 23–29, Mar. 3–7, 1920, DJ OG 379615, RG 65, NA.

33. 836, rep., Mar. 20, 1920, DJ OG 215915, RG 65, NA.

34. Hoover, Memo Upon the Work of the Radical Division, Aug. 1, 1919–Mar. 15, 1920, DJ OG 374217, RG 65, NA.

35. Powers, *Secrecy and Power,* l13–14, 116; William A. Gengarelly, "Resistance Spokesmen: Opponents of the Red Scare, 1919–1921" (Ph.D. diss., Boston University, 1972), 91–112; Dominic Candeloro, "Louis F. Post and the Red Scare of 1920," *Prologue* 11 (spring 1979): 40–46; Gengarelly, "William B. Wilson and the Red Scare," 321, 324–27.

36. Spencer to Burke, Feb. 28, Mar. 13, 1920, both DJ OG 215915, RG 65, NA; Coben, *Palmer,* 237–39; Williams, "The Bureau . . . and its Critics," 564–67.

37. R. G. Brown et al., *A Report Upon the Illegal Practices of the United States Department of Justice* (Washington: National Popular Government League, 1920). The other signers were Roscoe Pound, Ernst Freund, Francis Fisher Kane, Frank Walsh, Alfred S. Niles, David Wallerstein, and Tyrrell Williams. Powers, *Secrecy and Power,* 119–21; Athan Theoharis and John Stuart Cox, *The Boss: J. Edgar Hoover and the Great American Inquisition* (Philadelphia: Temple University Press, 1988), 66–67.

38. Hale Testimony, Sedition, 85–86, 98–99; *NYT,* July 4, 1937; *General Intelligence Bulletin* (Strictly Confidential), Apr. 16, 1921, DJ OG 374217, RG 65, NA.

39. Byron H. Uhl to Caminetti, Jan. 15, 1920; Caminetti to Uhl, Jan. 16, 1920; J. C. Knox, decision in *U.S. ex rel. John Johnson v. Byron H. Uhl, Acting Commissioner of Immigration at the Port of New York,* Feb. 6, 1920, all DJ, INS 54616/264, FOIA/PA.

40. Knox, *ex rel. John Johnson,* DJ Bureau of Immigration 54616/264, FOIA/PA.

41. Ibid.; Alfred Hampton to Hoover, Feb. 26, 1920; Charles Recht to Commissioner of Immigration, Ellis Island, Feb. 26, 1920; A. W. Parker to Caminetti, Feb. 27, Apr. 6, 1920; Caminetti to Parker, Mar. 3,

1920; same to Ruch, Mar. 11, 1920; same to Parker, Mar. 18, 1920; DeSilver to Post, Mar. 27, 31, 1920; Post to DeSilver, Mar. 30, 1920; Hampton to Commissioner, Ellis Island, Apr. 2, 1920; Post to same, May 19, 1920; Hampton to Hoover, May 19, 1920, all DJ INS 54616/264, FOIA/PA.

42. Parker to Caminetti, Apr. 6, 1920; Post to Parker, May 19, 1920; Assist. Commissioner-General of Immigration to Hoover, May 19, 1920; same to Marlborough Churchill, May 25, 1920, all DJ, INS 54616/264, FOIA/PA.

43. Spencer to Burke, Mar. 20, 1920; Hoover to Spencer, Mar. 26, 1920, both DJ OG 379615; Spencer to Burke, Mar. 27, 1920, all RG 65, NA. Ward became a Marxist and like Elizabeth Gurley Flynn was removed during the ACLU's purge of the leftists in 1940.

44. Spencer to Burke, Mar. 13, Apr. 3, 24, 1920, DJ OG 215915, RG 65, NA; Gentry, *Hoover,* 140; GFR memo for JEH, Mar. 22, 1920, DJ OG 18197, RG 65, NA.

45. Gengarelly, "William B. Wilson and the Red Scare," 327–29. For Post's appearance see U.S. Congress, House Committee on Rules, *Hearings on H. Res. 522, Investigation of Administration of Louis F. Post, Assistant Secretary of Labor, in the Matter of Deportation of Aliens,* 66th Cong., 2d sess., 1920.

46. Powers, *Secrecy and Power,* 118, 120–21.

47. Spencer to Burke, July 21, 1920, DJ OG 215915, RG 65, NA.

48. Same to same, July 27, 1920, DJ OG 379615, RG 65, NA.

49. Ibid.

50. Ibid.

51. Full-time Radical Squad agents remained in New York, Boston, Chicago, Philadelphia, Detroit, Pittsburgh, Spokane, and Seattle. The data are from letters, Hoover to the various SACs, July 26 or 27, 1920, DJ OG 374217, RG 65, NA.

52. Hoover to Spencer, July 26, 1920, DJ OG 374217, RG 65, NA.

53. *NYT,* Sept. 17, 18, 1920; *General Intelligence Bulletin,* Sept. 25, 1920, DJ OG 374217, RG 65, NA.

54. 836, reps., Nov. 7–15, 1918, Sept. 18, 1919; Speer, rep., May 9, 1919, all DJ OG 18197; 836, rep., Nov 24, 1918, Feb. 9, 1919, DJ OG 215915; same, rep., Jan. 22, 1919, DJ OG 314013, all RG 65, NA; same, reps., Nov. 16, 21–24, Dec. 2, 1918, MID 10110-199 RG 165, NA.

55. 1060 or 1069, reps., Oct. 18, 20, 1920, DJ OG 343013, RG 65, NA.

56. 1060 or 1069, reps., Oct. 18, 20, 1920, DJ OG 343013, RG 65, NA.

57. Spencer, rep., Nov. 8–11, 1920, DJ BSF 202600-918-1, RG 65, NA, refers to "1069" as "1060."

58. Ibid.

59. *Pittsburgh Post,* Dec. 10, 1919; Interchurch World Movement, *Public Opinion and the Steel Strike,* 103–04. Bob Judge later became part-owner and New York office chief of RAI. See U.S. Congress, Senate Subcommittee on Education and Labor, *Hearings to Investigate Violations of Free Speech and Assembly and Interference with the Right of Labor to Organize and Bargain Collectively,* 74th Cong., S. Res. 266, Exhibit 45, 249 (Washington: USGPO, 1937–1938).

60. Parchmenko said that his two accomplices were killed in a bank robbery at Castle Shannon. Minor differences improve the Parchmenko scenario over the Orwell incident. Parchmenko secures a car in advance and allows several days to case the town and the bank. The Monessen robbers had first failed to "borrow" the car they planned to use when its owner unexpectedly left town. Then they drove the one they finally got miles out of their way to Orville in Ohio instead of Orwell. And, in case Wendell was a stoolie, Parchmenko was careful not to reveal the bank's location to Wendell in advance of the holdup. 1069 or 1060, rep., Oct. 18, 1920, DJ OG 343013, RG 65, NA.

61. It was not unlike Wendell, Lenon, Spencer, and Burgoyne to sow false information in the files, but in this case, it is difficult to see why they would do so. Anyone would see that the Bureau was protecting Wendell-Walsh-836.

62. On November 11 Spencer speculated that Pittsburgh police had picked up Parchmenko two days earlier as part of their clean-up. Spencer, rep., Nov. 8–11, 1920, DJ BSF 202600-918-1, RG 65, NA. I found no mention in Pittsburgh newspapers of a bank robbery anywhere near Bessemer in early November 1920.

63. Hoover, Memo Upon the Work of the Radical Division, Aug. 1, 1919–Mar. 15, 1920, DJ OG 374217; Lenon, reps., Sept. 1, Oct. 27, 1920; Ruch, Memo for Hoover, Oct. 26, 1920, all DJ OG 215915; Clarence D. McKean to Chief, June 27, 1921, DJ BSF 202600-1768, all RG 65, NA.

64. Weekly rad. rep., Oct. 21–28, 1920, DJ OG 215915, RG 65, NA.

65. See Lenon or Ames, weekly rad. reps. and monthly resumés of radical literature, Feb.–Oct. 1921, DJ BSF 202600–1768, RG 65, NA.

66. See Lenon, weekly rad. rep., Sept. 17, 1921, DJ BSF 202600-1768, RG 65, NA. Williams, "The Bureau . . . and Its Critics," 575, credits Lenon with the ACLU reports, but it was Wendell's assignment. "836 is making up an extensive brief on the ACLU" wrote Spencer to Hoover, Apr. 3, 1920, DJ OG 215915, RG 65, NA.

67. By Magdeleine Marx (a pseudonym for Magdeleine Legendre Paz), translated from the French by Adele Szold Seltzer (New York: T. Seltzer, 1920); Lenon, weekly rad. rep., Apr. 30, 1921, DJ BSF 202600-39, RG 65, NA. For the FBI's literary interests, see Natalie Robins, *Alien Ink: The FBI's War on Freedom of Expression* (New Brunswick: William Morrow and Company, 1992).

68. Lenon, weekly rad. rep., Apr. 30, 1921, DJ BSF 202600-39, RG 65, NA.

69. Lenon, weekly rad. rep., Sept. 10, 1921, DJ BSF 202600-1768, RG 65, NA.

70. Sooner would be Haywood who fled to the Soviet Union in April 1921 while on bail pending the appeal of his Chicago conviction. Later would be Scarlett who stayed with the IWW in Canada until the late 1920s before joining the Communists. Avery, "British-born 'Radicals,'" 77–78; Joseph R. Conlin, ed., *Bread and Roses, Too: Studies of the Wobblies* (Westport, Conn.: Greenwood Press, 1969), 146–47; Renshaw, *The Wobblies,* 199; Nelson et al., *Steve Nelson,* 22, 25.

71. See Ralph Chaplin's condemnation of the Communists in his *Wobbly: The Rough and Tumble Story of an American Radical* (Chicago: University of Chicago Press, 1948), 285–86, 333–39.

72. Bird, Georgakis, and Shaffer, *Solidarity Forever,* 15, 159–62; and Thompson and Murfin, *I.W.W.,* 128, 136–37.

73. Lenon or Ames, weekly rad. reps., June 23, July 16, 23, Aug. 8, Sept. 3, 26, Oct. 15, 1921, all DJ BSF 202600-1768, RG 65, NA.

74. The last known reference to Walsh or 836 is Lenon, weekly rad. rep., Mar. 14, 1921, DJ BSF 202600-1768, RG 65, NA.

75. The name Walsh came up during questioning of General Motors executives about their use of detectives to thwart the union organizers in their plants. *Violations of . . . Right of Labor,* 1886. The Detroit City Directories give an address for L. M. Wendell, but not for Leo M. Walsh. The file referred to in Index MID 9961-7475 is missing. See also Maj. R. C. Park to G-2, June 27, 1940, RG 165, NA. In 1947 "M. M. Wendell" filed for incorporation of W. W. and B. with a common stock of $1,000, then failed to produce an annual report causing the corporation to be dissolved. "Wendell, Walsh, and Brown, Inc.," on file at Corporation and Securities Bureau, Michigan Department of Commerce, Lansing, Mich.

76. Lenon to Spencer, May 14, 1921, DJ BSF 202600-1768, RG 65, NA.

77. A.k.a. Joseph Miller, D. Miller, George Scander, and Joe Yadish. They spotted him because of the green and black scarf he always wore, even indoors. Lenon, rep., Feb. 7, 1921, DJ BSF 202600-939, RG 65, NA.

78. Lenon, weekly rad. reps. and supplemental reps., Feb. 7, 8, 10, 17, Apr. 21, 30, 1921; E. Stewart to D. J. Driscoll, Mar. 24, 1921; J. S. Apelman, rep., Apr. 1, 1921, all DJ BSF 202600-939; Lenon, weekly rad. reps., May 4, 10, 1921, DJ BSF 202600-1689; Lenon, resumé of activities, Pittsburgh, Penn., United Communist Party, June 6, 1921; weekly rad. reps., June 18, July 3, 9, 23, Aug. 20, Sept. 3, 10, 1921; McKean to Chief, June 27, 1921, all DJ BSF 202600-1768, all RG 65, NA.

79. Lenon, weekly rad. rep., Oct. 15, 1921, DJ BSF 202600-1768, RG 65, NA.

80. Theoharis and Cox, *The Boss,* 69.

81. Richard G. Powers, *Not Without Honor: The History of American Anticommunism* (New York: Free Press, 1995), 41.

9. "DEPORTING" MARGOLIS, 1919–1921

1. For the Pittsburgh better sort and the legal profession, see Joseph F. Rishel, *The Founding Families of Pittsburgh: The Evolution of a Regional Elite* (Pittsburgh: University of Pittsburgh Press, 1990), 102–04, 193–94.

2. Judge, rep., Feb. 4, 1918, DJ OG 18197, RG 65, NA.

3. *Pittsburgh Gazette-Times,* July 24, 1918. Federal officials were also interested in two other Pittsburgh lawyers, Phil Calley and John B. Fayne. Request for legal status, Apr. 6, 1918, MID PF19113, RG 165, NA.

4. Flood to DMI, Nov. 9, 16, Dec. 2, 1918; John M. Dunn to Daniel D. Roper, Dec. 6, 1918, all MID

10110-597; Howard A. Pace to Dunn, Dec. 12, 1918, MID 10110-199, all RG 165, NA; 836, reps., Aug. 12–14, 1918, DJ OG 18197, RG 65, NA.

5. *Pittsburgh Press*, Oct. 22, 1919; *NYT*, Oct. 23, 28, 1919. For the role of the press in the steel strike see Murray, "Communism and the Great Steel Strike of 1919," 445–66.

6. Ames, rep., Sept. 9, 1919; C. T. Sprague, rep., Sept. 11, 12, 16, 19, 1910; [?] memo for JEH, Oct. 18, 1919; M. E. Tucker, rep., Oct. 19–20, 1919; H. Alden, rep., Oct. 20, 1919, all DJ OG 18197, RG 65, NA.

7. Baldwin to Margolis, Jan. 6, 1920, Case of Jacob Margolis, vol. 139, roll 20, 1920, ACLU, PU. For the founding of the ACLU in January 1920 see Walker, *In Defense of American Liberties*, 46–47.

8. *Pittsburgh Press*, Apr. 29, 1920; JEH, memo for Haynes, Jan. 15, 1920; Burke [JEH] to Spencer, Jan. 17, 1920; JEH to same, Jan. 19, 1920, all DJ OG 18197.

9. JEH to R. A. Bowen, Jan. 22, 1920; Bowen to JEH, Jan. 24, 1920; Haynes, memo for JEH, Feb. 6, 1920; JEH to Churchill, Feb. 13, 1920; same to Morton, Jan 22, 1920; same to Spencer, Jan. 22, 1920; same to A. L. Barkey, Jan. 22, 1920; [?], memo for JEH, Jan. 1, 1920; FEH, memo for JEH, Jan. 19, 1920, all DJ OG 18197, RG 65, NA; transcript of speech on political prisoners at Automobile Workers' Union Hall, Detroit, Mich., Nov. 23, 1919; Hoover to George W. Lamb, Jan. 22, 1920, roll 65, *EGP*.

10. F. E. Haynes, memo for JEH, Jan. 30, 1920, DJ OG 18197, RG. 65, both, NA; To the U.S. Government of America from the Men of Deportation, Jan. 10, 1920, Agnes Inglis Papers, Labadie Collection, Special Collections Library, University of Michigan; Roy C. McHenry, rep., Feb. 14, 1920, DJ OG 379165, RG 65, NA. This file focuses on Todd, a disciple of Margaret Sanger, who took up the cause of the families left behind by the *Buford* deportees.

11. E. J. Williams, rep., Feb. 22, 1920, DJ OG 18197, RG 65, NA.

12. GFB [?] to JEH, Mar. 18, 1920; Burke to Spencer, Mar. 19, 1920; GFR to Spencer, Mar. 19, 1920; 836, rep., Mar. 20–23, 1920; GFR to JEH, Mar. 22, 1920; Barkey to Burke, telegram, Apr. 22, 1920; Burke to Barkey, Apr. 27, 1920; GFR to JEH, memo, Apr. 28, 1920; T. C. Wilcox, rep., Apr. 28, 1920, all DJ OG 18197, RG 65, NA.

13. *Pittsburgh Press*, Apr. 29–30, 1920; *Pittsburgh Gazette-Times*, Apr. 30–May 1, 1920. The judges were John D. Shafer, Thomas J. Ford, and Joseph M. Swearingen.

14. *Pittsburgh Press*, Apr. 29–30, 1920; *Pittsburgh Gazette-Times*, Apr. 30–May 1, 1920. The hearing took place on Apr. 29–30 and, after a hiatus, May 12–13.

15. *Pittsburgh Press*, Apr. 29–30, 1920; *Pittsburgh Gazette-Times*, Apr. 30–May 1, 1920.

16. *Pittsburgh Press*, May 12, 1920; *Pittsburgh Gazette-Times*, May 13, 1920; *Pittsburgh Telegraph*, May 12, 1920; *Pittsburgh Dispatch*, May 13, 1920; *Pittsburgh Sun*, May 13, 1920.

17. *Pittsburgh Press*, May 13, 1920; *Pittsburgh Sun*, May 13, 1920.

18. *Pittsburgh Press*, May 14, 1920.

19. *Pittsburgh Gazette-Times*, May 14, 1920.

20. ACBA Brief, 2–57, 61–63, 92–94, 105, 127, 130.

21. Ibid., 14–15, 80–81. In 1921 a change of editors moved *One Big Union Monthly* into the procommunist camp. Renshaw, *The Wobblies*, 200, 203.

22. ACBA Brief, 181–83, citing *Ex parte Wall*, 107 U.S. 265; 183–84, citing *State of Oregon v. Graves*, 73 Oregon 331.

23. ACBA Brief, 185, citing *In the Matter of Pierre Dormenon*, 2 Wheeler (U.S.) 344.

24. Ibid., 187–89.

25. "Brief on the Facts for the Respondent," Case of Jacob Margolis, vol. 139, roll 20, ACLU, PU.

26. Ibid.; Baldwin to Harry H. Willock, June 14, 1920; Case of Jacob Margolis, vol. 139, roll 20, ACLU, PU. For Anderson see Powers, *Secrecy and Power*, 116–17.

27. Later he was the main speaker in Cleveland. Spencer to Burke, July 17, 1920; Lenon, rep., Sept. 1, 1920, both DJ OG 215915, RG 65, NA.

28. "Order *in re* Jacob Margolis, An Attorney at Law," Case of Jacob Margolis, vol. 139, roll 20, ACLU, PU.

29. Spencer to Acting Director (telegram), Sept. 15, 1920; 836 to Ruch, Sept. 16, 1920, both DJ OG 18197; Rider to William J. Neale, Sept. 20, 1920, DJ OG 215915, all RG 65, NA; Scully to Coxe (Secret and Confidential), Sept. 20, 1920, MID 10110-199, RG 165, NA. Coxe acknowledged receipt, saying "We are very much interested, as you know, in the Margolis case, and this brief will be very helpful." Coxe to

Scully, Oct. 1, 1920, MID 10110-199, RG 165; Rider to Neale, Sept. 30, 1920, DJ OG 18197, RG 65, both NA; U.S. Department of Justice, *Annual Report of the Attorney General of the United States for the Year 1920* (Washington: USGPO, 1920), 178.

30. "U.S. Steel *v.* Margolis," *The Nation* 111 (Nov. 3, 1920): 498; Williams, "The Bureau . . . and its Critics," 570.

31. Margolis to Civil Liberties Bureau, Sept. 21, 1920, Case of Jacob Margolis; DeSilver to Margolis (copy), Sept. 23, 1920, both vol. 139, reel 20, ACLU, PU.

32. GFR, memo for JEH (confidential), Oct. 2, 1920, DJ OG 18197; Lenon, rep., Oct. 4, 1920, DJ OG 215915, both RG 65, NA.

33. 836, rep., Nov. 11, 1920; "DMN," rep., Oct. [?], 1920; Rider to Neale, Sept. 27, 1920; Lenon, rep., Dec. 7, 1920, all DJ OG 215915, RG 65, NA.

34. "Margolis's Case," *Pennsylvania State Reports* 269, Supreme Court of Penn., October Term 1920 and January Term 1921, 206, vol. 280 (1924), 296; Lenon, rep., Feb. 19, 1921, DJ BSF 202600-1768, RG 65, NA.

35. Margolis complimented Lenon for having "been rather decent to me when you consider the job you hold." He refused to say the same about Yankovich, who had once been with the hated Pennsylvania State Constabulary. Lenon got on badly with Yankovich and was doubtless pleased to report both the compliment and the insult. Lenon, rep., Feb. 19, 1921, DJ BSF 202600-1768, RG 65, NA.

36. Lenon, reps., Feb. 19, Mar. 5, 1921; same, weekly rad. rep., Mar. 12, 1921, all DJ BSF 202600-1768, RG 65, NA.

37. *General Intelligence Bulletin,* May 7, 1921, DJ OG 374217; Ames, reps., Aug. 20, 27, 1921; Lenon, rep., Mar. 5, 1921; same, weekly rad. rep., Sept. 10, 1921, all DJ BSF 202600-1768, RG 65, NA. In September Joe Ettor stayed with Margolis.

38. Lenon, weekly rad. rep., Mar. 12, 1921, DJ BSF 202600-1768, RG 65, NA.

39. Spencer, rep., May 29, 1923, roll 66, EGP; "In re Margolis," *Pittsburgh Legal Journal* (68): 609–11; Inglis to Goldman, Oct. 30, 1926; Goldman to Margolis, Dec. 28, 1926, both roll 16, EGP; Margolis to Goldman, n.d. (1928–1930), roll 19, EGP. In 1929, Margolis represented Italian anarchist Attilio Bortolotti in deportation proceedings in Detroit. Paul Avrich, *Anarchist Voices: An Oral History of Anarchism* (Princeton: Princeton University Press, 1996), 99. *Polk's* Pittsburgh City Directories (1927–1945) show his office in the Law and Finance Building until the late 1930s and then in the Grant Building.

40. In 1933 Agnes Inglis met Helen Hockett, wife of Ike Margolis, brother of her old ally Jake at the Chicago offices of the *Industrial Worker.* Agnes Inglis Card Catalog, Labadie Collection, Special Collections Library, University of Michigan. An inquiry of the *Industrial Worker,* now in San Francisco, produced no information.

41. Margolis to Goldman, Feb. 16, 1934, roll 30, EGP.

EPILOGUE

1. Irving Bernstein, *The Lean Years, A History of the American Worker, 1920–1933* (Boston: Houghton, Mifflin Company, 1960). See Melvyn Dubofsky, *The State and Labor in Modern America* (Chapel Hill: The University of North Carolina Press, 1994), chapters 3 and 4.

2. Murphy, *World War I,* 238–48; Howe, *Confessions of a Reformer,* 282.

3. Nelson et al., *Steve Nelson,* 21–25.

4. Oestreicher, "Working-Class Formation," 135–37.

5. Ibid., 136.

6. Total personnel dropped from 1,127 to 641 in the same period. Powers, *Secrecy and Power,* 137–39, 142–43; Walker, *In Defense of American Liberties,* 65–66. Sidney Howard's 1921 *New Republic* exposé of federal domestic spying sold thirty thousand copies in pamphlet form. Three years later he brought out a book-length version, *The Labor Spy.* The BI's image suffered further from the ACLU's accusatory pamphlet, *The Nationwide Spy System Centering in the Department of Justice.*

7. Gregory to Col. E. M. House, Jan. 14, 1927; House to Gregory, Jan. 23, 1927; Gregory to Jerome Miller, July 1, 1929, all Thomas Watt Gregory Papers, LC.

8. Theoharis and Cox, *The Boss,* 83–94. After his retirement in 1929 MID legend Ralph Van Deman oversaw a private radical surveillance operation drawing upon government sources, private detectives,

company secret services, and volunteers affiliated with groups such as the American Legion and the shadow successors to the APL. By 1940 this group had files on more than 125,000 persons and organizations. ONI also maintained an unpaid, largely volunteer, covert apparatus in many places including Pittsburgh. Weber, ed., *Van Deman*, xxii; *NYT*, July 9, 1971; Jensen, *Army Surveillance*, 198–99, 205; William Pencak, *For God and Country: The American Legion, 1919–1941* (Boston: Northeastern University Press, 1989), 2–144; Gordon Johnson to Churchill, rep. on United Americans, Jan. 14, 1920, MID 10261-144, RG 165, NA; Dorwart, *Conflict of Duty*, 81.

9. Interchurch World Movement, *Report on the Steel Strike*, 221, 225–26, and *Public Opinion and the Steel Strike*, 1–86.

10. For an assessment of Hoover's understanding of Communism, see Theoharis and Cox, *The Boss*, 61–62.

11. See Kazin, "Agony and Romance of the American Left"; John Patrick Diggins, *The Rise and Fall of the American Left* (New York: W. W. Norton & Company, 1992); Weinstein, *Decline of Socialism;* Bell, *Marxian Socialism*.

12. Jeffreys-Jones, "Profit Over Class," 248.

INDEX

DATE DUE